BIOGRAPHICAL DICTIONARY OF ANCIENT GREEK AND ROMAN WOMEN

BIOGRAPHICAL DICTIONARY OF ANCIENT GREEK AND ROMAN WOMEN

Notable Women from Sappho to Helena

Marjorie Lightman and Benjamin Lightman

Checkmark Books®

An imprint of Facts On File, Inc.

BIOGRAPHICAL DICTIONARY OF ANCIENT GREEK AND ROMAN WOMEN

Checkmark Books
An imprint of Facts On File, Inc.
11 Penn Plaza
New York NY 10001

Library of Congress Cataloging-in-Publication Data
Lightman, Marjorie.
      Biographical dictionary of ancient Greek and Roman women / by
  Marjorie Lightman and Benjamin Lightman.
         p.   cm.
  Includes bibliographical references and index.
  ISBN 0-8160-3112-6 (hardcover)
  ISBN 0-8160-4436-8 (paperback)
  1. Women—Rome Biography Dictionaries. 2. Women—Greece Biography
  Dictionaries. 3. Women Biography—To 500 Dictionaries.
  I. Lightman. Benjamin. II. Title.
  HQ1136.L54 1999
  305.4'092'24563—dc21   99-20682

Text and cover design by Cathy Rincon
Page layout by Grace M. Ferrara
Map by Jeremy Eagle
All photographs courtesy of The American Numismatic Society, New York.

Printed in the United States of America.

MP FOF 10 9 8 7 6 5 4 3 2 1
(pbk) 10 9 8 7 6 5 4 3 2 1

This book is printed on acid-free paper.

For our children

Suzanne, Timothy, and Andrew

CONTENTS

PREFACE

Over the past several years we often have been asked about our experiences of working and writing together. Long married, we always pursued separate professional lives. It was an unexpected opportunity that led us to this book. Much to our surprise, we found our professional skills complementary and the shared project a never-ending source of intense, albeit not always harmonious, discussion. At the very time when our previously largest project, raising three children, had reached a stage of relative completion, we found ourselves sitting in restaurants passionately arguing with each other over Julia's adultery or the military tactics of one or another of the Cleopatras. At dinner parties in Washington, D.C., during the impeachment hearings of President Bill Clinton, we offered ancient gossip as a far richer alternative to the Kenneth Starr inquiry.

None of our friends were surprised by our disagreements, especially on the subject of women's relationships with the men in their lives, nor that those women with whom we felt a special kinship were often the same we most heatedly defended against ancient accusations. The overall paucity of information generally left us free to develop the possibilities of our favorites' lives. Sometimes we presented our friends with a his-and-her version of the women, each of us convinced of our own interpretation.

We are grateful to everyone who listened to us and hope we have rescued at least one friend from belief in the passivity of ancient women, as well as at least one ancient woman from oblivion. There are some people, however, without whom there would have been no book. Frances Collin, a friend since she and Marjorie were at college together, with whom we spent many happy hours during the early years of our marriage, and who brought to us the idea for the book, cajoled us into writing the proposal. In her professional capacity as literary agent, she has eased the way at every step in the process. Our friend and colleague William Zeisel, who is Marjorie's business partner in Q.E.D. Associates and with whom Marjorie has collaborated since their first professional papers at the American Historical Association 1973, read and reread parts of the book. Ronald Cluett, who was completing his dissertation when we began and is now an assistant professor of classics and history at Pomona College in California, worked with us throughout the editing process and made invaluable contributions.

We wish to thank the librarians at the Library of Congress in Washington, D.C., for their unending patience and for their knowledge of the collections; also, we thank the American Numismatic Society in New York and especially Dr. William E. Metcalf, who guided us through the images of women on coins from which we selected the book's illustrations. While writing the biographical dictionary, we met with several editors at Facts On File, all of whom were encouraging and patient. During the past year, we have had an especially cordial relationship with Mary Kay Linge, who has spent long hours bringing the book to birth. Behind Ms. Linge are all the other specialists at Facts On File who have made this a beautiful book.

Finally, we want to acknowledge our children. Their frequent advice and help with our computers cannot be overestimated. Without their knowing, however, they also played an another role. It is they above all who have helped us understand the fragility of life and the chances of fortune. In loving them we found a bridge across the centuries.

—Marjorie Lightman and Benjamin Lightman

INTRODUCTION

In the Greco-Roman world during almost every generation a woman ruled somewhere. Some women led armies and captained ships, others made law and wrote poetry. Women joined conspiracies and priesthoods. They studied in the most famous schools of philosophy, traded in the marketplace, bought and sold land, and paid taxes. Also during centuries of peace and war, woman were raped, sold into slavery, and bartered as brides. More often than not they died young, frequently during pregnancy or from the consequences of childbirth.

Women were among the rich and poor, free and slave, educated and illiterate. Some were healthy, strong, and independent. Others, circumscribed by custom, wealth, and the politics of power in their times, were quiet and retiring. Probably most women never moved far from where they were born, but some traveled far and wide. Many became slaves of conquering armies, victims of the incessant wars; some committed suicide to save themselves from rampaging soldiers, prison, and torturous death. No more wanton than the men around them and no less cruel, still others were murderers, avengers, and women of fortune set upon amassing wealth and securing honor.

In these sympathetic biographical sketches that stretch imagination, we try to expand understanding of the circumstances that shaped a woman and her life. The stories are fragmentary, sometimes unusual or violent, and filled with emotional realities that influenced behavior and are often difficult, if not impossible, to grasp. Nonetheless, the 447 women included in this book, *Biographical Dictionary of Ancient Greek and Roman Women,* suggest the variety of women's experiences, the roles they played, and the often hard choices they faced in an unforgiving and harsh world.

The book is intended for all those interested in ancient women, from the novice student to the general reader and scholar. Each entry begins with a headnote that includes the woman's name; her dates, if known, or century in which she lived; her cultural identity—Greek, Roman or other; where she lived; and a descriptive phrase about her. When possible, the entry opens with a statement about what the woman did and to whom she was related. At the end of each entry are citations to ancient and modern sources of information. In the rear of the volume is an alphabetical registry that provides an easy guide to the women in this book and to the relationships among them, as well as an extended bibliography of ancient and modern works, and a glossary of less familiar Latin and Greek terms.

Unlike the study of a single woman or a specific group of women during one period of time or in one place, the entries include women across the sweep of Greco-Roman history from the seventh century B.C.E. to the early fourth century C.E. In the dictionary are women from small Greek city-states, Hellenistic empires, and Italian towns, as well as from the early republic of Rome and the empire that extended through the centuries over the older civilizations of North Africa, Syria, Egypt, and Judaea, up to Britain, along the Rhine and the Danube, and through to the Black Sea and into Asia. This inclusiveness emphasizes the unending cycles of war, political upheaval, and natural disasters, as well as relatively short interludes of peace and prosperity that marked more than a thousand years. The long frame of time and the wide spread of geography also suggests the repetition of behavior, both praised and condemned, that speaks to shared values, and the persistence of choices that distinguished the lives of women from men.

The dictionary draws on information about women from the surviving Greek and Latin literature. It was once a more extensive literature. Ancient public and private libraries collected poetry, history, philosophy, drama, letters, journals, and almost every other imaginable kind of written work. In Alexandria alone the library was said to have had as many as 40,000 texts. Wars, natural disasters, and successive waves of religious and ideological purges, however, have destroyed most ancient written records. In cities like Ephesus and Pergamum, near the coast of modern Turkey, the partially ruined monumental arches that were once the entrance to the cities' library still stand as silent sentinels to a literate past.

However limited, the surviving written works have provided the primary basis for our understanding of ancient philosophy, social relationships, the economy, religion, law, and custom. Some of the authors are more familiar to modern readers than others: the histories of Herodotus; the letters, speeches, and essays of Cicero; the multivolume history of Rome from its founding to the beginning of the empire by Livy; the scathing denunciations of the Julio-Claudian rulers by Tacitus; the letters from Pliny the Younger to friends and to the emperor Trajan; and the biographies of the famous Greeks and Romans by Plu-

tarch. Less familiar works include the histories written by Polybius, Sallust, and Dio Cassius, and the descriptions of women by Athenaeus or the women included by Josephus in his history of the Jews.

Except for some poetry, we have no literature written by Greek and Roman women, although we have many references to their writings. Among the fragments that have survived, the most famous are by the poet Sappho, who was universally admired. As a whole, women poets spoke with passionate voices, often from the perspective of the young woman, and about the central moments in women's lives. There is an immediacy that crosses the centuries and formal forms of presentation. Although extremely limited as a source of historical information, the poetry nonetheless provides a suggestive counterpoint to other narratives and constitutes a perspective otherwise largely absent from the historical literature.

Many surviving histories and commentaries reinforce the sense of a shared body of stories and historical references to places, events, customs, and people reaching in a continuous tradition over the long period of time. Ancient authors, most of whom wrote long after the events they narrate, sometimes hundreds of years later, tantalize us with allusions that assume familiarity with people and events, especially women to whom they may only briefly refer. The inference that a woman may have been well known to her contemporaries and even perhaps far less incidental to the narrated events than would appear, further highlights how limited is our information about the ancient world and in particular about ancient women.

In the face of limited ancient sources of information, the dangers of generalization are evident. They are even further exacerbated by the uneven distribution of surviving texts across the centuries and societies of the Mediterranean. Although sometimes there is more than one narration about the same individuals and events, for another reasonably well-documented period there may be only one source of information. For many periods of time and many places, there is no ancient literary source. This contributes to a seeming historical randomness. It heightens the possibility that a few women from a particular place and period may misrepresent the general condition of women. Alternatively, only a few women may be dismissed when their lives challenge traditionally held assumptions.

For some few historical eras there are portraits of women over several generations. The women of the Julio-Claudian period in the early Roman Empire are one such example. In the works of Tacitus and others, the social and economic class of the women included reflects the biases of the ancient authors toward the politically elite, the propertied, and the well born. Even in the best-informed periods, women from nonelite backgrounds only gained entry into the historical record when they amassed wealth and influenced men and events. The information about these women rarely includes the identity of their family, although they may have claimed an elite non-Greek or -Roman parentage. On occasion there may be information about the women's mother or the city in which she was born, but she was more likely to be described by her physical charms, her associations with great men, her artistic ability, and her intelligence.

Modern scholarship has not accorded equal value to the information from all the available historical narratives. Some of the extant literature is universally venerated. Among historians, Herodotus is considered the father of history. Tacitus and Thucydides stand without peer. All concur that the letters of Cicero and of Pliny the Younger vividly portray their times and echo the immediacy of concerns that dominated their lives. There are also lesser works of gossipy commentaries, histories, and biographies filled with incredible tales that mix fact and fiction so that they are neither reliable histories nor elegant literature. Embedded in these works, however, are references and information about women found nowhere else. The *Biographical Dictionary* draws on the testimony of the great writers, but it also incorpo-

rates lesser works, following a policy that information from an ancient author about a historical woman not self-evidently improbable nor contradicted by other evidence, either in the general circumstances or with regard to a particular woman, is important, regardless of the source. However, the dictionary does not include every woman mentioned by an ancient author. Rather, it includes the women about whom we have something to say. In some manner, these women have made history.

Since with some few valuable exceptions of women's own poetry, what we know about women comes primarily through the lens of men who wrote about and for other men, understanding ancient women is in some degree inseparable from understanding ancient men. What concerned men, especially elite men, were public life and military affairs, and these were the activities they most often recorded. Together these spheres of life were the milieu in which men pursed the triad of public honor, position, and wealth. In no small measure, political turmoil and military battles made men's name, fortune, and history.

Throughout the centuries and in every part of the Greco-Roman world, the pursuit of this treasured triad was set against a background of scarcity that dominated most lives, even among the elite. With an economy based on land and inefficient agriculture, communities and individuals lacked a safety net from the natural disasters of storms, floods, or droughts: Somewhere crops always failed and famine threatened. The endemic wars combined with the inelasticity of the economy to bankrupt landowners in recurring inflationary/deflationary cycles that fed discontent and contributed to further war. Finally, ancients did not clearly distinguish between private wealth and the public purse. The riches of ancient rulers was frequently co-equal with the wealth of the state and as such was not only insignificant by contemporary standards, but used in an economically unproductive fashion for ornament, display, and warfare.

In contrast with the contemporary experience, underpopulation, not overpopulation was the ancient problem. People and animals were the sources of power for production. Ships often used rowers to move for trade and war. Roads and cities were built and land was farmed, all without machines to augment power. In this world a supply of labor was fed with slaves gained through war and with children, who were the most precious and vulnerable members of the community. There were never enough slaves, never enough children.

In a world of scarce resources where life was manifestly insecure, the unique glory of women was inseparable from their power to bear children. Without children, the family had no future, and the deeds of men in their worldly pursuit of wealth, position, and honor, no immortality, especially before Christianity when death promised no glorious afterlife or redemption. Both men and women venerated and feared the sexual powers of women. The oldest priesthoods celebrated fertility. Ancient rites practiced by women assured the seasonal fertility of childbirth, and in a historical elision, fertility of the land. This power was invoked by the women poets and praised in every eulogy written by men about women. No glory was greater than to bear children.

Women were simultaneously at the center of ancient Greek and Roman society and outside the triad of public honor, position, and wealth that rewarded men. Repeatedly women become a background chorus to men's public deeds, and they received the conventional praise of forbearance, silence, beauty, support for the men around them, and above all, fecundity. Yet the narratives also attribute great import to women's behavior. Again and again there is the assumption that when times were good, it was because women were good, and conversely that rapacious women were omens of coming disaster. The narratives that praised or condemned women, whether for good or bad, always link the behavior with sexuality.

No less than in contemporary times, the ancients appreciated the strengths of individual women without altering their generalized assumptions about the women. In the realities of ancient life men welcomed women's active collaboration when they perceived them useful and condemned them when they were their opponents. With some notable exceptions, information about women coincided with the moments when women stepped into a public spotlight and like men, pursued the triad of wealth, power, and position either for themselves or in the name of the family. These women suffered periods of political favor and exile and maintained independent international networks of allies and clients that afforded them some protection in conflict and cushioned them in defeat. As with the men around them, they sometimes lost their battles and died. Unlike the men, however, they were often condemned and convicted of adultery when treason was the crime.

Sometimes, however, women's unique experiences come to the fore. Women's rites and priesthoods that were central to the well-being of the state persistently appear along the periphery of the historical narratives. There were women-only sanctuaries, and women were said to have powerful ways of securing compliance with fears of vengeance through magic. The importance of these institutions in the lives of women is only suggested by their recurrence across time and geography, and their power in the society, evidenced by the severity of punishments for priestesses who violated their oaths. On infrequent occasions, the endowments of the women's temples or the treasuries of the women's priesthoods also became economically important in one or another conflict.

More often than not women were on the side of reform, especially land reform, and were more willing than men to use wealth to buy their way out of armed conflict. With good reason. During wars or political purges, when the fighting men left the city, women stayed. They coped with the inflation in costs, the protection of the family's property, and the problems of securing food. When wars did not go well, they defended the city's walls and hid their wealth and children from the victors. They also became slaves of the victors and the greater number of refugees from slaughter. If lucky, they lived long enough after defeat to avenge their men, sometimes through revolutions and other times through the law courts. In the aftermath of civil wars, which were especially devastating for the elite, it often fell to mothers, daughters, sisters, and former sisters-in-law to rear, dower, and arrange the marriages of orphaned children who reestablished stability and re-created bloodlines from the past.

As women moved from youth through maturity they gained greater control over their own life and often had grown children who extended their reach. They used land, jewels, and gold to support husbands, fathers, and especially brothers and sons. They did not hesitate to barter their wealth for marital alliances or practice a self-interested serial monogamy. Personal wealth bought them not only husbands but also generals and armies who advanced their causes and fought under their banners.

The narratives repeatedly and in different contexts detail alliances of women within the family who sought power and protected kin. Among an elite that was always few in number, powerful female cliques were often multigenerational and could be deadly enemies. Alliances between mothers and daughters, both of whom could be married and bearing children during the same years, not only belie the traditional historical narratives that move from father to son, but suggest one of women's most frequent emotional and political relationships. Through death or divorce, both common happenings, women often married more than once. They married men closer to their own ages as they grew older, further complicating generational lines. Cross-generational alliances also extended to sisters, cousins, and sisters-in-law, all of whom could be enough younger or older from one another to have married men of different generations over the course of their life.

Often there is confusion in the stories about a woman's identity. Sometimes two women or two stories are conflated; frequently the women bear the feminine form of the same family name or have married collateral kin. We can infer a well-born woman's complete name if we know the name of her father or his family. Similarly, we can infer a less well-born woman's dependent relationship from her name and possibly, if another name is also known, her place of origin. However, there were many Cornelias and many Cleopatras alive at the same time, and a single reference, a reference without a complete name or with only a nickname, can leave open exactly which woman was meant.

The confusion is furthered when two or more women from the same family are allied to promote one man. Husband, father, or more likely brother were pushed into the spotlight of power by female-led family coalitions and opposed by other, equally powerful groups, also led by women. No less than men, women saw their children as their glory and frequently used children, especially sons, as their most valuable token in trade for power. Under the guise of promoting or advancing the interests of their children, they again and again acted as regent in name, and ruler, in fact.

Events such as wars, political scandals, murders, famines, shifting international alliances, and inherited family politics all help situate the women's lives. The careers of fathers, mothers, siblings, and children position a woman within a social context. In general each entry includes a full name, when it is known, as well as the name of her father and mother and the names of her husbands and children. The entries try to identify sisters and sometimes aunts, grandmothers, and daughters-in-law to help establish a female family context. The sources often lack information routine in records about women from the more recent past. Dates, places of birth or death, information about childhood or schooling, number of marriages, etc., are fragmentary or absent. For easy use, the women in the dictionary are listed in alphabetical order under the name by which they most generally appear in the ancient literature, even if it was not their full or formal name.

In a further effort to understand more clearly a woman's life, some of the language used in the *Biographical Dictionary* to describe women's status, relationships, and honors may differ slightly from older translations of the ancient authors and familiar modern histories. The entries refer to a woman as "ruler," or "woman ruler," or "coruler," rather than "queen," which carries historical meanings not part of the ancient world. In addition, titles such as "Augusta" are largely untranslated since they have no modern equivalent but are clear from context. Such terms as *husband, companion, lover, partner, ally, friend,* and *consort* describe specific and different kinds of relationships. Epithets such as *businesswoman, financial manager,* and *political actor* describe the modern names for activities in which the women engaged.

The *Biographical Dictionary of Ancient Greek and Roman Women* would not have been possible without the past century of research and scholarship in Europe and America. The standard texts of ancient authors and the extensive scholarly apparatus allowed the mention of a single name in an ancient source to become an entry. Dictionaries, commentaries, and encyclopedias were essential to following the labyrinth of references. Monographs about individuals, families, and groups of families linked over time provided outlines of relationships that opened the way to find and understand the position of women.

Although modern scholarship has long taken account of ancient bias in the study of culture, politics, and the military, until well into the 1960s it accepted the ancient vision of women. Scholars repeated the ancient authors' condemnation of blatantly immoral women as the cause of dire events and saw no place for women in the important institutions of ancient society. Recently scholars have sought to gain greater insight into the history of women. Scholars have begun to look more closely at the portrayal of women in the moral instruction through historical example that characterized ancient history texts, in the speeches to persuade jurors, the polemical tracts frequently written and widely circulated for one or another political end, and in the celebrations of a patronage. Their work has led to an expanded understanding of the centers of power and authority in Greco-Roman society that includes women. Their work has also been critical to our readings of the ancient texts and to our understanding of their meanings.

The *Biographical Dictionary of Ancient Greek and Roman Women* follows in this new tradition. The entries pay less attention to either the vitriolic attacks on women for the most extraordinary licentious behavior or praise for passive virtues. Instead, the focus is on what a woman did, who she was, and what the consequences of her actions were. These questions open the way to understanding the choices she faced and the consequences she suffered. When situated within the broadest possible historical context, we hope the entries in the dictionary invite readers to new discoveries about the lives of women over the long period of Greco-Roman civilization before the spread of Christianity.

LIST OF ABBREVIATIONS

A. General

cent.	century	q.v.	see also
c.	circa	v.	volume
ff.	following		

B. Authors and Books

And.	Andocides	**Ath.**	Athenaeus
	On the Mysteries	**Aul. Gell.**	Aulus Gellius
App.	Appian: *Roman History*	NA	*Noctes Atticae*
Bciv.	*Bella civilia (Civil Wars)*	**CAH**	*The Cambridge Ancient History*
Syr.	*Syrian Wars*	**Catull.**	Catullus
Apul.	Apuleius		Poetry, passim
Apol.	*Apologia*	**Cic.**	Cicero
Met.	*Metamorphoses (The Golden Ass)*	ad Brut.	*Epistulae ad Brutum*
		Amic.	*De amicitia*
Arist.	Aristotle	Att.	*Epistulae ad Atticum*
Pol.	*Politics*	Brut.	*Brutus*
Arr.	Arrian	Cael.	*Pro Caelio*
Anab.	*Anabasis of Alexander*	Cat.	*In Catalinum*
Succ.	*Successors*	Clu.	*Pro Cluentio*
Asc.	Asconius	De. or.	*De oratores*
Mil.	Commentary on Cicero's *Pro Milone*	Dom.	*De domo sua*
		Fam.	*Epistulae ad familiares*

Leg. agr.	*De lege agraria*	Grg.	*Gorgias*
Mil.	*Pro Milone*	Menex	*Menexemus*
Phil.	*Orationes Philippicae*	**Plin.**	Pliny the Elder
Q. Fr.	*Epistulae ad Quintum fratem*	NH	*Naturalis Historia*
Verr.	*In Verrum*		
Dem.	Demosthenes		
Dio.	Dio Cassius	**Plin.**	Pliny the Younger
Diod.	Diodorus Siculus	Ep.	*Epistulae*
Diog. Laert.	Diogenes Laertius	Pan.	*Panegyricus*
Ep. Caes.	*Epitome Caesaris*	**Plut.**	Plutarch
Eus.	Eusebius	**Mor.**	*Moralia*
Vit. Const.	*Vita Constantini*	Amat.	*Amatorius*
Eutr.	Eutropius	De fort. Rom.	*De fortunata Romanorum*
Fronto	Fronto	De mul. vir.	*De mulierum virtutibus*
Ep.	Epistulae	Quaest. Graec.	*Quaestiones Graecae*
Hdt.	Herodotus	Quaest. Rom.	*Quaestiones Romanae*
Isae.	Isaeus	Vit. dec. orat.	Vitae decem oratorum
Jos.	Josephus	Vit.	*Vitae Parallelae (Parallel Lives)*
AJ.	*Antiquitates Judaicae (Jewish Antiquities)*	Aem.	*Aemilius Paulus*
BJ	*Bellum Judaicum (Jewish Wars)*	Ages.	*Agesilaus*
Vit.	Vita	Alc.	*Alcibiades*
Just.	Justin	Alex.	*Alexander*
Epit.	*Epitome* (of Trogus)	Ant.	*Antonius*
Juv.	Juvenal	Arat.	*Aratus*
Lact.	Lactantius	Brut.	*Brutus*
MP	*De mortibus persecutorum*	Caes.	*Caesar*
Livy	Livy	Cat. Min.	*Cato Minor*
Epit.	*Epitome*	Cic.	*Cicero*
Per.	*Perioche*	Cim.	*Cimon*
Lucan	Lucan	Cleom.	*Cleomenes*
Phar.	*Pharsalia*	Crass.	*Crassus*
Macrob.	Macrobius	Dem.	*Demosthenes*
Sat.	*Saturnalia*	Demetr.	*Demetrius*
Mart.	Martial	Eum.	*Eumenes*
Nep.	Nepos	G. Gracch.	*Gaius Gracchus*
Att.	*Atticus*	Luc.	*Lucullus*
Cim.	*Cimon*	Mar.	*Marius*
OCD	*The Oxford Classical Dictionary*	Pel.	*Pelopidas*
Oros.	Orosius	Per.	*Pericles*
Paus.	Pausanias	Phoc.	*Phocion*
Pl.	Plato	Pomp.	*Pompeius*
Alc.	*Alcibiades*	Pyrrh.	*Pyrrhus*
Chrm.	*Charmides*	Sert.	*Sertorius*
Ep.	*Epistulae*	Sull.	*Sulla*

Them.	*Themistocles*
Ti. Gracch.	*Tiberius Gracchus*
Polyaenus	Polyaenus
Strat.	*Strategemata*
Poly.	Polybius
Prop.	Propertius
PW	A. Pauly, G. Wissowa, and W. Kroll, *Real-Encyclopadie d. Klassischen Altertumswissenschaft 1893–*
Quint.	Quintilian
Inst.	*Institutio Oratoria*
Sall.	Sallust
Cat.	*Bellum Catilinae (Catiline)*
Sen.	Seneca
Ad Marciam con.	*Ad Marciam consolatione*
Ben.	*De beneficiis*
Ep.	*Epistulae*
SHA	*Scriptores Historiae Augustae*
Alex. Sev.	Alexander Severus (Marcus Aurelius Severus Alexander)
Ant. Pius	Antoninus Pius
Aurel.	Aurelian
Comm.	Commodus
Did. Jul.	Didius Julianus
Gallien.	Gallienus
Gord.	Gordian
Hadr.	Hadrian
M. Ant.	Marcus Aurelius Antoninus (Caracalla)
Marc.	Marcus Aurelius Antoninus (Marcus Aurelius)
Max.	Maximinus
Pert.	Pertinax
TT	Tyranni Triginta (Thirty Tyrants)

Stat.	Statius
Silv.	*Silvae*
Suet.	Suetonius
Aug.	*Augustus*
Caes.	*Caesar*
Calig.	*Gaius Caligula*
Claud.	*Claudius*
Dom.	*Domitian*
Galb.	*Galba*
Gram.	*De grammaticis*
Jul.	*Julius*
Ner.	*Nero*
Oth.	*Otho*
Tib.	*Tiberius*
Tit.	*Titus*
Ves.	*Vespasian*
Virg.	*Virgil*
Vit.	*Vitellius*
Tac.	Tacitus
Agr.	*Agricola*
Ann.	*Annales*
Hist.	*Historiae*
Thuc.	Thucydides
Tib.	Tibulus
Ulp.	Ulpian
Val. Max.	Valerius Maximus
Vell. Pat.	Velleius Paterculus
Xen.	Xenophon
An.	*Anabasis*
Hell.	*Hellenica*
Zonar.	Zonaras
Zos.	Zosimus

North Sea

Baltic Sea

Brigantes
Lindum
Virocunium
BRITAIN
Isca
Iceni
London
Cassiterides
Thames River

English Channel

Batavians

GERMANIA
INFERIOR
Colonia
Agrippina
GERMANIA

Augusta
Treverorum
Mogontiacum
Vistula River

Paris
BELGICA
LUGDUNENSIS

Atlantic Ocean

GERMANIA SUPERIOR

Rhine River

Danube River

Lauriacum

GAUL
A L P S
RAETIA
NORICUM
PANNONIA
Iazyges
DACIA

Bay of Biscay
AQUITANIA
Lugdunum
Vienna
Taurasia
CISALPINE GAUL
Aquileia
Emona
Tergeste
Siscia
ILLYRICUM
Mursa
Sirmium

SPAIN
TARRACONENSIS
NARBONENSIS
Rhône River
Cremona
Genoa
Po River
APENNINES
ETRURIA
Ariminum
Pisa
DALMATIA
UPPER
MOESIA
Naissus

LUSITANIA
Caesaraugusta
Celtiberians
NEARER BAETICA
Nîmes
Narbo
Massilia

AEMILIA
ITALY
LATIUM
Corfinium
Rome
Adriatic Sea
Dyrrachium
MACEDONI

FARTHER BAETICA
CORSICA
Aleria
SAMNIUM
CAMPANIA
Capua
Naples
APULIA
Tarentum
Brundisium
Apollonia
CALABRIA
Canusium
EPIRUS

BALEARIC ISLANDS
SARDINIA
Tyrrhenian Sea
BRUTTIUM
Corcyra

MAURETANIA
TINGITANA
Caesarea
Mediterranean Sea
Messana
Locri
SICILY
Ionian Sea

MAURETANIA
CAESARIENSIS
Hippo
Regius
Utica
Carthage
Agrigentum
Syracuse

Cirta
Zama

NUMIDIA
Theveste
Thapsus

NORTH AFRICA

PROCONSULAR AFRICA

Oea
TRIPOLIS
Ptolemais
Arsinoë
Berenice

GERMANIA	Region
PANNONIA	Subregion or province
Syracuse	City or city-state
Brigantes	Tribe or ethnic group
A L P S	Mountain range

Inset map (top left)

THRACE
Adrianople •

MACEDONIA
• Dyrrachium
• Philippi
• Apollonia
• Pydna
THESSALY • Thessalonica
EPIRUS
Corcyra
Aegean Sea
Pharsalus •
Lesbos
• Thermopylae
LOCRIS Euboea
Thebes •
BOEOTIA
Sicyon ATTICA
Corinth • • Athens
Argos • Salamis
PELOPONNESE • Tegea
Sparta • GREECE
Ionian Sea
Samos

Main map

0 ——————————— 500
miles

SARMATIA

CARPATHIAN MTS.

DACIA

Getae

Danube River
LOWER MOESIA

THRACE
Adrianople
Byzantium
Constantinople
Sea of Marmara
Bosphorus
Nicomedia
Nicaea BITHYNIA
MYSIA
Pergamum
ASIA MINOR
PHRYGIA
Sardis
LYDIA
Aegean Sea Ephesus • Tralles
Lesbos Miletus
Samos CARIA
GREECE LYCIA
PISIDIA
PAMPHYLIA
Sea of Crete
Rhodes
CRETE

Mediterranean Sea

Apollonia
Cyrene
CYRENAICA

Tomi •

Heraclea •

Black Sea

Sea of Azov

CAUCASUS MTS.

COLCHIS IBERIA ALBANIA

Caspian Sea

Sinope • Trapezus •
PAPHLAGONIA
Amasia • PONTUS
Heraclea • Zela • Nicopolis •
Ancyra • LESSER ARMENIA
GALATIA CAPPADOCIA SOPHENE
LYCAONIA Persian Empire
Halys River Caesarea •
Iconium • CAPPADOCIA
Laodicea •
Samosata •
Edessa • ASSYRIA
Arbela •
Seleucid Empire
Tigris River
MESOPOTAMIA
Parthian Empire

ARMENIA

Antioch •
Apamea • COELE-SYRIA
Orontes River Emesa •
Palmyra •
SYRIA
Damascus •
PHOENICIA
Tyre •
Caesarea • Jerusalem •
PALESTINE-JUDAEA
Gaza •
Pelusium • Petra •
Alexandria Sais •
Sebennytus • ARABIA
Arsinoë •
Memphis •

EGYPT

Nile River

Red Sea

Euphrates River
Ctesiphon •
Babylon • BABYLONIA
Susa •

CYPRUS

A

ACTE, CLAUDIA

(1st century C.E.) Roman: Italy
Self-made woman

Acte was born a slave in Asia Minor. She and the handsome young emperor Nero became lovers in 55 C.E. Their passion put her in danger of Nero's disapproving and powerful mother, the younger Julia AGRIPPINA. Nero hid their affair. Nero's tutor and adviser, the philosopher Lucius Annaeus Seneca, and his friend Annaeus Serenus shared the secret. Acte, who claimed descent from the kingly Attalidae and had probably gained her freedom from the emperor Claudius, pretended that Serenus was her lover.

It was a short-lived deception. Agrippina discovered the relationship; she only inflamed Nero's passion however, by her attacks on Acte. Shifting tactics, Agrippina offered Nero her rooms for their assignations. Rumors spread that Agrippina sought to seduce her son. Acte, in fear of her life, told Nero that his mother boasted of committing incest and that the troops were grumbling about an incestuous emperor. Alarmed, Nero first avoided Agrippina and later had her killed, in 59 C.E.

Acte could not hold Nero's passion. Even before Agrippina's murder, Acte had been pushed aside. In 68 C.E., however, the extravagant and beautiful Nero came to an inglorious end. He returned from Greece to a corn shortage in Rome, an angry populace, and a senate that opposed him. Events soon escalated, and he was declared a public enemy. Finally, he committed suicide. It was the loyal and loving Acte, along with his old nurses, who dressed him in gold-embroidered white robes and carried his ashes to the Pincian Hill, where he was entombed. Acte, who had grown wealthy with estates in Sardinia and Italy, paid 2,000 gold pieces for the funeral of her lover.

Dio. 61.7.1.
Suet., Ner. 28.1, 50.
Tac., Ann. 13.12–13, 46; 14.2.
Balsdon, J. P. V. D., pp. 108, 128.
Bauman, R., p. 194.
OCD, p. 336.
PW 399.

ACUTIA

(1st century C.E.) Roman: Rome
Convicted conspirator

Acutia was convicted of treason in the trials that followed the downfall of Lucius Aelius Sejanus in the last years of the emperor Tiberius. Although her full name remains elusive, Acutia's husband was Publius Vitellius. He committed suicide in 31

C.E. after he had been charged with diverting military funds to support a conspiracy led by Sejanus.

The dour and aging emperor had retired to Capri and left Sejanus in Rome. As prefect of the Praetorian Guard he became the emperor's eyes and ears in the capital. His aspirations grew. He sought to marry his lover Livia Julia Claudia LIVILLA, the emperor's niece, and perhaps even become regent for her young son after the death of Tiberius. His plans had almost succeeded when the aged emperor charged him with treason. A purge followed. Prosecutors grew rich from the trials. In 37 C.E. Laelius Balbus prosecuted Acutia before the Senate for her presumed participation in the conspiracy. Although convicted, she may have escaped death. There is no record of her execution, and the tribune Junius Otho vetoed the usual reward taken by a successful prosecutor.

Tac., Ann. 6.47.
Levick, B., *Tiberius*, p. 216.
Marsh, F. B., p. 217.
Marshall, A. J., "Women on Trial," p. 348.

▣ AELIA IUNILLA

(?–31 C.E.) Roman: Rome
Political victim

Aelia Iunilla died because she was the daughter of APICATA and Lucius Aelius Sejanus. Her father, head of the Praetorian Guard, had become the most powerful man in Rome when he alone had the ear of the emperor after Tiberius retired to Capri in 27 C.E. He was also the lover of Livia Julia Claudia LIVILLA, widowed daughter-in-law (and niece) of Tiberius and mother of the emperor's infant grandson. Around Livilla and Sejanus a conspiracy grew. The ailing emperor learned of Sejanus's perfidy from the younger ANTONIA, Livilla's mother. Vengence followed quickly. In October of 31 C.E., the Senate voted to execute Sejanus.

Eight days after her father died, her mother killed herself. In December Iunilla and her young brother were seized on Senate orders that there be no descendants of Sejanus. Traditionally, the Romans did not kill virgins, and it was said that Iunilla was raped before she was strangled.

Dio. 58.11. 5.
Tac., Ann. 6.5, 9.
Levick, B., *Tiberius*, p. 178.

▣ AELIA PAETINA

(1st century C.E.) Roman: Rome
Political victim

Aelia Paetina married the future emperor Claudius during the years when it seemed unlikely he would rule. She had a daughter, ANTONIA (4), born in about 28 C.E. When Claudius's prospects improved in the reign of his nephew Gaius Caligula, he divorced Aelia to marry the better-connected Valeria MESSALLINA.

After Messallina's death in 48 C.E., the powerful freedman Narcissus proposed to the emperor that he remarry Aelia. Aelia, the daughter of Aelius Catus, consul in 4 C.E., posed no threat to the imperial freedmen who controlled the bureaucracy and exercised their influence over Claudius. Claudius, however, married the younger AGRIPPINA and Narcissus soon lost his position and his life.

Suet., Claud. 26.2, 3.
Tac., Ann. 12.1–2.
Balsdon, J. P. V. D., p. 122.
Levick, B., *Claudius*, pp. 25, 55, 70.
Syme, R., *Augustan Aristocracy*, index.

▣ AEMILIA (I)

(2nd century B.C.E.) Roman: Rome
Priestess

Aemilia was one of three Vestal Virgins charged with violating the vow of chastity in 114 B.C.E. A daughter of the clan of the Aemilii, she was one of the six virgins dedicated for a period of 30 years to protect the sacred flame of Rome in the temple of

Vesta, the goddess of the hearth, and one of the oldest temples in the Forum.

Aemilia had an affair with L. Veturius, a Roman equestrian, and induced two of her sister Vestals, LICINIA (4) and MARCIA (1), similarly to engage Veturius's companions. It was said that Aemilia had several lovers, including Licinia's brother. Tried before the *pontifex maximus*, Lucius Caecilius Metellus, Aemilia was found guilty and condemned to death. Licinia and Marcia, initially declared innocent, were retried and condemned the following year. Evidence against the women came from a slave, Manius, who felt insufficiently rewarded by the women for his role as their go-between.

Romans traditionally regarded violations of chastity by the Vestal Virgins as signs of ill omen. Tales of their promiscuity often accompanied other indications of impending trouble for the city-state and sometimes preceded periods of political instability. In 111 B.C.E. a fire destroyed much of Rome and during these years there was a war against Jugurtha of Numidia in North Africa.

Dio. 26.87.
Livy per 63.
Oros. 5.15, 20–22.
Plut., Quaest. Rom. 83.
Bauman, R. A., pp. 52–58.
PW 153.

AEMILIA (2)

(1st century B.C.E.)   Roman: Rome
Political wife

Aemilia was the daughter of CAECILIA METELLA (1) from the rich and powerful Metelli clan. Aemilia's father was Marcus Aemilius Scaurus, consul in 115 B.C.E. After the death of her father, Aemilia's mother married Lucius Cornelius Sulla, the general who later became dictator of Rome. It was considered the match of the season, a great coup for Sulla who gained critical political support and wealth from the Metelli. For Caecilia, it was a chance to play politics using her family's stature and wealth to support a newcomer from an old patrician family that had long been out of the limelight.

Sulla and Caecilia Metella persuaded Gnaeus Pompeius (Pompey the Great) to divorce his wife ANTISTIA (2) and marry Aemilia. At the time, Aemilia was pregnant and living with her husband, Manius Acilius Glabrio, future consul in 67 B.C.E. An alliance with Sulla and the Metelli through Aemilia clearly enhanced and enriched Pompey.

Aemilia's views on her divorce and remarriage are not known. She died during childbirth in 80 B.C.E. shortly after her marriage with Pompey.

Plut., Pomp. 9.2.
Plut., Sull. 33.3
Haley, S. P., pp. 103 ff.
PW 154.
Syme, R., *Roman Revolution*, pp. 31–32.

AEMILIA LEPIDA (1)

(1st century B.C.E.)   Roman: Rome
Political wife

Aemilia Lepida, daughter of Mamercus Lepidus Livianus, consul in 77 B.C.E., was jilted by Quintus Caecilius Metellus Pius Scipio. She then agreed to marry Marcus Porcius Cato Uticensis. The two men could not have been more dissimilar. Cato was a self-righteous, unpleasant ascetic, while Scipio was corrupt and depraved.

On hearing of her engagement, Scipio changed his mind, and they were married about 73 B.C.E. Cato wanted to sue Scipio. Dissuaded by friends, he instead wrote and widely circulated a satiric poem ridiculing his rival. The result was a lasting feud.

Aemilia Lepida's son, Metellus Scipio, died at 18; her daughter, CORNELIA (6), married Publius Licinius Crassus in 55 B.C.E. He died in 53. In 52, Cornelia married Gnaeus Pompeius (Pompey the Great). Aemilia's new son-in-law, one of the most powerful politicians in Rome, supported the election of her husband as consul. Scipio's election made him immune from any law suits. He thereby avoided a bribery charge, and Aemilia Lepida became the wife, as well as the daughter, of a consul.

Plut., Cat. Min. 7.
PW 166.
Syme, R., *Augustan Aristocracy*, p. 245.

▣ AEMILIA LEPIDA (2)

(1st century B.C.E.–1st century C.E.)   Roman: Rome
Unjustly convicted of adultery

Aemilia Lepida was successfully prosecuted before the Senate by her vindictive ex-husband in a curious case that had political overtones. An aristocratic woman of impeccable lineage, she was the daughter of CORNELIA (7) and the granddaughter of MUCIA TERTIA and Gnaeus Pompeius (Pompey the Great). Her father, Quintus Aemilius Lepidus, was the son of the triumvir Marcus Aemilius Lepidus and JUNIA (1). She had been affianced to Lucius Julius Caesar, the grandson of Augustus, but Lucius died before the marriage could take place.

Around 2 C.E., she contracted a less auspicious marriage with the much older, but wealthy, Publius Sulpicius Quirinus who had been consul in 12 B.C.E. Three years later they were divorced. She then married Mamercus Aemilius Scaurus, a distinguished orator with an unsavory reputation, who was the last living male of the republican Aemilii Scauri clan.

In 20 C.E., her divorced first husband, Quirinus, now an even more ancient relic, charged her with adultery, attempting to poison him, and falsely claiming that he was the father of her child. She was also accused of consulting astrologers about the imperial family, a treasonous offense under recent imperial Roman law. Her brother Manius Aemilius Lepidus defended her.

Aemilia Lepida earned a good deal of sympathy from women. Not only were the charges brought many years after the divorce, but she, the descendant of a great and noble family, was accused by a man of lesser distinction in tiresome old age.

The emperor Tiberius played a role in the affair. Appearing simultaneously magnanimous and condemnatory, he ruled that there was no evidence of treason. Aemilia was, however, convicted of falsely claiming Quirinus as the father of the child she bore during their marriage. By default, therefore, she was guilty of adultery during her marriage with Quirinus.

Aemilia was banished, but a plea by Scaurus, her current husband, waived the confiscation of her property. Tiberius later announced that her slaves confessed under torture that she had attempted to poison her first husband.

Suet., Tib. 49.1.
Tac., Ann. 3.22–23.
Balsdon, J. P. V. D., p. 220.
Marshall, A. J., "Women on Trial," p. 343.
PW 170.
Syme, R., *Augustan Aristocracy*, pp. 112, 115.

▣ AEMILIA LEPIDA (3)

(1st century B.C.E.–1st century C.E.)
Roman: Rome
Political victim

Aemilia Lepida was a woman of impeccable lineage. Her mother was JULIA (7), the child of the great general Marcus Vipsanius Agrippa, and JULIA (6), the daughter of Augustus and his first wife, SCRIBONIA. No less illustrious on her father's side, Aemilia Lepida was the daughter of Lucius Aemilius Paullus, the brother of Marcus Aemilius Lepidus, the triumvir.

Her engagement to the future emperor Claudius ended when her father was executed for treason in 8 C.E. and her mother was banished for adultery. She later married Marcus Junius Silanus Torquatus, who had a respectable career, including the consulship in 19 C.E. They had two daughters, JUNIA LEPIDA and JUNIA CALVINA, and three sons, Marcus Junius Silanus, Lucius Junius

Silanus Torquatus, and Decimus Junius Silanus Torquatus.

Aemilia Lepida's link to Augustus, however, led to the downfall of her children. Lucius was forced to commit suicide, Marcus was executed, and Junia Calvina was exiled, all through the machinations of the younger AGRIPPINA. Junia Calvina was later allowed to return to Rome by the emperor Nero. Nero, however, was responsible for the forced suicide of Decimus and the condemnation of Junia Lepida. Aemilia Lepida's own death is not recorded.

Suet., Aug. 19.1.
Suet., Claud. 26.1.
Tac., Ann. 12.4.
PW 169.
Syme, R., *Augustan Aristocracy*, index.

AEMILIA LEPIDA (4)

(1st century C.E.) Roman: Rome
Duplicitous wife

Aemilia Lepida and her younger brother, Marcus Aemilius Lepidus, were the last descendants of the great republican family of the Aemilii Lepidi. Aemilia married Drusus Julius Caesar, and Marcus married Drusus's sister, JULIA DRUSILLA (1). Drusus and his brother Nero Julius Caesar were the great-grandsons of Augustus and stood in direct line of succession to the elderly emperor Tiberius.

Aemilia Lepida was a reputed lover of and possible coconspirator with Lucius Aelius Sejanus, commander of the Praetorian Guard. In 30 C.E. while Sejanus still held power over Rome, her husband was imprisoned. Although the nature of the offense is not known he died while still in prison some three years later. In 31 C.E. Sejanus was charged with treason and executed. Aemilia remained safe under the protection of her father, Marcus Aemilius Lepidus, consul in 6 C.E. and a great favorite of Tiberius.

After her father's death, however, Aemilia was charged with adultery. She did not try to defend herself and committed suicide in 36 C.E. Her brother, the last of the Aemilii, died four years later, in 39, after having been accused of participation in a somewhat mysterious conspiracy led by Gnaeus Cornelius Lentulus Gaetulicus.

Dio. 58.3.8.
Tac., Ann. 6.40.
Levick, B., *Tiberius*, pp. 55, 170, 215.
PW 167.
Syme, R., *Augustan Aristocracy*, p. 136.

AEMILIA TERTIA

(2nd–1st century B.C.E.) Roman: Rome
Power broker

Aemilia Tertia's life was shaped by the wars against Carthage. Her father, Lucius Aemilius Paullus, consul in 219 and 216 B.C.E., died in Hannibal's defeat of the Romans in 216 at Cannae in Canusium. Her husband, Publius Cornelius Scipio Africanus Major, led the Romans to victory over Hannibal at Zama in North Africa in 202.

In 195 B.C.E., Aemilia supported, and possibly participated in, the popular effort to repeal the Oppian law. Passed by the Senate as an austerity measure after the defeat at Cannae, the law barred displays of status and wealth. Specifically the law forbade carriages within a mile of Rome or in Roman towns except for religious festivals, purple trim on women's clothing, or women's possession of more than a half an ounce of gold. Although after Hannibal's defeat, austerity laws directed against men were lifted, until the women protested the law remained in effect against them.

All of Aemilia's children left a mark on Roman history. The eldest, Publius Cornelius Scipio, who suffered ill health, which prevented him for following a military and political career, became an outstanding orator. The second son, Lucius Cornelius Scipio, was praetor in 174. Of her two daughters, the eldest, CORNELIA (1), married her cousin Publius Cornelius Scipio Nasica. The younger, CORNELIA (2), married Tiberius Sempronius Gracchus and was the mother of two of Rome's most famous reformers, Tiberius and Gaius Sempronius Gracchus. In the political battles around the land bills supported by her grandsons, her son-in-law, Scipio Nasica, emerged as a leader of the conservative faction that assassinated Tiberius.

An aprocryphal story about the marriage of the younger Cornelia possibly suggests something of Aemilia's expectations of her husband. Attending a dinner of senators, Scipio was urged by those present to arrange his daughter's marriage with Tiberius Sempronius Gracchus. He agreed, and the contract was concluded on the spot. On returning home he told Aemilia. She was furious because she had not been consulted. She added that it was improper for him to act without having consulted her, even if the bridegroom was the desirable Tiberius Sempronius Gracchus.

Aemilia outlived her husband and faced the political attacks against him that erupted after his death in the early 180s B.C.E. Since her daughter's marriage in fact happened after her husband's death she probably *was* consulted. She also freed her husband's slave/lover and arranged for her marriage. While not without precedent, it nonetheless speaks well for the woman.

Aemilia was independently wealthy, in part, from her dowry, gifts from her husband, and a wide circle of clients. Possibly she also benefited from the spoils of her brother, Lucius Aemilius Paullus Macedonicus, consul in 168 B.C.E., who led the Romans to victory in the Third Macedonian War. She was said to have lived and traveled in comfort, accompanied by a number of retainers. She left her fortune to Publius Cornelius Africanus Numantinus, her adopted grandson. The date of Aemilia's death is unknown.

Livy 38.57.5–8.
Poly. 31.26.1–6; 31.27.1–4.
Val. Max. 6.7.1.
Balsdon, J. P. V. D., *Roman Women*, pp. 47, 215.
Bauman, R. A., index.
Pomeroy, S. B., *Goddesses*, passim.
PW 180.

▣ AFRIANA (CARFANIA)

(?–48 B.C.E.) Roman: Rome
Advocate

Afriana, also called Carfania, represented herself and others in cases brought before the praetor. The wife of Licinius Bucco, a senator of the first century B.C.E., Afriana lived during a time of turmoil and civil war when many men were in flight, in the army, or dead. Families found themselves pulled apart by the passions of the times and sometimes on opposing sides. Afriana, like other women, moved into spheres of activity usually reserved for men: She went into the law courts.

Afriana's success irritated some and provoked others to ridicule, which reflected the Romans' contradictory views of women and the law. On one hand, women were assumed to be unknowing and in need of protection. On the other hand, ignorance of the law, even on the part of a woman, was not an acceptable defense in the courts.

By the later first century B.C.E., however, women owned property in their own name and increasingly both sued and were sued. After Afriana, however, the law was changed so that women could plead for themselves before a magistrate but were prohibited from representing others. Afriana died in 48 B.C.E.

Ulpian 11.1.232n.30.
Val. Max. 8.3.2.
Bauman, R. A., pp. 50–51.
Marshall, A. J., "Ladies at Law," pp. 38–54.

▣ AGARISTE (1)

(6th century B.C.E.) Greek: Sicyon
and Athens
Mother of Cleisthenes

Agariste was the daughter of Cleisthenes, ruler of Sicyon, a Greek city northwest of Corinth, in the years between 600–570 B.C.E. Cleisthenes determined that Agariste would marry the best man in all of Greece. At the conclusion of the Olympic Games in c. 576 B.C.E., he invited worthy contestants to arrive in Sicyon within the next 60 days and spend a year as his guests. At the end of that time, one among them would marry his daughter.

Thirteen eminent men from 12 cities accepted the challenge. Cleisthenes assessed their families, expectations, and cities of origin. He tested their prowess in wrestling and running. At the end of a year, he gave a banquet and invited everyone in the city.

His favorite appeared to be Hippocleides, described as the wealthiest and the most handsome of the Athenians. Under the influence of too much wine, however, Hippocleides danced on a table and stood on his head waving his legs. Outraged at this behavior, Cleisthenes instead chose Megacles, a member of the aristocratic Alcmaeonidae of Athens.

Agariste gave birth to two children: Cleisthenes, who became the Athenian statesman regarded as the creator of Athenian democracy, and Hippocrates, the father of AGARISTE (2).

Hdt. 6.126–31.
Blundell, S., p. 67.
Hammond, N. G. L., *History of Greece*, p. 148.
Pomeroy, S. B., *Goddesses*, pp. 34–35.

AGARISTE (2)

(c. 520/510 B.C.E.–?)   Greek: Athens
Mother of Pericles

Agariste was born between 520 and 510 B.C.E. She was the daughter of Hippocrates, the son of AGARISTE (1), after whom she was named. Her father was a member of the family of the aristocratic Alcmaeonidae, and her uncle was Cleisthenes, who was one of the founders of Athenian democracy.

She married Xanthippus, an Athenian politician and general who helped defeat the Persians at the battle of Mycale in 479. According to Herodotus, Agariste dreamed that her son was delivered by a lion. The son, born in 494 B.C.E., became the great Athenian statesman Pericles. She had two other children: Ariphron (II), named af-

ter her husband's father, and a daughter who died of the plague in 430.

Hdt. 6.131.
Plut., Per. 3.1–2.
Davies, J. K., pp. 456–57.

AGARISTE (3)

(5th century B.C.E.)   Greek: Athens
Witness

Agariste testified against the brilliant, dissolute, and popular general Alcibiades at his celebrated trial in Athens (415 B.C.E.). She was a member of the aristocratic Alcmaeonidae family and the wife of Alcmaeonides, a leading Athenian.

Agariste had witnessed Alcibiades and his friends in a drunken revel staging a travesty of the sacred Eleusinian rites for goddesses Demeter and Kore. The episode happened at night in the house of Charmides, a friend of Alcibiades. It is possible, and even probable, that Agariste was visiting kin when the event happened.

Few extant records record women's court testimony in fifth century Athens, nor are there many records of well-born women moving around the city after dark.

And. 1.16.
Plut., Alc. 19.1–2.
Macdowell, D. M., ed., p. 75.
Pomeroy, S. B., *Goddesses*, pp. 81, 119.

AGATHOCLEIA

(3rd century B.C.E.)   Greek: Samos and Egypt
Adventurer and murderer

Agathocleia came to Egypt from the island of Samos off the coast of Asia Minor with her brother, Agathocles, and their mother, OENANTHE. The name of their father is unknown. Agathocleia was a dancer, and her mother played the tambourine. Oenanthe became one of Ptolemy III's many lovers and brought her children into the life of the palace. Shortly after Ptolemy IV became reuler in 221 B.C.E., he became wildly infatuated with Agathocleia. It was rumored that through him she controlled Egypt.

In 205 B.C.E. Agathocleia and her brother arranged the murder of Ptolemy IV and his wife, ARSINOË III PHILOPATOR. The conspirators included Oenanthe and Sosibius, guardian of Ptolemy's son. The deaths were kept secret for several days while Agathocles had himself appointed regent. Philammon, a coconspirator and murderer of Arsinoë, left Alexandria, and Agathocleia and Oenanthe took over care of the five-year-old boy-ruler.

The murder of Arsinoë, even more than the death of Ptolemy, aroused the anger of the Greek troops and the Alexandrian populace. A crowd, eager for revenge, collected at the stadium. A naked Agathocleia, along with her mother, brother, sisters, and relatives, were turned over to the mob and torn limb from limb. The women, especially those who had been close to Arsinoë, led the slaughter.

Ath. 13.577.
Plut., Mor., Amat. 9.
Poly. 14.11.2; 15.25.3–33.
Pomeroy, S. B., *Women in Hellenistic Egypt.*, passim.

⊡ AGESISTRATA

(?–241 B.C.E.)   Greek: Sparta
Reformer

Agesistrata, and her mother Archidamia, and her daughter-in-law AGIATIS were among the wealthiest women in Sparta during the middle decades of the third century B.C.E. They were committed to reform, especially land reform. Along with their friends, retainers and dependents, they constituted an influential political bloc in support of Agis IV, who led a reformist revolution in 244 B.C.E. to overthrow the reigning ruler, Leonidas II.

Agis IV, who was Agesistrata's son, was deposed and killed in 241. After her son's death, Agesistrata and her mother were executed. She died willingly, her final wish being that her death benefit Sparta.

Plut., Agis 4.2; 7.7; 9.5–6; 20.7.
Mosse, C., pp. 138–53.

⊡ AGIATIS

(3rd century B.C.E.)   Greek: Sparta
Reformer

Agiatis, the wealthy daughter of Gylippos, a well-respected Spartan, was heir to her father's fortune. Committed to reform, she was part of an aristocratic and wealthy faction that also included her mother-in-law, AGESISTRATA, and the latter's mother, ARCHIDAMIA.

Her first husband, Agis IV, seized power from the ruler Leonidas II in 244 B.C.E. at a time when a small oligarchy controlled large estates, and held mortgages on much of the remaining farmland. It was also a period of declining population, which seriously depleted manpower for the military and labor for agriculture. Agis sponsored a number of reforms and abolished mortgages to relieve debt. A conservative revolt led by the deposed Leonidas in 241 resulted in the death of Agis and left Agiatis a widow with a small son.

Leonidas sought to marry Agiatis to his son Cleomenes, who was quite young. Agiatis who wanted no part of a marriage to Cleomenes or anyone else married under protest. In 235 Cleomenes followed Leonidas as ruler. Influenced by Agiatis and her circle, Cleomenes III pursued the reform policies that had been an anathema to his father, and in 227–226 he canceled debts, redistributed land, and extended citizenship to some of the indigenous population and resident aliens. During the same years he was also successful in war and expanded Spartan territory; however, his policies garnered opposition, and he was overthrown in 222. He fled to Egypt, where he committed suicide in 219. It is not known what happened to Agiatis or her son.

Plut., Agis 4.2.
Plut., Cleom. 1.1–3.

⊞ AGRIPPINA THE ELDER, VIPSANIA

(c. 14 B.C.E.–33 C.E.) Roman: Germany
and Rome
Political player and power broker

Vipsania Agrippina was an extraordinarily power-ful and ambitious woman fully conscious of her noble heritage and determined to see that she, her husband, and their children received the titles, honors, respect, and positions due them. She was the daughter of JULIA (6), the only child of Augustus and his first wife, SCRIBONIA. Her father was Marcus Vipsanius Agrippa, Augustus's greatest general and closest confidant.

Around 5 C.E., Agrippina married Germanicus Julius Caesar, whose lineage matched hers. He was the son of Nero Claudius Drusus and the younger ANTONIA. His father was the brother of the future emperor Tiberius; his mother, the daughter of Mark Antony and the independent-minded sister of Augustus, OCTAVIA (2). In 4 C.E., Augustus adopted Tiberius, who in turn, adopted Germanicus as his son to form a line of fictive kin and ensure the future of the family and state.

Agrippina accompanied her husband on his campaign to lower Germany in 14 C.E. She was generous and popular with the troops, whom she helped with food, clothing, and medical care. Stories about her echo the attributes of courage and strong character that marked the ancient heroines. In 15 C.E., as Roman troops retreated toward a bridge that crossed the Rhine, pursued by the Germans, Agrippina stationed herself at the head of the bridge and stopped the retreat. The troops stood their ground and won the battle.

In 18 C.E., Agrippina, pregnant with her ninth child, accompanied her husband to Syria, after Tiberius made Germanicus consul with responsibility for all the provinces in the East. A military man himself, Tiberius was not comfortable with Germanicus's overly aggressive tactics and sent his friend Gnaeus Calpurnius Piso as governor to encourage a more moderate policy. Piso went to Syria with his wife, MUNATIA PLANCINA, a woman as strong, outspoken, and arrogant as Agrippina. The two men did not like each other and did not get along. Nor did the two women.

The deified Vipsania Agrippina was commemorated with this coin after her death.

When Munatia criticized Germanicus before the troops, Germanicus ordered Piso and his wife to leave Syria. They went to the island of Cos off the coast of Asia Minor. On October 10, 19 C.E., Germanicus died of a mysterious illness in Antioch. Before he died, he accused Piso and Munatia of poisoning him. Piso and Munatia openly rejoiced at the death of Germanicus and immediately sought to reassert their authority.

Agrippina believed not only that Germanicus had been poisoned by Piso and Munatia, but also that Tiberius was behind the deed. She returned to Rome with her husband's ashes, determined to avenge his death and to promote the interests of her six surviving children: Drusus Julius Caesar, Nero Julius Caesar, Gaius Caligula, the younger AGRIPPINA, JULIA DRUSILLA (1), and JULIA LIVILLA. The population of Rome turned out to pay Germanicus homage. The emperor's mother, LIVIA DRUSILLA; the taciturn Tiberius; and Antonia, Germanicus's own mother, did not attend the ceremonies. People took their absence as confirmation that Tiberius might have had a hand in the death of Germanicus.

Agrippina brought formal charges against Piso and Munatia. Poisoning could not be proved so the main charge was treason. Tiberius presided over the trial in the Senate. Piso killed himself before the end of the trial after having written to Tiberius protesting his loyalty. Munatia's trial had been separated from that of her husband. Livia, her close friend, intervened; Tiberius told the Senate that his mother wanted no action taken against Munatia, and she escaped conviction. Agrippina was furious. She and Livia, who had long disliked each other, were further alienated.

Agrippina spent the years 19–29 C.E. in Rome working to promote her sons as heirs to Tiberius. Livia Julia Claudia LIVILLA and Lucius Aelius Sejanus, prefect of the Praetorian Guard, were her opponents. Livilla, the sister of Germanicus, was Agrippina's sister-in-law. She was the grand-niece of Augustus and the widow of Tiberius's son, Drusus Julius Caesar. Sejanus was a military man of equestrian background who had

become Tiberius's confidant, and after 27 C.E., when Tiberius retired from Rome to Capri, he controlled access to the emperor. Although an uncle on his mother's side had been a consul suffectus, Sejanus had neither family nor family connections in the senatorial class that allowed him any aspiration to achieve for himself the position of emperor. In the person of Livilla, he found an ally whose sons were possible successors. Sejanus and Livilla became lovers and schemed to make Livilla's son the successor to Tiberius.

Agrippina was at the center of a group of powerful people who hated and resented the enormous influence exercised by Sejanus. They regarded his background with arrogant distaste and his position as an impediment to their own power. The senatorial families who supported Agrippina acted in the belief that tradition was on their side. There may have been an attempted conspiracy to supplant Tiberius with Agrippina's oldest son, Drusus Julius Caesar.

In 24, Sejanus initiated a barrage of legal attacks against Agrippina and her supporters. In the subsequent trials, some were exiled; others committed suicide or were executed. Despite the coolness between Agrippina and Livia, however, so long as Livia remained alive, Sejanus could not directly attack her or her children. Short of the emperor, Livia alone could forestall Sejanus.

In 25, Tiberius refused Sejanus's request to marry Livilla. In 26, Tiberius also refused Agrippina's request to marry. Gaius Asinius Gallus, a widower and no friend of Tiberius, was the man most likely to have been Agrippina's choice. Her intention may well have been to ally herself with a man of suitable background who could and would promote her interests. Gallus was known to be ambitious, and married to Agrippina, he might become the stepfather of an emperor. Tiberius, however, hated Gallus, who had once married his former wife, VIPSANIA AGRIPPINA.

Sejanus harassed Agrippina and fed her belief that the emperor had poisoned her husband. She came to believe that Tiberius intended also to poison her. While dinning with the emperor, she did not eat and when offered some fruit by Tiberius, she instead handed it to her servants. Tiberius remarked to his mother that it would not be surprising if he took action against someone who thought he was trying to poison her.

Tiberius made no immediate move against Agrippina or her sons. Doing so would have caused a confrontation with his mother who was already in her 80s. After the death of Livia in 29, however, Tiberius sent a letter to the Senate in which he accused Agrippina of arrogance and pride and her son Nero of homosexuality. Supporters of Agrippina gathered outside the Senate with signs and shouted that the letter was a fabrication of Sejanus. The Senate did nothing. Sejanus informed Tiberius of the Senate's inaction and the behavior of the mob. Tiberius sent another letter that denounced the actions of the crowd and demanded that the matter be decided by him. Agrippina was exiled to the tiny island of Pandateria off the coast of Campania. Nero was banished to Pontia off the same coast and executed or forced to commit suicide in 31. In 30, Sejanus convinced Tiberius that Agrippina's son Drusus was also a threat and should be imprisoned. He was incarcerated under the palace.

In 31, the end came for Sejanus. Following receipt of information from the younger Antonia, mother-in-law to Agrippina and mother to Livilla, Tiberius ordered Sejanus imprisoned for treason. Sejanus was strangled on October 18. His death did not help Agrippina, who died of starvation in 33, as did her son Drusus.

After her death, Tiberius accused Agrippina of adultery with Gallus. Agrippina's reputation for chastity, however, was only equaled by that of Tiberius's mother, Livia. The very characteristics for which Tiberius hated Agrippina—ambition and determination—were those for which she was also most honored. She would have rejoiced to see that in the end it was her son Caligula who succeeded Tiberius as emperor of Rome.

Suet., Tib. 53.
Tac., Ann. 1.33, 69; 2.43, 55, 70, 72, 75; 3.1, 3–4, 17; 4.12, 17, 40, 52–54, 60; 5.3–4; 6.25.
Balsdon, J. P. V. D., passim.
Bauman, R. A., passim.
Levick, B., Tiberius., passim.
Marsh, F. B., passim.
OCD, p. 1,601.
Syme, R., Tacitus.

AGRIPPINA THE YOUNGER, JULIA
(15–59 C.E.) Roman: Italy
Augusta; political player

Julia Agrippina grew up under the influence of her formidable mother the elder, Vipsania AGRIPPINA. Like her mother, she was ambitious for herself and her son, and had witnessed the destruction wrought by ambition on members of her family and friends close to the emperor. No more ruthless than those around her, she was exiled and recalled, hated and adored. A brilliant woman, politically astute, charming on occasion, and cultured, she left a now lost memoir that justified her choices during the reigns of three different emperors, one of whom was her brother; the second, her husband; and the third, her son.

The younger Agrippina was born on November 6, 15 C.E., at Ara Ubiorum (modern Cologne), one of nine children and the eldest daughter of Agrippina and Germanicus Julius Caesar. Her father was Augustus's stepgrandson, and her mother was Augustus's granddaughter by his only child JULIA (6). Agrippina the Younger married Gnaeus Domitius Ahenobarbus in 28, when she was 13. He was described as despicable, cruel, and dishonest. He was also rich.

Only a year later, in 29, Agrippina's mother and brother Nero Julius Caesar were banished by Tiberius for plotting against him. In 31, Nero Julius Caesar died through either murder or suicide, and in 33, her mother died by starvation. Her brother Drusus Julius Caesar, imprisoned in 30, died in prison in 33.

Julia Agrippina's son Nero Claudius Caesar was born in 37, the same year that her one surviv-

Julia Agrippina

ing brother, Gaius Caligula, succeeded Tiberius as emperor. Caligula honored Agrippina along with his two other surviving sisters as honorary Vestal Virgins and raised their status and influence with an honor that was without precedent by adding their names to the annual oaths of allegiance to the emperor. When JULIA DRUSILLA (1), Caligula's favorite, died in 38, he deified her.

After her sister's death, Agrippina had an affair with her brother-in-law, Marcus Aemilius Lepidus, who may have had his eye on succession as perhaps did Agrippina. In 39, Caligula exiled Agrippina for joining a plot to assassinate him, although what actually happened remains a mystery. It is possible that Agrippina and her only surviving sister, JULIA LIVILLA, feared that their increasingly irrational brother might turn on them. Their position was further threatened by MILONIA CAESONIA, whom Caligula married in 40, already pregnant with a child.

Agrippina returned from exile when Claudius became emperor in 41 C.E., a year after her husband Domitius Ahenobarbus died. She set out to protect and promote the interests of her son, the future emperor Nero, and to find a new husband.

Possibly, she married Lucius Cornelius Sulla Felix, consul in 33, but if so, the marriage was short-lived. Servius Sulpicius Galba better fit her needs. He was very wealthy and liked by Claudius; however, he had a wife, Aemilia Lepida. Aemilia's mother was said to have slapped Agrippina in public over her forward behavior. Agrippina finally settled on Gaius Passienus Crispus, consul in 44, a very wealthy older man.

The fact that Passienus Crispus was already married to a most formidable woman failed to deter Agrippina. His wife, DOMITIA, Agrippina's former sister-in-law, was not a woman easily thrust aside. She and her sister DOMITIA LEPIDA had hated Agrippina since her earlier marriage to their brother, and they took every opportunity to undermine her. Their hatred was returned in full.

Agrippina was said to have poisoned Passienus Crispus for his wealth, and in 48, with the death of Claudius's wife Valeria MESSALLINA, she focused on her uncle. Never one to leave her affairs with men to chance, she used Marcus Antonius Pallas, one of the powerful freedmen surrounding Claudius, to further her influence. Successful in her pursuit, she married Claudius in 49, after the Senate removed the prohibition against marriage between uncle and niece. Possibly to her credit, the next years of his reign were marked by increased cooperation with the Senate and a decline in extrajudicial murder.

With Pallas's aid, she persuaded Claudius to adopt Nero. In 50, he became one of the emperor's two sons. The other, Britannicus, son of Valeria Messallina, was younger by several years. Agrippina also arranged to have Nero marry Claudia OCTAVIA, Claudius's daughter. Only nine years old at the time of Agrippina's marriage with Claudius, she had been affianced to Lucius Junius Silanus since infancy. With the help of Lucius Vitellius, Claudius's close confidant and adviser, Silanus was accused of incest with his sister JUNIA CALVINA. He committed suicide in 49, on the day that Agrippina married Claudius, and Junia Calvina was banished by her. Nero and Claudia Octavia married in 53.

Never one for half-measures, Agrippina eliminated real and potential enemies. She had Silanus's brother, the unambitious Marcus Junius Silanus, poisoned so that his connections to Augustus would not imperil her son's claim, as well as to prevent any possibility that he would seek to avenge his brother's death. She arranged the execution of the powerful freedman Narcissus, who had urged Claudius to marry another woman. She also rid herself of possible rivals and arranged to have the beautiful LOLLIA PAULINA, a former wife of her brother Gaius Caligula, and whom Claudius found attractive, charged with using magic, banished, and eventually killed.

With Nero positioned to become emperor, Agrippina would tolerate no rival for her son's affections. In 54 she had her old enemy Domitia Lepida accused of using magic and posing a threat to Italy from the slaves on her vast estates in Calabria. Domitia was the grandmother of Britannicus, Nero's rival for the emperorship, and she had pampered Nero during the three years his mother was in exile. She was put to death.

Agrippina received the title Augusta, only the second woman to be so honored while alive and the first to carry the title during her husband's lifetime. Despite widespread and malicious gossip that she had poisoned Claudius, Nero followed Claudius as emperor in 54. On every count Agrippina had succeeded. She was truly her mother's daughter.

She exercised enormous power during the early years of Nero's reign, generally viewed as Nero's best years. However, her domination of his life came to a predictable end. Nero had an affair with ACTE, a freedwoman, in spite of Agrippina's objections. Agrippina's lover, Pallas, lost his power, and Lucius Annaeus Seneca and Sextus Afranius Burrus, Nero's closest advisers, turned against her. In order to frighten Nero, Agrippina seems to have hinted that she might support efforts to supplant him with his younger stepbrother Britannicus. In 55, Nero had Britannicus murdered.

Nero then fell in love with POPPAEA SABINA (2), a woman whom Agrippina hated and feared

for her lowly origins and for her influence over Nero. Poppaea hated Agrippina, no less. She forced Nero to choose between herself and his mother. Nero had long been exasperated over his mother's attempts to dominate him and control his public behavior. The threat alone or in combination with other circumstances marked the end of Agrippina's dominion.

An elaborate plot was developed. A freedman, Anicetus, who hated Agrippina, arranged to have a ship on which Agrippina was to travel sink at sea and drown her. The plot failed. The ship did not completely sink, and Agrippina managed to swim ashore. Anicetus was less inventive the second time. Caught stretched out on her couch, she was repeatedly stabbed by Anicetus's henchmen. She was cremated the same night.

Dio. 52.1–14; 59.22.5–9; 60.4.2; 61.31.6, 8; 61.32.
Suet., Calig. 7.
Suet., Claud. 26.3; 39.2; 43.44.
Suet., Ner 5.2; 6.1–4; 28.2; 34.1–4.
Tac., Ann. 4.53; 12.1–9, 22, 25–27, 37, 41–42, 56–59, 64–69; 13.1–2, 5, 13–16, 18–21; 14.1–12.

Balsdon, J. P. V. D.
Barrett, A. A.
Bauman, R. A.
Ferrill, A., *Caligula*.
Levick, B., *Claudius*.
OCD, p. 777.
PW 556.
Syme, R., *Augustan Aristocracy*, p. 172.
Syme, R., *Tacitus*, passim.

ALBUCILLA

(1st century C.E.) Roman: Rome
Alleged conspirator; convicted adulterer

Albucilla, notorious for her many lovers, divorced her one and only husband, Satrius Secundus. In 37 C.E., Albucilla and three senators, Lucius Arruntius, Gnaeus Domitius Ahenobarbus, who was the husband of the younger AGRIPPINA, and Vibius Marsus, as well as several lesser men, were accused of adultery and treason against the emperor Tiberius. The charges appear to have been instigated by Quintus Naevius Cordus Sutorius

Macro, the prefect of the Praetorian Guard, without the knowledge of the already dying emperor. Macro presided over the questioning of witnesses and the torture of slaves.

The Senate deliberately moved slowly reflecting their sense that Macro had fabricated the charges and that the emperor had not long to live. All except Albucilla and Arruntius managed to escape punishment. Arruntius committed suicide. Albucilla, however, was not so successful. Carried into the Senate after a failed suicide attempt, she was convicted of adultery and died in prison.

Dio. 58.27.4.
Tac., Ann. 6.47–48.
Bauman, R. A., pp. 116, 164.
Levick, B., *Tiberius*, pp. 198–99.
Marsh, F. B., passim.
Marshall, A. J., "Ladies at Law," p. 348.

ALCE

(4th century B.C.E.) Greek: Athens
Self-made woman

Alce, born a slave, worked as a prostitute and succeeded in gaining freedom, respectability, and citizenship for her eldest son. Working in a brothel owned by Euctemon of Cephsia in Piraeus outside of Athens, she cohabited with another slave, Dion, and had two sons. After some sort of violent fracas, Dion fled to Sicyon. Alce continued to work for Euctemon until she became too old. He freed her, and she took over the management of his tenement in Athens.

In time, Euctemon left his wife and children and moved in with Alce, who persuaded him to have her eldest son by Dion recognized as his own. Philoctemon, the eldest son of Euctemon's first wife, objected to the boy's registration in his father's phratry, which was the prerequisite for citizenship and inheritance. Euctemon threatened Philoctemon that he would marry again and have a second family. Faced with the prospect of an unknown number of future stepsisters and -brothers that could significantly diminish his portion of the estate, Philoctemon capitulated.

Isae. 6.18–26.
Sealey, R., pp. 111–33.
Walters, K. R., pp. 203–4.

ALEXANDRA

(1st century B.C.E.) Jewish: Judaea
Conspirator

Alexandra gained the support of CLEOPATRA VII to oppose her son-in-law, Herod the Great, and died in an attempt to overthrow him. She was the daughter of John Hyrcanus II, the Hasmonaean high priest of Judaea (63–40 B.C.E.). Her daughter, Mariamme I, married Herod the Great after he thwarted an invasion of Judaea by Antigonus, an anti-Roman Hasmonaean leader.

Herod, appointed king of Judaea by Mark Antony and the Roman Senate, made an obscure Jew from Babylonia, Hananel, high priest. Angry that a Hasmonaean was not appointed, Alexandra appealed to Cleopatra, who always engaged in one or another intrigue against Herod in hope of extending her rule over Judaea. Alexandra was successful: Herod appointed her 17-year-old son Aristobulus, high priest.

Herod had Aristobulus drowned at a bathing party in Jericho in 36 B.C.E. Alexandra informed Cleopatra of his murder, and Cleopatra pressed Antony to right the wrong. However, Herod charmed Antony, who wanted a strong ruler to carry out his policies. Herod reappointed Hananel high priest. Thus ended Cleopatra VII's dream of acquiring control over Judaea.

Subsequently Herod fell ill, and Alexandra conspired with Herod's sons to seize control over the fortifications of Jerusalem, enabling them to usurp the rule of Herod. The plot failed, and Herod had Alexandra executed in 28 B.C.E.

Jos., A J 15.23–27, 35–40, 53–56, 62–65, 74–76, 247–52.
Grant, M., p. 69.
Jones, A. H. M., *Herods of Judaea*, passim.

Amastris

AMASTRIS

(4th–3rd century B.C.E.) Persian: Asia Minor
Ruler

Amastris was a prudent regent who ruled
Heraclea Pontica on the Black Sea after the death
of her husband. She was the daughter of Oxyartis,
the brother of the Persian king Darius III. Her first
husband, Craterus, was one of 80 Macedonian officers who had married women of the Persian nobility after Alexander the Great's victory at
Guagamela in 331 B.C.E. After the death of Alexander, they divorced, and Amastris married
Dionysius, tyrant of Heraclea Pontica (337–305
B.C.E.). She had three children: Clearchus,
Oxathres, and Amastris.

After Dionysius died, Amastris became regent.
She gained the support of Antigonus, who sought
control of Asia Minor after Alexander's death.
Later Amastris switched her allegiance to
Lysimachus, another of Alexander's former generals, who had become ruler of Thrace and northwest
Asia Minor. Lysimachus, who coveted her wealthy
city, offered her marriage to seal the alliance. In
302, they married and had a son, Alexandrus.

Lysimachus divorced Amastris to marry
ARSINOË II PHILADELPHUS, the daughter of Ptolemy I Soter who ruled Egypt. Amastris resumed
her rule over Heraclea, which she enlarged and
established a city named after herself.

In 289, Amastris was murdered by her sons.
Her former husband, Lysimachus, avenged her
death and took control of the city of Amastris.

Arr., Anab. 7.4.
Diod. 20.109.6–7.
Strabo. 12.3.10.
Cary, M., pp. 55, 98.
Der Kleine Pauly, pp. 289–90.

ANCHARIA

(1st century B.C.E.) Roman: Rome
Mother of Octavia

Ancharia was the first wife of Gaius Octavius and
the mother of OCTAVIA (1). Her husband came from
a wealthy equestrian family in Velitrae. After she
died, her husband married ATIA (1); their only son,
Octavian, became the emperor Augustus.

Plut., Ant. 31.
Suet., Aug. 4.

ANTEIA

(1st century C.E.) Roman: Rome
Stoic

Anteia belonged to the fourth generation of a Roman family noted for literary and philosophical
achievements and for principled acts rooted in
honor and commitment. She, like her predeces-
sors, experienced the wrath of the emperors.
Anteia was the wife of Helvidius Priscus the
Younger, a well-known Stoic of his day.

When Priscus was executed by the emperor
Domitian for presenting a farce that Domitian interpreted as criticism of his recent divorce, Anteia
remained in Rome. Her mother-in-law, FANNIA
(2), and her grandmother-in-law, the younger
ARRIA, were exiled. After Domitian's death,

Anteia collaborated with her husband's friend Pliny the Younger to charge Publicius Certus, whose accusations had led to her husband's death. She arranged for Fannia and Arria to press suit jointly with Pliny and testify. The Senate, after much debate, agreed to let Pliny proceed with the suit. However, the new emperor, Nerva, not wanting to rake up the past, prevented the case from going forward.

Cornutus Tetullius spoke in the Senate on behalf of the women. He explained that even if no legal penalty would be exacted, Certus should be disgraced and stripped of his honors. The women wanted a truthful and accurate rendering of how Publicius Certus had sought the death penalty for Helvidius to curry favor with Domitian. They succeeded at least insofar as Certus failed to become consul.

Anteia had three children, two of whom died in childbirth.

Plin., Ep. 9.13.
Suet., Dom. 10.

ANTIGONE

(3rd century B.C.E.) Greek: Macedonia, Egypt, and Epirus
Married to a ruler

Antigone married the deposed ruler of Epirus, Pyrrhus (319–272 B.C.E.). The marriage assured aid to Pyrrhus from Antigone's mother, BERENICE I. Berenice had married her own brother, Ptolemy I Soter, to become the second most powerful voice in Egypt. Pyrrhus had ruled Epirus while still a minor, but had been deposed in 302 B.C.E. and had fled to his brother-in-law Demetrius I in Macedonia. After having secured peace with Egypt, Demetrius had sent Pyrrhus to Egypt to cement friendly relations.

Married, Antigone and Pyrrhus returned to Epirus well equipped with men and funds. Rather than war, Pyrrhus offered to rule jointly with Neoptolemus, the usurper. Antigone learned of a plot by Neoptolemus to poison Pyrrhus from a

woman named Phaenarete and informed her husband. Forewarned, Pyrrhus invited Neoptolemus to dinner and killed him. Antigone had a son, named Ptolemy after her father. Her husband built a city and named it Berenicis in her honor.

Plut., Pyrrh. 4–6.

ANTISTIA (1)

(2nd century B.C.E.) Roman: Rome
Reformer

Antistia was the wife of the rich, arrogant, and powerful Appius Claudius Pulcher, who was consul in 143 B.C.E. and part of the reform faction around Tiberius and Gaius Sempronius Gracchus.

She and CORNELIA (2), the mother of the Gracchi, were contemporaries. Antistia's daughter CLAUDIA (2) married Tiberius. The marriage cemented a political alliance between her husband and son-in-law over agrarian reform. Another daughter, CLAUDIA (3), became a Vestal Virgin. She used the power of her office to shield her father from obstruction, thereby enabling him to celebrate a disputed triumph for the defeat of the Salassi in Cisalpine Gaul. Antistia was the grandmother, through her son, Appius Claudius Pulcher, consul in 79 B.C.E., of the beautiful and infamous CLODIA (2) and the brilliant, brash, amoral Publius Clodius Pulcher.

Plut., Ti. Gracch. 4.1–3.

ANTISTIA (2)

(1st century B.C.E.) Roman: Rome
Political victim

Antistia fell victim to an upper-class pattern of using serial marriages to move up the social and political ladder of power. In 86 B.C.E., her father, Publius Antistius, had been prosecutor against Gnaeus Pompeius (Pompey the Great) in a case of misappropriating public funds. He was so taken with Pompey's handling of his own defense that he sought him out as a son-in-law. The young Antistia and Pompey married.

In 82, Antistius was killed in the Senate on orders of the younger Gaius Marius during the armed conflict between the Marian forces and Lucius Cornelius Sulla after the death of the elder Marius. Pompey served under Sulla. Sulla, no less impressed than Antistius had been years earlier, persuaded Pompey to marry AEMILIA (2), the daughter of his wife CAECILIA METELLA (1). Pompey divorced Antistia. After the divorce, Antistia and her mother committed suicide.

App., Bciv. 1.88.
Plut., Pomp. 4.2–3; 9.1–2.
PW 60.

◫ ANTISTIA POLLITTA

(?–65 C.E.) Roman: Italy
Political victim

Antistia Pollitta and her husband were rumored to have plotted an overthrow of the emperor Nero. She was the daughter of Lucius Antistius Vetus, consul with Nero in 55 C.E. Her husband was the wealthy and philosophically inclined Rubellius Plautus. Both could trace their lineage to the beginning of the empire: she to Mark Antony and the independent-minded OCTAVIA (2), sister of the emperor Augustus, and he to LIVIA DRUSILLA, Augustus's powerful wife and Augusta in her own right.

Rumors of Rubellius Plautus's ambition were circulated by enemies of the younger AGRIPPINA, Nero's mother. It was said that Agrippina planned to remove Nero and install Plautus as emperor. There was hope that the rumors would effect a split between mother and son. Called upon to defend herself, however, Agrippina convinced her son of her unwavering allegiance. Nonetheless, reports of Plautus as a possible alternative to Nero did not cease. Alarmed, the emperor suggested

that Rubellius Plautus retire to his family estates in Asia where he could enjoy the life of contemplation. Antistia, along with a few of their friends, accompanied her husband.

Given the situation, Antistia's father urged her husband to take up arms against the emperor. There was discontent on which he could capitalize, and he was about to suffer the consequences of treason regardless of his behavior. Plautus refused. He had no taste for war, even though he understood it was only a matter of time before Nero had him killed. Perhaps he also hoped that if he remained passive, Nero would spare Antistia and their children.

In 62 C.E., Antistia stood by as a centurion beheaded her husband and sent his head to Nero in Rome. Thereafter, Antistia remained in mourning. In 65 Nero ordered the suicide of her father, who had retired with Antistia to his estate in Formiae. Antistia went to Nero in Naples to plead for her father's life. He refused even to receive her. Informed that there was no hope, her father divided his money among his slaves and ordered them to remove all furnishings except for three couches in one room. Antistia, Antistius Vetus, and his mother-in-law SEXTIA (2) severed their veins. Covered with a single cloth, they were carried to the baths, where they died. Antistia was the last to expire. Nero had the Senate indict them after their death.

Tac., Ann. 14.22, 58–59; 16.10–11.
Marshall, A. J., "Ladies at Law," pp. 351–52.

◫ ANTONIA (1)

(1st century B.C.E.) Roman: Rome
Captured by pirates

Antonia suffered the dangers of sea travel in the ancient world. She was captured by pirates. More fortunate than many others, she was ransomed by her father Marcus Antonius, a famous orator and consul in 99 B.C.E., who only a year earlier had celebrated a triumph for defeating the Cilician pirates.

Plut., Pomp. 24.

☒ ANTONIA (2)
(1st century B.C.E.) Roman: Rome
Adulterer

Antonia was divorced by Mark Antony, who became convinced that she was having an affair with his friend Publius Cornelius Dolabella. She was Antony's second wife, as well as his cousin. Antonia, the daughter of Gaius Antonius, coconsul with Marcus Tullius Cicero in 63 B.C.E., would not have been the only woman of the late republic to find Dolabella a desirable lover. The third husband of Cicero's daughter TULLIA (2), he was notoriously attractive, considered quite dissolute and, chronically short of funds, a well-known womanizer.

Antonia and Antony had a daughter, ANTONIA (3), who married the wealthy Pythodorus from Tralles.

Plut., Ant. 9.

☒ ANTONIA (3)
(c. 54/49 B.C.E.–?) Roman: Rome and Tralles
Political wife

Antonia, born between 54 and 49 B.C.E., was the daughter of Mark Antony and his second wife ANTONIA (2). It was intended that their daughter marry Marcus Aemilius Lepidus, the son of a fellow triumvir. However, as her father's alliance with CLEOPATRA VII focused his political ambitions in the East, an alliance between Antonia and Pythodorus of Tralles, a wealthy commercial city in Asia Minor, became more desirable. They married in 34 B.C.E.

Antonia and Pythodorus had a daughter, PYTHODORIS, who married the ruler of Pontus, Polemon, and later Archelaus, who ruled Cappadocia. Antonia died quite young, but her daughter ruled Pontus during the reign of Augustus.

Macurdy, G., pp. 10–11.
OCD, p. 113.
PW 113.

☒ ANTONIA (4)
(28 –66 C.E.) Roman: Rome
Political player; possible conspirator

Antonia, born in 28 C.E., was the only child of the emperor Claudius and his second wife AELIA PAETINA. Her position as the emperor's daughter opened the possibility of succession for her husbands. She could become the emperor's wife, if she survived.

Antonia married Gnaeus Pompeius Magnus, the son of Marcus Licinius Crassus Frugi, consul in 27 C.E., and Scribonia, about whom we only know her name. Antonia's husband belonged to the group of powerful aristocrats who opposed Claudius's wife Valeria MESSALLINA. By virtue of his own lineage cojoined with that of Antonia, Pompeius became a serious contender to succeed Claudius and challenged the primacy of Messallina's son, Britannicus, as the most favored heir. By 46 or early 47, Messallina convinced Claudius that Pompeius was dangerous. Both he and his parents were killed.

The widowed Antonia married Faustus Cornelius Sulla Felix, the lethargic half brother of Messallina, who posed no threat to the latter's ambitions. Sulla and Antonia outlived both Messallina and Claudius and for a time flourished. Sulla became consul in 52. However, in 58 he was banished and later killed by the emperor Nero.

In 66, Antonia was herself killed. Possibly she was a participant in the Pisonian conspiracy (65 C.E.) against Nero. Gaius Calpurnius Piso, the ineffectual figurehead of the conspiracy, supposedly promised to divorce his wife and marry Antonia after Nero's assassination. They were to meet in the temple of Ceres on the day of the planned assassination and proceed to the camp of the Praetorian Guard where Piso would be proclaimed emperor. The marriage would have clothed Piso in Antonia's lineage, and she would at last become the wife of an emperor.

Perhaps, however, she did not seek the role of emperor's wife and was not even among the conspirators. After Nero caused the death of his wife POPPAEA SABINA (2), he was said to have asked Antonia to marry him in an effort to repair his damaged reputation. Only after she refused did he order her death.

Suet, Claud. 27.1–2.
Suet, Ner. 35.4.
Tac., Ann. 13.23, 47; 14.57; 15.53.
Balsdon, J. P. V. D., p. 123.
Bauman, R. A., p. 172.
OCD, p. 113.
PW 115.
Syme, R., *Augustan Aristocracy*, passim.

▣ ANTONIA THE ELDER
(39 B.C.E.–?) Roman: Rome
Political player

Antonia, elder daughter of Mark Antony and the independent-minded OCTAVIA (2), sister of the emperor Augustus, grew up in a household filled with children from her parents' multiple marriages. Her parents had married to cement the pact of Brundisium in 40 B.C.E. that established a Roman state divided between her father and her uncle. The pact failed, leading to a renewal of civil war that pitted Roman against Roman and left many children of the senatorial class orphans and without clear claim or access to family or wealth.

Antonia was born in 39 B.C.E., when her parents were in Greece negotiating with her uncle Octavian. He sought Antony's aid in a campaign against Sextus Pompeius Magnus, the son of Gnaeus Pompeius Magnus (Pompey the Great) and leader of the remaining republican forces. After her parents' divorce in 32, Antonia and her younger sister ANTONIA stayed with their mother in a household that also included the three chil-

dren from Octavia's previous marriage to Gaius Claudius Marcellus, an opponent of Caesar and supporter of Pompey, who had died in 40 B.C.E. After Antony's defeat at Actium in 31, and his subsequent suicide in 30, Octavia's household grew to include the son of Antony's deceased wife, FULVIA (2), and the son and daughter of Antony and CLEOPATRA VII.

Antonia married Lucius Domitius Ahenobarbus, to whom she had been affianced since about 24 B.C.E. Ahenobarbus, of an old republican family, has been characterized, like many of his ancestors, as arrogant, cruel, addicted to chariot racing, and rich. He held the consulship in 16 B.C.E. and died in old age in 25 C.E.

It was Antonia's only marriage. She had three children, all of whom took a place in the politics of their time: Gnaeus Domitius Ahenobarbus, consul in 32 C.E. and father of the future emperor Nero; and two forceful women, DOMITIA, wife of Gaius Sallustius Crispus Passienus, and DOMITIA LEPIDA, the mother of Valeria MESSALLINA.

OCD, p. 113.
PW 113.
Syme. R., *Augustan Aristocracy*, passim.

▣ ANTONIA THE YOUNGER
(January 31, 36 B.C.E.–May 1, 37 C.E.)
Roman: Italy
Augusta; power broker

Antonia was an enigmatic woman who made difficult, and sometimes even inexplicable, life choices. In many ways Antonia epitomized the ideal Roman *matrona*. She was a woman of strong character and impeccable morality; she was intelligent and married only once. Twice she was named Augusta. She refused the title offered by her grandson Gaius Caligula when he became emperor 37 C.E. After her death the title was again bestowed, this time by her son, the emperor Claudius.

Antonia was the younger daughter of OCTAVIA (2) and niece of Augustus. She was born

Antonia the Younger and her son Claudius

January 31, 36 B.C.E., when her father, Mark Antony, was in Egypt with CLEOPATRA VII. After the civil war and Antony's death in 30, Antonia lived in her mother's household with the children of her parents' multiple marriages, including those of her father and Cleopatra.

Antonia married Nero Claudius Drusus, the son of LIVIA DRUSILLA, and the stepson of the emperor Augustus, in 16. Drusus was a popular young leader, and his marriage with Antonia made him a likely successor to Augustus. After Drusus's unexpected death while campaigning in Germany in 9 B.C.E., Antonia remained a widow despite her youth and the urging of Augustus to remarry. She lived with Livia who helped raise her children: Germanicus Julius Caesar, Livia Julia Claudia LIVILLA, and Claudius, the future emperor.

Her eldest son Germanicus became as popular as had been his father and married the elder AGRIPPINA, a granddaughter of Augustus. By then, Tiberius, Antonia's brother-in-law, was emperor. Germanicus, who was the most likely heir

to Tiberius, died as had his father before him, campaigning in Germany. Agrippina brought his ashes back to Rome convinced that Tiberius had arranged her husband's death. Inexplicably, Antonia made no appearance at the public honors for her dead son. Nor did Tiberius or Livia. Their absence fed rumors of conspiracy.

Antonia's daughter Livilla married Drusus Julius Caesar, the son of Tiberius and his first wife, VIPSANIA AGRIPPINA, in 4 C.E. Livilla and Drusus had a daughter, JULIA (8), and twin sons, Germanicus and Tiberius Gemellus. Antonia's daughter was later widowed and left with a grown daughter and one living son, Tiberius Gemellus.

Antonia watched the struggle that developed between her widowed daughter, Livilla, and her widowed daughter-in-law, Agrippina, as each competed to secure her own son as successor to Tiberius. They became the center of factions that gave no quarter. Agrippina surrounded herself with an elite circle of the Senate, and Livilla joined forces with her lover, Lucius Aelius Sejanus, the prefect of the Praetorian Guard and the most powerful man in Rome in the years after the departure of the emperor Tiberius for Capri. Antonia stepped in when catastrophe occurred.

Agrippina was forced into exile and suicide. Two of her grandsons, Nero Julius Caesar and Drusus Julius Caesar, died; the former was executed, and the latter starved himself to death while imprisoned. Antonia took the three remaining children of Germanicus and Agrippina—the future emperor Gaius Caligula and his sisters, JULIA DRUSILLA (1) and JULIA LIVILLA—into her household.

Certainly Antonia must have been affected by the exile of her daughter-in-law and the death of her two grandsons. She must also have known of her daughter's alliance with Sejanus and the harm that would befall her if he fell from power. Nonetheless, Antonia arranged to smuggle a letter to Tiberius in Capri, accusing Sejanus of unknown charges that may have led to his arrest and death by strangulation. Tiberius placed Livilla in the custody of Antonia, and she witnessed Livilla's suicide by starvation.

Although both her daughter and daughter-in-law were dead, her son Claudius and grandson Gaius Caligula lived, and Antonia remained a significant person of influence and wealth. She supported the political career of Lucius Vitellius who came from an equestrian background, gained power in the reign of her grandson Gaius Caligula, and was consul three times. She also fostered the career of the future emperor Tiberius Flavius Vespasian.

Antonia maintained extensive connections in the East and owned a great deal of property in Egypt. BERNICE (1), the daughter of SALOME and niece of Herod the Great, was one of her clients and friends. Berenice and her young son, Marcus Julius Agrippa, lived in Rome during the reign of Tiberius, and Agrippa stayed in Antonia's household for a few years. Later Antonia came to his aid and lent him 300,000 drachmas to pay a debt owed to the imperial treasury.

Antonia died on May 1 in 37 C.E., only months after her grandson became emperor. It was just as well. Caligula's behavior became increasingly bizarre, and in 38 he ordered the execution of Antonia's grandson, Tiberius Gemellus. Rumors spread that he had driven Antonia to commit suicide by his ill-treatment or that he had had her poisoned.

Dio. 58.3.9.
Jos., A J 18.156, 161–67, 181 ff., 204, 237.
Suet., Calig. 1.1; 10.1; 15.2; 23.2; 24.1.
Suet., Claud. 1.6; 3.2; 4.1–4; 11.2.
Tac., Ann. 2.43, 84; 3.3; 4.3; 10, 12, 39–41.
Balsdon, J. P. V. D., passim.
Bauman, R. A., pp. 138–39.
Ferrill, A., *Caligula*, passim.
Leon, Harry J., p. 20.
Levick, B., *Claudius*, passim.
Levick, B., *Tiberius*, passim.
Marsh, F. B., passim.
OCD, p. 113.
PW 114.

ANTONIA TRYPHAENA

(1st century C.E.)   Roman: Asia Minor
Ruler

Antonia Tryphaena was the daughter of PYTHODORIS and Polemon I of Pontus, a kingdom in northwestern Asia Minor; she was the great-granddaughter of Mark Antony and his second wife, ANTONIA (2). Antonia Tryphaena married Cotys, the ruler of Thrace.

When Cotys was murdered, Antonia accused his uncle Rhascuporis of committing the crime in order to annex her husband's territory. Antonia gave testimony at the trial held before the Roman Senate in 18 C.E. Rhascuporis was found guilty and banished.

Antonia left her three sons in Rome to be raised with the future emperor Gaius Caligula, and she went to Cyzicus on the island of Arctonnesus in the Black Sea. Very wealthy she used her money to pay for civic improvements including dredging the channel between the city and the mainland. She also became a priestess of

Livia DRUSILLA in whose household in Rome resided her children.

After her father died, Antonia returned to Pontus and ruled as guardian and regent for her son Polemon II. Her head and name appeared on the obverse of coins in accord with Pontus's status as a client kingdom of Rome.

Tac., Ann. 2.64–67.
Macurdy, G., pp. 10–11.
Magie, D., p. 513.
Marshall, A. J., "Ladies at Law," p. 355.

▣ ANTYE

(3rd century B.C.E.) Greek: Tegea
Poet

Antye was a well-known and well-respected poet of the third century B.C.E. Born in Tegea, a city on the southern Greek peninsula, she was said to have written in the traditional form and to have mirrored Homer in her grammar and sentence structure. However, she was attracted to the bucolic themes that were characteristic of the emerging traditions of the period after the death of Alexander the Great.

Although Antye's lyric poems have been lost, 19 Doric epigrams are extant. They are grave in tone and restrained in style. Her quatrains, possibly used as funerary inscriptions, are sensitive without being sentimental.

Lyra Graeca, v. 2, p. 241.
Der Kleine Pauly, p. 417.
Fantham, E., et al., p. 166.
Geoghegan, D., passim.
Gow, A. S., and Page, D. L., v. 2, pp. 89 ff.
OCD, p. 78.

▣ APAMA (1)

(4th–3rd century B.C.E.) Persian: Persia
and Antioch
Progenitor of Seleucid dynasty

Apama was the ancestor of the Seleucids, who ruled over portions of Asia for some 250 years. Her father, the Bactrian Spitamenes, organized a serious revolt in Sogdiana against Alexander the Great. Defeated in 328 B.C.E., he fled into the territory of his allies, the Messagetae. They cut off his head and sent it to Alexander as a token of submission.

Apama, however, survived and became one of the 80 elite Persian women married to Alexander's Macedonian officers at Susa in 324 in an effort to erase the distinction between the conquered and conqueror. Her husband, Seleucus I, was commander of the Silver Shields, which guarded the right flank of Alexander's army. After Alexander's death, Seleucus and Apama were the only couple not to divorce.

Seleucus conquered Babylon, Media, and Susiana to establish the Seleucid Empire. He named a number of cities after Apama. In 298, for strategic reasons, he also married the much younger STRATONICE (2), the daughter of Demetrius I, ruler of Macedonia. According to the ancient sources, Apama's son Antiochus I fell in love with Stratonice. Apama regained her former position in 293, when her husband allowed her son and Stratonice to marry.

Seleucus may have decided that he could no longer govern his eastern provinces from Antioch. He made Antiochus his partner and as coruler, sent him with Stratonice to govern the eastern territories. Antiochus I eventually succeeded his father and with Stratonice secured a dynasty that ruled parts of Asia Minor for over two centuries.

App., Syr. 59–62.
Plut., Dem. 38.
Cary, M., pp. 43, 54.
Macurdy, G.
OCD, p. 118.

▣ APAMA (2)

(3rd century B.C.E.) Greek: Cyrene
Ruler

Apama ruled Cyrene, in North Africa, after the death of her husband. She was overthrown by her daughter. Apama was the daughter of STRA-

TONICE (2) and Antiochus I, ruler of the Seleucid Empire in Asia. In 275 B.C.E., she married Magas, the ruler of Cyrene and the stepbrother of Ptolemy II Philadelphus of Egypt. She had a daughter, BERENICE II OF CYRENE, whom her husband affianced to the future Ptolemy III to secure a union of Egypt and Cyrene. Magas died in 258, and Apama became the ruler of Cyrene. Antigonus Gonatus, ruler of Macedonia and an enemy of Egypt, sent his half brother, the handsome Demetrius, to make an offer of marriage to Berenice and to foil a union with Egypt.

Apama welcomed Demetrius. She favored the house of the Seleucids from which she came, against a union with Egypt which was generally opposed also by the independent-minded Cyrenicians. There is some confusion as to whether Apama married Demetrius or became his lover after he married her daughter. In any case, Berenice, afraid of losing power, led a rebellion in which Demetrius was killed in Apama's bedroom as she tried to shield him with her body.

Apama's life was spared by her daughter, and nothing further is known about her.

Just. 26.3.8.
Cary, M., pp. 84, 138.
Macurdy, G., pp. 131 ff.

APEGA

(3rd–2nd century B.C.E.) Greek: Sparta
Political player

Apega was collaborator, supporter, and agent for the reform policies of her husband, Nabis, ruler of Sparta (207–192 B.C.E.). Nabis canceled debts, redistributed property, and extended citizenship to select indigenous and foreign residents. Apega traveled to Argos to collect gold jewelry and cloth from women to provide funds to support her husband's reforms.

The opposition accused Nabis of prosecuting the wealthy and confiscating land. They also charged Nabis with seizing their wives for the pleasure of his supporters and mercenaries. A curious tale that suggests the determination of Nabis, and perhaps Apega, to extract wealth from the rich has survived. Nabis supposedly constructed a replica of Apega. With the replica at his side, he summoned wealthy men and asked for contributions. Any who refused were required to take the hand of the replica, whose clothing concealed sharp nails. Using a spring mechanism, the replica embraced the recalcitrant donors and drove nails into their flesh. Contributions were usually forthcoming and those who refused were killed by the replica of Apega.

Poly. 13.6–7; 18.17.

APICATA

(1st century C.E.) Roman: Rome
Avenger

Apicata took revenge on her husband and his lover. Her lineage is unknown. Her husband was the infamous Lucius Aelius Sejanus, prefect of the Praetorian Guard and confidant to the emperor Tiberius. After Tiberius went to Capri in 27 C.E., Sejanus became the main conduit for information to the emperor and consequently the most powerful man in the city.

Sejanus collected a discontented faction around him and divorced Apicata when it appeared possible that he might marry his lover and coconspirator, Livia Julia Claudia LIVILLA, the widowed daughter-in-law and niece of Tiberius. In October of 31, however, Sejanus fell out of favor and was charged with crimes sufficiently heinous to cause his immediate execution. Apicata's eldest son Strabo was killed six days later, and Apicata committed suicide the next week. The two younger children, AELIA IUNILLA and Capito Aelianus, were strangled in December on orders of the Senate so that Sejanus might leave no heirs.

Before her death, Apicata extracted revenge. She sent a letter to Tiberius accusing her husband and Livilla of poisoning Livilla's husband, Drusus Julius Caesar, eight years earlier in 23. Drusus had been Tiberius's son. His death was a critical turning point in Tiberius's life now compounded by the discovery of the conspiracy led by Sejanus in whom he had placed his trust. He took the accusation seriously enough to extract a confirmation of the murder in confessions gathered under torture from Livilla's doctor and a slave even though it was already some eight years after the event.

Dio. 58.11.5–7.
Tac., Ann. 4.3.
Bauman, R. A., p. 147.
Levick, B., *Tiberius*, pp. 161, 201, 274; notes 71, 72.
Syme, R., *Tacitus*, p. 402.

APPULEIA VARILLA

(1st century B.C.E.–1st century C.E.) Roman: Rome
Convicted adulterer

Appuleia Varilla was indicted on charges of treason and adultery in 17 C.E. She was one of several people also accused of slander against the emperor. Her father was Sextus Appuleius, consul in 29 B.C.E. and proconsul of Asia; her mother was Quinctilla, a niece of OCTAVIA (1), the half sister of Augustus. The name of Appuleia's husband is unknown. The name of her lover, however, was Manlius.

Appuleia was accused of defaming the new emperor Tiberius and his mother LIVIA DRUSILLA as well as Augustus, only recently deified after his death two years earlier in 15 C.E. Tiberius informed the Senate that neither he nor his mother wished to pursue the charges of slander or treason. The apparently less frivolous charge of adultery stood. If convicted Appuleia could have lost half her dowry and a third of her property, and could also have been banished. Tiberius, however, suggested that she simply be handed over to her family and be removed at least 200 milestones from Rome. Her lover was banned from living in Italy or Africa.

Tac., Ann. 2.50.
Levick, B., *Tiberius*, p. 197.
Marsh, F. B., passim.
Marshall, A. J., "Women on Trial," p. 342.
PW 33.
Syme, R., *Augustan Aristocracy*, passim.

APRONIA

(1st century C.E.) Roman: Rome
Murder victim

Apronia was probably murdered by her husband, the praetor Plautus Silvanus, sometime in 24 C.E. for unknown reasons. She died by falling or being thrown out of a window in her husband's house. Her father Lucius Apronius, who had been a legate to the emperor's adopted son Germanicus Julius Caesar, quickly brought Silvanus up on charges before the emperor Tiberius. Silvanus claimed that Apronia must have committed suicide. He had been fast asleep at the crucial time, and moreover, he suffered from spells inflicted upon him by his long-divorced first wife, Fabia NUMANTINA, whom he was in the process of suing.

Tiberius visited the scene of the crime. He examined the room and window where the event had occurred and found evidence that Apronia had been forcefully ejected. He referred the case to the Senate. Before the case was heard, URGULANIA, the grandmother of Silvanus and a close friend of LIVIA DRUSILLA, the mother of Tiberius, sent Silvanus a dagger. Urgulania, a formidable woman whose arrogance was backed by her influence, left Silvanus little choice. After a fruitless attempt at suicide, Silvanus arranged for someone to open his arteries. With his death the charges against his first wife were dismissed.

Tac., Ann. 4.22.
PW 10.

ARCHIDAMIA

(3rd century B.C.E.) Greek: Sparta
Reformer

Archidamia and her daughter AGESISTRATA were the two wealthiest women in Sparta during the middle decades of the third century B.C.E. Respectively the grandmother and mother of the reformist king Agis IV, they used wealth and position to secure political and economic reform.

With friends and kin, including AGIATIS, the king's wife, Archidamia formed a political alliance that supported land redistribution and the reduction and cancellation of debts. The reformers met strong opposition from those who had vastly increased their wealth through inheritance and foreclosure during the preceding decades, when a declining citizen population found it increasingly difficult to pay mortgage installments. In 241 B.C.E., after Agis initiated his land and debt policies, he was overthrown and killed. Archidamia and her daughter Agesistrata were executed.

Plut., Agis 4.2; 7.5–7; 9.5–6; 20.7.
Mosse, C., pp. 138–53.

⊡ ARCHIPPE (1)

(6th–5th century B.C.E.) Greek: Athens
Political wife

Archippe was the wife of Themistocles (528–462 B.C.E.), the famous Athenian politician and military leader who was exiled in the decade after the battle of Salamis in 479 B.C.E. Probably Themistocles first wife, her father was Lysander from the deme of Alopece. Archippe had three sons: Archeptolis, Polyeuctus, and Cleophantes. Plato characterized Cleophantes as good at horseback riding and not much else.

Her exiled husband left Athens for Persia, where he convinced the king of his usefulness, despite having been responsible for the strategy that defeated the Persians at Salamis. He settled in Magnesia, where he appears to have had a second family. Themistocles killed himself when it became clear that he could no longer serve the Persians without endangering the Greeks.

Although Archippe appears not to have lived in Asia, it is unclear if her marriage was ended by divorce or death.

Pl., Meno p. 93d–e.
Plut., Them. 32.1–2.

⊡ ARCHIPPE (2)

(*c.* 410 B.C.E.–?) Greek: Athens
Self-made woman

Archippe was an Athenian, probably born in 410 B.C.E. or soon after. Although she died a rich woman and a citizen with sons to inherit her wealth, she did not come from a wealthy background nor was she from a family of Athenian citizens.

Archippe married Pasion, who was some 20 years her senior, around 395. An Athenian money changer, Pasion had started life as a slave and he became an Athenian citizen after 391. At the time of their marriage, however, he was already considered the wealthiest banker and manufacturer in Athens. Sources estimate that Pasion earned 100 minae per year through money changing and between 20 and 60 minae from his shield workshop at a time when 60 minae equaled 1 talent, the approximate cost of building an Athenian battleship.

Archippe and Pasion had two sons, Apollodorus and Pasciles. The former was 24 and the latter 10 when their father died. Pasion left real estate worth 20 talents and capital of almost 40 talents. He left his estate to his sons after Archippe had received a large dowry plus property. In his will he appointed Phormion, his business manager, as one of two legal guardians of Archippe's wealth and instructed her to marry him.

Archippe married Phormion, who was not an Athenian citizen. Her son Apollodorus objected to his mother's marriage. The marriage may well have effectively removed Apollodorus from control over his mother's wealth and may also have forced a restructuring of the estate to pay out her dowry. In an effort to annul the marriage, the son charged Phormion with adultery. Since Athenian law prohibited a legal marriage between a citizen woman and a noncitizen, by implication Archippe had gained citizenship through her first husband.

Although the court stipulated that Phormion's sons would have no claim over any of the residual inheritance, the suit failed to annul the marriage or eliminate Archippe's portion under the will.

Ten years later, Phormion was granted citizenship. The two sons born to Archippe and Phormion also became citizens. When Archippe died those sons inherited her property.

Dem. 45.28, 74; 45.3; 46.21.
Godolphin, F. R. B., ed., v. 2, pp. 765–66.
Lacey, W. K., passim.
PW 541–42.

⊞ ARCHO

(2nd century B.C.E.) Greek: Thessaly
War victim

Archo's life was inextricably linked with that of her sister THEOXENA. Their father Herodicus, a leading citizen, had died fighting the invasion of Thessaly by Philip V of Macedon in the late second century B.C.E. Archo's husband also died opposing Philip. As part of a policy of consolidation of his sovereignty, Philip forced whole villages and towns to move. Uprooted from her ancestral home, Archo left with a small child. She married Poris, a prominent citizen from Aenea in northeastern Greece and had several more children before she died.

Archo's sister, widowed in the same invasion, also had a son but chose not to remarry. After Archo's death, Theoxena married Poris to consolidate the estate and to be mother to all the children. In 182 B.C.E., the entire family died in new violence unleashed by Philip V.

Livy 40.3–4.

⊞ ARETAPHILA

(1st century B.C.E.) Greek: Cyrene
Avenger

Aretaphila retired to her loom after avenging her husband's murder. Born into a distinguished family in Cyrene in North Africa during the first century B.C.E., she married Phaedimus, a well-born Cyrenian. He was murdered by Nicorates, the tyrant of Cyrene.

Nicorates forced Aretaphelia to marry him after the murder. Determined to avenge the death of Phaedimus, she tried to poison Nicorates. Caught, she claimed that the draught was a love potion and stood by her story under torture. Despite the misgivings of Nicorates' mother, Calbia, who distrusted Aretaphila, she succeeded not only in saving her life, but also in regaining her position as the tyrant's wife. Fearful of any further direct attack on Nicorates, Aretaphila used her daughter to entice Nicorates' brother Leander into marriage. Her daughter then convinced him that even he, the brother of the tyrant, was not safe. Leander arranged for Nicorates' murder and became tyrant.

Leander proved no better a ruler than Nicorates, and Aretaphila determined that his tyrannical rule over the people of Cyrene must also end. She sought out the African ruler Anabus and encouraged him to attack Cyrene. Then she bribed him to arrange a meeting with Leander on the pretext of making peace. Instead, in accordance with his agreement with Aretaphila, Leander and his mother were turned over to the people of Cyrene. They were both killed.

Aretaphila was asked by the people of Cyrene to rule. She, however, having achieved her goals, retired to private life.

Plut., Mor., De mul. vir. 257d–e.
Polyaenus, Strat. 38.

⊞ ARETE (1)

(5th–4th century B.C.E.) Greek: Cyrene
and Greece
Philosopher

Arete was a philosopher in Athens at the end of the fifth century B.C.E. She was a disciple of her father, Aristippus, a teacher of rhetoric, who was a companion of Socrates. Although Socrates left no written work, Plato portrayed Socrates and his companions in vivid dialogues. The dialogues indicate that Socrates questioned previously unexamined assumptions.

Arete taught philosophy to her son Aristippus, whom she named after her father. He became a founder of the Cyrenaic school, which held that pleasure of the senses was the supreme good, since only sensory impressions are knowable and pleasure preferable to pain.

Diog. Laert. 2.86.

▣ ARETE (2)

(4th century B.C.E.) Greek: Syracuse
Political player

Arete and her mother, ARISTOMACHE, shared tumultuous turns of fortune. Arete was the daughter of Dionysius I and the wife of Dion, both of whom ruled Syracuse, Sicily, in the third century B.C.E. After the death of Thearides, her first husband and her father's brother, she married Dion, who was her mother's brother.

Dion, who held an influential position under her father, Dionysius I, and his successor, Dionysius II, was attracted to the philosophy of Plato. He persuaded Dionysius II to invite Plato to Syracuse in 366 B.C.E. Fearful that Dion wanted to supplant him and become Plato's ideal philosopher-king, Dionysius II exiled him. Plato left Syracuse soon after. Arete and her mother remained behind.

In 361, Dionysius threatened to seize the exiled Dion's property unless Dion persuaded Plato to return to Syracuse. Arete and her mother convinced of Dionysius' seriousness, urged Dion to act quickly. Plato returned and requested that Dion be brought from exile. Instead, Dionysius sold Dion's property. Plato again left Syracuse.

Dionysius also forced Arete, still in Syracuse, to marry his friend Timocratus. In 357/356 B.C.E., Dion captured Syracuse while Dionysius was in Italy. Fearful of her reception, Arete went with her mother to meet him. Her mother informed Dion that Arete had been forced into a second marriage. Dion embraced Arete as his true wife.

Dion's rule became increasingly authoritarian, and opposition increased. The two women were aware of unrest in city, but Dion would not heed their counsel. Callipus, a former supporter of Dion was one of the leaders of the opposition. He feared Arete and her mother and swore his loyalty to them with a sacred oath. He then treacherously murdered Dion in 354. Arete and her mother were imprisoned. Arete gave birth to boy while incarcerated.

Soon Calliopus was killed. Arete and Aristomache were released. They found support from Hicetas, a friend of Dion. However, enemies persuaded him to send Arete and her mother to Greece. Once on board the ship, they were murdered.

Diod. 14.44.8; 16.6.4.
Pl., Ep. 7.345c–347.
Plut., Dion 3.3–4; 6.1–2; 21.1–6; 51.1–5; 57.5; 58.8–10.

▣ ARISTOMACHE

(4th century B.C.E.) Greek: Syracuse
Political player

Aristomache was at the center of a struggle for control over Syracuse, in Sicily, during the fourth century B.C.E. She, her daughter, and her brother, who was also her daughter's husband, constituted a faction influenced by Plato and his ideal of a philosopher-king. Their struggles began after the death of Dionysius I in 376 B.C.E. and ended with their own murders sometime after 354.

Aristomache, the daughter of Hipparinus, a notable of Syracuse, was the wife of the tyrant Dionysius I. She was a cowife, married on the same day that Dionysius also married DORIS of Locri, the daughter of Xenetus, from a leading family in Locri. Dionysius was said to have dined with both women and then bedded each in turn. Other sources claim that Dionysius feared the women and slept with them only after they were searched.

Aristomache bore no children until Dionysius killed Doris's mother, who allegedly had used drugs to prevent Aristomache from conceiving a child. Of her subsequent two daughters, it is known that Sophrosyne married Dionysius II. The other, ARETE (2), was her mother's lifetime ally. Her first husband was Thearides, the brother of Dionysius I. Her second husband was Dion, Aristomache's brother.

After the death of Dionysius I, Aristomache threw in her lot with Arete and Dion, who held a high position at the court of Dionysius II. Influenced by Plato, Dion sought to make Dionysius II a philosopher-king and in 366, he persuaded Dionysius to invite Plato to Syracuse. However, Dionysius exiled Dion in 365 after he became convinced that Dion intended his overthrow. Dion went to Athens, and Plato soon followed.

Aristomache and her daughter remained in Syracuse, where they lobbied on behalf of Dion and protected his wealth as best they could. Dionysius demanded that Dion persuade Plato to return. It was both promise and threat. If Plato returned, Dion would no longer be threatened, but if he refused to come, Dion's estate in Syracuse would be confiscated. Aristomache and Arete were vulnerable and alarmed. They wrote Dion to urge Plato's return.

Even though Plato returned, Dionysius confiscated Dion's estate. He also forced Arete to marry his friend Timocratus. When Plato had difficulty leaving, Dion had no choice but to raise a mercenary army and wage war against Dionysius. In 357–356, Dion marched on Syracuse while Dionysius was in Italy. Aristomache met him. Since Arete was uncertain of her reception, Aristomache assumed control over the situation and informed her brother of Arete's forced marriage. Dion embraced Arete as his wife.

Aristomache remained close to her daughter and brother during his rule of Syracuse and Dion might well have come to a less bloody end had he listened more closely to her advice. Dion sought to emulate a philosopher-king. He lived modestly with his wife and sister and eschewed the ribald and coarse entertainments of his military companions. He also sought to circumscribe the dem-

ocratic assembly of citizens. His attempt to establish an aristocratic government bred discontent. In a critical error of judgment he allowed the murder of Heracleides, who had once won a naval victory over Dionysius but had had become Dion's opponent. Filled with remorse over the slaying, Dion failed to listen closely to Aristomache when she and Arete reported a plot against him led by Callippus, a man who Dion believed to be a friend.

Hearing that Aristomache and Arete had become convinced of his treachery, Callippus approached the women. He proclaimed his loyalty. The women demanded a binding oath in the sanctuary of Demeter and Persphone, where the sacred rites were performed. Callippus donned the purple vestments of the goddesses and recited the oath while holding a blazing torch. All to no avail.

Callippus had Dion murdered in 354 B.C.E. Aristomache and Arete were imprisoned. There Arete gave birth to a boy, a posthumous son of Dion. No sooner had Callippus set out on military campaigns, however, than he lost control over Syracuse. In another turn of fortune, Aristomache, Arete, and the baby were released from prison into the friendly care of Hicetas of Syracuse, a friend of Dion. This, however, was the act of treachery that ended their lives.

Hicetas, persuaded by opponents of the Dion faction, sent the women with the baby to Greece. No doubt the women agreed, since their lives and that of Dion's posthumous son hung by a thread in Syracuse. Once on board ship, the three were murdered, either by sword or by drowning.

Diod. 14.44.8; 16.6.4.
Pl., Ep. 7.345c–347.
Plut., Dion 3.3–6; 6.1–2; 18.6–9; 19.8; 21.5–6; 51.1–5; 56.1–6; 58.8–10.
Val. Max. 9.13.4.

ARRECINA TERTULLA
(1st century C.E.) Roman: Rome
Young wife

Arrecina Tertulla was the daughter of Arrecinus Clemens, one of the two prefects of the Praetorian

Guard under the emperor Gaius Caligula. She married the future emperor Titus in the 60s C.E. She died before his father, Vespasian, became emperor. They had no children.

Suet., Tit. 4.2.
Levick, B., *Claudius*, pp. 37–38.

◫ ARRIA THE ELDER

(1st century C.E.) Roman: Italy
Stoic

Arria lived a life of passionate commitment shared by her daughter, the younger ARRIA, and her granddaughter, FANNIA (2). Living in the most influential political circles of her time, her behavior underscored traditions of character, family loyalty, and honor admired and rarely practiced in the conflicts that racked elite Roman society during the middle decades of the first century C.E.

Educated and articulate, Arria and her husband, Caecina Paetus, followed the teachings of the Stoics. They believed in the dignity of the Senate and the responsibility of senators to speak out about the affairs of the empire. In 42 C.E. Paetus sided with Lucius Arruntius Camillus Scribonianus, legate in Dalmatia and consul in 32, when Scribonianus led two legions in an ill-conceived and ill-fated revolt against the emperor Claudius. Even though Arria was a friend of Valeria MESSALLINA, the wife of Claudius, she traveled with Paetus to Dalmatia in support of the insurgency. The legions, however, refused to march on Rome, and the revolt was quashed in four days. Scribonianus was killed, and Paetus was taken prisoner.

Arria sought to accompany her husband on board the ship taking him to Rome. She argued that a man of his rank, even though a prisoner, should be accorded several slaves for his toilet and table. Were she present, she would be able to serve him. When the soldiers refused her request, Arria hired a small fishing boat and followed behind her husband's ship to Rome. There, at the emperor's palace, she encountered Vibia, the wife

of Scribonianus, also newly returned from Dalmatia, who had testified against her own husband in the resulting inquiry. When the woman approached, Arria turned away, declaring that she would not suffer conversation with a woman who clung to life although her murdered husband had died in her arms.

Arria's strength of character rested on her conviction that marriage bound her with her husband in public as well as in private life. Her husband and their beloved son were both critically ill, and the son died. Arria arranged for the funeral and kept the news from Paetus so that grief would not tip the scales in his own struggle to live.

Her death was as noble as her life. Awaiting her husband's conviction for treason, she refused to appeal to her friend Messallina and made it clear to her family that she planned to die with him. Her son-in-law, Publius Clodius Thrasea Paetus, sought to dissuade her. He asked if she would tell her daughter to die in similar circumstances. Arria responded that she would, if her daughter had as harmonious a shared life with her husband as Arria had with hers. When her family sought to protect her from herself, she beat her head against a wall until she lost consciousness, making plain that they could not force her to live.

When the time came for Paetus to die, Arria was by his side. She took the sword and plunged it into her breast, sealing her immortality by telling him that it did not hurt.

Dio. 60.16.5–7.
Plin., Ep. 3.16.
Mart. 1.13
OCD, p. 175.
Pomeroy, S. B., *Goddesses*, p. 161.

◫ ARRIA THE YOUNGER

(1st century C.E.) Roman: Italy
Stoic

Arria belonged to a circle of distinguished men and women who shaped the literary and philosophical ideas of the period and who were active in the politics of the day. Often, they risked their fortunes and their lives to oppose the emperors. Her mother, the elder ARRIA, and her father, Caecina Paetus, had committed suicide in 42 C.E. after her father had been convicted of treason against the emperor Claudius.

By marrying Publius Clodius Thrasea Paetus, consul suffectus in 56, Arria, who was related to the Stoic satirist Aulus Persius Flaccus (34–62 C.E.), entered into a senatorial family that reinforced the union of honor, politics and Stoic discourse. Her husband upheld the family tradition when he walked out of the Senate after a self-serving letter was read in which the emperor Nero enumerated the charges that justified the death of his own mother, the younger AGRIPPINA.

The almost inevitable happened in 66. Thrasea Paetus was accused in the Senate of treason. Helvidius Priscus, the husband of Arria and Thrasea Paetus's only child, FANNIA (2), was also accused. Priscus, a fellow student of Stoicism, had married Fannia in about 55. The accusation that he shared Thrasea Paetus's views was no doubt justified. Arria's husband was condemned to death, and Priscus was banished. Thrasea Paetus learned of his fate while hosting a dinner. He urged his guests to leave so as not to be implicated in his affairs and turned his attention to committing suicide. Arria intended to follow her mother's example and die with her husband, but he convinced her to live for the sake of their daughter. She and Fannia were closely linked thereafter. Since Fannia was already a grown woman and married, Arria may have used her own wealth to augment the losses to her daughter from the confiscation of both Thrasea Paetus's and Priscus's estates.

In 66, Arria and Fannia left Rome voluntarily with the banished Priscus. The three returned in 68, when Galba supplanted Nero as emperor. Priscus immediately began a prosecution of Marcellus Epirus, who had received 5 million sesterces for his earlier successful prosecution of Priscus and Thrasea Paetus. Fortune as well as honor was at stake. Among the senators, more

than a few had financially benefited from the late persecutions and were themselves vulnerable to attack from newly returned exiles. The Senate was divided, and Priscus withdrew his case on the advice of friends.

Priscus continued to attack Epirus outside the Senate. Around 75, the emperor Vespasian, angered by Priscus's attacks and claiming that he did the state no service by constantly harping on wrongs from the past, again exiled him. Fannia and Arria left with him. Soon after, Priscus was executed, although sources note that Vespasian had sent a letter that arrived too late to prevent the execution.

Arria and Fannia returned to Rome after the death of Vespasian, and they once more entered on a collision course with the emperor. At the time of Thrasea Paetus's death, Junius Arulenus Rusticus, then plebeian tribune, had offered to veto the Senate's resolution condemning Thrasea Paetus. His offer had been refused, for Thrasea Paetus did not wish to jeopardize the young man at the beginning of his career by causing him to directly oppose the Senate and the emperor. In 93, the emperor Domitian ordered the execution of Rusticus, who had been consul suffectus in 92, for his praise of the dead Thrasea Paetus and the elder Helvidius Priscus. He also ordered the execution of the younger Helvidius Priscus, Fannia's stepson, and he expelled all philosophers from Rome in an attempt to rid himself of Stoic sympathizers. Arria and Fannia were among those exiled.

More specifically, Arria and Fannia were expelled for commissioning a laudatory memoir of the younger Helvidius Priscus. Fannia attempted to take full blame and to spare her mother another exile, to no avail. The women, however, once more outlived their tormentor and returned to Rome in 96. At the request of the younger Pliny, Arria and Fannia joined with ANTEIA, the widow of the younger Helvidius Priscus, in a suit to clear the latter's name. Pliny brought the matter before the Senate, but no action was taken.

Arria died before Fannia, although the exact date is unknown.

Plin., Ep. 3.11; 9.13.
Tac., Ann. 16.21–29, 33–35.
Tac., Hist. 4.3–9.
Suet., Dom. 10.
Suet., Ves. 15.
Balsdon., J. P. V. D., p. 58.
OCD, p. 175.

▥ ARRIA FADILLA

(1st–2nd century C.E.)   Roman: Gaul
Mother of Antoninus Pius

Arria Fadilla was from Nemausus (Nimes) in Roman Gaul. She was a member of the new provincial elite that came to power with the emperor Trajan and that formed the dynasty of the Antonines. She was well educated and very wealthy. Like many of the women in these elite families, she successfully managed her own business affairs with property inherited from her father's as well as her mother's sides of the family.

Her father, Arrius Antoninus, had been consul suffectus in 69 C.E. and proconsul of Asia. He was a friend of the emperor Marcus Cocceius Nerva, under whom he served a second time as consul, and with whom he shared an interest in Greek poetry. His poetry was sufficiently well known for Pliny the Younger to have commented favorably upon it. Arria Fadilla's mother was Boionia Procilla, whose family probably had connections to the emperor Trajan.

Arria Fadilla married Aurelius Fulvus, a man also from a provincial consular family in Nimes. It was a successful marriage. Their son, Titus Aurelius Fulvus Boionus Arrius Antoninus, became the emperor Antoninus Pius (reigned 137–61) after his adoption by Hadrian.

Plin., Ep. 4.3.
SHA, Ant. Pius 1.4
PW 44
Syme, R., *Tacitus*, pp. 604–5.

▥ ARSINOË

(4th century B.C.E.)   Greek: Macedonia
Progenitor of Ptolemaic line

Arsinoë was the mother of the Ptolemaic line of Greek rulers in Egypt that lasted from 323 B.C.E., after the death of Alexander the Great, until Egypt became a Roman province in 30 B.C.E. She was probably a lover of Philip II, ruler of Macedonia (359–336 B.C.E.). She married a Macedonian named Lagus, who was the father of her son Ptolemy. Ptolemy, a general in Alexander's army, became Ptolemy I Soter, ruler of Egypt.

OCD, p. 1,271.
PW 24.

▥ ARSINOË I

(300 B.C.E.–?)   Greek: Greece and Egypt
Political player

Arsinoë I and her sister-in-law, ARSINOË II PHILADELPHUS, vied for power in the generation born after the death of Alexander the Great. Born in 300 B.C.E., she was the daughter of NICAEA (1) and Lysimachus, one of Alexander's generals. In 289 or 288 she married Ptolemy II Philadelphus and had three children: Ptolemy III Euergetes, BERENICE SYRA, who married the Seleucid king Antiochus II, and Lysimachus.

Arsinoë was no match for her sister-in-law. After escaping from her husband/stepbrother Ptolemy Ceraunus, who ruled Macedonia, Arsinoë II persuaded Ptolemy II to become her husband and banish Arsinoë on trumped up charges of conspiracy. The very wealthy Arsinoë went to Coptus in Upper Egypt where she lived in great splendor and exercised considerable power. Her eldest son ruled Egypt after his father's death.

Poly. 25.5.
Cary, M., passim.
Macurdy, G., pp. 109–11.
OCD, p. 177.

🏛 ARSINOË II PHILADELPHUS
(c. 316–270 B.C.E.) Greek: Egypt
and Macedonia
Coruler; deified

Arsinoë II played an important role in the complicated marital and political coalitions formed in the generation born after the death of Alexander the Great in 323 B.C.E. She was the daughter of Ptolemy I Soter of Egypt and BERENICE I. In 300 or 299 B.C.E., she married Lysimachus, a companion of her father and of the late Alexander. Her husband had became ruler of Thrace and had gained control of Macedonia and Thessaly in the years since Alexander's death. He shed his second wife to marry Arsinoë and cement relations with her father.

Arsinoë was about 16 when she married; Lysimachus was 60 or 61. She strongly influenced her elderly husband who gave her the towns of Heraclea, Tius, Amastris, and Cassandria. They had three sons. Determined that one of her sons would succeed her husband, she convinced Lysimachus to eliminate Agathocles, his eldest son by a previous marriage. He charged the boy with treason and put him to death in 283.

Arsinoë II

Lysimachus was killed in battle in 281. Arsinoë, who was in Ephesus, dressed her maid in royal clothing while she darkened her face and dressed in rags. With her three sons, she went to the shore where ships were waiting to take them to Macedonia. She escaped and the maid, whom she left behind, was killed. Settling in Cassandreia, she raised a mercenary army from her own wealth.

Arsinoë married Ptolemy Ceraunus, her half brother, who ruled Macedonia and Thrace after having killed Seleucus I to become king. The distrustful Arsinoë forced Ceraunus to marry her in front of the Macedonian troops outside the gates of Cassandreia. Shortly thereafter, Ceraunus killed two of her sons even as she held them. The eldest, who had warned his mother against the marriage, had escaped to Illyria before the wedding. Fearful of Arsinoë's brother, Ptolemy II Philadelphus, Ceraunus spared Arsinoë. She, however, mindful of her vulnerable position, left for Egypt.

Almost 40 years old, Arsinoë married her brother Ptolemy II after persuading him to banish his wife, ARSINOË I. Theirs was the first sibling marriage among the Greek rulers of Egypt. Prior to the marriage, Ptolemy II had been defeated by Antiochus I, and Egyptian forces had been driven from Syria. After the marriage, Arsinoë energized her new husband to lead the Egyptians to a victory that included the capture of Phoenicia and most of the coast of Asia Minor from Miletus to Calycadnus in Cilicia. She also strengthened Egyptian sea power to expand the sphere of Egypt's influence.

She and her husband ruled for about five years. She was the first Greek woman ruler of Egypt to have her portrait appear along with that of her husband on coins. She and her husband were also the first Ptolemaic rulers to deify themselves during their lifetime. She was considered an incarnation of the Egyptian goddess Isis. Poets composed verses about her, and the court of Alexandria flourished. Arsinoë wanted her son Ptolemy, whose father was Lysimachus, to become king of

Macedonia, but she died in 270 B.C.E. before she could succeed.

Just. 24.2–3.
Polyaenus, Strat. 18.57.
Burstein, S. M., pp. 197–212.
Cary, M., passim.
Macurdy, G., passim.
OCD, p. 177.
Pomeroy, S. B., *Women in Hellenistic Egypt.*, passim.
Tarn, W. W., *Hellenistic Civilization*, passim.

▣ ARSINOË III PHILOPATOR

(3rd century B.C.E.)   Greek: Egypt
Ruler

Arsinoë III, a brave, beloved, and virtuous ruler, was victimized by her brother/husband and eventually murdered in a conspiracy headed by her husband's lover and brother. Born in 235 B.C.E., she was the daughter of BERENICE II OF CYRENE and Ptolemy III Euergetes. In 217 Arsinoë, who was still a young woman, was present on the battlefield of Raphia in Coele-Syria where she rallied the troops and prevented a defeat by Antiochus III the Great in the Fourth Syrian War. After the battle, she married her brother, Ptolemy IV Philopator. Arsinoë, who was much younger than her brother, gave birth to a boy in 210.

The marriage was not happy. Ptolemy was addicted to drink and debauchery. He became besotted with AGATHOCLEIA, who had come to Egypt from Samos with her mother and brother. Along with her mother, OENANTHE, and her brother, Agothocles, Agathocleia murdered Ptolemy and Arsinoë in 205. Enraged primarily at the death of Arsinoë, whom they admired, the army and the people of Alexandria tore the assassins limb from limb.

Ath. 276b.
Poly. 5.83–84; 15.33.
Macurdy, G., pp. 136–41.
OCD, pp. 177–78.
Pomeroy, S. B., *Women in Hellenistic Egypt*, pp. 50–51.

▣ ARSINOË AULETES

(65 B.C.E.–43/40 B.C.E.)   Greek: Egypt
Coruler; insurgent leader

Arsinoë Auletes engaged in a struggle with her older sister CLEOPATRA VII for control over Egypt that cost her life. Her mother was possibly CLEOPATRA VI TRYPHAENA, and her father was Ptolemy XII Auletes. She was born about 65 B.C.E. She seems to have been as strong-willed as Cleopatra VII but without her charm, allure, diplomatic skills, or culture. In 48, when Julius Caesar decreed that Cleopatra VII and her brother Ptolemy XIII, should be joint rulers of Egypt and marry each other, he also made Arsinoë Auletes and her other brother, Ptolemy XIV, joint rulers of Cyprus. Arsinoë was kept under watch by Caesar.

Jealous of Cleopatra VII's more prominent role, she escaped to Alexandria aided by the eunuch Ganymede. She was about 17 when the Egyptian forces in Alexandria, led by their commander-in-chief Achillas, declared her ruler of Egypt. Not satisfied with a secondary role, she soon vied with Achillas over control of the armed forces. She had him killed and took charge. She appointed Ganymede head of the armed forces in the fight against Caesar. The Egyptian forces, unhappy under the control of a woman and a eunuch, asked Caesar to send the young Ptolemy XIII, Arsinoë's brother, to discuss peace terms. Instead, the Egyptian forces rallied around Ptolemy XIII. Arsinoë was defeated after a hard struggle.

Fearful that Arsinoë would again rally the Egyptians, Caesar took her to Rome and paraded her in regal attire and chains in his triumph. In 41, he allowed Arsinoë to go free, and she became a suppliant in the temple of Artemis at Ephesus. After Caesar's death, Mark Antony, at the request of Cleopatra VII, ordered that she be taken from the temple and killed.

App., Bciv. 5.9.
Dio. 42.35, 39–40, 42; 43.19.2–4.
Jos. AJ 15.89–90.
Macurdy, G, passim.
PW 28

◨ ARTACAMA

(4th century B.C.E.)   Persian: Persia
Political wife

Artacama married Ptolemy, the future ruler of Egypt, when he was still a general in the army of Alexander the Great. Artacama was the daughter of Artabazus (387–325 B.C.E.), who was appointed satrap of Dascylium by Artaxerxes II, king of Persia. After subduing the Persians, Alexander arranged to have 80 of his most distinguished Macedonian officers marry women of the Persian aristocracy in an effort to meld conquerors and conquered.

The marriages, including that of Aretaphila and Ptolemy, took place in 324 at Susa. After the death of Alexander in 323, the experiment in union through marriage fell apart. Artacama and Ptolemy divorced.

Arr., Anab. 7.4.
Cary, M., p. 250.

◨ ARTEMESIA I

(5th century B.C.E.)   Greek: Asia Minor
Ruler

Artemisia captained five ships in Xerxes' Persian fleet at the battle of Salamis against the Greeks in 480 B.C.E. Widowed, and with a young son, she ruled Halicarnassus, Cos, Nisyrus, and Calyndus in southwestern Asia Minor. Her father was Lygdamis of Halicarnassus, and her mother was thought to be of Cretan background. She assumed rule over Halicarnassus, whose inhabitants were Greek, after the death of her husband. Although she ruled under Persian suzerainty, it was not necessary for her to bring a fleet into battle.

Artemisia provided ships as well as wise and practical counsel for Xerxes. She was the only one of his naval commanders to urge him—correctly—not to engage the Greek fleet in the straits of Salamis. She escaped after the Persian defeat by sinking an enemy vessel. Later she transported part of Xerxes' family to Ephesus.

A white marble figure was erected in the portico of the temple of Artemis in Sparta to commemorate her actions at Salamis.

Hdt. 7.95–100.
Paus. 3.11. 3.
Hammond, N. G. L., *History of Greece*, p. 239.
OCD, p. 184.

◨ ARTEMISIA II

(4th century B.C.E.)   Greek: Asia Minor
Ruler

Artemisia ruled Caria, a virtually independent satrapy of Persia in southwest Asia Minor, after the death of her brother/husband, Mausolus, in 353 or 352 B.C.E. In memory of her husband, she continued to build a mausoleum he had begun in Halicarnassus that would become one of the Seven Wonders of the Ancient World.

The foundation of the Mausoleum was about 100 by 140 feet with a high base upon which stood a colonnade of some 36 Ionic columns supporting a pyramidlike cap that reached a height of about 140 feet. The architect was Pythius, who was said to have sculpted a major chariot group frieze for the structure. Other well-known sculptors of the time, including Scopas, Bryaxis, Timotheus, and Leochares, were also said to have contributed to the project.

Following in her husband's Panhellenic literary, scientific, and artistic path, Artemisia sponsored a competition in oratory attended by the leading figures of the day, including Isocrates. The winner was Theopompus. She also must have had an interest in horticulture and named a plant after herself.

An attack on Rhodes by exiles expecting support from Athens gave Artemisia reason for attacking and conquering Rhodes. She died a short time later in 351 B.C.E.

The Mausoleum, with its sculptured groupings of animals and human figures, was destroyed in an earthquake before the 15th century C.E. In 1857 the site was excavated by C. T. Newton. Among the pieces brought to the British Museum were colossal statutes of Mausolus and Artemisia.

Aul. Gell., NA 10.18.1–6.
Plin., NH 25.36; 36.30–32.
OCD, p. 184.

◫ ARTONIS

(4th century B.C.E.) Persian: Persia
Political wife

Artonis was one of 80 noble Persian women who married the elite Macedonian officers of Alexander the Great in a mass ceremony in Susa in 324 B.C.E. She was the daughter of Artabazus, who defected to Alexander the Great and was made satrap of Bactria.

Artonis married Eumenes, a Greek from Cardia, who was Alexander's principal secretary. Eumenes divorced Artonis after Alexander died.

Arr., Anab. 7.4.

◫ ARTORIA FLACCILLA

(1st century C.E.) Roman: Rome
Loyal wife

Artoria Flaccilla lived among the rich, the educated, and the imperial elite. Her husband, Novius Priscus, was a close friend of the philosopher Lucius Annaeus Seneca. For some eight years at the beginning of Nero's reign, Seneca and Sextus Afranius Burrus were the emperor's two most important advisers. Burrus died in 62 C.E., and Seneca fell from favor as Nero's behavior became more extreme. In 65, Nero falsely accused Seneca of participating in the Pisonian conspiracy to kill the emperor and forced him to commit suicide. Nero sent Priscus into exile, and Artoria Flaccilla voluntarily went with her husband.

Tac., Ann. 15.71.

◫ ASPASIA

(5th century B.C.E.) Greek: Athens
Self-made woman

Aspasia was the most famous woman of Athens during the height of its democracy in the fifth century B.C.E. She was clever, intelligent, sophisticated, cultured, and politically astute. Her father, Axiochus, was from Miletus on the southwest coat of Asia Minor. Aspasia was Pericles' companion and lived with him from 445 B.C.E., some five years after he divorced his wife, HIPPARETE (1), until his death in 429.

Very much a part of the public life of the city, she participated in its intellectual and political ferment. She visited with Socrates and his disciples. There is some indication that several of the men who visited with her may even have been accompanied by their wives or other female companions. She is also said to have educated a group of young women, possibly resident foreigners or freedwomen.

Pericles, always open to political attack, was especially vulnerable in his relationship with Aspasia. Her public presence so close to him and among the elite of the city drew comments, sometimes amusing, other times derisive and biting. In the winter of 441–440 B.C.E., war broke out between Samos and Miletus, Aspasia's birthplace, over possession of the city of Priene. Aspasia was accused of persuading Pericles to make war against the Samians after the Milesians lost and appealed to Athens for help. According to treaty, Athens had no right to intervene; nevertheless, Pericles conquered Samos.

After Pericles died, Aspasia joined forces with Lysicles, a popular leader described as a low-born sheep dealer who became famous through his association with her. He died in 428.

Aspasia had two children, one with Pericles and the other with Lysicles. Pericles had been the author of the Athenian law that restricted citizenship to children born of two citizen parents. However, Aspasia and Pericles' son became a citizen after the death of Pericles' two sons from his earlier marriage. The child took Pericles' name and grew up to become an Athenian general.

The exact date of Aspasia's death is not known.

Ath. 5.219b–c.
Pl., Menex. 235e–236d; 249d, e.
Plut., Per. 24.2–6; 25.1; 32.1–3.
Blundell, S., p. 148.
Davies, J. K., p. 458.
OCD, p. 192.
Pomeroy, S. B., *Goddesses*, pp. 89–90.

ATIA (1)

(1st century B.C.E.) Roman: Italy
Mother of Octavia and Augustus

Atia can truly be said to be a woman known by her children. She was the mother of Octavian, who became the emperor Augustus, and OCTAVIA (2) and the stepmother of OCTAVIA (1). Atia was the elder daughter of Marcus Atius Balbus and JULIA (4), the younger sister of Julius Caesar. Her first husband, Gaius Octavius, died in 58 B.C.E., leaving her with two children. She then married Lucius Marcius Philippus, who was consul in 56.

When Caesar was murdered, Octavian was in Apollonia on the Adriatic Sea, where he had been sent by his uncle for experience in campaigning. Atia and Philippus wrote advising him to come to Rome with dispatch, but to keep a low profile and assess the situation. Atia, concerned that the Senate had decreed not to punish the assassins, advised Octavian to use wiles and patience rather than seek confrontation.

Octavian took their advice and first stopped at Brundisium, where he discovered that he was Caesar's heir. Atia supported Octavian's plan to accept his inheritance and avenge Caesar's death. The 19th-year-old Octavian began his march on Rome.

Octavian was 20 years old and serving his first consulship when Atia died in 43. She had a public funeral. Octavian conferred the highest posthumous honors on her.

App., Bciv. 3.13, 14.
Suet., Aug. 61.
OCD, p. 207.
PW 34.

ATIA (2)

(1st century B.C.E.) Roman: Italy
Niece of Julius Caesar

Atia and her older sister ATIA (1), the mother of the emperor Augustus, were the nieces of Julius Caesar through their mother JULIA (4), Caesar's sister. Their father was Marcus Atius Balbus.

Atia married Lucius Marcius Philippus, consul suffectus in 38 B.C.E. He was the stepson of her sister, who had married Philippus's father after the death of her first husband. They had a daughter, MARCIA (3), who later married Paullus Fabius Maximus, consul suffectus in 45 B.C.E.

OCD, p. 207
PW 35.
Syme, R., *Augustan Aristocracy*, passim.

ATILIA

(1st century B.C.E.) Roman: Italy
Accused adulterer

Atilia, the daughter of Serranus Gavianus, tribune in 57 B.C.E., married Marcus Porcius Cato Uticensis in 73 B.C.E. He was on the rebound from AEMILIA LEPIDA (1), who had unexpectedly rejected him. Cato, an unpleasant person, was 22 years old. Atilia was about 16. Plutarch wrote that Cato was a virgin; presumably so was Atilia. Although not unusual for a woman, it was indicative of an unusual man.

At first the marriage was sufficiently successful for Atilia to wish to accompany Cato on a political mission for the Senate in the East, and to be concerned for his safety when he went without her. There were several children. Nonetheless, the marriage ended in divorce, with Cato accusing Atilia of infidelity.

Plut., Cat. Min. 7.3; 9.1–2; 24.1.
PW 79.

⊡ ATTIA VARIOLA

(1st century C.E.) Roman: Rome
Litigant

Attia Variola sued her father for her patrimony. She was born into an aristocratic family and married a member of the Praetorian Guard. Her father, a lovesick old man, remarried at the age of 80. Eleven days later, he disinherited Attia. The case was tried before the entire Centumviral Court, consisting of 180 jurors. Attia was represented by Gaius Plinius Caecilius Secundus (Pliny the Younger), who gave one of his best speeches. The stepmother and her son both lost any right to inherit.

Plin., Ep. 6.33.

⊡ ATTICA, CAECILIA

(51 B.C.E.–?) Roman: Rome
Heiress

Caecilia Attica was the beloved only child of Titus Pomponius Atticus, whose lifetime friendship with Marcus Tullius Cicero included a correspondence that provides rare insight into personal and family life during the late republic. Her father came from a wealthy equestrian family and inherited additional wealth from an uncle who had adopted him. He married PILIA in 56 B.C.E., when he was 53. She came from an old family in the city of Cora not far from Rome. It was his first marriage. Their daughter Attica was born in 51.

The extant correspondence from 68 to 43 B.C.E. between Atticus and Cicero covers both personal and professional concerns. As Attica was growing up, the letters traced the seasonal movements from city to country, the trips with her mother to visit friends and family in and out of Rome, and concern with the various illnesses she suffered.

In 37 Attica married Marcus Vipsanius Agrippa, a close friend of Atticus and a lifelong supporter, friend, and leading military commander of Octavian, the future emperor Augustus. The marriage made Agrippa immensely wealthy. Her father gained a relationship with the closest circle around Octavian. One can only guess at the relationship between the lively 14-year-old Attica and the austere Agrippa. In 31, Attica gave birth to a daughter, VIPSANIA AGRIPPINA.

After her father's death in 32, Attica was suspected of having an affair with her tutor, Quintus Caecilius Epirota, a learned freedman. She was either divorced or died young. Agrippa contracted another marriage in 28 B.C.E.

Cic., Att. 12.1, 6, 13, 33; 13.14, 19, 21a, 52; 14.16.11.
Cic., Brut. 17.7.
Suet., Gram. 16.
OCD, p. 267.
PW 78.

⊡ AURELIA (1)

(2nd–1st century B.C.E.) Roman: Rome
Mother of Julius Caesar

Aurelia came from the patrician family of the Aurelii Cottae, whose members included two consuls between the years 76 and 74 B.C.E. She married Gaius Julius Caesar, who died in 85 B.C.E. She never remarried. They had three children: a son, the great Gaius Julius Caesar, who was 16 when his father died, and two daughters, JULIA (3) and JULIA (4).

It was Aurelia who detected the presence of the notorious Publius Clodius Pulcher disguised as a woman in Caesar's house during the Bona Dea rites, a traditional festival restricted to well-born women.

Aurelia died in 54 while Caesar was campaigning in Britain.

Plut., Caes. 10.
Balsdon, J. P. V. D., p. 244.
OCD, p. 219.
PW 219.

37

◫ AURELIA (2)

(1st century C.E.) Roman: Rome
Woman of means

Aurelia appears at the moment she was about to sign her will in a vivid and humorous letter written by Pliny the Younger. Even though a *tutor*, functioning in the role of agent, probably was still necessary or customary for some kinds of transactions, Aurelia, like many Roman women of the later first century, controlled her own affairs and could make bequests of her own choosing. The signing of a will moreover, was an occasion when propertied and wealthy women dressed in an elaborate fashion, clothing being itself valuable as well as indicative of wealth. Marcus Regulus, an advocate, seemingly made it a habit to persuade people to include him in their wills. He was present as one of the witnesses on the festive occasion of the signing. He asked Aurelia to leave him her dress. Aurelia thought he was joking, but he was insistent, and so she wrote the bequest of her dress into her will while he stood by. Pliny concluded his letter with the report that Aurelia was still alive and Regulus still awaited his bequest.

Plin., Ep. 2.20.

◫ AURELIA ORESTILLA

(1st century B.C.E.) Roman: Rome
Possible conspirator

Aurelia Orestilla was the wife of Lucius Sergius Catilina when he led an uprising against the Senate in 63 B.C.E. Her father was Gnaeus Aufidius Orestes, consul in 71. She married, had a daughter, and was widowed. Left wealthy, she married the impovished but well-born Catiline in 68. Vicious rumors circulated around the marriage; one accused Catiline of having murdered his son to marry Aurelia because she refused to become the stepmother of a grown son.

Catiline had a varied political career. Increasingly impoverished, however, he rallied a political base among the indebted, both low and high born.

The combination of inflation with the rigidity of a land-based economy and the absence of a flexible money supply resulted in indebtedness and mortgaged estates that fed frustration and became politically charged. Catiline became the leader of a conspiracy against the Senate to ease debt. The conspiracy was uncovered and Catiline fled Rome in 62.

Catiline was said to have written his friend Quintus Lutatius Catullus that he had sufficient funds to meet his own obligations. However, Aurelia and her daughter paid some part of the debt incurred by others on his behalf, and he left Aurelia vulnerable to law suits stemming from the conspiracy. Catiline was subsequently put to death without a trial. Whatever her role in the conspiracy, or the resulting law suits, Aurelia remained unharmed, her wealth intact.

App., Bciv. 2.2
Cic., Cat. 114
Cic., Fam. 8.7.2
Sall., Cat. 15.2; 35.3, 6
PW 261

◫ AURELIA SEVERA

(?–213 C.E.) Roman: Rome
Priestess

Aurelia Severa was tried and convicted of violating her vow of chastity. One of four Vestal Virgins convicted in 213 C.E. by the emperor Marcus Aurelius Antoninus, she and her colleagues CANNUTIA CRESCENTINA, CLODIA LAETA, and POMPONIA RUFINA, caused a major scandal. In an earlier age, the conviction of four out of six Vestals would have been regarded as a sign of approaching calamity, but times had changed. Although still regarded as part of ancient tradition, awe had given way to greater skepticism. Nonetheless, Aurelia was buried alive in the ancient tradition.

Dio. 78.16.1–3.

AXIOTHEA (1)

(4th century B.C.E.)   Greek: Greece
Philosopher

Axiothea came from the city of Philius on the Peloponnese, the peninsula in southern Greece. She studied philosophy under Plato at the Academy he established in Athens.

Diog. Laert. 3.46.

AXIOTHEA (2)

(4th century B.C.E.)   Greek: Cyprus
Heroine

Axiothea died rather than surrender when the city of Paphos was seized in a war among Alexander the Great's successor generals. She was the wife of Nicoles of Paphos on the island of Cyprus. Nicoles had sided with Antigonus, who controlled most of Asia Minor after the death of Alexander, against a coalition led by Ptolemy I Soter of Egypt, Cassander of Macedonia, and Lysimachus of Thrace. Nicoles committed suicide in 310 B.C.E. when Ptolemy's army surrounded his palace.

Ptolemy had issued no instructions about the women. As his army stormed the palace, Axiothea killed her daughters so that it would be impossible for the enemy to rape them. She urged her sisters-in-law to join her in committing suicide. After they killed themselves, the brothers of Nicoles set fire to the palace and perished in the blaze.

Axiothea was praised by the ancient historians for her bravery in choosing death for herself and her children over a life of slavery.

Diod. 20.21.1.
Polyaenus, Strat. 8.48.

B

BALBILLA, JULIA

(2nd century C.E.) Greek: Asia Minor
Poet

Julia Balbilla was a poet who accompanied the imperial entourage of Vibia SABINA and her husband, the emperor Hadrian, on a trip to Egypt in 130 C.E. She inscribed five epigrams on the left foot of the Colossus of Memnon in Thebes.

Her epigrams were in Aeolian Greek, the language used by the great poet SAPPHO eight centuries earlier. They juxtapose the mortal and the immortal. They tell the story of Memnon, a mythical king of Ethiopia who was killed by Achilles at Troy and whom Zeus made immortal. Balbilla claimed for herself piety and a royal lineage to Balbillus the Wise and the ruler Antiochus. On the Colossus, she hoped that her words would last forever, and she, a mortal descendant of a king, would become immortal.

Balsdon, J. P. V. D., p. 140.
Bowie, E. L., p. 63.
Fantham, E, et al., pp. 353–54.
PW 559.

BARSINE (1)

(4th century B.C.E.) Persian: Asia Minor
and Egypt
Adventurer

Barsine lived an adventurous life in difficult times. She was the daughter of Artabazus, a Persian, who succeeded his father, Pharnabazus, as satrap of Dascylium, a city on the Black Sea in Asia Minor. She married a Rhodian mercenary leader, Mentor, who along with his brother Memnon had entered the service of Artabazus in a revolt of the satraps (362–360 B.C.E.) quelled by the Persian ruler Artaxerxes III.

In 353 Barsine, Memnon and Mentor fled. Barsine and Mentor went to Egypt where Mentor assembled an army of Greek mercenaries. In 344, while supposedly guarding the city of Sidon in Phoenicia against an attack by Artaxerxes, he instead helped Artaxerxes capture the city. Artaxerxes rewarded him by appointing him general. In this position Mentor helped Artaxerxes conquer Egypt in 343. He also secured a position for his younger brother, Memnon. After Mentor's death, probably in 342 B.C.E., Barsine married Memnon. Memnon fought successfully against

Philip II of Macedon in 336 and became commander-in-chief of the Persian forces under Darius. He died suddenly around 333 B.C.E.

Barsine was captured by Alexander the Great in Damascus after the death of Memnon. Her high birth, beauty, Greek education, and amiable disposition brought her to his personal attention. She was said to be the only woman with whom Alexander had a sexual relationship prior to his marriage. Alexander married the daughter of Barsine and Mentor to his naval commander, Nearchus.

After Alexander's death Barsine lived in Pergamum in Asia Minor and took part in the struggles for power among Alexander's generals. Her pawn in these struggles was Heracles, whom some claimed was her son by Alexander. Although probably not the son of Alexander, and possibly not even the son of Barsine, the 17-year-old boy was taken by Alexander's former general Polyperchon from Pergamum to use as a bargaining chip with Cassander when he sought to gain control over Macedonia. Polyperchon reached an agreement with Cassander to kill Heracles in exchange for land, support, and additional troops. Heracles was murdered in 309 B.C.E. Polyperchon also killed Barsine.

Diod. 10.20.1–4; 10.28.1–4.
Just. 11.10; 15.2.
Plut., Alex. 21.7–11.

▣ BARSINE (2)

(4th century B.C.E.) Persian: Persia
Wife of Alexander the Great; political victim

Barsine, called Stateira by Plutarch, was the eldest daughter of Darius, the ruler of Persia. In 324 B.C.E., after having conquered Persia, Alexander the Great arranged a mass marriage of his most distinguished officers to 80 aristocratic Persian women in a revolutionary effort at ethnic harmony. He married Barsine even though he already had a wife, ROXANE, whom he had married in 327. Barsine's sister DRYPETIS married Hephaestion, Alexander's closest companion.

After the death of Alexander, Barsine was a potential rallying point in the bitter battles for power that erupted among Alexander's generals. To protect the position of her infant son, Roxane had Barsine and her sister murdered and hid their bodies in a well.

Arr., Anab. 7.4
Diod. 17.6
Plut., Alex. 70.1–3.
Burn, A. R., *Alexander the Great,* pp. 122, 170, 182.

▣ BASTIA

(1st century B.C.E.) Roman: Rome
Hard-hearted woman

Bastia lived through the Social War (90–88 B.C.E.) and the proscriptions that followed in the dictatorship of Lucius Cornelius Sulla. She was the wife of Gaius Papius Mutilus, a Samnite from southern Italy and one of the two leading generals in the armies fighting Rome. Despite passage of a law that granted Italians full Roman citizenship, Mutilus refused all Roman offers of peace and led resistance in the last stronghold in 80 B.C.E. in the city of Nola.

His final defeat by Sulla coincided with the onset of the proscriptions, a bloodbath precipitated by the Roman system of rewarding informers for uncovering the whereabouts of people on the lists of those wanted by the state. Papius Mutilus was listed, but Bastia was not. He came in disguise to Bastia's house to seek refuge. She would not admit him. It is unclear if she also threatened to report him. He stabbed himself to death on her doorstep. Her death is not recorded.

Livy 89.

▣ BERENICE (1)

(1st century B.C.E.–1st century C.E.) Jewish: Judaea
Political client

Berenice, the daughter of SALOME and the niece of Herod the Great of Judaea, had close ties with the

Roman imperial family through her friend, the younger ANTONIA. After Berenice's husband, Aristobulus, was executed in 7 B.C.E., she brought Marcus Julius Agrippa, her young son and future ruler of Judaea, to Rome and placed him in Antonia's care. He grew up with Tiberius's son Drusus Julius Caesar, with whom he became a close friend, and Antonia's son, the future emperor Claudius. These relationships stood him, his sister HERODIAS, and their kin in good stead over the course of his political life.

When Berenice died, she left her freedman Protos in the service of Antonia. It was not an unusual bequest from a client, especially to a patron such as Antonia, who had business interests in the East. It was probably also an effort on Berenice's part to assure security for Protos.

Jos., AJ 17.12; 18.143, 156, 164–65.
Leon, H. J., p. 20.
Levick, B., *Claudius*, p. 12.

▣ BERENICE (2)

(1st century C.E.) Jewish: Judaea and Rome
Political player

Berenice might have become Augusta had she not been a foreigner and a Jew. Politically astute, intelligent, charming, and beautiful, Berenice had great influence with the emperors Vespasian and Titus. Born in 29 C.E. she was the oldest daughter of Marcus Julius Agrippa I, the king of Judaea, and Cypros, the granddaughter of Herod the Great. She had a younger sister, DRUSILLA (2) with whom there was a lifelong sibling rivalry. In 41 she married into a very wealthy Jewish family in Alexandria. When her husband died she married her uncle Herod, the king of Chalcis in Lebanon, with whom she had two sons. After Herod died she lived with her brother, Agrippa II, who succeeded her husband as king of Chalcis. To quiet rumors of incest, Berenice married Polemon, priest-king of Olba in Cilicia, whom she soon left.

She was responsible for the appointment of her former brother-in-law, Tiberius Julius Alexander, to the post of procurator of Judaea in 46. However, her attempts to persuade Gessius Florus, procurator of Judaea appointed by the emperor Nero in 64, to change his policies toward the Jews failed. When the Jews revolted against his harsh rule, Berenice barely escaped.

In 67, Vespasian, accompanied by his son Titus, arrived in Judaea to quell the rebellion. Titus fell in love with Berenice, who at 39 was some 11 years his senior, although age had evidently made no inroads on her beauty, charm, or diplomatic skills. She and her brother, Agrippa, sided with Vespasian in his successful attempt to become emperor in place of Vitellius. Berenice accompanied her brother to Berytus (Beirut) where Vespasian was encamped, charmed the emperor, and plied him with gifts.

After conquering Jerusalem in 70, Titus returned to Rome in triumph to share the emperorship with his father. Berenice came to Rome in 75 and lived with Titus for several years. Widespread criticism of the liaison forced its end. When Titus became emperor in 79, Berenice returned to Rome, but once again criticism ended the relationship. Berenice has been called the "mini-Cleopatra"—though Titus and Vespasian were no Julius Caesar and Mark Antony.

Jos., AJ 18.132; 19.267–77, 354; 20.104, 145–46.
Jos., BJ 2.217, 220–22, 310–14.
Grant, M.
OCD, p. 4.
Perowne, S., passim.

▣ BERENICE I

(340–281/271 B.C.E.) Greek: Macedonia and Egypt
Political player; deified

Berenice I was the most influential woman in Egypt at the end of the fourth and beginning of the third centuries B.C.E. She supplanted her cousin EURYDICE (3) in the affections of her stepbrother

Ptolemy I Soter. Born in 340 B.C.E., Berenice was the granddaughter of Cassander, a general under Alexander the Great, and the great-granddaughter of Antipater, one of Alexander's successors. Her mother was Antigone, and her father, a Macedonian named Lagus.

Berenice married Philippus, a Macedonian, and had several children, among whom were Magas, later king of Cyrene, and ANTIGONE. Widowed, she came to Egypt as a companion to her aunt Eurydice, who had married Ptolemy I Soter as part of a plan by Antipater to secure marital alliances among the successors to Alexander and thereby re-create his empire.

Berenice, some 26 years his junior, became Ptolemy's lover in 317 and persuaded him to reject her aunt. Their love was celebrated in the Seventeenth Idyll of the leading poet of the period Theocratus of Syracuse. She bore two children, ARSINOË II PHILADELPHUS and Ptolemy II Philadelphus. Ptolemy designated their son as heir and appointed Ptolemy Philadelphus joint ruler in 285.

Berenice married her daughter Antigone to Pyrrhus, later ruler of Epirus, who sought a close relationship to secure Ptolemy's support. He returned to Epirus with money and an army. Just as Ptolemy named a town in Berenice's honor in Egypt, so too Pyrrhus named a town in her honor in Epirus.

Berenice died between 281 and 271 and was deified by her son, who built temples to honor his parents.

Plut., Pyrrh. 4.4; 6.1.
Macurdy, G., pp. 103–9.
OCD, p. 239.
Pomeroy, S. B., *Women in Hellenistic Egypt.*
PW 9.

▣ BERENICE II OF CYRENE
(c. 273–221 B.C.E.) Greek: Cyrene and Egypt
Ruler

Berenice was a woman of courage, great strength of character, and enormous ambition. She overcame the treachery of her mother, APAMA (2), to

Berenice II of Cyrene

become ruler of Cyrene, in North Africa, and succeeded in linking Cyrene with Egypt through her marriage to Ptolemy III Euergetes.

Born in 273 B.C.E., Berenice was part of the tangled web of relationships among five generations of successors to Alexander's empire. Her father, Magas, king of Cyrene, was the great-grandson of Cassander, one of the generals in the army of Alexander. Her grandmother BERENICE I had gone to Egypt after her father's birth. Already a widow with several children, her grandmother became the wife of Ptolemy I Soter and mother of Berenice's stepuncle Ptolemy II Philadelphus—and consequently the most influential woman of her day.

Ptolemy II had been responsible for her father's rule over Cyrene. Before her father died, he arranged her marriage to Ptolemy III, the future ruler of Egypt, for the union would extend the alliance between Cyrene and Egypt into the next generation. Berenice's mother, Apama, came from the house of the Seleucids, also successor rulers to Alexander with an empire centered in Asia Minor. She opposed Berenice's marriage, as did Antigonus Gonatus of Macedonia, who had concluded an alliance with the Seleucids. The marriage was also opposed by the home-rule partisans of Cyrene.

After her father's death, Berenice's mother invited the half brother of Antigonus Gonatus, the handsome Demetrius the Fair, to come to Cyrene and marry Berenice. Sources, sometimes unclear about this web of relationships, especially with regard to the women, differ as to whether Apama or Berenice married Demetrius. They agree that he became Apama's lover.

Fearful of the intentions of her mother and Demetrius, Berenice, who was about 18 years old, led a successful revolt in 255. Demetrius was killed in Apama's bedroom, despite Apama's attempt to shield him with her own body. Berenice prevented any harm to her mother.

In 247, shortly after he became ruler, Berenice married Ptolemy III. They had four children. One son, Magas, was scalded to death in his bath by another son, the future Ptolemy IV Philopator, who felt that Berenice favored Magas. A daughter, ARSINOË III PHILOPATOR, married her brother Ptolemy IV, and another daughter, Berenice, died in 238. In all accounts, Berenice's marriage was successful. It has given rise to one of the famous stories of antiquity. When Ptolemy embarked on a campaign to Syria in aid of his sister, BERENICE SYRA, Berenice vowed to dedicate to the gods a lock of her hair if he returned safely. According to a literary tradition that the Roman poet Catullus was said to have borrowed from the earlier poet Callimachus, Berenice deposited her tresses at the temple of Aphrodite in Alexandria. The hair disappeared, and Conon, a Greek astronomer residing in Alexandria in the imperial service, rediscovered the tresses in a constellation of stars he named the Lock of Berenice. It is known today as the Coma Berenices.

After the death of her husband in 221, Berenice ruled jointly with her son Ptolemy IV. Her power was soon challenged by one of the ministers, Sosibius. Rivalry between mother and minister dominated imperial affairs. Chafing under his mother's domination, Ptolemy IV had Sosibius

assassinate Berenice in 221 B.C.E. A decade later in 211 or 210 he established an eponymous priesthood and a special cult in her honor.

Catull. 66.
Just. 26.3
Poly. 5.36.1.
Cary, M., passim.
Macurdy, G.
OCD, p. 239.
Pomeroy, S. B., *Women in Hellenistic Egypt*, passim.

BERENICE III CLEOPATRA
(2nd–1st century B.C.E.) Greek: Egypt
Ruler

Berenice III Cleopatra ruled Egypt jointly with her father and then for short time independently. Her mother was either CLEOPATRA IV or CLEOPATRA V SELENE. Her father was Ptolemy IX Soter II, also known as Lathyrus.

She remained in Egypt after her father was driven into exile and in 102 or 101 B.C.E. married her uncle, Ptolemy X Alexander I. In the twisted web of relationships among the Ptolemies, Alexander was the youngest son of Berenice's grandmother. The marriage took place shortly after the death of her grandmother, who had been coruler with Alexander. Berenice fled with Alexander after he was deposed in a popular revolt in 89. They went to Syria, where he was killed the next year. She returned to Egypt, where her father had once again assumed control, and became coruler with him. He died in 80, leaving Berenice his heir.

The women around Berenice were anxious that she marry a male kinsman and appoint him coruler. There was good reason for concern. Rome depended on Egypt for its corn and was positioned to exert its influence over Egyptian affairs. Taking the initiative, Lucius Cornelius Sulla, then dictator of Rome, sent a son of Ptolemy X Alexander to Egypt to marry Berenice and become Ptolemy XI Alexander II.

Neither Berenice nor the people of Alexandria welcomed the new arrival. Nineteen days after he wedded Berenice, in 80 B.C.E., he had her murdered. Angered by the murder of Berenice, whom they admired, the Alexandrians revolted, and Ptolemy XI Alexander II, the last direct male descendant of Alexander the Great's general Ptolemy I, died in ignominy.

App., Bciv. 1.102.
Cic., Leg. agr. 2.42.
Macurdy, G., passim.

▣ BERENICE IV CLEOPATRA

(1st century B.C.E.) Greek: Egypt
Ruler

Berenice ruled Egypt for two to three years before she was murdered in a struggle for power with her father, Ptolemy XII Neos Dionysus Auletes. She was either the daughter or the sister of CLEOPATRA VI TRYPHAENA. Auletes was a weak man. He used bribes that depleted his own wealth and placed tax burdens upon the populace to strengthen his claim to rule. In 58 B.C.E. he went to Rome to seek Roman support against a threatened revolt. In his absence Berenice and Cleopatra VI Tryphaena were recognized as joint rulers by the Alexandrians. The latter died after one year, and Berenice ruled for two more years (58/57–56/55 B.C.E.).

The Alexandrians insisted that Berenice marry. They sought to both strengthen Berenice's position and preclude the claims of Auletes. Choices were limited, and two potential matches fell through. A hasty marriage was arranged for Berenice with a Seleucid whose behavior was so crude that the Alexandrians called him "Fish-packer." Berenice had him strangled within a few days. In the meantime, Auletes had journeyed to Ephesus where he hoped to bribe Gabinius, the Roman proconsul of Syria, to secure his position in Alexandria. Gabinius restored Auletes in 55, and her father immediately ordered Berenice's execution.

Dio. 39,57.
Jos., AJ 13.13.1; 15.1.

Strabo 12.3.34.
Macurdy, G., passim.
Pomeroy, S. B., *Women in Hellenistic Egypt*, p. 24.
Skeat, T. C., pp. 37–39.

▣ BERENICE SYRA

(c. 280–246 B.C.E.) Greek: Egypt
and Antioch
Ruler

Berenice struggled to control the Seleucid Empire and failed. Born about 280 B.C.E. to ARSINOË I and Ptolemy II Philadelphus, in 252, she became the pawn in a dynastic marriage arrangement between Ptolemy and the Seleucid Antiochus II. With a dowry so large that she was referred to as "Dowry Bearer" (Phernophorus), Ptolemy hoped her marriage would neutralize Antiochus as he pursued war against Antigonus Gonatus in Macedonia.

Berenice's dowry probably encompassed the territory Ptolemy had previously captured from Antiochus. Since she was almost 30, it was said that Ptolemy also sent jars of Nile water to encourage her fertility. Despite wealth and the birth of a son, the union was no bargain for Antiochus or the Seleucids. The marriage opened a conflict between Berenice and LAODICE I, Antiochus's first wife, whom he had repudiated as a condition for the alliance with Berenice.

The women's conflict rent the empire. Laodice, with whom Antiochus had had four children, moved herself and her family from Antioch to Ephesus. Henceforth, both cities served as capitals of the empire. In 251, after Antiochus assured Berenice that her infant son would be his heir, he returned to Laodice and declared the latter's 20-year-old son his successor. Antiochus promptly died.

Berenice, who remained in Antioch, charged that Laodice had poisoned Antiochus and pressed the claims of her son. A number of cities in Syria, including Antioch, supported her. She also appealed for aid to her father, Ptolemy II. Her message reached Egypt shortly after her father's death. Her brother, Ptolemy III Euergetes, sent a fleet to aid her.

Laodice bribed the chief magistrate of Antioch to kidnap Berenice's son. Berenice pursued the kidnappers in a chariot, striking the chief magistrate with a spear and killing him with a stone. The child, however, was dead. Berenice appealed to the people. The magistrates who had colluded in the murder became fearful. They produced a child whom they claimed was Berenice's son, but they refused to release him to Berenice.

Berenice moved into a palace in Daphne, a suburb of Antioch, guarded by Galatian soldiers and her women retainers and supporters. In 246, assassins sent by Laodice attacked and murdered Berenice, despite the efforts of the women to shield her with their bodies. As a final note, although her brother's fleet arrived too late to save her, her retainers concealed her death until his arrival and thereby enabled her brother to rally to his side all those in Syria who supported Berenice, precipitating the Third Syrian War (246–241 B.C.E.).

App., Syr. 65.
Just. 27.1, 4.
Polyaenus, Strat. 8.50
Val. Max. 9.10.1.
Bevan, E. B., pp. 181 ff.
Cary, M., pp. 86–88.
Macurdy, G., pp. 87 ff.
OCD, p. 239.
Pomeroy, S. B., *Women in Hellenistic Egypt*, pp. 14, 17.
PW 10.

BILISTICHE

(3rd century B.C.E.) Greek or Phoenician: Egypt
Self-made woman

Bilistiche's background is uncertain. Her beauty and astuteness, however, are well attested. She had once been a slave brought to Alexandria. Described as an Argive freedwoman much sought after by men, her name suggests she may have been Macedonian or Phoenician in origin or ancestry.

She grew rich and famous as the favored lover of Ptolemy II Philadelphus. She was the First woman of her background to sponsor horses in the Olympic games. Her horses won the four-horse chariot race in 268 B.C.E. and the two-horse race at the next festival. She managed her wealth well. There is a record of her having made a loan in 239 or 238 when she was well into old age.

Among other honors, she was appointed to an eponymous priesthood, and Ptolemy II dedicated shrines and temples to Aphrodite in her honor. The date of her death is not known.

Ath. 13.596.
Plut., Mor., Amat. 753f.
Harris, H. A., pp. 178–79.
Pomeroy, S. B., *Women in Hellenistic Egypt*, pp. 53–55.

BOUDICCA

(1st century C.E.) Celtic: Britain
Ruler

Boudicca led a revolt of the Iceni in East Anglia against the Roman settlements in Britain. She was the wife of Prasutagus, whom the Romans had made a client-king. He died in 59 or 60 C.E., and in his will he named the emperor Nero co-heir with Boudicca and her daughters in the hope that this would insure the stability of his lands and his family.

His effort was in vain. Roman imperial agents whipped Boudicca and raped her daughters. They pillaged the lands of the Iceni and confiscated estates of prominent families. Heavy Roman taxation, complicated by the harsh demands of money lenders who supplied the silver and gold against the security of land, caused others to ally themselves with the Iceni.

Led by Boudicca, the Iceni, assisted by the Trinovantes, revolted in 60 C.E. A large woman with long tawny hair flowing down to her hips, a harsh voice, and blazing eyes, she held a spear ready while leading her troops into battle, and she terrified the Romans. Her forces plundered the

Roman strongholds at Colchester, Verulamium, and London.

In time, she was defeated by a large and organized Roman force and she committed suicide. Damned with faint praise, the ancients wrote that she possessed greater intelligence than most women.

Dio. 62.1–12.
Tac., Agr. 16.1–2.
Tac., Ann. 14.31–37.
Dudley, D., and Webster, G., passim.
OCD, p. 256.

🔲 BUSA

(3rd century B.C.E.)   Roman: Italy
Patriot

Busa was a woman of unknown background and great wealth. In 216 B.C.E. she resided in Canusium, the town in Apulia to which the Roman general Publius Cornelius Scipio retreated in disarray with some 10,000 soldiers after their devastating defeat by Hannibal at Cannae.

Townspeople provided shelter for the fleeing soldiers. To regroup, Scipio needed more than shelter; Busa gave him food, clothing, and financial support, providing the means to raise new soldiers and rearm. Busa was honored by the Roman Senate at the end of the war.

Livy 22.52.7; 54.1–3.
Val. Max. 4.8.2.
Bauman, R. A., p. 23.

C

CAECILIA
(1st century C.E.) Roman: Italy
Mother of Pliny the Younger

Caecilia was with her son in Misenum on the Bay of Naples when Mount Vesuvius erupted in August 79 C.E. She begged her son to leave her, but the 18-year-old Pliny refused. Together they walked out of the town. Both escaped unharmed.

Caecilia was a member of the Plinii, a provincial family that was wealthy and well connected. Her husband owned estates in Comum (Como). Widowed when her son was still young, there is no indication that she married again. Her son was adopted by his uncle, Pliny the Elder, a famous writer and naturalist. The elder Pliny stayed too long to observe the eruption of Mount Vesuvius and was killed.

Plin., Ep. 6.20.

Caecilia Metella (1)
(2nd–1st century B.C.E.) Roman: Rome
Power broker

Caecilia Metella was a widow already 50 years old when she married Lucius Cornelius Sulla. It was the marriage of the Roman social season. She gained a political husband on the way up; he gained a wife with wealth and connections. The subsequent years may well have been more difficult and bloody than she had anticipated; however, only death ended their relationship.

Sulla was not her first husband. Born into the Metelli clan, her relatives held the office of consul or censor and celebrated triumphs 12 times within a 12-year period. Her father was Lucius Caecilius Metellus Delmaticus, consul in 119 B.C.E. Her first husband, Marcus Aemilius Scaurus, was wealthy, a consul, and a *princeps senatus,* the senior member of the Senate. They had three children, including AMELIA (2). Caecilia Metella married Sulla in 88 B.C.E., after the death of Scaurus. With the support of the Metelli, the 50-year-old Sulla became consul in the same year. She was his fourth wife, and as with his earlier marriages, he had married her to forge an alliance with her influential and wealthy family. With Sulla she had twins: Faustus Cornelius Sulla and FAUSTA.

When Lucius Cornelius Cinna seized control of Rome in 87 and ordered Sulla removed from his command, Caecilia Metella escaped from Rome with her children and a year later, in 86 joined Sulla in Greece. Although their property in Rome was attacked and their houses burned, Sulla refused to accept Cinna's authority. They returned to Italy, and Sulla's army defeated the opposition forces. He entered Rome victorius. In 82 he became dictator.

Caecilia Metella did not live long after his victory. She died from an illness that Sulla may have transmitted to her and that was sufficiently contagious for the priests to have forbidden him to be with her or to have her funeral in the house. To avoid ritual contamination, to observe the strict letter of the law, and perhaps to satisfy his own fears, he transported her to a neutral house and divorced her posthumously. Her funeral, however, allowed no misunderstanding of his feelings. Ignoring his own recent funerary law, he spared no expense on her burial.

Plut., Sull. 6.10–12; 22.1; 35.1–2.
OCD, p. 267.
PW 134.
Syme, R., *Roman Revolution*, pp. 20, 31.

CAECILIA METELLA (2)

(2nd–1st century B.C.E.) Roman: Rome
Political player

Caecilia Metella, born into one of Rome's wealthiest and most illustrious families, died with an unsavory reputation. Her father was Lucius Metellus Calvus, consul in 142 B.C.E., and her husband was Lucius Licinius Lucullus, praetor in 104. Her husband was convicted of bribery, and she was reputed to be promiscuous.

She had two sons. The eldest, Lucius Licinius Lucullus, supported and served under the general Lucius Cornelius Sulla. He was an excellent soldier and administrator and served as consul in 74. The younger son was Marcus Terentius Varro Lucullus, consul in 73.

Plut., Luc. 1.

CAEDICIA

(1st century C.E.) Roman: Rome
Possible conspirator

Caedicia was exiled from Italy without a trial in the aftermath of the Pisonian conspiracy against the emperor Nero in 65 C.E. Her husband, Flavius Scaevinus, was the conspirator designated to stab Nero. Scaevinus was a man of senatorial rank whose mind was said to have been destroyed by debauchery. He was betrayed by a servant. The exact role played by Caedicia in the conspiracy is unclear.

Tac., Ann. 15.49, 53–55, 70–71.

CAENIS ANTONIA

(?–75 C.E.) Roman: Rome
Self-made woman

Caenis Antonia spanned the decades from Julio-Claudian rule to the Flavians. She was a mature woman when she became the lover of the future emperor Vespasian. Earlier, in 31 C.E., she was a freedwoman secretary of the younger ANTONIA, and it was she who was said to have carried the letter from Antonia to the emperor Tiberius describing the treachery of the emperor's confidant Lucius Aelius Sejanus. When Antonia demanded that Caenis Antonia destroy the message about Sejanus after Tiberius had the information, she was said to have responded that she could not erase her memory.

Caenis Antonia and Vespasian became lovers during the lifetime of his wife, DOMITILLA FLAVIA (1). After her death, they lived as husband and wife. She was a woman reputed to like money and power. During her years with the emperor Vespasian, she acquired vast sums by selling state priesthoods and offices including positions as governor, general, and procurator. She died in 75 C.E.

Dio. 64.1–4.
Suet., Ves. 3.
Balsdon, J. P. V. D., p. 131.
PW 126.

CALPURNIA (1)

(1st century B.C.E.) Roman: Rome
Wife of Julius Caesar

Calpurnia married Gaius Julius Caesar in 59 B.C.E. to cement an alliance between Caesar and her father, Lucius Calpurnius Piso Caesoninus, consul in 58. She was 18 years old and Caesar's third wife.

She remained attached to Caesar even as he contemplated a marriage with the daughter of Mark Antony in 53. She warned him against going to the Senate on the fateful Ides of March 44 B.C.E. After his assassination, she turned his papers over to Mark Antony along with a large sum of money.

Plut., Caes. 63.
Suet., Caes. 21; 81.
OCD, p. 279.
PW 279.

▣ CALPURNIA (2)

(1st century C.E.)   Roman: Rome
Self-made woman

Calpurnia revealed to the emperor Claudius the scandalous behavior of his wife Valeria MESSALLINA and her lover Gaius Silius. Calpurnia was one of Claudius's two favorite freedwomen. Bribed with promises of gifts and influence by Messallina's political enemy Narcissus, the powerful freedman secretary of the emperor, Calpurnia described the mock marriage that had taken place between Messallina and Silius. Claudius had both Messallina and Silius put to death in 48 C.E.

Tac., Ann. 11.29–30.
Levick, B., *Claudius*, p. 67.

▣ CALPURNIA (3)

(1st–2nd century C.E.)   Roman: Rome
Wife of Pliny the Younger

Calpurnia married Pliny the Younger after the death of his second wife in 97 C.E. Her grandfather, Calpurnius Fabatus, and Pliny both came from Comum. Pliny described Calpurnia to her aunt, CALPURNIA HISPULLA, in rapturous terms. He praised Calpurnia's discerning interest in his books and writings. She was supportive when he was involved with a case and glad to have his com-

pany when he was free. She was, he claimed, an ideal woman.

Calpurnia had a miscarriage and went to Campania to recover. Pliny waited for her letters and begged her to write as often as twice a day. Her husband attributed her miscarriage to her youthful ignorance of the hazards of pregnancy. Calpurnia accompanied Pliny to Bithynia-Pontus in northwest Asia Minor, where he had been sent by the emperor Trajan in 110 to reorganize the disorderly province. She returned to Italy on news of the death of her grandfather.

Plin., Ep. 4.19; 6.4, 7; 7.5; 8.10, 11, 19; 9.36; 10.120.
OCD, p. 279.
PW 130.

▣ CALPURNIA HISPULLA

(1st–2nd century C.E.)   Roman: Italy
Woman of means and character

Calpurnia Hispulla was a close friend of Pliny the Younger and his family, especially his mother, CAECILIA. Although they owned estates in different parts of Italy, her father, Calpurnius Fabatus, had been born in Comum, the same town that was the home of Pliny's family. She raised her niece, CALPURNIA (3), who at a relatively young age became Pliny's third wife. Pliny attributed many of the qualities of his wife's character to the influence of Calpurnia Hispulla.

Plin., Ep. 4.19; 8.11.

▣ CALVIA CRISPINILLA

(1st century C.E.)   Roman: Rome
Political survivor

Calvia Crispinilla prospered by pandering to the tastes of the times. Her lineage is unknown, but she lived within the imperial circle under Nero, survived the transition to the Flavians, and died a rich old woman. During the reign of Nero, Calvia arranged entertainments, apparently lascivious in nature. Under her care was the young Greek eunuch Sporus, who resembled Nero's wife POPPAEA SABINA (2), whom he had killed in a fit of anger.

Calvia joined the conspiracy against Nero. She encouraged Lucius Clodius Macer, the governor in Africa, to revolt in 68 C.E. and supported his policy of cutting off the corn supply to Rome. Despite her visibility, she avoided retribution after Clodius Macer was killed by orders of Servius Sulpicius Galba, who supplanted Nero. She was said to have used her popularity to secure a husband behind whose propriety she could stand invisible.

Calvia managed to survive the reigns of Galba, Otho, and Vitellius and to become richer with each regime. As time passed, her wealth and the absence of any children as heirs made her very attractive to men whose fortunes had waned or been lost, as well as to all other kinds of adventurers and fortune hunters. She was courted until she died.

Dio. 62.12.3–4.
Tac., Hist. 1.73.
Charles-Picard, G., p. 162.

▣ CALVINA

(1st–2nd century C.E.) Roman: Italy
Financial head of household

Calvina settled her father's estate and faced insolvency. Her father was C. Plinius Calvinus, part of the Plinii, a well-known provincial landowning family whose most famous members were the naturalist Pliny the Elder and his letter-writing nephew Pliny the Younger.

Calvina's father had left his estate encumbered and Calvina strapped for cash to meet the outstanding notes. She wrote Pliny the Younger about the situation. Although not fully knowledgeable of the total encumbrances on the estate, Pliny agreed that Calvina might have no choice but to sell land. If, however, he was the only creditor or the principal one, he would surrender his claim and consider the 100,000 sesterces that he had loaned her father a gift. Pliny also surrendered

claim to a second 100,000 sesterces raised by her father for her dowry.

Pliny encouraged Calvina to accept his offer and protect her father's memory. As a friend, he would not her father's memory sullied by his having died insolvent. He assured her that the gift would not leave him in straitened circumstances; although his fortune was small, his expenditures were similarly restricted.

Plin., Ep. 2.4.
PW 5.

▣ CANNUTIA CRESCENTINA

(?–213 C.E.) Roman: Rome
Priestess

Cannutia Crescentina was one of four Vestal Virgins condemned in 213 C.E. for violating the vow of chastity. The Vestal Virgins guarded the flame of Vesta in one of the oldest temples in the Forum.

In earlier times pollution among Vestal Virgins was believed an ill omen for the city. By the third century C.E., these old beliefs had declined or given way to new kinds of religious experience. Nonetheless, the power of tradition and the historical association between the chastity of the Vestal Virgins and the well-being of Rome exceeded the life of the ancient religious belief and maintained a hold over the imagination of Rome.

Crescentina was convicted with AURELIA SEVERA, CLODIA LAETA, and POMPONIA RUFINA and condemned to die in the ancient rite of being buried alive. She, however, committed suicide by jumping off the roof of her house.

Dio. 78.16.1–3.

▣ CARTIMANDUA

(1st century C.E.) Brigantian: Britain
Ruler

Cartimandua led the Brigantes, the most populous tribe in Britain, for some 26 years, between 43 and 69 C.E. The last surviving member of the family who had traditionally led the tribe, she negotiated a treaty with the emperor Claudius to become a client state. The treaty brought peace to the northern border of Roman Britain and prosperity to the Brigantes for six years.

Her alliance with the Romans, however, was controversial. Venutius, her husband, favored greater independence. There was a series of political crises. In 51 Cartimandua turned over to the Romans a defeated Welsh leader, Caratacus, who had fled to the Brigantes. A quarrel ensued between Cartimandua and Venutius. Twice between the years 52 and 57 Rome intervened on her behalf, and the two were reconciled.

In 69, when Cartimandua discarded Venutius in favor of his armor-bearer, Vellocatus, whom she made joint ruler, she effectively separated her husband from his most important client-chief and provided herself with male support more favorable for her policy of close ties with Rome. However, in 68–69, while the Roman forces in Britain were otherwise occupied, Venutius and his supporters defeated Cartimandua in battle.

Rome rescued her but did not restore her to her former position, and thereby lost the opportunity to maintain a strong and friendly buffer state on its northern British border.

Tac., Ann. 12.36.
Tac., Hist. 3.45.
OCD, pp. 296–97.
Richmond, I. A., pp. 43 ff.

▣ CASTA, CAECILIA

(1st–2nd century C.E.) Roman: Rome
Acquitted of corruption

Caecilia Casta was indicted along with her husband, Caecilius Classicus, her daughter, and her son-in-law on charges of malfeasance for behavior and acts incurred during her husband's tenure as provincial governor in Baetica, Spain. It was quite usual for Roman officials to augment their personal fortunes when serving abroad; it also was not unusual for them to be sued on their return to Rome, particularly if they had been especially avaricious. Only after Rome became an empire, however, did women frequently join their husbands on posts abroad and become subject to suit.

Casta's husband died before the trial began. Pressed by the Baeticians, the Senate voted to allow the prosecution to proceed against Casta, her daughter, her son-in-law, and her husband's estate. Pliny the Younger acted for the Senate as one of two prosecuting counsels.

There was direct evidence against Caecilius Classicus. Letters were found among his papers boasting of the amounts of money he had taken. In one, addressed to a woman in Rome, he claimed that he would return to Rome with 4 million sesterces. To gather evidence against Casta, the Baeticians had secured the services of Norbanus Licinianus, known as the Inquisitor for his style in court. During the trial in 100 C.E., however, one of the witnesses accused Norbanus of conspiring with Casta to upset any case against her.

The disposition of the charges rested with the Senate, and the consequences could be quite dire, ranging from the confiscation of property to death or exile. The Senate found the daughter and son-in-law not guilty. Classicus's estate was stripped of any gains, and the confiscated funds were to be divided among the victims. Any payments made to creditors in the period since the end of his governorship were similarly to be returned. His residual estate, which consisted mostly of his debts, was awarded to his daughter.

Much to Pliny's disgust, Casta was found not guilty. Since her daughter, not she, was the residual legatee, she escaped unscathed, not even responsible for the unpaid debts on her husband's estate. Norbanus, however, was found guilty of colluding with Casta and was exiled.

Plin., Ep. 3.9.
Marshall, A. J., "Women on Trial," pp. 350–51.

CELERINA, POMPEIA

(1st–2nd century C.E.)   Roman: Rome
Friend and wealthy mother-in-law of Pliny the Younger

Pompeia Celerina, the daughter of Pompeius Celer, was a wealthy woman. She married twice. Her daughter was the second wife of Pliny the Younger. The daughter died about 97 C.E., but Celerina and Pliny remained friends. He was probably closer to her age than that of her daughter.

Celerina owned several villas in Umbria and Perusia. Pliny considered the purchase of a nearby estate. The price was 3 million sesterces. Somewhat strapped for cash since his wealth was chiefly in land, he planned to borrow from Celerina. He felt quite comfortable using her money as if it were his own. Celerina, in turn, used Pliny's connections with the emperor Trajan. She requested the appointment of her kinsman, Caelius Clemens, to a proconsulship.

Plin., Ep. 1.4; 3.19; 10.51.
PW 126.

CHAERESTRATE

(4th century B.C.E.)   Greek: Samos
Mother of Epicurus

Chaerestrate was the mother of Epicurus, the famous philosopher and founder of one of the great ancient schools of philosophy. Her husband was Neocles, an Athenian schoolmaster, who immigrated to Samos, an island off the west coast of Asia Minor. Possibly, she read charms for people.

Chaerestrate had four sons. Epicurus was born in 341 B.C.E. The others, whose dates are uncertain, were Neocles, Chaeredemus, and Arisobulus.

Diog. Laert. 10.1–4.

CHELIDON

(1st century B.C.E.)   Greek: Sicily
Office manager

Chelidon was of Greek origin and an associate of Gaius Verres, praetor in 74 B.C.E. and governor of Sicily from 73 to 71. In 70, after his return to Rome, Verres was tried on charges of corruption while holding the office of praetor. Marcus Tullius Cicero, noted orator and statesman, was one of the prosecutors.

Chelidon had already died by the time of the trial; nevertheless, she was very much a part of Cicero's speech to the court. Cicero disparaged her as a *meretrix*, a "street-walking prostitute," and attacked Verres for his relationship with her. Cicero's description of her role in Verres's administration, however, belied his disparagement. She had her own household, and Verres used her household as his headquarters. She was surrounded by people seeking favors, as was the praetor himself. She was a person with whom people transacted their business: She oversaw payments and promissory notes.

In short, Cicero's description suggests she may have been closer to Verres's office manager than a prostitute. Chelidon also may well have had the intelligence for business that the corrupt Verres found useful. In a final irony, Chelidon left Verres a legacy in her will.

Cic., Verr. 2.1, 120 ff., 136 ff.; 2.2, 116.
Bauman. R. A., pp. 66–67.
Hillard, T., pp. 42–45.

CHILONIS (1)

(7th century B.C.E.)   Greek: Sparta
Heroine

Chilonis allegedly switched places with her husband to allow him to escape from prison. Chilonis married the Spartan ruler Theopompus (720–675 B.C.E.). After Theopompus was captured by the Arcadians, Chilonis traveled to Arcadia. Impressed by her fortitude and audacity in undertaking such a trip, the Arcadians allowed her to visit her husband in prison. Chilonis exchanged clothes with her husband, and he escaped while she remained behind. Theopompus later captured a priestess of Diana in a procession at Pheneus. He exchanged her for Chilonis.

Polyaenus, Strat. 8.39.
Der Kleine Pauly, p. 1,146.

▣ CHILONIS (2)
(3rd century B.C.E.)   Greek: Sparta
Heroine

Chilonis was willing to commit suicide rather than fall into the hands of her ex-husband. She was the granddaughter of a deceased ruler of Sparta and had married Cleonymus, son of the former king of Sparta, Cleomenes II. She was much younger than her husband and beautiful.

After she fell in love with Acrotatus, whose father ruled Sparta, she left her husband. Her desertion and the politics of succession led Cleonymus to ally himself with Pyrrhus against Sparta in 272 B.C.E. When an attack was imminent, Chilonis was said to have kept a rope around her neck so that she could kill herself rather than suffer capture by her former husband. Through a defense strategy aided by the city's women, the attack on Sparta was repelled. Chilonis was spared.

Plut., Pyrrh. 26.8–9; 27.5; 28.1–3.

▣ CHILONIS (3)
(3rd century B.C.E.)   Greek: Sparta
Heroine

Chilonis twice chose exile. She was the daughter of the Spartan king Leonidas II, who was a foe of the land and debt reforms initiated under his predecessor, Agis IV. She married Cleombrotus, who supplanted her father as king and forced him into exile. Chilonis went into exile with her father. When her father returned and ordered Cleombrotus exiled in 241 B.C.E., she again went into exile, this time with her husband.

Plut., Agis 17 ff.
Plut., Cleom. 38.5–12.
Mosse, Claude, pp. 146, 147.

▣ CHIOMARA
(4th century B.C.E.)   Galatian: Asia Minor
Avenger

Chiomara was the wife of Ortiagon, a chief of the Tectosagi Gauls in Asia Minor. They were defeated by the Romans near what is now Ankara, in Turkey. Chiomara was taken prisoner and raped by a centurion, who afterwards arranged for her ransom.

During the exchange, she instructed the Gauls to kill the centurion. His head was cut off, and Chiomara wrapped it in the folds of her dress. When she returned to her husband, she threw the head at his feet and revealed the rape. Chiomara was admired for her intelligence and spirit.

Livy 38.24
Plut., De mul. vir. 22.
Poly. 21.38.

▣ CLAUDIA (1)
(3rd century B.C.E.)   Roman: Rome
Possibly tried for treason

Claudia was born into a proud patrician family and is remembered for her arrogance. Her father was Appius Claudius Caecus, the famous censor of 312 B.C.E. who opened the citizen rolls to include a far larger number of Romans and who was responsible for building the Appian Way.

Her brother, Publius Claudius Pulcher, led a Roman naval battle against the Carthaginians at Drepana in 249 B.C.E. during the First Punic War. After disparaging unfavorable omens, he suffered a defeat and lost 93 out of 123 ships. The story is told that before the battle when the sacred chickens would not eat, he threw them into the sea, saying that they could drink instead.

Claudia revealed a similar disregard for tradition. Caught amid the crowds in 246 while attending the games in Rome, she was reputed to have said that she only wished the crowd could be put aboard another fleet and her brother brought back from the dead so that he could drown them all and clear the mobs from Rome.

Romans of the third century B.C.E. did not take such remarks lightly. Claudia was fined and possibly tried for treason.

Aul. Gell. 10.6.1.
Suet., Tib. 2.2–4.
Val. Max. 1.4.3; 8.1.4.
Balsdon, J. P. V. D., p. 43.
PW 382.

▣ CLAUDIA (2)

(2nd century B.C.E.)   Roman: Rome
Reformer

Claudia was part of the movement for land reform in the politics of Rome during the 130s B.C.E. Her parents were ANTISTIA (1) and Appius Claudius Pulcher, consul in 143 B.C.E. Her sister was CLAUDIA (3). Claudia married the tribune Tiberius Sempronius Gracchus. The union cemented his alliance with her father in a coalition that supported an agrarian law to regulate private usage of public land and to distribute public land to the landless.

The reforms addressed the need for citizens, especially veterans to have sufficient land to support themselves and to disperse the increasing numbers of landless who were collecting in Rome and transforming Roman life. The alliance of Claudia's husband and father deeply divided her husband's family. Although the brothers Gaius and Tiberius Gracchus, cousins of Claudia's husband, were in accord, their sister SEMPRONIA (1) was married to Publius Cornelius Scipio Aemilianus, who bitterly opposed the land commission.

The marriage between Claudia and Tiberius Gracchus was said to have been arranged by their fathers over dinner. Antistia, Claudia's mother, was furious at not being consulted. She was said to have relented, however, since Tiberius was seen as a very desirable "catch." (There was a similar story told about AEMILIA TERTIA and her daughter CORNELIA [2]. Since Tiberius Gracchus was the son of this same Cornelia, a remarkable women in her own right, the story would appear to be a confusion among a group of strong women all of whom were kin, albeit of different generations, and all in search of desirable marital partners for their daughters.)

Tiberius Gracchus was murdered by his cousin Publius Cornelius Scipio Nasica. Hundreds of his supporters were also murdered. Nothing is known about the widowed Claudia.

Plut., Ti. Gracch. 4.
Richardon, K., pp. 41, 46.
PW 385.

▣ CLAUDIA (3)

(2nd century B.C.E.)   Roman: Rome
Priestess

Claudia was a Vestal Virgin and sister of CLAUDIA (2). Chosen from among the very young women of elite families, the Vestal Virgins maintained the flame that assured the continuity and purity of the city. They served Vesta, the goddess of the hearth. Living in one of the oldest temples in the Forum, their well-being was equated with the well-being of the city. Impropriety by any one of them was an omen of misfortune for Rome.

They were not, however, immune to the calls of honor demanded by family. Claudia was a daughter of ANTISTIA (1) and Appius Claudius Pulcher, consul in 143 B.C.E. He had led an army in Cisalpine Gaul against the Salassi, whom he defeated at the cost of several thousand Roman soldiers. The Senate refused him permission to celebrate so costly a victory with a procession in

Rome. He chose to defy the Senate and mount a triumph at his own expense.

According to Roman tradition, a tribune could intervene on behalf of the citizenry. In this case, Claudia learned that a tribune would intervene and prevent her father's triumph. She mounted her father's chariot, threw herself into his arms, and was carried in the procession. The sanctity of her person protected her father from any interference. Claudia appears to have been the first Vestal Virgin to use her power to frustrate the will of the Senate.

Cic., Cael. 34
Suet., Tib. 2.4.
Val. Max. 5.4. 6.
Balsdon, J. P. V. D., pp. 42–43.
Bauman, R. A., p. 47.
PW 38.

▣ CLAUDIA (4)

(1st century B.C.E.) Roman: Rome
Political player

Claudia was a member of the family who divided between republicans and Caesarians during the Roman civil wars of the late first century B.C.E. Bound together by complicated natal family ties further entangled by marriages, divorces, remarriages, and love affairs, Claudia and the women of her generation had multiple and sometimes conflicting allegiances.

Claudia's mother was a Servilia of the Caepio family. Claudia's father was the unprincipled and arrogant Appius Claudius Pulcher. Her uncle was the notorious tribune Publius Clodius Pulcher, and her aunt was CLODIA (2), the woman Gaius Valerius Catullus portrayed in poetry as his faithless lover Lesbia. Claudia was also a niece of CLODIA (1) and CLODIA (2).

Claudia married Marcus Junius Brutus in 54 B.C.E., and SERVILIA (1) became her mother-in-law. Brutus was quaestor to her father in Cilicia in 53 and, like her father, joined the republicans under Gnaeus Pompeius Magnus (Pompey the Great) against Gaius Julius Caesar. In 49, the men went with Pompey to Greece, leaving the women behind. As the city sat poised between Ceasar and the republicans, women such as Claudia sought to protect family assets and to assure their family's future, whoever the victor.

Her father died in Greece. After Caesar's defeat of Pompey at Pharsalus in 48, Brutus accepted the pardon offered by Caesar and assumed control over a provincial command. However, her husband was a complicated, even tortured and brooding, man, who felt conflicted loyalties between his mother, a woman of substantial power in Caesar's camp, and his step-uncle, the republican Marcus Porcius Cato. Brutus, against his mother's wishes, divorced Claudia in 45. After her divorce she disppeared from the historical record.

PW 389.
Syme, R., *Augustan Aristocracy*, p. 198.
Syme, R., *Roman Revolution*, pp. 58–59.

▣ CLAUDIA (5)

(53 B.C.E.–?) Roman: Rome
Political pawn

Claudia, or Clodia as she may possibly have been called, was the stepdaughter of Mark Antony and a niece of CLODIA (1), CLODIA (2), and CLODIA (3). In 43 B.C.E., when she was about 10, Antony arranged her marriage with Octavian, the future emperor Augustus, in order to cement the Second Triumvirate, the alliance established that year among himself, Octavian, and Marcus Aemilius Lepidus.

Claudia's father was the notorious Publius Clodius Pulcher, who had been killed in 52 B.C.E. by his hated rival and political enemy Titus Annius Milo when they passed each other on the road. Her mother was FULVIA (2), who in 45 married Antony and unsuccessfully undertook to protect her husband's interests against the other triumvirs while he was in the East. However, the triumvirate lasted only for a five-year period, before the events of the civil war overtook the accord. Octavian formally divorced Claudia, without ever having consummated the marriage, in 41 B.C.E. Although Claudia would have reached a marriageable age anytime after 41 or 40, with her mother dead and her stepfather deeply enmeshed with CLEOPATRA VII and his new family in the East, there is no record of marrying: She may well have died young.

Suet., Aug. 62.1.
Balsdon, J. P. V. D., p. 178.
Delia, D., p. 202.
PW 390.

▣ CLAUDIA (6)

(1st century C.E.) Roman: Italy
Member of artistic circle

Claudia had two husbands, each of whom was an artist. Her first husband composed poetry to music. After his death, she married Publius Papinius Statius (c. 45–96 C.E.), who came from Naples to settle in Rome where he established a reputation as a poet.

She and Statius mingled in eminent circles and were part of a group associated with the emperor Domitian. Although not wealthy, Statius had sufficient means to live well. His poetry addressed the pleasant possibilities of life. In one poem he urged Claudia to leave Rome and return with him to Naples; in another he praised her for nursing him through an illness.

Claudia had one daughter with her first husband, but no children with Papinius Statius.

Stat., Silv. 3.5.
Der Kleine Pauly, p. 396.
OCD, p. 1,439.

▣ CLAUDIA PULCHRA

(1st century C.E.) Roman: Rome
Political player; exiled

Claudia Pulchra was a victim in the ceaseless struggles for position and power during the reign of Tiberius. She was a grandniece of Augustus and the daughter of Messalla Appianus, consul in 12 B.C.E., and the younger Claudia MARCELLA, Augustus's niece. She became the third wife of Quinctilius Varus, who owed his career to her connections. A military man, he ultimately suffered an ignominious defeat in Germany and committed suicide. They had a son, also named Quinctilius Varus.

The widow Claudia had wealth and standing. She was a close friend of her second cousin, the elder AGRIPPINA, who had a high profile in the politics of the times. Agrippina opposed Tiberius, who she believed had caused the death of her husband. Her enemies became the enemies of her friends. One of them, Gnaeus Domitius Afer, accused Claudia in 26 C.E. of illicit relations with an otherwise unknown man named Furnius, of engaging in a plot to poison the emperor Tiberius, and of using magic against the emperor. This was a familiar triad of accusations used in political battles of the period.

Agrippina interceded with Tiberius on Claudia's behalf. She met Tiberius as he was sacrificing to a statue of Augustus and demanded to know why he would allow Claudia Pulchra to be convicted. Claudia, she argued, was a living person, more of an image of Augustus than any senseless statue. She was not successful. Claudia Pulchra was convicted of lewdness and probably exiled. The following year, Afer brought suit against Claudia's son, who had inherited his father's substantial wealth. By that time, Tiberius had left Rome, and the Senate allowed the suit to lapse.

Tac., Ann. 4.52.
Bauman, R. A., pp. 147–49.
Levick, B., *Tiberius*, pp. 165 ff.
Marshall, A. J., "Women on Trial," p. 344.
Syme, R., *Augustan Aristocracy*, passim.

▣ CLEITO

(5th century B.C.E.) Greek: Greece
Mother of Euripides

Cleito was thought to be well born. She was the mother of the great Greek tragedian Euripides, who was born in 485 B.C.E. Her husband was a mechant named Mnesarchus or Mnesarchides.

Murray, G., p. 35.

▣ CLEOBOULE

(c. 407/400 B.C.E.–?) Greek: Athens
Fraud victim; mother of Demosthenes

Cleoboule was probably an Athenian. She was born between 407 and 400 B.C.E. Her father, Gylon, had committed treason and fled to the Bosporus after being condemned to death in Athens. After 403 B.C.E., his death sentence was commuted to a heavy fine.

Although her father may never have returned to Athens, he provided Cleoboule and her elder sister Philia with substantial dowries of 5,000 drachmas. She married a man named Demosthenes sometime early in the 380s. He was a well-to-do Athenian citizen; his wealth, with the exception of his house, was not in land but in the manufacturing of cutlery, pursued mainly in a home factory with slave labor.

In 385–384 or 384–383, Cleoboule gave birth to a son, also named Demosthenes, who became the greatest orator of Athens. She later gave birth to a daughter. Her husband died in 377, when her son was about seven, and her daughter, about five years old. She was left a large estate worth nearly 14 talents, although its exact amount was kept deliberately unclear since her husband sought to protect his estate from any claims on her absent father. He also left a will in which he appointed his brother Aphobus one of three guardians of his estate along with another brother, Demophon, and a friend, Therippides.

Under the terms of the will, Cleoboule was to have 8,000 drachmas to marry Aphobus. When her daughter came of age, she was to have a dowry of 12,000 drachmas and marry Demophon. Both men failed to fulfill the terms of the will: Aphobus did not marry Cleoboule, and Demophon did not marry her daughter. They did, however, embezzle the inheritances of both women and, in addition, depleted the residual estate, which was to go to Demosthenes.

Cleoboule raised the children without adequate resources. Their finances were so extreme that at one time even the fees of Demosthenes' tutor were unpaid. Her situation was further complicated by her son's constant illnesses.

Cleoboule looked to her son to right the wrong done them. When Demosthenes came of age, he took the executors to court. He sued and finally won his case after some five years of litigation. In the end, however, the family received only a small portion of the original estate.

Plut., Dem. 3.4.1–5.
Davies, J. K., pp. 113–41.

▣ CLEOBULINE

(6th century B.C.E.) Greek: Rhodes
Poet

Cleobuline wrote riddles in verse in imitation of her father, the philosopher Cleobulus of Rhodes. Her father advocated the education of women. Cleobuline was a literate woman in the sixth century B.C.E., a time when few men and fewer women could read or write. She was mentioned by Cratinus, one of the greatest poets of Old Attic comedy, who named one of his plays after her.

Diog. Laert. 1.89.91.
Pomeroy, S. B., *Goddesses*, p. 56.

▣ CLEODICE

(6th century B.C.E.) Greek: Greece
Mother of Pindar

Cleodice was the mother of the great Greek poet Pindar. She gave birth in Boeotia, in central Greece, in 518 B.C.E. Her husband was Daiphantus. All that is known of her background comes from the extant lines of Pindar's poetry, he claimed to be of the Aegidae tribe of Sparta, which would mean that his parents came from aristocratic families.

Hdt. 4.149.

▣ CLEOPATRA (1)

(5th century B.C.E.) Greek: Macedonia
Victim of family violence

Cleopatra married Perdiccas II, ruler of Macedonia (c. 450–413 B.C.E.). Widowed with a young son in 413, she married Archelaus, her grown stepson. Although his mother was reputed to have been a slave, Archelaus succeeded Perdiccas and was guardian of Cleopatra's young child—her former husband's heir.

Archelaus was ruthless. Fearing his ward, he pushed him into a well and was said to have claimed that he had fallen and drowned while chasing his pet goose. Cleopatra's fate after the death of her son is unknown.

Arist., Pol. 5.131b.
Pl., Grg. 471c.
Thuc. 2.100.
Macurdy, G., pp. 15–16.

▣ CLEOPATRA (2)

(4th century B.C.E.) Greek: Macedonia
Political player

Cleopatra suffered the fury of OLYMPIAS (1) after the death of Philip II. Cleopatra was the niece of Attalos, one of Philip's prominent Macedonian generals. Younger than Olympias, she married Philip II when Olympias's son by Philip, Alexander the Great, was a grown man.

The enmity between the two women and their respective supporters was already evident at Cleopatra's wedding feast, which Alexander attended. Attalos proposed a toast calling upon the Macedonians to ask that the gods grant the bride and groom a son so that there would be a legitimate heir to the throne. Incensed at the implication, Alexander threw a glass of wine in

Attalos's face. Philip drew his sword and made for Alexander. Drunk, Philip tripped and fell on his face.

Cleopatra lived in Macedonia, but Olympias and her children, including Alexander, went to Epirus. Philip and Alexander later reconciled, and Cleopatra gave birth to a son. After the murder of Philip II in 336 B.C.E., however, it was Alexander, not Cleopatra's child, who became ruler. After Alexander established his rule, Olympias returned to Macedonia.

While Alexander was campaigning, Olympias killed Cleopatra's infant son and took her revenge on the younger woman. Cleopatra either committed suicide by hanging herself or was dragged over a bronze vessel containing charcoal until she roasted to death. Alexander was said to have felt that the death was too harsh. He, however, ordered her uncle and a number of her kinsmen put to death.

Just. 9.7, 12.
Paus. 8.7.5.
Plut., Alex. 9.6–11.
Burn, A. R., pp. 44–45, 64.
Macurdy, H., pp. 30, 32.
Tarn, W. W., *Alexander the Great,* pp. 2–3.

▣ CLEOPATRA (3)

(c. 354–308 B.C.E.) Greek: Macedonia, Epirus, and Asia Minor
Coruler

Cleopatra was a daughter molded by a powerful mother. Lifetime allies, Cleopatra and her mother OLYMPIAS (1) fought to rule Macedonia. Born in 354 B.C.E., the child of Olympias and Philip II (359–336 B.C.E.), Cleopatra was the sister of Alexander the Great. In 336, at 18 years of age, she married her uncle Alexander I, ruler of Milossia (c. 342–330 B.C.E.) in Epirus.

Her husband was 28 years old and a notable general. The marriage cemented the alliance between Epirus, the center of her mother's influence, and Macedonia, ruled by her father, Philip

II. Although her father was assassinated during the wedding celebration, her brother assumed control over Macedonia and the alliance held. Cleopatra remained in Epirus and gave birth to two children, Neoptolemus and Cadmeia. Six years later, after her husband's death in 330, she ruled in the name of her young children along with her mother.

In 325, Olympias assumed the roles of guardian over Cleopatra's children and regent of Epirus while Cleopatra went to Macedonia. Alexander, already traveling in the East, had appointed the general Antipater ruler of Macedonia in his absence. Olympias and Cleopatra were hostile to Antipater, and Cleopatra sought to raise support against him. Alexander, however, only scoffed at Cleopatra's quest and is said to have remarked that their mother had gotten the best of the deal: Their mother ruled Epirus while Cleopatra was sent on a fool's errand, since Macedonia would never accept a woman ruler.

The death of Alexander in 323 inaugurated a period of political turmoil. Three of Alexander's generals, Antipater, Craterus, and Perdiccas, vied for control of his empire, with Perdiccas in the dominant position and Antipater in control of Greece. Cleopatra could have chosen any one of them as a husband, although each would have objected to her marriage with any of the others.

Instead, she pursued a different path. Pushed by Olympias, and with her eyes still on Macedonia, Cleopatra invited Leonnatus, a handsome Macedonian general in Alexander's army who had distinguished himself in Asia, to become her husband. Related to the ruling house and governor of Phrygia in Asia Minor, Leonnatus modeled himself after Alexander. He was only too happy to accept Cleopatra's offer, recognizing it no doubt as a stepping stone for both of them in pursuit of a larger sphere of power. He died in a battle with Greek insurgents before the marriage could take place.

With Macedonia still the sought-after prize, and a score to settle with Antipater, Olympias and Cleopatra upset plans for a marriage between NICAEA (1), Antipater's daughter, and Perdiccas. Instead, Olympias organized a marriage between Perdiccas and Cleopatra. Cleopatra left for Sardis in Asia Minor in 322 B.C.E.

Perdiccas evidently feared the enmity of Antipater more than he desired the alliance with Cleopatra and Olympias. He decided to marry Nicaea. He also, however, secretly promised Cleopatra that he would later divorce Nicaea and marry her. News of the secret arrangement came to the attention of Antipater and caused a permanent breach between the two men. Cleopatra was kept under watch in Sardis to prevent her from marrying Perdiccas. Sources differ over whether or not Perdiccas married Nicaea before his assassination in 321.

The drama of Perdiccas, and Antipater on the one side, and Olympias and Cleopatra on the other was watched by other generals of the late Alexander's army, all of whom sought their own spheres of power. Eumenes, a Greek general, supported Cleopatra, but she prevented him from attacking Antipater to preserve favor with the Macedonian populace. Eumenes' death in 316 left her without allies.

Tired of her semiconfinement in Sardis, Cleopatra planned to leave for Egypt in 308 to marry Ptolemy I Soter, one of the most successful of Alexander's successors. With orders from Antigonus, who controlled a large portion of Asia Minor, not to allow her to leave, the commander in Sardis arranged for a group of women to murder her. Antigonus quickly put the women to death to hide his involvement, and he gave Cleopatra a splendid funeral.

Arr., Succ. I.24, 40
Diod. 16.91.3; 18.23.1–3; 20.37.3–6.
Just. 13.6.
Plut., Alex. 68.4.
Plut., Eum. 3.8.
Carney, E. D., "What's in a Name?" p. 157.
Cary, M., p. 12.
Macurdy, G., index.

▣ CLEOPATRA (4)

(1st century C.E.) Roman: Rome
Self-made woman

Cleopatra belonged to the group of freedmen and -women who attained power under the emperor Claudius. She was said to be Claudius's favorite, a position she shared with CALPURNIA (2), another freedwoman. Her access to the emperor made her a useful ally in the intrigues of imperial life. At the same time, access had a price, and Cleopatra expected to retire a rich woman.

When the behavior of Valeria MESSALINA, the emperor's wife, appeared to open the way for a revival of power for the senatorial elite, the powerful freedmen felt threatened. Narcissus, one of Claudius's two most important secretaries, paid Cleopatra to vouch for Calpurnia's report that Messallina and her lover Gaius Silius had undergone a marriage ceremony. If this was true, it would mean at the least that Messallina had made the emperor appear a fool. Possibly, it was more, and the ceremony was the first move in a conspiracy.

Silius and Messallina died in the wake of the affair, and Cleopatra was all the richer from it.

Tac., Ann. 9.30.

▣ CLEOPATRA (5)

(1st century C.E.) Roman: Rome
Political client

Cleopatra was a friend and client of the wealthy, smart, and beautiful POPPAEA SABINA (2), one of the many lovers, and later the second wife, of the emperor Nero. Cleopatra married a well-to-do Roman businessman, Gessius Florus, from Clazomenae, a city on a small island off the southern shore of the Gulf of Smyrna. She used her relationship with Poppaea to secure from Nero an appointment for her husband as procurator of Judaea in 64 C.E.

Poppaea, though thought to have Jewish sympathies, did the Jews no service: Cleopatra's husband, Florus, was a ruthless governor.

Jos., AJ 20.252.
Jones, A. H. M., *Herods of Judaea*, pp. 235 ff.
OCD, p. 635.

▣ CLEOPATRA I (THE SYRIAN)

(c. 215–176 B.C.E.) Greek: Asia Minor and Egypt
Ruler

Cleopatra I, known as the Syrian, was the first woman of the Ptolemaic line to act as regent for her son and to mint coins in her own name. Born in Syria, the daughter of LAODICE III and Antiochus III, whose ancestor Seleucus I was a general under Alexander the Great, she was one of three daughters strategically married to insure her father's alliances.

Her father had defeated Ptolemy IV Philopator at the battle of Panium in 200 B.C.E. and regained Coele-Syria, which he had previously lost to Ptolemy at the battle of Raphia in 217. With the Romans on the horizon, Antiochus sought peace on the Egyptian/Syrian border. The marriage of Cleopatra and the future Ptolemy V Epiphanes was arranged when they were still children.

Cleopatra and Ptolemy married at Raphia in 193. She was 22, and he was about 17. Antiochus gave her Coele-Syria as part of her dowry, no doubt to assuage Egyptian sensibilities. The marriage was successful. Cleopatra was the bolder, more vigorous, more ambitious, and more intelligent of the two, and they shared power. After her husband's death in 180 B.C.E., Cleopatra became sole regent for her young son, who was about six years old at the time. She proved to be an able ruler. Under her rule, Egypt remained peaceful. She discarded her husband's plan to campaign against her brother Seleucus IV in Syria and kept peace with both Syria and Rome.

Her two sons later ruled Egypt as Ptolemy VI Philometor and Ptolemy VIII Euergetes II, and her daughter, CLEOPATRA II PHILOMETOR SOTEIRA, became one of the greatest long-reigning woman rulers of Egypt. She died in 176 B.C.E.

Jos., AJ 12.154–55.
Macurdy, G., pp. 141–47.
Pomeroy, S. B., *Women in Hellenistic Egypt,* p. 23.
OCD, p. 346.

CLEOPATRA II PHILOMETOR SOTEIRA
(c. 185?–115 B.C.E.) Greek: Egypt
Ruler

Cleopatra II was one of the ablest rulers of Hellenistic Egypt, ruling for 57 years. Born between 185 and 180 B.C.E., the daughter of CLEOPATRA I (THE SYRIAN) and Ptolemy V Epiphanes, she overcame extraordinary obstacles in her quest for power.

After the death of her mother, who had been regent for her children, Cleopatra married her younger brother Ptolemy VI Philometor in 175 or 174. Two eunuchs from Coele-Syria, Eulaeus and Lenaeus, assumed the regency for the young household. Their governance was a disaster, and they were defeated in a battle with Cleopatra's uncle, the Seleucid Antiochus IV. The defeated Eulaeus persuaded Cleopatra's brother/husband, the young Ptolemy VI, to withdraw with him to the island of Samothrace. Her youngest brother went to Alexandria, where Cleopatra joined him. They were declared joint rulers by the populace, and he took the title of Ptolemy VIII Euergetes II.

Antiochus continued to meddle in Egyptian affairs in an effort to exercise control. He supported Ptolemy VI, who now resided in Memphis, and launched an attack on Cleopatra and Ptolemy VIII in Alexandria. Cleopatra and Ptolemy VIII sent envoys to Rome to plead for Roman intervention. In the meantime, Ptolemy VI, fearful of Antiochus's intentions, contacted Cleopatra and his brother to arrange a settlement between them. Cleopatra, the eldest of the three, brokered a peace.

Cleopatra ruled along with her two brothers from 170 to 164 B.C.E., after the Romans forced Antiochus to withdraw to Syria. Cleopatra and Ptolemy VI were supported by the powerful Jewish community of Alexandria and put their army under the control of two Jewish generals. A resumption of the quarrel between the brothers, resulted in a victory for Ptolemy VI. Cleopatra and he ruled jointly from 164 onward, while Ptolemy VIII withdrew from Egypt to Cyrene.

Cleopatra had four children with Ptolemy VI, one of whom, Ptolemy Eupator, ruled jointly with his father for a brief time. Another became Ptolemy VII Neos Philopator and became joint ruler with his father in 145 and sole ruler after his father died in battle in the same year. There were also two daughters, CLEOPATRA III and CLEOPATRA THEA.

After the death of Ptolemy VI, Ptolemy VIII returned to Alexandria from Cyrene, murdered the 17-year-old Ptolemy VII, and bowed to the demands of the Alexandrians to marry his sister Cleopatra. Cleopatra III also married Ptolemy VIII, her uncle and her mother's second husband, in 142, while her mother was still his wife. Furious at this slight, Cleopatra bided her time for 10 years. Then in 132, with the support of the Jews, she organized a revolt in Alexandria, and in 130 Ptolemy VIII fled to Cyprus.

Cleopatra III and her children went with Ptolemy. Cleopatra II's four-year-old son with Ptolemy VIII was also taken. Ptolemy murdered the boy and sent pieces of his body packed in a hamper as a birthday present to Cleopatra in Alexandria. A year later, after Ptolemy VII returned to Egypt with Cleopatra III and captured Alexandria, Cleopatra fled to Antioch, bringing with her vast wealth to secure support from her former son-in-law, Demetrius II. Demetrius had been married to her daughter Cleopatra Thea. He rose to her defense but was killed in battle.

Cleopatra eventually returned to Alexandria and reconciled with her brother/husband to reign peacefully with him and with her daughter Cleopatra III. Reforms were issued in the names of the three rulers. Among these were a prohibition against imprisonment without trial, a decrease in taxes, improved judicial proceedings, and reforms in housing and ownership of land.

Cleopatra died in 115 B.C.E., shortly after her husband's death. She was more than 70 years old.

Diod. 33.13.1; 34.14.1.
Livy 44.19.6–14; 45.9–13.1–9.
Poly. 28.1, 20–21.
Cary, M., p. 222.
Macurdy, G., index.
OCD, pp. 346–47.
Pomeroy, S. B., *Women in Hellenistic Egypt.*

⊞ CLEOPATRA III

(c. 165?–101 B.C.E.) Greek: Egypt
Ruler

Cleopatra III let no one stand in the way of her quest for power. Her life was shaped by struggles with her mother and her children to become the dominant ruler of Egypt. Enormously wealthy she was the daughter of CLEOPATRA II PHILOMETOR SOTEIRA and her husband/brother, Ptolemy VI Philometor. Born between 165 and 160 B.C.E. in 142, she became the wife of her uncle, Ptolemy VIII Euergetes II, who was simultaneously her mother's second husband. She was the sister of CLEOPATRA THEA.

After 10 years of marriage marked by discord between the women, Cleopatra II led a successful revolt in 132, and Ptolemy VIII was forced to flee Alexandria. Cleopatra III supported her husband and fled with him to Cyprus accompanied by her five children: Ptolemy IX Soter II Lathyrus, Ptolemy Alexander, CLEOPATRA TRYPHAENA, CLEOPATRA IV, and CLEOPATRA V SELENE. They also brought to Cyprus Ptolemy VIII's four-year-old son from his marriage with Cleopatra II. The boy was murdered, and parts of the body were sent to the boy's mother in Alexandria.

In 129 Ptolemy VIII reconquered Alexandria, and eventually both Cleopatras reconciled. Over the next 13 years, mother and daughter ruled together with their joint husband. In the name of the three rulers there were reforms in the courts, in debt, in land holdings, and in taxes. At his death in 116, Ptolemy VIII left Cleopatra III, the younger of the two women, in control of Egypt with the right to choose either one of her sons as coruler. Her mother died soon after, and left her the unchallenged ruler.

She was forced by the populace in 116 to name her son Ptolemy IX Soter II as coruler instead of the younger Ptolemy Alexander, whom she found more pliable. She sent her younger son to Cyprus but asserted her position by presenting her name and image before that of her older son on official documents and other iconography. She also made his life miserable.

Ptolemy IX had married his sister, Cleopatra IV, whom he dearly loved. Cleopatra found that this daughter had a mind of her own and was not to be dominated. In a short time, Cleopatra succeeded in securing her son's divorce and a new marriage to his younger sister, Cleopatra V Selene, whom she more easily controlled. In 110, Cleopatra also secured the agreement of Ptolemy IX to accept her younger son, Ptolemy X Alexander I, as his joint ruler. Soon, however, they quarreled, and Ptolemy Alexander returned to Cyprus.

Ptolemy IX sought to counter his mother's power by siding against the Jews, who were the second most privileged group in Alexandria after the Greeks and were her supporters. He received a request from Antiochus IX Cyzicenus, his cousin and the ruler of Antioch, for help in fighting against the forces of John Hyrcanus, the Jewish high priest, who was attacking the Greeks in Samaria. Ptolemy sent 6,000 troops without telling his mother.

In 108, Cleopatra accused Ptolemy IX of seeking to poison her. She incited a mob and Ptolemy IX was driven into exile. She recalled her younger son, Ptolemy X, from Cyprus as her coruler and sent an army to capture Ptolemy IX. The troops, with the exception of the Jews, revolted, and Ptolemy IX became ruler of Cyprus. Cleopatra put the commander of the troops to death.

Cleopatra and Ptolemy X quarreled. In 102 B.C.E. her older son, Ptolemy IX, invaded Palestine from his base in Cyprus, captured Judaea, and advanced toward Egypt. Cleopatra collected her grandchildren along with her will and a large amount of treasure, which she deposited in the temple of Aesculapius on Cos, an island off the coast of southern Asia Minor. She then led an army into Palestine where she halted Ptolemy's advance. She was only dissuaded from trying to regain Coele-Syria by her Jewish advisers, who threatened to withdraw their support if she captured Alexander Jannaeus, the brother of John Hyrcanus, who controlled the area. Instead, she signed a treaty of alliance and mutual aid with him.

Cleopatra was worshiped as Isis, the great mother of the gods, and cults were established in her honor. She provided funds for an expedition by Eudoxus of Cyzicenus to India for a shipment of precious stones and perfumes. She died at about 60 years old, before Eudoxus's return in 101. She may have been murdered, perhaps by Ptolemy X.

Jos., AJ 13.285, 287, 328, 331, 348–55.
Livy 14.67.
Cary, M., pp. 222–23.
Macurdy, G., index.
OCD, p. 347.

▣ CLEOPATRA IV

(2nd century B.C.E.) Greek: Egypt and Syria
Insurgent leader

Cleopatra IV threatened the power of her mother in Egypt and her sister in Syria. She was the daughter of CLEOPATRA III. Her father, Ptolemy VIII Euergetes II, was also her great-uncle. She married her brother, Ptolemy IX Soter II Lathyrus, who became coruler with her mother after her father's death in 316 B.C.E.

Her mother sought to exercise control over Ptolemy IX, who was her oldest son. In the conflict between mother and wife, her husband reluctantly sided with his mother and agreed to reject Cleopatra in favor of marriage with a younger sister, CLEOPATRA V SELENE, who was more amenable to his mother's influence. Cleopatra left Egypt for Cyprus, where another brother, Ptolemy Alexander, ruled.

Like many of the Cleopatras, Cleopatra IV had enormous wealth. In Cyprus she raised an army and took it to Syria. At this time the half brothers Antiochus IX Cyzicenus and Antiochus VIII Grypus were waging war against each other. Both were first cousins of Cleopatra IV through their mother, CLEOPATRA THEA, who was the sister of Cleopatra III. Grypus was married to another of Cleopatra's own sisters, CLEOPATRA TRYPHAENA. The other half brother was available.

In Antioch, Cleopatra offered her support to Cyzicenus and married him. Grypus captured Antioch and Cleopatra in 112 B.C.E. He might not have murdered Cleopatra, but her sister, fearing Cleopatra would seduce her husband, had Cleopatra killed even though she had sought sanctuary in the temple of Artemis. Later, Cleopatra's husband Cyzicenus recaptured Antioch. He had his sister-in-law Cleopatra Tryphaena killed to appease the spirit of his murdered wife.

Just. 39.3.
Downey, G., p. 129.
Macurdy, G.

▣ CLEOPATRA V SELENE

(c. 131/130–69 B.C.E.) Greek: Egypt
and Syria
Political player

Cleopatra V Selene engaged in a series of matrimonial alliances to secure a sphere of power in the politics of Egypt and Syria. She was the youngest daughter of CLEOPATRA III and Ptolemy VIII Euergetes II, who was also her great-uncle. In 116 B.C.E., when she was about 14 or 15 years old, her mother arranged her first marriage with her brother Ptolemy IX Soter II Lathyrus, in the belief that she would be more malleable to her mother's machinations than his previous wife, her older sister CLEOPATRA IV.

In 108, with the support of the Jews of Alexandria, her mother incited a successful revolt to drive Ptolemy IX Soter II from Egypt. Cleopatra remained in Alexandria with her mother. Her deposed husband assembled an army in Cyprus, where he had fled. He defeated the Jewish army in Syria and conquered Judaea. Sometime during this period Cleopatra, who was still in Alexandria, divorced Ptolemy IX. Threatened by his advancing army, she left Alexandria for Syria. With her mother's support, she brought troops with her and carried a large dowry of treasure to Antiochus VIII Grypus in Antioch.

Grypus was kin by a former marriage and was a partner who could offer Cleopatra and her mother an alternative base of power in their war against Ptolemy. At the time, there was almost continuous warfare for control over the Seleucid Empire between two half brothers, Antiochus VIII Grypus and Antiochus IX Cyzicenus. Cyzicenus had been married to Cleopatra IV. She had been murdered by order of her sister CLEOPATRA TRYPHAENA, who was Grypus's wife. To avenge the murder of Cleopatra IV, Cyzicenus murdered Cleopatra Tryphaena.

Cleopatra V married Grypus, but the union was short-lived. He was murdered in 96 B.C.E. by his leading general, Heracleon of Beroea, during an attempted coup. Meanwhile in Egypt, Cleopatra's mother was murdered, possibly by one of her sons. Cleopatra became a free agent, able to choose her allies. She married Cyzicenus, her husband's half-brother and bitterest enemy, who occupied Antioch soon after her husband's death.

She was not his wife for long either. Cyzicenus died in battle along with the eldest son of Grypus in about 95 or 94. Antiochus X Eusebes, the son of Cyzicenus, staked his claim for power. He conquered Antioch and reigned from 94 to 92. Cleopatra married Eusebes, once more negotiating her enormous wealth for political power. Although Eusebes died fighting in 92, Cleopatra survived. She moved to Ptolemais in Phoenicia

and lived in great luxury with her children for nearly two decades.

In 75, she sent her two sons by Eusebes to Rome where they contested the legitimacy of Ptolemy XII Neos Dionysus (Auletes), son of Ptolemy IX. The Romans refused to support their claim. Cleopatra also sought to place her son, Antiochus Asiaticus, in power in Syria. Tigranes I the Great of Armenia, who controlled Syria, campaigned against her in Phoenicia. In 69 she was captured in Ptolemais by Tigranes, who brought her to Seleuceia on the Euphrates and had her killed. Her son ruled over Syria from 69 to 68 B.C.E. after Tigranes withdrew from Antioch.

App., Syr. 49.69.
Cic., Verr. 4.27.
Jos., AJ 13.6.5; 365, 367, 370–71.
Strabo 16.7, 49.
Macurdy, G., index.

CLEOPATRA VI TRYPHAENA

(?–57 B.C.E.) Greek: Egypt
Coruler

Cleopatra VI Tryphaena was the daughter of Ptolemy IX Soter II Lathyrus. Her mother was one of his lovers. Cleopatra married her half-brother Ptolemy XII Neos Dionysus (Auletes) in 80 or 79. A weak man, Ptolemy XII's rule was challenged by CLEOPATRA V SELENE, who was living in Ptolemais and looking to settle her sons by Antiochus X Eusebus.

Cleopatra was very young when she married, and her brother/husband was only about 15 when he became ruler. Much of his time and money was spent bribing Romans to support his claims to the throne. The heavy taxes levied to pay for these bribes left him highly unpopular. Rome finally recognized his rule in 59 B.C.E., after Julius Caesar, who was consul in that year, received a large settlement. When the Alexandrians threatened revolt, Ptolemy XII went to Rome to seek support. Cleopatra shared power with BERENICE IV CLEO-

PATRA in Egypt for about a year until she died in 57.

Cleopatra may have been the mother of ARSINOË AULETES and the most famous Cleopatra, CLEOPATRA VII. She may also have been the mother or sister of Berenice IV Cleopatra. In addition, she had two sons, Ptolemy XIII and Ptolemy XIV.

Dio. 39.12.
Macurdy, G., index.
Pomeroy, S. B., *Women in Hellenistic Egypt*, p. 24.
Skeat, T. C., p. 35.

▣ CLEOPATRA VII

(c. 69–30 B.C.E.)   Greek: Egypt, Asia Minor, and Italy
Ruler

Cleopatra VII is one of the most famous women of history, the subject of legend and literature. A protagonist in the politics and wars that marked the end of the Roman republic and an independent Egypt, she was courageous, intelligent, arrogant, clever, and charming. She had a facility for languages and was possibly the only Ptolemaic ruler who spoke fluent Egyptian. She was also extremely rich. The last in the long line of Ptolemaic rulers, many of whom were powerful women, she was born in 69 B.C.E. and ruled Egypt from 51 to 30. Ambitious for Egypt, she used Julius Caesar and Mark Antony to solidify her rule and extend her empire. In turn, she offered them her treasury. She exhibited some of the characteristics of Alexander the Great, and had Antony followed her advice, together they might well have ruled a world empire.

Cleopatra was the daughter of Ptolemy XII Neos Dionysus (Auletes). Her mother's identity has remained uncertain. The most likely candidate is CLEOPATRA VI TRYPHAENA, who married Auletes in 80 or 79 B.C.E. Possibly, she was the daughter of one of Auletes' lovers. However, none of the ancient sources, which were some-

times quite hostile toward Cleopatra, challenged her legitimate right to rule Egypt.

Cleopatra was 14 in 55 B.C.E. when her father returned to power in Egypt with the support of Rome. Ptolemy XII was a weak man who had spent several years and a great deal of money bribing Romans to support him over the objections of the Alexandrians. He had left Egypt for Rome in 58. In his absence, the Alexandrians recognized as joint rulers his wife Cleopatra VI Tryphaena and BERENICE IV CLEOPATRA, who was either the aunt, sister, or stepsister of Cleopatra. Cleopatra VI died a year later. Berenice IV Cleopatra ruled alone until Auletes returned and murdered her.

Before her father died in 51, he named the 17-year-old Cleopatra and her brother, Ptolemy XIII, joint rulers of Egypt. Cleopatra was seven years older than her brother; she married him within the year. The young rulers were surrounded by three men who expected to exercise power: Prothinus, a court eunuch; Theodolltus, a Greek from Chios who was Ptolemy's tutor; and Archillas, who commanded the army in Alexandria. Conflict was not slow in coming. From the beginning, Cleopatra allied herself with the Romans. In 49 she supplied Gnaeus Pompey, the son of the republican general Gnaeus Pompeius (Pompey the Great), with 60 ships in addition to money and supplies of corn. The advisers, fearful that she might achieve an independent basis of power supported by the Romans, alleged that she sought to rule alone.

With the help of an Alexandrian mob, Cleopatra was expelled from the city in 48 B.C.E. Undeterred, she raised a mercenary army and returned to fight her brother. In 48, Julius Caesar arrived in Egypt in pursuit of Gnaeus Pompeius (Pompey the Great) and found the armies of Cleopatra and her brother arrayed against each other. Caesar sent a message to Cleopatra encamped in Pelusium. To escape assassination, Cleopatra wrapped herself in bedclothes and used a small boat to smuggle herself into Alexandria to meet Caesar. She secured his support.

Cleopatra VII and Mark Antony

In an effort to appease the Alexandrians, who were affronted by the Romans marching through the city, and to calm conflict between Cleopatra and her brother, Caesar read to an assembled group of Alexandrians a copy of Auletes' will that had been left in his care. He affirmed Auletes' instructions and made Cleopatra and her brother corulers of Egypt under the protection of Rome.

In a further effort to assure peace within the ruling clique in Alexandria, Caesar proposed that Cleopatra's younger sister, ARSINOË AULETES, and their youngest brother, Ptolemy XIV, leave Egypt and become joint rulers of Cyprus. Arsinoë Auletes, however, jealous of Cleopatra, fled to Alexandria and joined up with the Egyptian army, which declared her ruler. She quarreled with the general Archillas, had him murdered, and assumed control over the army. The mercenary army had no liking for a woman commander and welcomed the young Ptolemy XIII, who came from Alexandria under a ruse of bringing the army to Caesar's side. War followed. In 47 Caesar de-

feated the army and captured Arsinoë, whom he brought to Rome. Ptolemy drowned in the Nile trying to escape.

By now Caesar had become Cleopatra's lover, and she was pregnant with his child. Born in June 47, the child was named Ptolemy Caesar. He became known as Caesarion. Cleopatra married her younger brother, Ptolemy XIV, who was about 12 years old at the time, and Caesar returned to Rome leaving Alexandria quiet and Cleopatra in power, supported by three Roman legions. In 46 Cleopatra joined Caesar in Rome along with her young son and her husband, Ptolemy XIV. She lived in one of Caesar's houses and held court. After his assassination in 44, she returned to Egypt. Shortly thereafter, she had her husband poisoned and named her son, the three-year-old Caesarion, joint ruler.

During the ensuing Roman civil war, Cleopatra sided with the Caesarians. She supplied Publius Cornelius Dolabella with four legions and excused herself from helping his opponent Gaius

Cassius Longinus the Tyrannicide on the grounds that there was famine in Egypt. After the defeat of Dolabella, she tried to sail with her fleet to join Mark Antony and Octavian, but a storm destroyed many of her ships. An illness prevented her from sailing again, and the victory of the Caesarians made further aid unnecessary.

In 41 Cleopatra was summoned by Antony to Tarsus. Antony's mission was to consolidate power and raise revenues to pay for the war. Cleopatra convinced him that she had supported the Caesarians, probably provided him with immediate material aid, and successfully seduced him. Antony spent the winter of 41–40 with her in Egypt. At her request, he arranged for the murder of her sister Arsinoë Auletes, who was in Ephesus and who Cleopatra felt might be a future threat. In the spring of 40, Antony left Egypt to return to Rome.

Between 40 and 37 B.C.E., Cleopatra remained in Egypt. In 37 Antony was again in the East, and he summoned Cleopatra to meet him in Antioch where they formed an alliance. She agreed to provide him with aid and in return received control over Coele-Syria, Cyprus, and a part of Cilicia. Antony also acknowledged that he was the father of their twins, CLEOPATRA SELENE and Alexander Helios.

In 35 OCTAVIA (2), who had married Antony in 40 to seal the pact of Brundisium and who under Roman law was still his wife, brought Antony reinforcements from her brother, Octavian. She came with far fewer troops than Antony had expected and Octavian had promised. Antony told her to stop at Athens: The alliance with Cleopatra provided for his needs, and Cleopatra had no interest in Octavia's presence. With Cleopatra's resources, Antony mounted a successful eastern campaign against the Armenians in 34. Afterward, Antony and Cleopatra divided power. She and Caesarion continued to be corulers of Egypt, Cyprus, Libya, and Coele-Syria. Alexander Helios was given Armenia, Media, and Parthia, and little Ptolemy Philadelphus, their other son, was named ruler of Phoenicia, Syria and Cilicia. Coins were

struck with Antony on one side and Cleopatra on the other.

Cleopatra had succeeded. She was joint ruler with the most powerful Roman in the East and had an empire that extended well beyond her patrimony of Egypt. She crowned her success with marriage to Antony after he divorced Octavia in 32.

Octavian declared war against Cleopatra. He could not leave Antony and Cleopatra in control of the East, the richer and more populous part of the ancient Greco-Roman world. Octavian needed the resources of the East and the corn of Egypt to feed Rome. However, Octavian feared declaring war directly against Antony who remained popular among Romans, especially those in the army. Cleopatra wanted Antony to focus on the East, but she reluctantly supplied Antony with money, men, and ships to fight Octavian. Antony adopted a two-part plan in which he would proceed against Octavian and, only if that failed, would he fall back on extending his rule in the East.

Romans supporting Antony met with him and Cleopatra at Ephesus. They were clear: They wanted Cleopatra to return to Egypt. They adamantly opposed recognizing Caesarion as the legitimate son of Caesar and Cleopatra and as a possible coruler of Rome. However, Cleopatra was furnishing 200 of the 800 ships of the fleet as well as 2,000 talents. She refused to go back to Egypt. She claimed that the Egyptians would be insulted and that her soldiers would not fight. Perhaps she also feared that Antony might be persuaded to abandon her if she was not physically present. Antony stood by Cleopatra, much to the disgust of his Roman army.

In the battle of Actium in 31 B.C.E., Antony's Roman troops wanted the navy to attack Octavian's ships. If they won, Octavian would be forced to send his army into battle. If Octavian's fleet won, the army under Antony would withdraw to the interior, forcing Octavian to follow. Cleopatra's ships were stationed in the rear. Antony put treasure aboard fast ships that were also stationed in the rear. This aroused suspicion among the troops, and some of Antony's fleet deserted him at the beginning of the battle. Cleopatra ordered her ships back to Egypt, and Antony, probably thinking that his army might desert him, abandoned the fight, boarded a fast ship, and followed her. The rest of his army surrendered. Antony committed suicide before Octavian arrived in Egypt.

On August 10, 30 B.C.E., Cleopatra killed herself by poison from an asp rather than face being paraded as a captive in Octavian's triumph.

App., Bciv. 4.61–63, 82; 5.8–9.
Dio. 42.35 ff; 49.41.
Jos., AJ 15.4.1.
Plut., Ant. 25–29; 30; 53–86.
Plut., Caes. 49.
Plut., Pomp. 78.
Suet., Caes. 52.
Macurdy, G., index.
OCD, p. 347.
Pomeroy, S. B., *Goddesses*, pp. 187–88.
Pomeroy, S. B., *Women in Hellenistic Egypt.*, index.
Syme, R., *Roman Revolution*, index.

▣ CLEOPATRA SELENE

(40 B.C.E.–? C.E.) Greek: Egypt, Italy and Mauritania
Coruler

Cleopatra Selene ruled the Roman client kingdom of Mauritania with her husband, Juba. She and her twin, Alexander Helios, were born in 40 B.C.E. to CLEOPATRA VII and Mark Antony. After the battle of Actium and the death of her parents when she was about 11 years old, she walked with her brother in Octavian's triumph. Alexander died shortly thereafter, and OCTAVIA (2), the ex-wife of Mark Antony, raised Cleopatra in her own household.

In 20 B.C.E., Octavian, now Augustus arranged a marriage between Cleopatra Selene and Juba of Mauritania. Juba had been paraded in a triumph of Julius Caesar in 46 B.C.E. and, like his new wife, had been brought up since childhood in Rome. Augustus was fond of him and, before becoming emperor, had granted him Roman citizenship and had taken him on some of his campaigns.

Juba was an extraordinarily cultured man who wrote many books, all now lost. He and Cleopatra brought Roman and Greek culture to Mauritania. They had a son named Ptolemy who succeeded his father as king and ruled until 40 C.E. He was killed on orders of the emperor Gaius Caligula, who wanted his wealth. They also had a daughter, DRUSILLA (1), who married Marcus Antonius Felix, a freedman of the younger ANTONIA, the mother of the emperor Claudius. As procurator of Judaea, Felix was the judge at the trial of St. Paul.

Cleopatra issued coins in her own name with Greek inscriptions. Her husband's coins were in Latin. She was the last Cleopatra, and her son was the last royal Ptolemy. It is not known when she died, but the iconography of her coins suggests she might have been alive as late as 11 C.E.

Jos., AJ 13.420.
Jos. BJ 1.116.
Tac., Hist. 5.9.
Balsdon, J. P. V. D., index.
Grant, M., p. 159.
Macurdy, G., index.
OCD, p. 347.

▣ CLEOPATRA THEA

(2nd century B.C.E.) Greek: Egypt and Syria
Coruler

Cleopatra Thea was used by her father to enhance his power in Syria and then took control of her own destiny and sought to find an able man to rule the Seleucid Empire. She was the daughter of CLEOPATRA II PHILOMETOR SOTEIRA. Her father was her mother's brother and husband Ptolemy VI Philometor.

In 162 B.C.E., Demetrius I Soter gained control over Syria, but he soon became unpopular. Alexander Balas, an impostor who bore a remarkable resemblance to Antiochus IV, the former ruler of Syria, was put forward as the rightful heir. In exchange for influence and possibly even territory,

Ptolemy VI arranged for Alexander's marriage with Cleopatra Thea. Alexander Balas defeated Demetrius with support from Egypt, Pergamum, and the Jews. He and Cleopatra Thea had a son, Antiochus.

Alexander proved to be an incompetent ruler who immersed himself in luxurious living and debauchery. In 147, Demetrius II, the eldest son of the defeated Demetrius I, led an army of mercenaries from Crete into Syria. At this point, Ptolemy VI quarreled with Alexander and recalled his daughter. Cleopatra Thea then married Demetrius II, who was several years her junior.

Alexander was defeated. Forced to flee, he took his and Cleopatra Thea's son, whom he left with desert chiefs. Ptolemy persuaded the people of Antioch to recognize Demetrius as ruler. Alexander returned to fight Demetrius. Alexander and Ptolemy VI died in battle.

The young Demetrius was another inept ruler. He too became highly unpopular, blamed for the persecution of Alexander Balas's supporters and the cruelty of his mercenary troops. Diodotus, the governor of Syria, gained possession of Cleopatra Thea's son, drove Demetrius from Antioch and proclaimed little Antiochus ruler. However, Diodotus had the boy murdered a year or two later since Antiochus was a threat to his power.

Cleopatra Thea, who had two sons with Demetrius, Seleucus V and Antiochus Grypus, accompanied her inept husband to Seleuceia-in-Pieria, a port city in Syria, after his defeat by Diodotus. In 139, her husband was captured by Mithradates and the Parthians. Fearing Demetrius lost and that Diodotus (now renamed Tryphon) might secure his position, she invited her brother-in-law, Antiochus VII Sidetes from Rhodes, to Sleuceia-in-Pieria to marry her and become ruler.

Sidetes accepted Cleopatra Thea's offer, was welcomed by the people, and proved to be an able ruler. In 138 he defeated Tryphon, who committed suicide. The couple returned in triumph to Antioch and order was restored to the rest of the country. Sidetes also reconquered Judaea. Cleopatra Thea gave birth to a son, Antiochus Cyzicenus.

Cleopatra Thea and her first husband, Alexander Balas

Cleopatra Thea and her son Antiochus VIII Grypus

Over the next several years nothing is known about Cleopatra Thea. Her husband, however, campaigned against the Parthians and among them discovered his brother Demetrius II alive. He had become a favorite of Mithradetes, who had betrothed him to his daughter Rhodogune. Sidetes secured Demetrius's freedom before he died in battle in 129. Demetrius II returned to reign in Syria. It was at this time that Cleopatra Thea's mother Cleopatra II arrived in Antioch. She sought support from Demetrius II in her struggle with her husband/brother Ptolemy VIII Euergetes, who was also Cleopatra Thea's uncle. Cleopatra Thea hated Demetrius and certainly did not welcome her mother. Her mother, Cleopatra II, however, brought with her enough wealth to secure cooperation from Demetrius, who set out with an army to fight for her cause. The people of Antioch revolted as soon as he left.

Taking advantage of the situation in Antioch, and in revenge against Cleopatra II, Ptolemy VIII declared an impostor, Alexander Zebinas, ruler of Antioch in 128. Zebinas defeated Demetrius II. Demetrius fled to Ptolemais and sought refuge with Cleopatra Thea. She refused to receive him. She then arranged for his murder by the governor of Tyre. She also murdered their son Seleucus V lest he aspire to rule. Given the climate of the times, she might have been seeking to avert her death at Demetrius's hands, as he would no doubt have sought to avenge the earlier death of his father, Demetrius I.

Ptolemy VIII quarreled with Alexander Zebinas and switched his support to Cleopatra Thea, who became joint ruler of Syria with her son Antiochus VIII Grypus in 125. Cleopatra Thea issued silver coins with her head, name, and titles. She was the first Hellenistic woman ruler to strike coins in her own name. On later coins her head appeared with that of Grypus; her head, however, was in front of her son's.

In 123, she believed that she faced a final challenge to her position. CLEOPATRA TRYPHAENA, the daughter of Ptolemy VIII, and Grypus were betrothed. She was said to have offered her son a drink containing poison after he came in from a hunt. He became suspicious and offered her the drink instead. She refused. Afraid of her machinations, Grypus had her killed in 121 or 120 B.C.E.

Without her powerful presence neither of her sons, Grypus nor Antiochus IX Cyzicenus, were able to rule successfully. They waged war against each other, killed each other's wife, and succeeded in destroying the power of the Seleucids.

App., Syr. 67–69.
Diod. 28; 32.9c; 33.
Jos., AJ 13.80–82, 109–10, 137, 221–22.
Just. 39.2.
Livy, Epit. 60.
Downey, G., pp. 119–29.
Macurdy, G., index.

▣ CLEOPATRA TRYPHAENA

(2nd century B.C.E.) Greek: Egypt and Asia Minor
Military leader

Cleopatra Tryphaena murdered her sister CLEOPATRA IV and was, in turn, murdered by her sister's husband. She was the daughter of CLEOPATRA III. Her father, Ptolemy VIII Euergetes II, was also her uncle. The viciousness of her relationship with her sister reflected their mother's earlier struggle for power.

In 125 B.C.E., her father had installed her aunt CLEOPATRA THEA as joint ruler of Syria with one of her aunt's sons, Antiochus VIII Grypus. Two years later, in 123, he arranged a marriage between Cleopatra Tryphaena and Grypus. Cleopatra Thea perceived the advent of another woman as a threat to her power. She sought to poison her son. He had her murdered in 121 or 120, and the marriage went forward. Cleopatra Tryphaena moved to Antioch.

Her father died in 116, and her mother forced an end to the marriage between Cleopatra Tryphaena's sister Cleopatra IV and her brother Ptolemy IX Soter II Lathyrus. Her sister went to Cyprus, where their mother had previously placed another brother in charge. There she raised a mercenary army, which she led to Antioch and offered to Grypus's half-brother, Antiochus IX Cyzicenus. She also married him. She was now her sister Cleopatra Tryphaena's enemy.

Grypus drove Cyzenicus out of Antioch in 112 and captured Cleopatra IV. Cleopatra Tryphaena could not have had any illusions about her sister or what she could buy with her wealth. She feared that her husband would become her sister's pawn. She insisted that Cleopatra IV be killed.

Cyzicenus later recaptured Antioch and killed Cleopatra Tryphaena to appease the spirit of his murdered wife.

Just. 39.3.
Downey, G., pp. 127–28.
Macurdy, G., index.

▣ CLEORA

(5th–4th century B.C.E.) Greek: Sparta
Wife of ruler

Cleora was the wife of Agesilaus II of Sparta, who came to power in 399 B.C.E. She had two daughters, Eupolia and Proanga, and a son, Archidamus, who succeeded his father in 360 B.C.E.

Plut., Agis 19.5.

▣ CLODIA (1)

(1st century B.C.E.) Roman: Rome
Political wife

Clodia was the eldest of three sisters, all named Clodia, and the only one of them to lead a life free of notoriety. Her mother was from the powerful and aristocratic Metelli clan, and her father was Appius Claudius Pulcher, consul in 79 B.C.E. When Clodia married Quintus Marcus Rex, consul in 68, her father was still alive and the family intact. However, he died soon after and left debts that far outweighed assets. Even though her oldest brother assumed family responsibility

worked to restore their fortunes, it was a financial disaster for her two sisters, CLODIA (2) and CLODIA (3), and transformed their lives.

PW 72.
Syme, R., *Roman Revolution,* pp. 20, 23.

▣ CLODIA (2)

(95 B.C.E.–?) Roman: Italy
Adventurer

Clodia was well born, smart, and educated. She lived her life with scant regard for tradition amid the rich, famous, and notorious in the last decades of the republic. One of six children, she was born in 95 B.C.E. into the aristocratic Metelli clan. Her mother's name is unknown. Her father was Appius Claudius Pulcher, consul in 79 B.C.E. He died in 76, leaving the family in poverty. Her eldest brother, Appius Claudius Pulcher, sought to restore the family's fortunes and was regarded as corrupt even in an age known for its corruption. Publius Clodius Pulcher, her younger brother, became tribune, curried popular favor, and enforced populist laws with armed mobs.

With little more than her beauty and her brains, Clodia married her first cousin Quintus Metellus Celler by 62 B.C.E. and was widowed in 59, when her husband unexpectedly died before he assumed his proconsulship of Transalpine Gaul. Although it is unclear at what point she became part of the social set that included the well born, the notorious, the rich, and the cultured, she began an affair with the poet Gaius Valerius Catullus toward the end of her husband's life when she was about 35 years old, and Catullus, some 6 to 10 years younger.

Her lover was one of Rome's greatest poets, and his life marked the opening of the richest period in Latin poetry. Born around 85 B.C.E. in the vicinity of Verona, he lived his adult life primarily in Rome. He wrote in the years that preceded full-scale civil war, when festering political, social, and economic problems already made a patent mockery of the historical ideals of the republic. His poetry, built on Alexandrine literary traditions that had come into Roman culture from the East, often portrayed the political intrigue and gossip of the clannish Roman elite with a vivid and witty sting. Above all, however, his poetry recorded his love for Lesbia.

Lesbia was his name for Clodia. It was a reference to SAPPHO, the greatest woman poet of the ancient world, and a tribute to Clodia's beauty and intelligence. The Lesbia poems followed the demand of poetic love for a grand passion of a mostly unhappy kind and may or may not reflect a progression that fully matched the reality of their relationship. Catullus largely portrayed himself as an adoring lover who suffered the imperious and unfaithful attentions of his adored. He portrayed Lesbia as the dominant partner in the relationship and as a woman unlikely to surrender herself for very long to idylls of love with a poet.

The Lesbia poems also convey a timeless emotional reality. Catullus's aching love for Clodia/Lesbia stands historically marked by lyrical lines of wanting. The less ardent love of Lesbia/Clodia wraps itself around her demands for gifts of value and her calculated uses of the love-struck poet for her own ends. One of Catullus's repeated laments, and sometimes the subject of his most wickedly funny poems about Lesbia/Clodia, is her unwillingness to be faithful to him alone.

Among her other men was Marcus Caelius Rufus. Some 8 to 10 years her junior, Caelius was a part of the same social set. He had come to Rome as a protégé of Marcus Tullius Cicero and had been on the periphery of the conspirators around Lucius Sergius Catilina in 63 B.C.E. He held several political offices and was aedile under Cicero in Cilicia in 50. An acknowledged orator, he had a caustic wit and charm, and was a brilliant prosecutor.

Clodia began an affair with him after she was widowed, and the younger Caelius rented a house next door to her brother Publius. The relationship lasted about two years. It ended acrimoniously. In 56, Caelius was charged with a five offenses including killing the Egyptian ambassador, robbing Clodia, and attempting to poison her. Clodia was among those who brought the charges.

Both Clodia and her brother Clodius were enemies of the orator and statesman Cicero, consul in 63 B.C.E. Cicero had testified against Clodius after the Bona Dea scandal in 61 (see TERENTIA [1]) and had made clear his dislike for Clodia's lifestyle. Her brother gained revenge when he was tribune in 58 and passed a bill that exiled Cicero. Among Caelius's defenders was Cicero, only recently returned from exile and now presented with an opportunity to attack his enemy Clodia.

Cicero's speech in favor of Caelius was a model courtroom oration. Vivid, clever, and very funny, the speech destroyed Clodia's credibility and her reputation. Cicero addressed her as if he were her most illustrious ancestor, the famous censor Appius Claudius. He instantly reduced her, a woman close to 40 years old, to the status of a child whose behavior was unsuitable for a woman. Cicero accused her of behaving in the manner of a prostitute. He very carefully never accused her of actually being one, only of having a lifestyle associated with immoral women. He pointed to her household, to her travels to the resort town of Baiae, to her collection of jewels, and to her friendships with men. He described her as the Medea of the Palatine who had led a mere youth astray, although Caelius was hardly an innocent. As a final blow, he insinuated that she and her brother, his sworn enemy, had an incestuous relationship.

Caelius was acquitted, and nothing more was heard of Clodia. However, the information in the speech, when viewed without malice, also makes clear that Clodia had succeeded. She used her beauty and brains to offset her father's financial debacle and lived an independent, rich, and varied life, loved by one of Rome's greatest poets and with close ties to her family, especially her brother Clodius.

Cic., Att. 12.38, 42.
Cic., Cael., passim.

Plut., Cic. 29.1–5.
Balsdon, J. P. V. D., pp. 54–55.
Bauman, R. A., pp. 69–73.
Grimal, P., pp. 148–56.
OCD, p. 350.
PW 66.
Quinn, K., pp. 54–203.

▣ CLODIA (3)

(1st century B.C.E.) Roman: Rome
Convicted adulterer

Clodia was divorced for adultery after her brother incited rebellion among the troops under her husband's command. Her parents came from aristocratic families. Her mother's name is unknown, but it is certain that she came from the Metelli family. Her father was Appius Claudius Pulcher, consul in 79 B.C.E. Tragedy struck her family when her father died destitute in 76. She was the youngest of three sisters, all named Clodia. CLODIA (1) married Quintus Marcus Rex, consul in 68; CLODIA (2) was the lover of the poet Catullus, among others. Her youngest brother, Publius Clodius Pulcher, was a populist politician whose base of power lay with armed mobs and urban plebs.

Clodia married Lucius Licinius Lucullus, consul in 74. Her husband, a relative on her mother's side, was an able soldier, politician, and provincial administrator, lacking only the gift of evoking loyalty from troops and colleagues. He held military commands in Africa and Asia from which he greatly enhanced his personal wealth. He appears to have been among the few Romans of the time to have understood that strangling the cities with usurious interest rates, tax, or tribute to Rome was economically counterproductive. He successfully reorganized the debts owed Rome with a payment plan at moderate interest rates for the cities in the East.

Clodia's wealthy husband and her populist brother ran on a collision course. In 68 B.C.E., when her husband was in Armenia and his troops were ready to mutiny, her brother incited rebellion. The war had been longer than anticipated, and its end was not in sight. Although the army had gained significant victories, there was a sense that Lucullus had benefited far more than had the soldiers. This was just the kind of situation in which her brother thrived. Gifted with articulating the discontent of Romans, her brother also believed that Lucullus had failed to adequately reward him. Moreover, the leadership in Rome had turned against Lucullus. Led by the equites, whose incomes suffered from his financial reorganization, they successfully clamored for him to be relieved of his command.

Lucullus returned to Rome a frustrated and angry man who had to fight for a triumph. Shortly after he returned, he divorced Clodia for adultery. She had been in Italy for several years alone at a time when women were increasingly able to have independent social lives. Her sister Clodia (2) the lover of the poet Catullus, was part of a literary and social circle regarded by others as dissolute. With whom Clodia engaged in adulterous relationships is not clarified in the sources, which simply assert her immorality. Their hostility toward her probably reflects their conservative nature and is an extension of their view of her brother and sister.

Clodia had a son with Lucullus who died fighting on the side of Marcus Junius Brutus against Octavian and Mark Antony at Philippi in 42 B.C.E.

Cic., Mil. 73.
Plut., Luc. 34.1; 38.1.
Balsdon, J. P. V. D., p. 186.
PW 67.

▣ CLODIA (4)

(1st century B.C.E.–1st century C.E.) Roman: Rome
Long-lived woman

Clodia was the wife of an otherwise unknown Claudius Aufilius during the late republic. She survived her husband and her 15 children. She was said to have died at the age of 115.

Plin., NH 7.48, 158.
PW 68.

◨ CLODIA LAETA

(?–213 C.E.) Roman: Rome
Priestess

Clodia Laeta was one of four Vestal Virgins accused of sexual misconduct in 213 C.E. by the emperor Marcus Aurelius Antoninus (Caracalla). Clodia protested, claiming that Antoninus knew her to be a virgin. Still, she and her three sister Vestals, AURELIA SEVERA, CANNUTIA CRESCENTINA, and POMPONIA RUFINA, were condemned. Clodia suffered the traditional punishment of being buried alive. In contrast with earlier times, the improprieties of Clodia and her sister Vestal Virgins raised few fears of omens of disaster for Rome. Nonetheless, loyalty to tradition survived religious faith and an expectation of chastity from the Vestals remained the norm.

Dio. 78.16.1–3.

◨ CLOELIA (1)

(6th century B.C.E.) Roman: Rome
and Etruria
Heroine

Cloelia led a group of Roman hostages to freedom. A heroine from the sixth century B.C.E., before the union of Etruria and Rome, she was among the hostages sent by Rome to the Etruscans as surety for a peace treaty. In a story that may well be apocryphal, Cloelia successfully organized some of the hostages to swim back to Roman territory across the Tiber. The furious Etruscan ruler, Porsenna, demanded that Cloelia be returned; but in admiration of her daring, he promised her safety.

Cloelia returned. Porsenna allowed her to chose one-half of the hostages to take back to Rome. With the approval of the hostages, she chose the younger boys, because, she argued, they were the most vulnerable. Cloelia was honored by the Romans with a statue on the Via Sacra.

Livy 2.13.6–11.
Polyaenus, Strat. 31.
OCD, p. 254.

◨ CLOELIA (2)

(1st century B.C.E.) Roman: Rome
Faultless wife; divorced

Cloelia suffered divorce from the future dictator Lucius Cornelius Sulla in 88 B.C.E., ostensibly because she was childless. Faultless in marriage, she secured Sulla's praise and gifts of value as part of the divorce. Within a few weeks of the divorce, her ex-husband married his fourth wife, CAECILIA METELLA (1), who was both very wealthy and better connected.

Plut., Sull. 6.10, 11.
Syme, R., *Roman Revolution*, p. 20.

◨ COESYRA

(6th century B.C.E.) Greek: Athens
Political wife

Coesyra was the daughter of Megacles from the aristocratic Athenian clan of the Alcmaeonidae and was ready for marriage at a critical political moment. In 560 B.C.E. her father and his ally Lycurgus had deposed Pisistratus, the tyrant of Athens. When the relationship between Lycurgus and Megacles soured, her father offered the deposed Pisistratus an alliance. Marriage with Coesyra sealed the bargain.

Pisistratus, however, already had grown sons and had neither the need nor the desire for more children—especially with Coesyra, for her family suffered under an ancient curse. An ancestor, also named Megacles, had been an archon in Athens in 632 B.C.E. He had promised to spare the lives of a group of men who had seized the Acropolis. Instead, he induced some of them to leave the sacred precinct of Athena and killed a number of others at the altar of Eumenides. No good would come of any descendants of Megacles, it was said.

Coesyra reported to her mother that her husband's sexual behavior inhibited conception. Her father again changed sides and joined the opposition that drove Pisistratus out of Athens.

Hdt. 1.60–61.

CONSTANTIA, FLAVIA JULIA

(?–c. 329 C.E.) Roman: Italy, eastern Roman Empire, and Rome
Augusta; early Christian

Flavia Julia Constantia, a half sister of the emperor Constantine the Great, was a participant in the political and religious controversies of the early Christian church. She was greatly influenced by the Alexandrian priest Arius, whose teaching that Christ the Son was subordinate to God the Father was the most serious doctrinal controversy of the period. She was one of six children. Her father Constantius I had been appointed Caesar in the West under Maximian by the emperor Diocletian. Her mother was Flavia Maximiana THEODORA. In 313 C.E. Constantia married Valerius Licinius, the emperor of the East, to bolster his alliance with Constantine.

The marriage of Constantia and Licinius in Milan spurred Valerius Maximinus Daia to begin a war. His defeat left her husband and half brother the two supreme rulers of the empire, and Constantia became Augusta in the East. Using her position, she sought to foster a reconciliation in the church. She corresponded with Bishop Eusebius of Caesarea, a leader of the Arian sect and today recognized as the church's first historian, and brought Eusebius to meet with Arius before the Council of Nicaea in 325.

The alliance between her half brother and husband faltered, and Constantine defeated her husband in battle at Chrysopolis in 324. She fled with her husband but intervened with her brother and secured her husband's freedom. Her efforts were short-lived. Her husband, allowed to rule over a much smaller area with its capital at Nicomedia in Asia Minor, was later put to death after being accused of plotting against Constantine.

After the death of her husband, she and her two children, Licinius and Helena, returned to Rome and lived in Constantine's court. She exercised sufficient influence for her half brother to mint coins with her likeness and to name the port city of Gaza after her. Her work with church leaders continued. She was present at the Council of Nicaea in 325 and persuaded her Arian friends to formally recognize the doctrine of the unity of God the Father and Son, and to take confession. She died about 329. Her young son, Licinius, was executed on orders of Constantine for unknown reasons.

Eutropius 10.5, 6.
PW 13.

CORELLIA HISPULLA

(1st–2nd century C.E.) Roman: Italy
Affluent woman; litigant

Corellia Hispulla, the daughter of HISPULLA and Corellius Rufus, enjoyed a lifelong friendship with Pliny the Younger. They engaged in business and shared family successes and concerns. Corellia married their mutual friend Mucinius Justus. Throughout her life she bought and sold shares in property that she had inherited from family and friends. At one time she expressed an interest to Pliny in owning land on Lake Comum (Como). Instead of disposing of a recent legacy of five-twelfths of an estate, he offered it to Corellia at whatever price she wished to pay. She gave him 700,000 sesterces for the land. Later, when she found out that Pliny could have received 200,000 more, she offered him the difference, but he refused.

In the legalisitic society of the first century C.E., many if not most propertied people probably found themselves in court at one time or another. Pliny defended Corellia in a suit brought against her by the consul-elect Caecilius. The content of the suit is unknown, but Pliny maintained friendly relations with Caecilius. After her husband's death from painful gout, she assumed responsibility for her children and continued to correspond with Pliny about their education.

Plin., Ep. 1.12; 3.3; 4.17; 7.11, 14.

CORINNA

(3rd century B.C.E.) Greek: Tanagra
Poet

Corinna was a poet from Tanagra, in Greece, who probably lived in the third century B.C.E. Her parents were Procatia and Acheloadorus. She wrote lyric poems in a local Boeotian dialect. Her subjects were the legends of gods and heroes presented in a simple and straightforward narrative without metaphors or similes. Unlike SAPPHO's work, her poetry was neither passionate nor personal.

In the works of Pausanius and Plutarch there are references to her life that place her in the sixth century B.C.E. as a contemporary of the Greek poet Pindar, against whom she was said to have won five competitions. Pausanius wrote that in her tomb at Tanagra there was a painting that portrayed her in the gymnasium at Thebes binding her hair with a fillet in honor of her victory over Pindar. He credited her victory to her beauty and to the Aeolian dialect of her poetry, which he claimed was understood better than the Doric used by Pindar. However, her name first appeared in the first century B.C.E., possibly as a later addition to the compendium of women poets originally collected by the Alexandrians. The third century B.C.E. is now considered a more likely time period for her life.

Knowledge of her poetry has come mainly from papyrus texts written in the first three centuries C.E. Propertius and Ovid, Roman poets of the first cen-tury C.E., named their poetic lovers Corinna in celebration of her beauty, gracefulness and intelligence.

Ovid passim.
Paus. 9.22.3.
Propertius passim.
Campbell, D. A., v. 4, pp. 1–3, 19–23.
Fantham, E., et al., pp. 166–67.
OCD, p. 290.
Page, D. L., *Corinna.*
Pomeroy, S., *Goddesses,* p. 52.

CORNELIA (I)

(2nd century B.C.E.) Roman: Rome
Political player

Cornelia was widowed after her husband killed her nephew and then committed suicide. She was the elder daughter of AEMILIA TERTIA and the great Publius Cornelius Scipio Africanus Major, the conqueror of Hannibal and sister of CORNELIA (2). Her father was attracted to Greek philosophy and literature, and educated his children, including his daughters, in the controversial new learning of the period.

Cornelia married a cousin, Publius Cornelius Scipio Nasica, consul in 138 B.C.E. Her husband and her nephew Tiberius Sempronius Gracchus, the son of her sister Cornelia (2), were opponents. Faced with a growing landless population that collected in Rome, Tiberius and his brother Gaius led the effort to reform the use of public land and forgive debts. Their powerful opposition was led by conservative landed interests. Cornelia's conservative husband was in the forefront of the mob that killed Tiberius.

Scipio Nasica left Rome to escape popular anger. Eventually he committed suicide in Pergamum. Cornelia remained in Rome and later lived with her mother on their estates in southern Italy.

Plut., Ti. Gracch. 19.1–6; 21.3–4.
PW 406.
Richardson, K., pp. 94–95.

⊞ CORNELIA (2)

(c. 190s–121 B.C.E.) Roman: Italy
Political player

Cornelia was both formidable and influential. Born in the 190s B.C.E. into one of Rome's most distinguished families, Cornelia was the second daughter of AEMILIA TERTIA and the general who had conquered Hannibal, Publius Cornelius Scipio Africanus Major. Her father was attracted to Greek culture and gave his daughters, Cornelia and her sister CORNELIA (1), an education in Greek literature and philosophy, which was still unusual even for men. She married only once, raised her children as a widow, and bore the death of both her sons with courage and fortitude.

Cornelia was a wealthy woman. She received 25 talents from her mother on her marriage and another 25 talents after her mother's death. She married well, the wealthy and much older Tiberius Sempronius Gracchus who was comfortable with an unusually well-educated wife. He was a fine soldier and an excellent provincial governor, consul twice, in 177 and 163, and censor in 169. Her marriage gave rise to an apocryphal story. As repeated by the historian Livy, Cornelia's father arranged her marriage at the urging of Roman senators without the prior approval of her mother. Her mother, furious at not having been consulted, only forgave her husband when she discovered that the bridegroom was the illustrious Tiberius Sempronius Gracchus.

Her husband died in 154 B.C.E., and Cornelia became a sought-after widow. She remained interested in the East, and Ptolemy VIII Physcon, ruler of Cyrene, offered her marriage in 154. Almost continually at odds with his older brother, Ptolemy VI Philometor, he no doubt rightly believed that his influence in Rome would be greatly enhanced through a marital alliance with Cornelia. So too would his purse. After her husband's death, however, Cornelia devoted herself to her children and managing her estates. She employed Greek tutors for her children to pro-

vide an education for them like her own in philosophy and mathematics. In a famous story that is most probably apocryphal, when a visitor possibly Ptolemy, displayed to her a collection of magnificent jewels, Cornelia pointed to her children and replied that they were her jewels.

Of the 12 children she had borne before her husband's death, only three survived into adulthood. Her two sons, Tiberius and Gaius Gracchus became the most famous men of their day. They led Rome in an effort for land reform and debt forgiveness that would stem the growing problems of a landless urban poor. Both were killed, but not before politics had also rent the family. Her son Tiberius was killed by his political opponent and uncle, the husband of Cornelia's sister. Her only daughter, SEMPRONIA (1), married Scipio Aemilianus in 129, another opponent of the reforms. It was an unhappy marriage, and his sudden death provoked rumors that Sempronia and Cornelia had murdered him. The two women were close and lived together after Sempronia was widowed.

Historians have differed over Cornelia's politics about land reform, which had so dominated the life and death of her sons. On one hand, in a fragment of a letter that she was purported to have written and that had been preserved by the historian Cornelius Nepos, she chastised her son Gaius for policies that were destroying the state. On the other hand, the validity of the letter has been seriously challenged since Nepos wrote at a time when the ruling oligarchy wanted the Gracchi discredited. Plutarch, moreover, reported that Cornelia hired men from abroad to come to Rome disguised as reapers and aid Gaius. What has never been disputed was her influence on the behavior of her children. Although Gaius attacked the tribune Marcus Octavius for his veto of Tiberius's agrarian reforms in 133 B.C.E., he also withdrew the bill that might have meant exile for the same tribune, claiming it was at the request of his mother.

After the assassination of Tiberius, Cornelia retired to her estate in Misenum on the Bay of

Naples where she entertained notables of the day. While there, she received news of Gaius's death. Cornelia wrote voluminously, and her letters were published, although only the challenged fragment quoted by Nepos remains. She died in 121. The Romans honored her with a bronze statue.

Cic., Brut. 104, 211.
Livy 38.57.5–8.
Nep., "Letter of Cornelia," in Horsfall, N., pp. 41–43.
Plin., NH 34.31.
Plut., G. Gracch. 4.1; 13.2.
Plut., Ti. Gracch. 1.4–5; 4.1–3; 19.1–6; 21.3–4.
Poly. 31.27.
Val. Max. 4.4.
Bauman, R. A.
OCD, p. 392.
PW 407.
Stockton, D., pp. 24–25.

CORNELIA (3)

(2nd–1st century B.C.E.) Roman: Rome
Great-great-grandmother of Tiberius

Cornelia was the great-grandmother of the powerful, independent, and wealthy LIVIA DRUSILLA, the wife of Augustus and mother of the emperor Tiberius. Cornelia married Marcus Livius Drusus, consul in 112 B.C.E., who successfully opposed the election of Gaius Gracchus as tribune. Widowed during her husband's consulship, she also outlived her son, who was tribune in 91. Her son was assassinated after proposing reforms for which the ruling oligarchy would be credited.

PW 409.

CORNELIA (4)

(2nd–1st century B.C.E.) Roman: Rome and Italy
Businesswoman

Cornelia was the daughter of the Roman general and dictator Lucius Cornelius Sulla. In 82–81 B.C.E., her father led a ruthless proscription that solidified his power and eliminated key opposition families. Cornelia benefited from the sudden surplus of properties available on the market and bought for a relatively small sum a beautiful villa at Baiae, one of the most desirable locations on the Bay of Naples, which figured prominently in the lives of the Roman elite during the last century B.C.E. The property she acquired had once belonged to Gaius Marius, the brilliant general and major opponent of Sulla, who died in 86. Cornelia later sold the property to Lucius Licinius Lucullus, the husband of CLODIA (3), for some 33 times the original sum. This is an unusually vivid illustration of the inflation that accompanied life throughout the century and that was the cause of at least some of the political instability.

Cornelia was the wife of Quintus Pompeius Rufus, son of her father's coconsul in 88 B.C.E. With her husband, who was murdered at the end of 88, she had two children: Quintus Pompeius Rufus, tribune in 52, and POMPEIA (1), who became the wife of Julius Caesar and was a suspect in the Bona Dea scandal of 62.

In 51, her son became involved in a public trial and sought from her several farm properties that she held in trust for him. Initially she refused, but an emissary convinced her to change her mind. It remains unclear whether she was rapacious, as reported by the ancient commentator Valerius Maximus, or simply a good businesswoman.

She spent much of her life in Baiae and died there.

Plut., Mar. 34.2.
Val. Max. 4.2.7.
PW 412.

CORNELIA (5)

(?–68 B.C.E.) Roman: Rome
Brave woman

Cornelia was the granddaughter of Lucius Cornelius Cinna, consul in 87–84 B.C.E. and political ally of the general Gaius Marius. In 84 she married Julius Caesar, the nephew of JULIA (1) and

Marius. For both it was a first marriage. He was 16 years old; she was probably slightly younger. They had one daughter, JULIA (5).

These were difficult years. After Marius's death and Lucius Cornelius Sulla's victory over Cinna, Sulla initiated a proscription against Marian supporters. Cornelia was vulnerable. Caesar could provide little support. He had rejected Sulla's demand that he break with the Marian faction and divorce Cornelia. Stripped of his priesthood and forbidden his inheritance, he went into hiding and left Rome for Asia where over the next decade he studied and honed his military skills. Cornelia, despite her husband's proscription from public life and the loss of her dowry, remained in Italy, if not Rome. Possibly she was aided by Caesar's aunt Julia.

Several years before Cornelia's death Sulla pardoned Caesar, and he returned to Rome and his wife. She died in 68 B.C.E. Caesar gave the funeral oration.

Plut., Caes. 1.1–2.
Suet., Caes. 1.1–3.
PW 413.

CORNELIA (6)
(1st century B.C.E.) Roman: Rome
Cultured woman

Cornelia was the beautiful and cultured daughter of AEMILIA LEPIDA (1) and the corrupt Quintus Caecilius Metellus Pius Scipio, consul in 52 B.C.E. Said to be educated in mathematics and philosophy, she married Publius Licinius Crassus, the younger son of the triumvir, in 55 B.C.E. He died in 53 fighting the Parthians in Syria. The following year she married Gnaeus Pompeius (Pompey the Great). Her new husband sought an alliance with Cornelia's prominent, rich, and aristocratic family. He also rescued her father from a bribery charge and made him his coconsul.

The marriage was successful. When Pompey left Italy at the head of the republicans in 49, Cornelia and their young son, Sextus, went to the island of Lesbos. After Caesar defeated Pompey at

Pharsalus in 48, Cornelia met her husband in Mitylene, the chief city of Lesbos. Together they sailed to Cilicia in southern Asia Minor and then to Egypt, where she witnessed his fatal stabbing as he landed on September 28, 48 B.C.E.

Cornelia left Egypt for Cyprus and then, with Caesar's permission, returned to Italy bearing her husband's ashes.

App., Bciv. 2.83, 85.
Plut., Pomp. 55, 66, 74, 76, 78–80.
OCD, p. 392.
Pomeroy, S. B. *Goddesses*, p. 171.
PW 417.
Syme, R., *Roman Revolution*, p. 40.

CORNELIA (7)
(c. 46 B.C.E.–?) Roman: Rome
Political wife

Cornelia was the daughter of POMPEIA (2) and Faustus Cornelius Sulla. Her grandfathers were Lucius Cornelius Sulla, the formidable dictator of Rome, and Gnaeus Pompeius (Pompey the Great), consul in 70 and the leader of the republican forces against Caesar.

Born no later than 46 B.C.E., she married Quintus Aemilius Lepidus and joined in the most politically active circle of women in Rome. Her father-in-law was a member of the Second Triumvirate, established in 43 B.C.E., together with Mark Antony and Octavian. Her mother-in-law, JUNIA (1), was the daughter of SERVILIA (1). Servilia, once the lover of Julius Caesar, was the half sister of Cato Uticensis, and the mother of Marcus Junius Brutus.

Cornelia's two children, AEMILIA LEPIDA (2) and Manius Aemilius Lepidus, consul in 11 C.E. survived the civil wars and became public figures in the early empire.

Tac., Ann. 3.22.1.
Syme, R., *Augustan Aristocracy*, index.

CORNELIA (8)

(?–16 B.C.E.) Roman: Rome
Eulogized by Propertius

Cornelia was eulogized by Propertius in a long poem commissioned by her husband after her death in 16 B.C.E., during the consulship of her brother, Publius Cornelius Scipio. Presented in the form of a funeral oration or a long epitaph, Cornelia speaks for herself from the grave. She accounts for her life and measures herself against the highest of traditional Roman ideals. Proudly she describes herself as an *univira*, a woman married only once. She admonishes her two children to know their history and to carry on the noble family tradition, to assure the immortality of her name.

Cornelia gives her lineage on both her mother's and her father's side. She reaches back into Roman history of the second century B.C.E. and to her ancestor the great general Publius Cornelius Scipio Africanus Major, who conquered Hannibal. She identifies her parents as SCRIBONIA and her second husband, Publius Cornelius Scipio, consul suffectus in 35 B.C.E. She speaks movingly of her marriage and her husband, Paullus Aemilius Lepidus, consul suffectus in 34 and censor in 22. She figuratively soothes his sorrow and assures him that it will pass.

Cornelia was the half sister of JULIA (6). Her two sons were Lucius Aemilius Paullus, consul in 1 C.E., and Marcus Aemilius Lepidus, consul in 6 C.E. Lucius Aemilius Paullus married the granddaughter of Augustus, JULIA (7), in 4 B.C.E.

Propertius 4.11.36, 61–72.
PW 419.
Syme, R., *Augustan Aristocracy,* index.

CORNELIA (9)

(1st century B.C.E.–1st century C.E.) Roman: Rome
Loyal wife

Cornelia, a member of the Scipiones family, married Lucius Volusius Saturninus, consul in 3 C.E.

In 24 C.E., when her husband was 62, she bore him a son, Quintus Volusius Saturninus, who became consul in 56. Her husband died in the year his son became consul when he was 93 years old.

Plin., NH 7.62.
PW 423.
Syme, R., *Augustan Aristocracy,* pp. 252 ff.

CORNELIA (10)

(1st century C.E.) Roman: Rome
Priestess

Cornelia received a dowry of 2 million sesterces when she became a Vestal Virgin in 23 C.E. The commitment to the priesthood was optional after 30 years. Since Cornelia became a priestess at a young age, she could later marry. Moreover, her wealth would remain intact throughout her priestly years, and she could leave the priesthood a very wealthy woman.

Tac., Ann. 4.16.
PW 422.

CORNELIA (11)

(1st century C.E.) Roman: Rome and Germany
Adulterer

Cornelia went to Germany with her husband, Gaius Calvisius Sabinus, consul in 26 C.E. and then governor of Pannonia. Although by this time it was not uncommon for wives to accompany their husbands, military camps at night were largely off-limits to women. With the complicity of the tribune Titus Vinius, Cornelia entered the camp after dark disguised as a soldier. She watched the drills and, according to Tacitus, committed adultery in the general's headquarters.

Returning to Rome in 39 C.E., Cornelia was charged with accompanying the sentries on their rounds and watching them drill. Her husband was accused of abetting her. They both committed suicide before the trial.

Dio. 59.18.4.
Tac., Hist. 1.48.
PW 424.

▣ CORNELIA (12)

(?–90 C.E.) Roman: Rome
Priestess

Cornelia was the head of the college of Vestal Virgins when the emperor Domitian began a purity campaign in 83 C.E. to improve public morality. He attacked the Vestal Virgins and the temple in the Forum as a sinkhole of immorality that had existed from before his reign. Three of the Vestal Virgins, the two sisters OCULATA and VARRONILLA, were forced to choose how they should die. Cornelia was found innocent of any charges.

Domitian was determined that she be found guilty. He renewed the charges in 90 and convened the pontiffs at his villa in the city of Alba Longa, some 15 miles southeast of Rome, rather than in the pontifical court in Rome. Cornelia was condemned and sentenced to death for incest without being present to rebut the charges. Such was Domitian's hostility to Cornelia that he also decreed that the punishment should be entombment while still alive, instead of allowing her to choose her own manner of death.

Cornelia protested her innocence as she was led to her burial place. Celer, the Roman equestrian accused of consorting with her, protested his innocence as he was whipped to death in a public square.

Plin., Ep. 4.11 ff.
Suet., Dom. 8.
Balsdon., J. P. V. D., p. 241.
PW 426.

▣ CORNIFICIA

(?–211 C.E.) Roman: Rome
Political victim

Cornificia was the daughter of the younger Anna Galeria FAUSTINA and the emperor Marcus Aurelius. A period of unrest followed her father's death in 180 C.E. In 193 Septimius Severus became emperor. He died in 211 leaving two sons who hated each other; the brothers, Marcus Aurelius Antoninus, known as Caracalla, and Septimius Geta, quarreled over succession.

Their mother was JULIA DOMNA, with whom Cornificia maintained at least a formal friendship. Julia Domna sought to mediate between her sons. After calling for a meeting with Geta and his mother, Caracalla instead sent centurions who murdered Geta in his mother's arms. Cornificia visited Julia Domna to mourn Geta's death. Caracalla took offense. Geta, he claimed, had committed treason, and anyone who wept for his death also committed treason.

He ordered that Cornificia die. She was allowed to commit suicide. Cornificia opened her veins and went to her death mindful that she was a daughter of the great emperor Marcus Aurelius, and calling upon her spirit that was soon to be free of her body.

Dio. 78.16.6a.
Herodian 4.6.3.
Balsdon, J. P. V. D., p. 154.

▣ CRATESICLEIA

(3rd century B.C.E.) Greek: Sparta and Egypt
Reformer

Cratesicleia was a Spartan aristocrat who gambled her life and fortune in support of reform during the third century B.C.E. She was the wife of the Spartan ruler Leonidas II, who led a conservative faction that opposed debt relief or land and citizenship reform. Her son Cleomenes III (260–219 B.C.E.), who followed his father in 235, pursued reformist policies. To support him, Cratesicleia pooled her property with that of other family members and allowed a redistribution of the land to ease the burden of debt that was driving many into poverty.

Although she did not seek a second husband, a marital alliance with Aristonous X assured her son support from one of the most prominent citizens of Sparta. When Cleomenes sought the aid of Ptolemy III Euergetes of Egypt in a war against

Antigonus III, ruler of Macedonia, Ptolemy demanded Cratesicleia and Cleomenes' children as hostages. Willingly she went.

After Cleomenes' defeat in 222 B.C.E., he went to Egypt where Ptolemy III promised ships and money. Ptolemy III died in 221, and his successor, Ptolemy IV Philopator, was no friend. Cleomenes led a group of Spartans in an attack to free the hostages. They killed a number of Egyptians but failed to ignite a revolt in Alexandria. Rather than face capture, Cleomenes and his soldiers killed themselves.

Ptolemy IV ordered Cratesicleia, her women attendants, and her grandsons killed. Although she requested that she die first, she was the last to be killed.

Plut., Cleom. 6.1–2; 11.1–2; 22.3–7; 38.3–6.
Mosse, C., pp. 145–46, 148.

CRATESIPOLIS

(4th century B.C.E.)   Greek: Sicyon
Ruler

Cratesipolis became ruler of the Greek city of Sicyon in 314 B.C.E. after the death of her husband, Alexander, the son of Polyperchon—a general under Alexander the Great. On her husband's death, she was welcomed by the soldiers, who esteemed her highly for her acts of kindness, her practical skills, and her daring.

When the people of Sicyon revolted, she crushed the rebellion. The name Cratesipolis, meaning conqueror of the city, was conferred on her after her victory. She also ruled Corinth until she was defeated by Ptolemy I Soter in 308.

Diod. 19.67.1–2; 22.37.1.
Macurdy, G., pp. 106, 233.

CRISPINA

(1st century C.E.)   Roman: Rome
Brave woman

Crispina ransomed her father's body after his death. Her father, Titus Vinius, consul in 69 C.E.,

was a close adviser of the emperor Servius Sulpicius Galba. He was murdered by the soldiers of Marcus Salvius Otho when they assassinated Galba in 69. Taking responsibility for the burial rites, she negotiated payment with the slayers and retrieved his body.

Tac., Hist. 1.47.

CRISPINA BRUTTIA

(2nd century C.E.)   Roman: Rome
Political player

Crispina Bruttia lived and died by intrigue. Her father was Gaius Bruttius Praesens, consul in 180 C.E., and her husband, Lucius Aelius Aurelius Commodus, was the elder son of the emperor Marcus Aurelius. She married in 177, the same year that her husband became joint ruler with his father. Three years later, after the death of her father-in-law, her husband became emperor.

Her sister-in-law Annia Aurelia Galeria LUCILLA vied with Crispina for position and influence. About 182, Lucilla organized a plot to assassinate her brother. It failed. She was exiled and then executed. In 187, Crispina suffered a similar fate. She was found guilty of adultery and banished to Capri, where she was killed.

Dio. 72.33.1; 73.6.
Herodian 1.8.4.
SHA, Comm. 5.11.
SHA, M. Ant. 27.8.
Balsdon, J. P. V. D., pp. 147–48.
PW 17.

CYNANE

(?–322 B.C.E.)   Greek: Macedonia and Asia Minor
Political player

Cynane vied with OLYMPIAS (1) to rule Macedonia after the death of Alexander the Great. She and Alexander were half siblings through their father, Philip II. Her mother was Audata from Illyria along the Adriatic Sea opposite Italy. Cynane was said to have fought by the side of her father when he campaigned in Illyria, and she killed Caeria, an Illyrian woman ruler, in combat. She married Amyntas, Philip's nephew, and had a daughter, EURYDICE (2) (ADEA). Alexander had Amyntas killed, probably to solidify his claim to Macedonia after his father's death. Cynane did not marry again.

Cynane was independently wealthy and after Alexander's death determined to use her daughter to lay claim to Macedonia. Her plan was simple: The generals had declared two children, Philip Arrhidaeus and Alexander IV, joint rulers of Macedonia in 323. Alexander was the son of Alexander the Great and ROXANE. He was an infant and fiercely protected by his mother. Philip Arrhidaeus, however, was the son of Philip II and PHILINNA, less protected and not fully competent. Cynane decided to marry her daughter Eurydice to Philip. In 322, she organized an army and took her daughter to Asia where Philip resided under the control of Alexander's general Antipater, who had been appointed regent for the two heirs.

Antipater failed to stop Cynane and her army from crossing the Strymon River. She came face to face with the Macedonian forces under Alcestas, who ordered her to withdraw or be killed. Cynane declared herself ready to die unless Alcestas met her demand that Philip Arrhidaeus marry Eurydice. On orders of Alcestas, she was killed before her own daughter and the Macedonian troops.

Shocked by what had happened, the troops threatened to revolt unless the marriage took place. Perdiccas, who held the chief executive authority after the death of Alexander, acquiesced, even though he had hoped to marry CLEOPATRA (3), the daughter of Olympias and full sister of Alexander, and claim the Macedonian throne for himself.

Polyaenus, Strat. 8.16.
Carney, E. D., "The Career of Adea-Eurydice," pp. 496–98.
Macurdy, G., pp. 48–52.
Pomeroy, S. B., *Women in Hellenistic Egypt*, pp. 6–7.

▣ CYNISCA

(4th century B.C.E.) Greek: Sparta
Self-made woman

Cynisca, a wealthy woman, was the daughter of the Spartan ruler Archidamus and the sister of Agis II, who succeeded her father. She was among the first women to breed horses and the first to gain an Olympic victory.

At the beginning of the fourth century B.C.E., when the owner of the horses and the racing driver no longer needed to be the same person, the races opened to women. Cynisca's horses won the four-horse chariot race and two other victories. Her name was inscribed on the victor lists. She erected a memorial of bronze horses at Olympia to celebrate her victory, as well a statue of herself in Elis sculpted by Apelles.

Paus. 3.8.1–2; 3.15.1; 6.1.6.
Harris, H. A., p. 178.
Pomeroy, S. B., *Goddesses*, p. 130

▣ CYTHERIS VOLUMNIA

(1st century B.C.E.) Roman: Rome
Self-made woman

Cytheris Volumnia was a famous, beautiful, and wealthy freedwoman of the late Roman republic. A talented mime, she was the lover of several politically important men including Mark Antony and Marcus Junius Brutus. In a letter to his friend Lucius Papirius Paetus, written in 46 B.C.E., Marcus Tullius Cicero mentioned her presence at a dinner party he had attended. Years later, the poet Virgil composed his Tenth Eclogue on the theme of Cornelius Gallus's obsession with Cytheris.

Plut., Ant. 9.5.
Cic., Amic. 9.26.2.
Pomeroy, S. B., *Goddesses*, pp. 198–99.

D

◫ DANAE

(3rd century B.C.E.) Greek: Athens and Syria
Political player

Danae saved her lover and died a traitor. Her mother, LEONTION, rivaled Theophrastus, Aristotle's successor, as the leading philosopher in Athens. Her father, Metodorus, was the most important disciple of Epicurus. Her father died several years before his teacher, who took responsibility for Danae's future. In his will, Metodorus left Danae a dowry and instructions to his executors to arrange a marriage for her with another member of the Epicurean school when she came of age.

Nothing is known of the intervening years before Danae became the favored attendant of the powerful LAODICE I in Antioch. The very wealthy Laodice had established her own household after her husband, Antiochus II, had married a younger woman. Later reconciled with him, he mysteriously died before he could renege on his promise to appoint her son his heir.

Among the cities under Laodice's control was Ephesus. She appointed a man named Sophron to govern the city. He and Danae were lovers. For unknown reasons, Laodice became suspicious of Sophron and summoned him to Antioch, intending to kill him. Danae signaled him a warning during his audience with Laodice. Sophron grasped the situation and requested that Laodice give him two days to contemplate their discussion. He escaped. Later he helped the Egyptians take Ephesus and became a commander in the Egyptian navy.

Laodice discovered Danae's treachery and ordered her thrown off a cliff. While she was being led to her death, Danae was reputed to have said that it was no wonder the gods were despised. She had saved her lover and was to be killed, while Laodice had murdered her husband and was rewarded with glory and a kingdom.

Ath. 593c–d.
Diog. Laert. 10.19–20.
McCurdy, G., pp. 85–86.

◫ DEINOMACHE

(5th century B.C.E.) Greek: Athens
Mother of Alcibiades

Deinomache was the daughter of Megacles of the aristocratic family of the Alcmaeonidae. She married Cleinias, who outfitted a trireme and fought against the Persians at Artemisium in 480 B.C.E. Widowed in 447 when her husband was killed in a battle with the Boeotians, she had a son,

Alcibiades, known for his beauty, his treachery, and his leadership of the Athenians.

Plut., Alc. 1.1.

▣ DEMARETE

(5th century B.C.E.) Greek: Syracuse
Political player

Demarete was immortalized on coins issued by her husband, Gelon, who ruled Gela and Syracuse, two of the greatest Hellenic cities in Sicily during the fifth century B.C.E. Demarete was the daughter of Theron (488–472 B.C.E.), who ruled Acragas located in southwest Sicily. After she married Gelon, he conquered Syracuse in 485 and made it his seat of power.

An alliance between Demarete's father and husband defeated the invading Carthaginians under Hamilcar at Himera. The victory was celebrated throughout the Greek world. Her husband issued celebratory coins in gratitude to the gods. The large silver decadrachms called Demareteia depicted Demarete on the reverse.

She and her husband were buried on her estate. A costly tomb, erected by the people, was destroyed by the Carthaginians in 396 B.C.E.

Hdt. 7.153–66.
Diod. 11.38.3–4.
Hammond, N. G. L., *History of Greece*, p. 270.

▣ DOMITIA

(?–59 C.E.) Roman: Rome
Political player

Domitia was contentious, proud, and unforgiving. She was the eldest daughter of ANTONIA THE ELDER and the arrogant Lucius Domitius Ahenobarbus, consul in 16 B.C.E. Augustus was her great-uncle and her grandparents were Mark Antony and OCTAVIA (2). She may have had two early marriages: to Decimus Haterius Agrippa, consul in 22 C.E., and to Quintus Junius Blaesus,

consul suffectus in 26 C.E. In a contentious suit against her brother, Gnaeus Domitius Ahenobarbus, consul in 32 C.E., she was defended by her third and last husband, the famous orator Gnaeus Passienus Crispus, consul in 44 C.E.

Domitia and her sister, DOMITIA LEPIDA, had opposed the marriage of their brother and the younger Julia AGRIPPINA. After her brother's death, Agrippina settled on Domitia's husband, Passienus Crispus, as a likely replacement. Dislike between the two women turned into enmity when Domitia and Crispus divorced largely on account of Agrippina's interference.

In 54 Domitia Lepida was put to death by Agrippina. A year later, Domitia joined with an enemy of Agrippina, JUNIA SILANA, in a plot to turn Agrippina's son, the emperor Nero, against his mother. They planned to convince the emperor that his mother was conspiring with Rubellius Plautus to supplant him. A freedman of Domitia, the actor Paris, carried the damning report about Agrippina to Nero. Nero ordered that his mother be killed. However, the prefect of the Praetorian Guard, Sextus Afranius Burrus, persuaded Nero that Agrippina be given a hearing. She managed to convince Nero of her innocence.

Although Domitia succeeded in outliving Agrippina, Nero had her poisoned in 59 C.E., when she was more than 60 years old, so that he could acquire her property.

Dio. 62.17.1–2.
Suet., Ner. 34.5.
Tac., Ann. 13.19–21.
Balsdon, J. P. V. D., index.
PW 90.
Syme, R., *Augustan Aristocracy*, index.

▣ DOMITIA LEPIDA

(?–54 C.E.) Roman: Rome
Political player

Domitia Lepida was the beautiful younger daughter of ANTONIA THE ELDER and the arrogant Lucius Domitius Ahenobarbus, consul in 16 B.C.E. Her lineage was of the highest order. Her grandmother was OCTAVIA (2) and her great-uncle was Augustus. She inherited the traits of her father's family—pride in ancestry, arrogance, ambition, and an implacable hatred for enemies—which shaped a lifetime of conflict in the most intimate circles of imperial power. She vied with her daughter, the strong-willed Valeria MESSALLINA, and her sister-in-law, the younger Julia AGRIPPINA, for influence over the emperor Claudius.

Domitia Lepida, before she was 20 and sometime after the birth of Messallina, had been left a widow by Marcus Valerius Messalla Barbatus. Her second husband was Faustus Cornelius Sulla. They had a son, Faustus Sulla, consul in 52 C.E., and their marriage ended either by death or divorce.

The marriage of the emperor Claudius and her daughter Messallina placed Domitia in the privileged position of mother-in-law to the emperor and subsequently as grandmother to Britannicus, the heir apparent. In 41 Claudius arranged a third marriage for his widowed or divorced mother-in-law with his friend Gaius Appius Junius Silanus, consul in 28 C.E. The marriage may well have aroused Messallina's fears. Silanus, a good friend of Claudius and now the husband of her powerful and manipulative mother, posed a clear threat to her dominant position of influence over the aging emperor. A year after the marriage, in 42, Silanus was charged with treason and executed. Messallina and Narcissus, one of Claudius's powerful freedmen secretaries, had orchestrated his removal.

The resulting estrangement between mother and daughter was never healed. Although Domitia hurried to Messallina's side when her daughter was accused of treason for enacting a marriage ceremony with her lover, Gaius Silius, she simply advised her daughter to kill herself. Finally killed by one of the soldiers in 48 Domitia took her body for burial.

Years before her daughter's death, Domitia Lepida and her sister, DOMITIA, had opposed the marriage of their brother with the younger Agrippina. After her brother's death in 39, the widowed Agrippina was herself exiled by her own brother, the emperor Gaius Caligula. During her exile, Domitia had cared for her nephew, the future emperor Nero. Agrippina was recalled by Claudius in 41. She never forgave Domitia for opposing her marriage and now further resented any influence she might have acquired over Nero. When Agrippina married Claudius, her dislike for Domitia was further exacerbated by Domitia's relationship with Britannicus, Claudius and Messallina's son.

Agrippina, desirous of enhancing the position of her son Nero at the expense of Britannicus, and fearful that Domitia's influence with the elderly Claudius would favor Britannicus at the expense of Nero, arranged to have her old enemy found guilty of using magic and posing a threat to the peace in Italy by failing to curb the slaves on her estates in Calabria. She was put to death in 54 C.E.

Suet., Ner. 6.3; 7.1.
Tac., Ann. 12.64–65.
Bauman, R. A., index.
Levick, B., *Claudius*, p. 76.
PW 102.
Syme, R., *Augustan Aristocracy*, index.

⊞ DOMITIA LONGINA

(?–c. 140 C.E.) Roman: Rome
Augusta

Domitia Longina lived a long life and was successful at imperial intrigues, including murder. She was the daughter of a distinguished general, Gnaeus Domitius Corbulo, whom the emperor Nero ordered to commit suicide in 66 C.E. She divorced her first husband, the patrician Lucius Aelius Lamia Aemilianus, at the insistence of the future emperor Domitian. She married Domitian in 70 C.E., and they had a son and a daughter, both of whom died. Domitian awarded her the title Augusta and divorced her. There were rumors that Titus, the brother of Domitian, had been her lover. She appears to have taken as a lover the freedman actor Paris, who was the rage of Rome and a very desirable lover. Around 84, Domitian had Paris executed and remarried Domitia, claiming that it was the will of the people.

Domitia feared that Domitian would kill her. She joined a conspiracy that murdered her husband in 96. Domitia lived another 40 years and died shortly before 140. A temple in her honor was built in Gabii with a donation of 10,000 sesterces by one of her freedmen on the condition that a celebration would be held annually on her birthday.

Dio. 65.4; 67.3.1–2; 67.15.2.
Suet., Dom. 1.3; 3.1; 14.1.
Suet., Tit. 10.2; 67.15.2–4.
Balsdon, J. P. V. D., pp. 131–32.
PW 103.

◨ DOMITIA LUCILLA

(?–155/161 C.E.) Roman: Rome
Political player

Domitia Lucilla was a very rich woman at the center of a network of connected families that came to the fore under the emperor Trajan. According to her son, she was educated and also fluent in written Greek. She corresponded with Fronto, her son's teacher, and was a friend of his wife, Gratia, whom she invited in 143 C.E. to celebrate her birthday in Naples where she was staying with her son.

She had only one husband, Marcus Annius Verus, whose father, also named Marcus Annius Verus, was consul in 126 C.E. They had two children: a daughter, Annia Cornificia Faustina, and a son, Marcus Annius, born in 121. Marcus became the emperor Marcus Aurelius (161–180 C.E.) after he had been adopted by his aunt Annia Galeria, the elder FAUSTINA and her husband, the emperor Antoninus Pius.

Domitia Lucilla managed her own business affairs, especially after the death of her husband around 124. She had inherited her wealth from her mother, also named Domitia Lucilla, who had been adopted by her great-uncle Publius Calvius Tullus, consul in 109. The family's fortune had originated with her great-grandfather, Gnaeus Domitius Afer, an orator and businessman who had a large tile factory outside Rome.

She remained on good terms with both her children and gave advice on family affairs. When her daughter Faustina married, she asked her son to give his sister as a dowry the inheritance left to him by his father, since he would have his grandfather's fortune. Marcus agreed, noting that his sister should not be poorer than her husband.

Domitia Lucilla evidently was an influential woman. The future emperor Marcus Didius Julianus was brought up in her house, and she helped to secure his appointment to the Board of Twenty, a court that decided cases of inheritance. He later became a wealthy senator, and then emperor for a brief period. Domitia Lucilla died between 155 and 161 C.E.

SHA, Did. Jul. 1.3–4.
SHA, Marc. 1.3.
Birley, A. R., *Marcus Aurelius*, index.
OCD, p. 152.

◨ DOMITIA PAULINA (1)

(1st century C.E.) Roman: Spain
Political player

Domitia Paulina came from Cádiz in Spain; nothing is known of her parentage. She was the wife of Publius Aelius Hadrianus Afer. They had a daughter, DOMITIA PAULINA (2), and a son who became the emperor Hadrian. Domitia Paulina died when Hadrian was 10 years old, and Hadrian became a ward of the future emperor Trajan.

SHA, Hadr. 1.1–2.
PW 107.

◨ DOMITIA PAULINA (2)

(?–130 C.E.) Roman: Rome
Political player

Domitia Paulina was the sister of the future emperor Hadrian and the daughter of Publius Aelius

Hadrianus Afer and DOMITIA PAULINA (1). She married Lucius Iulius Ursus Servianus, who was about 30 years her senior. Trajan considered her husband a possible successor. Her husband, consul in 102, sought to further his prospects at the expense of his brother-in-law Hadrian, whom he accused of extravagance and debt. This turned out to be a serious error of judgment, especially once his brother-in-law became emperor.

When Paulina died in 130, Hadrian paid her no public honor. He also showed no favor to her grandson, Gnaeus Pedianus Fuscus, born to her daughter Julia. When he adopted Lucius Aelius as his successor, he had the already 90-year-old Servianus and his 18-year-old grandson Fuscus put to death for challenging the adoption.

Dio. 69.17.1–2.
SHA, Hadr. 1.1–2; 2.6; 15.8; 23.8.
Balsdon, J. P. V. D., p. 139.
OCD, pp. 786–87.
PW 108.

▣ DOMITILLA, FLAVIA (1)

(1st century C.E.)   Roman: Italy and North Africa
Mother of two emperors

Flavia Domitilla was born in Ferulium, Italy. Her father, Flavius Liberalis, was a scribe or law clerk in a praetor's court. He went before a board of arbitration and successfully gained for her full Roman citizenship.

Before she married the future emperor Vespasian, Domitilla had a de facto marriage with Statilius Capella, a Roman equestrian from Africa. When she married Vespasian, he was an army officer. She had two sons, Titus and Domitian, and a daughter, Flavia Domitilla. Domitilla and her daughter both died before Vespasian became emperor in 69 C.E. Her sons, Titus and Domitian, succeeded their father.

Suet., Ves. 3.

▣ DOMITILLA, FLAVIA (2)

(1st century C.E.)   Roman: Italy and Pandateria
Political player, exiled

Flavia Domitilla was the niece of the emperor Titus Flavius Domitian. She married Flavius Clemens, the emperor's cousin. They had two young sons whom Domitian favored as successors. Shortly after her husband's consulship in 95 C.E., the couple was accused of denying the traditional gods in favor of Jewish or Christian rites. Her husband was executed, and she was exiled to Pandateria. Nothing more is heard of the children.

Dio. 67.14.1–3.
Grant, M., pp. 225–56.
OCD, p. 600.
PW 227.

▣ DORIS

(5th–4th century B.C.E.)   Greek: Syracuse
Political player

Doris married Dionysius I, the tyrant of Syracuse, in Sicily (c. 430–367 B.C.E.). She was the daughter of Xenetus, from the leading family of Locri in Greece. On the same day that she married Dionysius, he also married ARISTOMACHE, who came from Syracuse. Gossip circulated that Doris's mother gave Aristomache potions to prevent pregnancy and that Aristomache only became pregnant after Dionysius had Doris's mother killed.

Dionysius was said to have been devoted to his wives. He dined with them both and slept with each in turn. It was also said that Dionysius was so fearful of the women that he had each wife searched before going to bed with her.

Despite the great support for Aristomache among the people of Syracuse, on Dionysius's death, Doris's son Dionysius II succeeded his father.

Diod. 16.6.
Plut., Dion 6.3.
Val. Max. 9.13.4.

▣ DRUSILLA (1)

(39 C.E.–?) Roman: Mauritania and Judaea
Political wife

Drusilla was the granddaughter of CLEOPATRA VII and Mark Antony, the daughter of CLEOPATRA SELENE and Juba II, who ruled the Roman client state of Mauritania in North Africa. Born in 39 C.E., she married Marcus Antonius Felix, a freedman of the younger ANTONIA. Her husband was appointed procurator of Judaea sometime after 52.

After her death her husband married DRUSILLA (2), the daughter of Agrippa I, king of Judaea.

Jos., AJ 20.7.2.
Tac., Hist. 5.9.
Perowne, S., p. 59.
PW 2.

▣ DRUSILLA (2)

(1st century C.E.) Jewish: Judaea and Rome
Political player

Drusilla competed with her older sister, BERENICE (2), for influence, wealth, and power. A member of a great Jewish dynasty, she was the daughter of Cypros and Agrippa I, king of Judaea (41–44 C.E.), and the granddaughter of Mariamme and Herod the Great. Her brother, Agrippa II, ruled the territories north of Judaea and often was the focus of the sisters' conflict, especially after the twice-widowed Berenice went to live with him.

Drusilla married Azizus, ruler of Emesa, after he agreed to be circumcised and follow the Jewish faith. She left her husband to become the second wife of Marcus Antonius Felix, a freedman of the younger ANTONIA. Felix had been appointed procurator of Judaea by the emperor Claudius in 52 C.E. He remained procurator for eight years,

and toward the end of his tenure, he presided over the preliminary hearing of Paul on charges of creating disturbances and profaning the Jewish Temple. Felix sought Drusilla's advice. Both listened to Paul testify.

Drusilla left Judaea for Rome with Felix at the end of his procuratorship and did not return. Felix's brother Pallas, an ally of the younger Agrippina, was Claudius's financial secretary and was among the richest, most powerful men in Rome. Drusilla used her influence to shield Felix when Pallas fell from power in Rome after the death of Agrippina.

Drusilla gave birth to a son named Antonius Agrippa, who died during the eruption of Vesuvius in 79.

Jos., AJ 19.354–55; 20.139, 141.
Tac., Hist. 5.9.
Grant, M., index.
Perowne, S., index.

▣ DRYPETIS

(4th century B.C.E.) Persian: Persia
Political player

Drypetis was one of the daughters of Darius III, ruler of Persia, who was defeated by Alexander the Great. She was among some 80 women of the Persian aristocracy married to Macedonian officers of Alexander's army at Susa in 324 B.C.E. Drypetis married Hephaestion, Alexander's childhood friend and closest companion, while Alexander married her sister BARSINE (2).

After the death of Alexander, Hephaestion divorced Drypetis. Subsequently, Drypetis and her sister were murdered by ROXANE, the wife of Alexander, to eliminate any rivals to Roxane's infant son.

Arr., Anab. 7.4.
Diod. 17.6.
Burn, A.R., *Alexander the Great*, p. 182.

▣ DURONIA

(2nd century B.C.E.) Roman: Rome
Accomplice to embezzlement

Duronia was infatuated with her second husband, Titus Sempronius Rutilus, and abetted him in fraud. Rutilus was guardian for the estate of Publius Aebutius, Duronia's son by her first husband. He had misused the funds, and her son was about to come of age.

Duronia set about discrediting Aebutius so as to prolong Rutilus's guardianship and thereby avoid an accounting of the estate. She told her son that some while ago when he was seriously ill, she had taken a vow that if he recovered she would have him initiated into the rites of the Bacchae. In 186 B.C.E. Romans feared the Bacchic rites, which were secret, restricted to the young and virile, and generally regarded as licentious, even dangerous to the well-being of the state. Aebutius's initiation into the cult may well have been judged as leaving him unfit to assume responsibility over his own estate.

Aebutius, who appears to have been a somewhat naive young man, told his freedwoman lover HISPALA FAECENIA of his mother's vow. Before Hispala had gained her freedom, she had accompanied her mistress to the rites and knew the ceremonies to be not only licentious or dangerous but also violent. She convinced Aebutius to refuse his mother's request. Together they went to Aebutius's aunt, who in turn went to the consul. Aided by the testimony of Hispala Faecenia to the consul Postumius, a scandal with serious political implications was uncovered, and a number of people were executed. Exactly what happened to Duronia and her second husband, however, remains unknown.

Livy 39.9.2–12.
Balsdon, J. P. V. D., pp. 37–41.

E

⊞ EGNATIA MAXIMILLA

(1st century C.E.) Roman: Rome
Loyal wife

Egnatia Maximilla, the wealthy wife of Glitius Gallus, accompanied her husband into exile after he was implicated in a failed conspiracy to assassinate the emperor Nero. She and her husband settled on the island of Andros in the Aegean Sea. An inscription found on the island indicates that they were held in high esteem by the island community despite the fact that her wealth had been confiscated.

Tac., Ann. 15.71.

⊞ ELPINICE

(c. 510 B.C.E.–?) Greek: Athens
Well-known Athenian

Elpinice was born around 510 B.C.E. Her father was Miltiades, the Athenian politician and general responsible for the great Greek victory over the Persians at Marathon in 490. Her mother, HEGESIPYLE, was the daughter of Olorus, ruler of Thrace.

Shortly after Marathon, her father led the naval forces in an unsuccessful attack on the island of Paros. Seriously wounded and too ill to testify on his own behalf, he was fined 50 talents in a trial prompted by political rivals after his defeat. He died in prison in 489 B.C.E. with the fine unpaid. The family was left in poverty. Without a dowry, Elpinice had no choice but to live with her brother, Cimon, a leader in Athenian politics and also a renowned general. His political rivals linked their names in scandalous gossip that was only heightened by her beauty. It was rumored that the painter Polygnotus, a friend of her brother, used her face for the portrait of Laodice in his painting of the Trojan women. In time, her brother paid off his father's fine, and Elpinice married one of Athens's wealthiest men, Callias, who waived a dowry for an alliance with the illustrious Phileidae.

Elpinice remained very much a visible woman after her marriage. Twice she lobbied Pericles. In 463, she sought to protect her brother after he was charged with taking bribes from Alexander I. After Pericles defeated the Samians, she upbraided him for spending Greek lives against Greek allies and not, like her brother, against a foreign foe.

Elpinice and Callias may have divorced. They had one son, Hipponicus. On his father's death, Hipponicus inherited his estate and became the richest man in Greece.

Nep., Cim. 1.2.
Plut., Cim. 4.1, 3, 5–7; 14.4.

92

Davies, J. K., pp. 302–3.
Walters, K. R., pp. 194–214.

⊡ ENNIA THRASYLLA

(? B.C.E./C.E.–38 C.E.)   Roman: Rome
Political player

Ennia Thrasylla was the granddaughter of Tiberius Claudius Thrasyllus, a famous astrologer from Alexandria. Her grandfather gained Roman citizenship from the emperor Tiberius, whom he had originally met on the island of Rhodes. When Tiberius retired to Capri, Thrasyllus followed. Ennia married Quintus Naevius Cordus Suetonius Macro, prefect of the *vigiles,* the large fire and police force stationed in Rome. Tiberius used Macro to capture Lucius Aelius Sejanus, the former prefect of the Praetorian Guard, whom Tiberius had come to suspect of treacherous designs.

Macro then became prefect of the Praetorian Guard. He was close to Gaius Caligula, Tiberius's most likely successor. Macro and Ennia worked as a husband-and-wife team to assure their future position. It was rumored that Ennia seduced the young Caligula after the death of the latter's wife, JUNIA CLAUDILLA, and even promised him marriage as part of a plan to expand her and her husband's sphere of influence. Alternatively, Caligula might have seduced Ennia in order to secure her husband's support and may even have agreed in writing to marry her if he became emperor.

Caligula appointed Macro prefect of Egypt. In 38 C.E. Caligula rid himself of the powerful couple by forcing them to commit suicide.

Suet., Calig. 12; 26.
Tac., Ann. 6.45.
Levick, B., *Tiberius* pp. 174, 215.

⊡ EPICHARIS

(?–65 C.E.)   Roman: Rome
Conspirator

Epicharis was an imperial freedwoman who participated in a failed conspiracy to kill the emperor Nero in 65 C.E. Impatient at delays by the assassins, she approached Volusius Proculus, one of the men used by Nero to kill his mother, the younger AGRIPPINA. Although Proculus had been made an officer of the fleet, he was known to be dissatisfied with the emperor's reward. Epicharis solicited his participation in the plot without revealing the names of her coconspirators.

Proculus reported his conversation with Epicharis to Nero. She denied any wrongdoing, and there was no apparent corroborating evidence. Nero ordered her taken into custody. Soon, however, several of the conspirators confessed and began to implicate others. Nero ordered Epicharis tortured. She refused to speak. On the second day, no longer able to stand, she was dragged in a chair before her inquisitors. She managed to strip the strap band from her chest and put it around her neck, and then tipped the chair and killed herself.

She is remembered for her courage in keeping silent when well-born men were betraying those close to them.

Tac., Ann. 15.51, 57.

⊡ ERINNA

(4th century B.C.E.)   Greek: Telos
Poet

Erinna was an esteemed poet who lived on the Greek island of Telos, off the coast of western Asia Minor. She wrote about her personal life and feelings. Her most famous poem, "Distaff," consisted of 300 hexameters. It was written before she was 19 years old. Only a few fragments have survived. They movingly relate childhood experiences with her friend Baucis and lament Baucis's death shortly after her marriage. She also wrote two funeral epigrams to Baucis.

Erinna died young and never married.

Fantham, E., et al., pp. 164–65.
Gow, A. S., and Page, D. L., v. 2, pp. 281 ff.
OCD, p. 556.
Pomeroy, S. B., *Goddesses,* pp. 137–39.

🔲 EUBOEA

(3rd–2nd century B.C.E.) Greek: Euboea
Political player

Euboea, the daughter of Cleoptolemus of Chalcis, located on the island of Euboea off the coast of Greece, was well born and beautiful. In 192–191 B.C.E. Antiochus III the Great of Syria occupied the island prior to invading Greece. Euboea charmed him. At the age of 50, he married her and spent the whole of the winter with her in Chalcis. After his defeat by the Romans, he retreated to Ephesus with Euboea.

Ath. 10.439e, f.
Poly. 20.8.

🔲 EURYDICE (1)

(4th century B.C.E.) Illyrian: Illyricum and Macedonia
Political player

Eurydice used her intelligence, prestige, and wealth to protect herself and her children in the struggles over succession in Macedonia. The grandmother of CLEOPATRA (3) and Alexander the Great through her son Philip, she probably was from Illyria, northwest of Macedonia. The daughter of Sirrhas, she may have been descended from a branch of the Bacchiadae clan, originally of Corinth, some of whom migrated to Illyria and founded the royal family of Lyncestis. As an adult Eurydice learned to read and write, a rare accomplishment, especially for a woman, and one for which she justly was both grateful and proud.

She married twice. Her first husband was Amyntas III, ruler of Macedonia (393–370 B.C.E.). Their marriage strengthened the relationship between Illyria and Macedonia. She had three sons, Alexander, Perdiccas, and Philip, each of whom would in turn rule. She also had a daughter, Eurynoë.

She was widowed in 370, and her son Alexander succeeded his father. She married her daughter's husband, Ptolemy of Alorus, for dynastic

reasons. It is not known what happened to Eurynoe, but it is known that Ptolemy killed Eurydice's son Alexander in 368 B.C.E. Never declared ruler, Ptolemy governed as regent over her other two sons for the next three years.

During Ptolemy's regency, a usurper named Pausanius attempted to claim the throne of Macedonia. Eurydice called on the Athenian general Iphicrates, whom her first husband had adopted as a son, to support the claim of her two remaining sons as the legitimate rulers of Macedonia. She put her two surviving children in his arms and pleaded their case. He drove out the usurper.

Later, when her son Perdiccas became old enough to rule, he had the regent Ptolemy killed. Perdiccas died in battle and was succeeded by her third son, Philip II, in 359. It remains unclear when Eurydice died.

Diod. 15.71.1; 77.5.
Just. 7.4–5.
Plut., De liberis educandis. 20.14.
Strabo. 7.7, 8.
Macurdy, G., index.

🔲 EURYDICE (2) (ADEA)

(c. 337–317 B.C.E.) Greek: Macedonia
Political player

Eurydice fought to rule Macedonia. She allied herself with Cassander during the turmoil in the decade after the death of Alexander the Great. Eurydice, originally called Adea, was the granddaughter of Philip II of Macedon and an Illyrian princess, Audata. Her mother was CYNANE, and her father, Amyntas, was Philip's nephew. She learned the skills of hunting and fighting from her mother, who had hunted and fought at the side of her grandfather.

In 322 B.C.E., Eurydice and her mother joined the complicated struggle for power that resulted from the unexpected death of Alexander a year earlier. Their interest was Macedonia. The generals of Alexander's army had already carved up his empire, and Philip Arrhidaeus, the son of Philip II and PHILINNA, and the infant son of Alexander the Great and Roxane, had been declared the joint rulers of Macedonia. The general Antipater, who had represented Alexander in Europe during the Asia campaign, was declared regent and the effective ruler of Macedonia.

Cynane raised an army and went to Asia. To further Eurydice's claim over Macedonia, Cynane was determined that Eurydice marry the weak Philip. Cynane was killed in front of the troops on orders of Alcestas, the brother of Perdiccas who had been the second in command of Alexander's army. Outraged by the murder, the army demanded that Eurydice and Philip Arrhidaeus be allowed to wed. Once married, Eurydice followed her mother's footsteps. She inflamed the troops against Antipater. By the time Antipater returned to Triparadessus, he found the troops unpaid and close to revolt. Somehow he turned the situation around and persuaded Eurydice and her husband, as well as Roxane and her infant son, to return with him to Macedonia.

Antipater died in 319, and Eurydice, now in Macedonia, found herself allied with his heir Polyperchon. Disagreements between them led to her offering an alliance to Cassander, who was seeking to overthrow Polyperchon. She arranged for her weak husband to proclaim Cassander regent. At the same time her stepgrandmother OLYMPIAS (1), who ruled in Epirus and who had unsuccessfully sought to control Macedonia for decades, allied herself with Polyperchon and raised an army against Eurydice.

At the border of Macedonia Eurydice met the army of Olympias. The soldiers regarded Olympias as sacred. They refused to fight. Olympias imprisoned Eurydice and tortured her. She sent her a sword, a noose, and hemlock and ordered her to commit suicide. Eurydice damned Olympias with the same fate that befell her and hanged herself with the straps of her gown. She had not yet reached 20 when she died in 317.

In 316, Cassander defeated Olympias and had her murdered. He gave Eurydice a royal burial at Aegae.

Arr., Succ. 1.30–33, 42, 44.
Diod. 18.39.2–4; 18.49; 19.11, 1–8.
Just. 14.5.1–4, 8–10.
Carney, E., "The Career of Adea-Eurydice," pp. 496–502.
Macurdy, G., pp. 40 ff, 48–52.
OCD, p. 575.

◫ EURYDICE (3)

(4th–3rd century B.C.E.) Greek: Macedonia, Egypt, and Miletus
Political player; military leader

Eurydice experienced several turns of fortune during her life. Her father, Antipater, claimed Greece and Macedonia after the death of Alexander the Great in 323 B.C.E. Antipater cemented alliances with marriages for his three daughters. Eurydice married Ptolemy I Soter in 322 or 321 B.C.E. Her sister NICAEA (1) married Lysimachus, who governed Thrace; PHILA (1) married Demetrius, who later ruled Macedonia.

Eurydice was probably the third or fourth wife of Ptolemy I and bore four children: a son, Ptolemy Ceraunus, and three daughters, LYSANDRA, Ptolemais, and Theoxena. Eurydice had brought with her to Egypt her younger cousin BERENICE I. Her elderly husband fell in love with Berenice, who in 317 persuaded Ptolemy to make her son his successor.

Supplanted by the younger woman, the wealthy Eurydice never remarried. She went to live in Miletus, a city in Asia Minor, where she had considerable influence. In 286 she arranged the marriage of her daughter, Ptolemais, with Demetrius I, the widower of her sister Phila and the sometime ruler of Macedonia. The alliance enhanced the position of her ambitious son, who was said to have been violent and cruel. For a short while Ceraunus ruled Macedonia. Eurydice moved to Cassandreia in Macedonia. She controlled the city with her army and was honored with a festival called Eurydicaea.

Polyaenus, Strat. 6.72.
Cary, M., pp. 13, 43, 55, 58.
Macurdy, G., pp. 102–4.

EURYDICE (4)

(4th–3rd century B.C.E.) Greek: Thrace and Macedonia
Political player

Eurydice was a participant in the unending conflict for control over Macedonia in the generations after the death of Alexander the Great. She was the daughter of NICAEA (1) and the granddaughter of Antipater, the general Alexander had assigned to rule Europe when he went to Asia on his last campaign. Her father, Lysimachus, ruled Thrace and married her mother to enhance the ties between Antipater and himself. Her sister was ARSINOË I. Eurydice married her cousin, also named Antipater who was the son of THESSALONICE and Cassander, ruler of Macedonia. Her marriage thereby extended into the next generation the historical link between Thrace and Macedonia.

On the death of her father-in-law, her mother-in-law divided Macedonia between Eurydice's husband, Antipater, and his brother, Alexander. Her husband, the elder brother, felt that he should have inherited all of Macedonia. He killed his mother and fought with his younger brother. Alexander appealed for help to the general Demetrius, who had his own ideas as to who should rule Macedonia. He arrived with his troops, murdered Alexander, drove Antipater and Eurydice out of the country, and made himself ruler.

Eurydice and Antipater fled to her father in Thrace. Lysimachus eventually made peace with Demetrius, which resulted in a quarrel with his son-in-law, Antipater. He had Antipater killed and then imprisoned Eurydice for siding with her husband. She probably died there, since she ceased to be an actor in the Macedonian drama.

Just. 16.1, 2.
Macurdy, G., pp. 55–58.

EURYLEONIS

(4th century B.C.E.) Greek: Sparta
Self-made woman

Euryleonis was a wealthy Spartan woman. She was one of the first three women whose horses won races at the Olympic Games. Her name was inscribed on the lists of victors and on inscriptions that she erected. A statue of Euryleonis commemorating her victory in a two-horse chariot race stood in the temple of Aphrodite in Sparta.

Paus. 3.17.6.
Pomeroy, S. B., *Goddesses*, p. 130.

EUTHYDICE (EURYDICE)

(4th–3rd century B.C.E.) Greek: Athens, Cyrene, and Macedonia
Political player

Euthydice (also called Eurydice) fared well in the turbulent Greek political world of the late fourth century B.C.E. She came from a prominent Athenian clan, the Philaidae. Her father, Miltiades, traced his ancestry to the general of the same name who had won the decisive victory over the Persians at Marathon in 490 B.C.E. She married Ophellas, a Macedonian officer in the army of Alexander the Great and who had joined Ptolemy when he became ruler of Egypt after Alexander's death. She went with her husband when Ptolemy sent Ophellas to Cyrene in North Africa where he subdued a revolt and became a virtually independent ruler, albeit under the suzerainty of Ptolemy.

Her husband and Agathocles, the tyrant of Syracuse, joined in a campaign to conquer Carthage. Her name was well known in Athens, and therefore many Athenians joined Ophellas's force. The expedition was not a success. The troops marched through the desert, and in 309 Agathocles murdered her husband.

After her husband's death, Euthydice returned to Athens. She married the handsome Demetrius I, who ruled Macedonia, had collected three wives, and was at a high point in his turbulent career. She gave birth to a son, Corrhagus.

Plut., Dem. 14.2; 20.40; 53.4.
OCD, p. 1,068.

EUTROPIA, GALERIA VALERIA
(3rd–4th century C.E.)   Roman: Syria, Italy,
and Judaea
Wife of the co-emperor, early Christian

Galeria Valeria Eutropia outlived her husband
Maximian, coruler of the Roman Empire with
Diocletian, and died a devout Christian. She was
part of a circle of strong, independent, and wealthy
women that included two Augustas—her daughter
Flavia Maxima FAUSTA, and HELENA FLAVIA JULIA,
who was the mother of Constantine—and
Constantine's half sister, Flavia Julia CONSTANTIA.
All of them influenced the political events and religious controversies of the day.

Eutropia was born in Syria. Her husband, a
general under the emperor Diocletian, was appointed Caesar in the West and then
co-Augustus. In addition to her daughter Fausta,
she had a son Maxentius. On May 1, 305 C.E., the
emperor Diocletian retired. Her husband reluctantly followed, and she settled with him in the
court of Constantine. Maxentius, passed over for
succession in favor of Galerius and Constantine,
immediately took up arms and within the year
persuaded his father to support him. The following years were filled with unsuccessful reconciliations and wars over succession. In 307, her
daughter Fausta married the future emperor
Constantine as part of her husband's effort to
form an alliance between himself and Maxentius.
The effort failed, and Eutropia found her children
on opposite sides of the struggles for control over
the empire, or some part of it.

Five years later, in 310 Maximian attempted to
seize power and assassinate his son-in-law
Constantine. Fausta revealed the plot to her husband. It failed, and soon after Maximian committed suicide. In 311, Eutropia's son, Maxentius,
engaged in an armed struggle with her son-in-law.
A year later, in 312, Constantine defeated him at
the Milvian Bridge in one of the most famous battles of the later Roman Empire. It was not much of
a battle; Maxentius died by drowning in the Tiber.
However, this was the military encounter in
which Constantine was said to have successfully
tested the power of Christianity to bring him victory. Thereafter, Christianity, despite setbacks,
was on the rise.

All during these conflicts among her kin, before and after her husband's death, Eutropia appears to have remained at Constantine's court.
She, her daughter, Constantine's half sister, and
his mother formed a nucleus of Christian women
around whom probably gathered women of lesser
rank and clerics. Constantia and Helena were
close to the priests Arrius and Eusebius, and Helena has long been credited by some with bringing
Christianity to her son.

After the death of her husband, Eutropia traveled to visit Christian holy places. Her life becomes
less well documented although she is known to have
visited the site of Mambre, revered by Jews and
Christians. Constantine arranged for shrines to be
erected after she reported that the site was being defiled by Jews and pagans with their markets and fairs.
She probably died soon after.

Barnes, T., *New Empire of Diocletian*, pp. 33, 34.
Lane Fox, R., p. 674.

F

🔳 FABIA

(1st century B.C.E.) Roman: Rome
Priestess

Fabia was a Vestal Virgin at the temple of Vesta in the Forum. In 73 B.C.E. she was accused of licentious behavior with Lucius Sergius Catilina, a young Roman patrician who led a conspiracy against the Senate that was successfully squelched by Fabia's brother-in-law Marcus Tullius Cicero, consul in 63 B.C.E. Fabia was exonerated.

In 58 she gave her half sister TERENTIA (1), Cicero's wife, sanctuary during the turbulent year of her husband's exile. She and Terentia were well-to-do women, and Fabia may have provided Terentia with cash until she could raise money from her own estates.

Asc. 91c.
Cic., Cat. 3, 9.
Balsdon, J. P. V. D., p. 239.

🔳 FADIA

(1st century B.C.E.) Roman: Italy and Greece
Ignored wife

Fadia was the de facto wife of Mark Antony during the period when he studied in Athens. They had at least one child, and their relationship was sufficiently well acknowledged for Marcus Tullius Cicero to attack Antony in the second Philippic as the son-in-law of a lowborn freedman. Fadia's father was the freedman Quintus Fadius.

Cic., Phil. 2.2,4.
PW 3.

🔳 FANNIA (1)

(1st century B.C.E.) Roman: Rome
Litigant

Fannia married Gaius Titinius from the city of Minturnae, located on the coast southeast of Rome. He divorced her and in 100 B.C.E., applied to retain her dowry on account of her immoral character. Fannia argued that Titinius had known her character before they married. The adjudicator was the consul Gaius Marius, the famous general.

Marius established that Titinius had married Fannia fully aware of her reputation and with the intention of divorcing her and keeping the dowry. He advised him to drop the case. Titinius refused. Marius fined Fannia a small sum and fined Titinius an amount equal to the value of the dowry to be paid to Fannia.

In 88 Fannia returned the favor by hiding Gaius Marius in her house when he was fleeing after his defeat by Lucius Cornelius Sulla.

Val. Max. 8.2.3.
Balsdon, J. P. V. D., p. 220.
Bauman, R. A., pp. 49–51.

FANNIA (2)

(?–107 C.E.) Roman: Italy
Stoic; exiled

Fannia was an educated, cultured, and determined woman who lived a principled life. She was the daughter of the younger ARRIA and Publius Claudius Thrasea Paetus, as well as the granddaughter of the elder ARRIA and Caecina Paetus. Like her parents and grandparents, she was a follower of the Stoics.

Fannia married the elder Helvidius Priscus, who was already 55 years old and had a son, Helvidius Priscus, and a daughter-in-law, ANTEIA. Fannia and her mother voluntarily accompanied her husband into exile in 66 C.E. after the death of her father, Thrasea Paetus. They returned after the accession of the emperor Galba in 69. Her husband became praetor in 70 while still a supporter of Vespasian, who had become emperor after Galba's assassination in 69. Vespasian became increasingly angered with Priscus's persistent efforts to prosecute and discredit those whose false charges had brought about his own exile and the death of his father-in-law during the previous regime. On Vespasian's orders, Priscus was again exiled, and Fannia and her mother again left with him. He was killed while in exile.

Fannia and Arria returned after the death of Vespasian. The new emperor, Domitian, was no friend of art, philosophy or dissent, principled or otherwise. In relatively short order, Fannia's stepson, the younger Helvidius Priscus, was condemned for writing a farce that Domitian believed to be a reflection on his own divorce. In 93 Domitian executed Priscus and in an effort to rid himself of dissenters, ordered all philosophers out of Rome.

A laudatory memoir of Priscus began to circulate in Rome. Fannia and her mother were tried for their support of the memoir written by Herennius Senecio. At the trial, Senecio declared that he had written the work at the behest of Fannia, which she corroborated and added that she had not only commissioned the work but had made private material available to Senecio. In her testimony Fannia sought to exonerate her mother from any responsibility; both were nonetheless exiled. Fannia retained a copy of the memoir, despite the Senate's order that all copies be destroyed.

In 96, after Nerva succeeded Domitian, Fannia and Arria returned to Rome. At the request of Pliny the Younger, a family friend, Fannia and Arria joined Anteia in a suit to restore Priscus's name and recover damages. The case was controversial, and the Senate was split. Pliny was pressed to drop the charges. Many among the elite felt that, should he succeed, they too would then be exposed to similar prosecution.

Fannia probably died in 107. She had contracted tuberculosis from nursing her relative JUNIA (3), who was a Vestal Virgin.

Tac., Ann. 16.34–35.
Plin., Ep. 3.II.16; 7.19.
Balsdon, J. P. V. D., pp. 58–59.
PW 6.

FAUSTA

(1st century B.C.E.) Roman: Rome
Political player

Fausta and her twin brother, Faustus Cornelius Sulla, were children of the general and dictator Lucius Cornelius Sulla and CAECILIA METELLA (1) of the wealthy and prominent Metelli family, who bankrolled part of her husband's rise to power. She was a half sister of AEMILIA (2). Fausta's first husband was Gaius Memmius, who served as tribune and later as praetor. They were divorced in 55 B.C.E.

In 54 Fausta married Titus Annius Milo. Her husband's fiercest political opponent, Publius Clodius Pulcher, campaigned to become tribune while her husband sought election as consul. In January 52, Fausta was with her husband when the two men and their entourages met accidentally on the street. A fight ensued, and Milo had Clodius killed. Milo was charged, tried, and exiled.

Fausta remained in Rome while Milo went into exile. Milo asked his colleague, Marcus Tullius Cicero, to take care of his confiscated estate and provide that Fausta would secure the portion of the property that was reserved for her. Cicero fulfilled his obligations and left Fausta with modest means to support herself.

Rumors swirled around Fausta. It was whispered that she had not been true to either of her husbands and that Milo had found her in bed with the historian Sallust. However, she and Milo never divorced, despite stories about her sexual exploits that continued into the last days of the republic, some even attributed to her twin brother.

Asc., Mil. 28.55
Aul. Gell., NA 17, 18.
Cic., Att. 5.8, 2f.
Cic., Mil. 28.55.
Macrob, Sat. 2.2, 9.
Balsdon, J. P. V. D., p. 55.
PW 436.

⊞ FAUSTA, FLAVIA MAXIMA

(289/290–324/325 C.E.) Roman: Italy, Gaul, Asia, and North Africa
Augusta

Flavia Maxima Fausta died on orders of her husband, the emperor Constantine, for reasons that are obscure. Born in 289 or 290 C.E., she was the daughter of the co-emperor Maximian and his wife, Galeria Valeria EUTROPIA. Fausta and the future emperor Constantine signed a marriage contract in 293 when her father sought to strengthen relations with Constantine after his elevation to the status of Caesar. Fausta was 3 or 4 years old at the time of the contract signing, and Constantine, 19. They married 14 years later in 307, by which time her father had once retired and then re-entered the fray of armed conflict in support of his son who had been passed over for succession. A closer union with Constantine, however, remained desirable. In 311, Fausta warned Constantine that her father plotted to murder him while he slept. Maximian was seized and allowed to commit suicide. Her mother remained at Constantine's court.

Around 324, after Constantine became sole emperor, Fausta and her mother-in-law, HELENA FLAVIA JULIA, assumed the title of Augusta. Fausta, Eutropia, Helena, and Constantine's half sister Flavia Julia CONSTANTIA formed a powerful group of independent-minded and wealthy women around Constantine. Although nothing has been recorded of Fausta's religious persuasion, the other three women were active Christians and very much a part of the evolving church.

The events of the subsequent years are unclear. In 326 when Fausta was 36 or 37 years old something sparked her death. Possibly at the urging of her mother-in-law Helena, Fausta died, scalded to death in the baths, either by accident, suicide, or intention. Constantine also poisoned his popular son, the 20-year-old Crispus, whose dead mother had been Constantine's longstanding lover before he married Fausta. At the same time, Licinius, the 12-year-old son of his half sister Constantia, was killed. Later commentators have speculated that Fausta had been involved in the death of Crispus and Licinius to protect her own sons. Alternatively, conflict between Fausta and her powerful mother-in-law may have erupted into conspiracy or confrontation with Constantine.

Fausta had three sons—Constantine II, Constantius, and Constans—and two daughters—Constantia, who married Gallus Caesar (351–354), and Helena, who married the emperor Julian (361–363).

Ep. Caes. 41.11 ff.
Eutr. 6.10
Zos. 2.29
Balsdon, J. P. V. D., pp. 167, 169–70.
Barnes, T., *New Empire of Diocletian.*

▣ FAUSTINA THE ELDER, ANNIA GALERIA

(c. 94–140/141 C.E.) Roman: Baetica/
Narbonensis, Italy, and Asia
Augusta

Annia Galeria Faustina lived a privileged life that brought her honor, influence, and wealth during a period without any wars of succession or civil strife. Educated and intelligent, she came from the new elite of distinguished provincial families that emerged with the emperor Trajan and became the Antonine dynasty. She was the daughter of Marcus Annius Verus, consul in 126 C.E. Her mother, Rupilia Faustina, was descended from republican nobility. At about 16 years old, around 110, she married the future emperor Antoninus Pius. They had four children, two sons and two daughters, one of whom was the younger FAUSTINA, the future wife of the emperor Marcus Aurelius.

Faustina's husband was twice her age and very wealthy. They lived primarily on their estates in Italy and in the oldest settled parts of Spain and Gaul. They traveled together, and she accompanied her husband to Asia for his proconsulship. Some 18 years after her marriage, her husband was chosen by Hadrian as his successor. Hadrian adopted her husband, and her husband, in turn, adopted both the later emperor Marcus Aurelius and Lucius Verus to establish a line of succession. When it became obvious that Verus would not become the next emperor, her husband left to her the delicate negotiation that arranged for their daughter Faustina's marriage to Marcus Aurelius, instead of to Verus as had been originally planned.

Becoming the imperial couple dramatically transformed their lives. Although always wealthy, there nonetheless was a significant dif-ference between the lifestyle of a private couple and that of an imperial couple. The household now included the feeding and housing of all those closely associated with the emperor. Moreover, the entire household moved with the emperor. Immediately after he assumed the role of emperor, it was reported that Faustina approached her husband about insufficient funds for household expenses, to which he was said to have replied that now that he was emperor there would never be sufficient funds.

The couple was always in the spotlight and faced with malicious court gossip. Her husband consistently ignored what he heard that suggested Faustina's sexual or other kinds of moral deficiencies.

In 138 Faustina was honored by the Senate with the title of Augusta and accorded the right to have coins struck in her name. She died shortly thereafter in 140 or 141 C.E. A temple was built and dedicated to her with suitable endowments and a priesthood. In 145, her husband named a new charity after her, Puellae Faustinianae, for destitute girls. Gold and silver statues of her voted by the Senate were paid for by her husband, who did not remarry. She left her personal fortune to her daughter, Faustina.

SHA, Ant. Pius 1.7; 3.8; 5.2; 6.7–8.
Balsdon, J. P. V. D., pp. 142, 144, 145.
OCD, p. 99.
Syme, R., *Tacitus,* p. 605.

▣ FAUSTINA THE YOUNGER, ANNIA GALERIA

(125/130–175 C.E.) Roman: Italy, Asia,
Gaul, and Germany
Augusta

Faustina was born between 125 and 130 C.E. to the emperor Antoninus Pius and the elder FAUSTINA. On both sides of her family she came from provincial nobility, and her parents intended that she be the wife of her father's successor. She was originally affianced to Lucius Verus, but her mother arranged, after her father became emperor, that she instead wed her cousin Marcus Aurelius. The agreement took place in 139. They married in 145. One of their daughters was Annia Aurelia Galeria LUCILLA.

Faustina was intelligent, well educated, and independently wealthy since childhood, with an inheritance from her mother who had unexpectedly died in 140 or 141 C.E. An active woman, she traveled widely with the emperor despite regular pregnancies and the birth of 12 children. Faustina was granted the title of Augusta and the right to mint coins in 147. During her lifetime she accrued additional titles from cities around the empire. Her presence, with one of her young daughters, at the German front in Sirmium where her husband was campaigning near the Danube between 170 and 174, led to her title "Mother of the Camp."

From fragments of Faustina's letters to her husband reported in the ancient sources, it is clear that they regularly discussed the affairs of state, even military affairs. They sometimes disagreed. She urged Aurelius to impose the fullest possible extent of punishment on Gaius Avidius Cassius, the supreme military commander in the East who raised a revolt. Her husband, however, granted clemency to Cassius's family.

She was the most visible woman in the empire and always subject to gossip. On more than one occasion she was denounced to the emperor for treason or adultery. When faced with one such accusation, the emperor was said to have responded that if he were to divorce Faustina, she could reclaim her dowry, and since his position as emperor rested on his adoption by her father, he wondered whether he would have to return to her the empire.

Faustina died suddenly in 175 far from home in Cappadocia near the Taurus Mountains. Marcus Aurelius had her consecrated by the Roman Senate and established an endowment for poor girls in her name, as one had been endowed in the name of her mother.

SHA, Aurel. 6.2.6; 19.2–9; 26.5–9; 29.1–3.
Balsdon, J. P. V. D., pp. 141–47.
OCD, p. 99.

▣ FLORA

(1st century B.C.E.) Roman: Rome
Self-made woman

Flora, whose origins, status, and family remain unknown, was so beautiful that the rich and illustrious Caecilius Metellus included a portrait of her among the decorations in the Forum's ancient temple of Castor and Pollux, with which his family was associated.

She was the lover of Gnaeus Pompeius Magnus (Pompey the Great), an often-married man whose appeal to women was well attested by the caring and devotion of his wives. Flora was reputed to have said that she never left the embraces of Pompey without the marks of his teeth to evidence his passion. She refused the advances of Pompey's friend Geminus, claiming devotion to Pompey. Geminus went to Pompey,

Annia Galeria Faustina the Younger

who offered no opposition. To her great distress, he also ended his affair with her.

Plut., Pomp. 2.3.

▣ FLORONIA

(?–216 B.C.E.) Roman: Rome
Priestess

Floronia was one of the six Vestal Virgins serving in 216 B.C.E. in the temple of Vesta, one of the oldest temples in the Forum. She and a sister priestess, OPIMIA, were convicted for licentious behavior. Floronia's lover, Lucius Cantilius, a scribe and a member of a minor order of the priestly college, was beaten to death. She was either buried alive or committed suicide before she could be entombed.

The improper behavior of the Vestals was considered a harbinger of ill omen for the city. The devastating defeat of the Romans by Hannibal and the Carthaginians at Cannae in the same year was perceived as retribution for Floronia and Opimia's misdeeds.

Livy 22.57.2–5.

▣ FULVIA (1)

(1st century B.C.E.) Roman: Italy
Political player

Fulvia was a member of a prominent Roman family and socialized with the political elite of her day. Her lover was Quintus Curius, also from a prominent family. Curius had financial problems, and it was rumored that Fulvia needed more money than he could provide. After he was ejected from the Senate, Curius joined the conspiracy led by the thwarted patrician Lucius Sergius Catilina in 63 B.C.E. From his boastful and threatening behavior, Fulvia drew from Curius information about the developing conspiracy.

Catiline was in debt and had failed in his attempts to win high office. He began to organize discontented veterans and small landowners. He was joined by a group of men and women from respectable and even elite families who also suffered from the effects of inflation on fixed incomes. They planned to take over Rome.

Fulvia arranged with Marcus Tullius Cicero, consul in 63, to act as a conduit of information about the conspiracy. Cicero promised Fulvia that her lover Curius would be rewarded for his role as informant. As their situation became more desperate, Catiline and his conspirators decided to set fire to Rome and murder Cicero. The plot failed. Fulvia informed Cicero of the planned attempt on his life. Catiline left Rome, and he and his followers were declared public enemies by the Senate. Julius Caesar convinced the Senate that Curius should not receive the large reward that had been promised by Cicero.

Catiline was killed in battle, and five of his ringleaders were executed in Rome after Cicero obtained written evidence of their plot. Nothing more is heard of Fulvia.

Sall., Cat. 23.3 ff.; 26.3; 28 2.
Balsdon, J. P. V. D., p. 49.
Bauman, R. A., pp. 67–69.
PW 113.

▣ FULVIA (2)

(?–40 B.C.E.) Roman: Italy and Greece
Political player

Fulvia was indomitable and fearless. She had an implacable determination and possessed a spirit and strength of character unmatched by any of her three husbands. Among the many strong and independent women of the late republic, Fulvia holds a unique position. She alone among these Roman women crossed the gender boundary and stepped into the male preserve of military action during civil war.

Fulvia was the wealthy daughter of Marcus Fulvius Bambalio and Sempronia, both from atrophying ancient families. Her mother was the sister of SEMPRONIA (2), who was said to have had a part in the conspiracy of Lucius Sergius Catalina in 63 B.C.E. Fulvia's first husband was the brash, tempestuous, and sometimes brilliant aristocrat Publius Clodius Pulcher. His oratory in favor of populist positions was supported by armed bands in his tribuneship of 58 B.C.E.

Clodius again campaigned for tribune while a bitter enemy, Titus Annius Milo, campaigned for consul. They accidentally met on the road in January 52. Fulvia was with her husband surrounded by their retinue. A dispute ensued, and Milo had Clodius killed. Fulvia brought Clodius's body back to Rome, where she placed it in the courtyard of their house and incited the crowd with a display of his wounds. The body was carried into the Senate and burned as the Senate house itself caught fire.

Milo was tried. He was defended by Marcus Tullius Cicero, consul in 63 and the man responsible for thwarting the earlier conspiracy led by Catiline in which Fulvia's aunt may have had some part. There was a history of enmity, however, between the opposing sides in the trial. Nearly a decade earlier, Cicero had spoken on behalf of the prosecution against Clodius, who had been caught in the house of Julius Caesar disguised as a woman during the women-only rites of the Bona Dea. Rumor had it that Clodius was there for an assignation with Caesar's wife, POMPEIA (1). He was declared innocent by a heavily bribed jury. Clodius became Cicero's sworn enemy; as tribune in 58, he secured Cicero's exile. At the trial, Fulvia testified. She also arranged the public lamentations of her mother, among others, that aroused the sympathies of the onlookers. Milo was convicted and sent into exile. Cicero transferred his enmity from Fulvia's husband to her.

With Clodius, Fulvia had a daughter, CLAUDIA (5), and a son, Publius Claudius, who later became praetor. Her second husband was Gaius Scribonius Curio, tribune in 50 B.C.E. and another brilliant orator. He became an ally of Julius Caesar from whom he received a large monetary gift. He served under Caesar in 49 and was

killed in a military campaign in Africa. Their son, Scribonius Curio, was executed by Octavian after his victory at Actium in 31 B.C.E.

After her second husband's death, Fulvia married Mark Antony by 45 B.C.E. A year later, in 44, Cicero accused Fulvia and Mark Antony of taking bribes and selling properties and favors for vast sums of money. The attack was directed against Fulvia. Cicero claimed that Fulvia conducted property auctions in the women's quarters of Antony's house and that Antony preferred an avaricious Fulvia to the Roman Senate and people. In January 43, enemies of Antony, led by Cicero, attempted to have the Senate declare Antony a public enemy. Fulvia, her mother-in-law, JULIA (2), and their supporters visited the houses of key senators during the night to secure their vote against the motion. The next morning, dressed in mourning clothes, they buttonholed senators on their way to the Senate with lamentations and cries. Their claim that it was contrary to Roman law to declare a citizen a public enemy without a trial, no doubt persuaded some. All in all the women enabled Antony's supporters to defeat the bill.

After Antony's defeat at Mutina in April 43, however, he left Italy and was declared an outlaw by the Senate. In Rome, Antony's enemies instituted a series of lawsuits against Fulvia to deprive her of her property. Titus Pomponius Atticus, Cicero's closest friend and one of the wealthiest and most generally respected men in Rome, aided Fulvia. He accompanied her to court, provided the necessary surety to assure her future legal appearances, and lent her money without interest or security to enable her to make the payments due on the estate that she had purchased before Antony's exile.

Fulvia worked to enhance Antony's position in relation to the two other members of the ruling Second Triumvirate, Octavian and Lepidus. In 43, when the triumvirate was formed, Claudia, Fulvia's daughter with Clodius, was to become the first wife of Octavian and cement the alliance. The triumvirs proscribed Cicero, and he was killed on December 7, 43. It was said that his head was sent to Fulvia and Antony. The ancient sources are uniformly hostile to Fulvia and embroidered her response to Cicero's death in gruesome detail. They depict her as avaricious and cruel. Her avarice was specifically blamed for the death of Quintus Salvidienus Rufus. After his name appeared on the lists, he offered her his house, said to be the reason she had had him proscribed. It was to no avail. He was killed.

Proscriptions raised needed money as well as rid the triumvirs of real and imagined enemies. Still, money was a problem. At one point, the triumvirs ordered the 1,400 richest women in Rome to provide an evaluation of their property preparatory to a special tax. The women protested. The women's arguments, as articulated by HORTENSIA, spoke to their unique position. They argued that this was not a war against an outside enemy, as had been the war against Hannibal when women willingly surrendered their personal wealth. This was a civil war in which husbands and sons fought against brothers and cousins. This was not *their* war, according to the women. They were supported by Antony's mother, Julia, and by the independent-minded OCTAVIA (2), who was Octavian's sister, but not by Fulvia.

Lucius Antonius, the brother of Antony, became consul, along with Publius Servilius, in 41, while Antony went to the East. Fulvia and Lucius worked together closely in Antony's interests. They largely dominated the political scene in Rome. They especially sought to assure Antony honor for the distributions to the troops, since he, not Octavian, had been responsible for the defeat of Brutus and Cassius at the battle of Philippi in 42. Their anti-Octavian policy extended into the prosperous regions of Umbria, Etruria, and the Sabine country north of Rome. They attempted to form a coalition there of soldiers and property owners against Octavian after protests against Octavian's confiscations for the resettlement of veterans.

Furious at Fulvia's opposition, Octavian officially divorced Claudia in 41, after a two-year marriage that was never consummated. She had been a child at the time of the union, which was primarily a politically symbolic act, as was the divorce. Octavian also publically read a copy of the pact Antony had made with the soldiers in Rome who were against war and demanded a settlement. With Antony still in the East, however, Fulvia backed Lucius Antonius in support of the Italian cities against Octavian. The Perusine War ensued. Lucius Antonius marched into Rome without opposition and then left to advance north in order to link up with Antony's generals, who controlled the Gallic provinces.

Fulvia and Lucius Antonius sent messages to Antony. They urged his generals in Italy and Gaul to assist them. Octavian was in a precarious position both on land and at sea. If Antony's cohorts had united against him, Octavian could not have received reinforcements and most probably would have been defeated. However, without direct instructions from Mark Antony, most of the generals did not act. Lucius Antonius went to the ancient city of Perusia north of Rome, where he was surrounded by the forces of Octavian. Fulvia, who was not in Perusia, persuaded some of Antony's forces to aid Lucius.

Octavian launched a vitriolic and obscene attack on Fulvia as the main instigator in the Perusine War since she was the most vulnerable. Octavian feared to offend Antony, and Lucius Antonius's republican principles made an attack on him equally undesirable. Lucius Antonius surrendered early in 40, and Octavian appointed him governor of Spain in order to maintain good relations with Antony. Fulvia fled to Greece with her children. Antony blamed her no less than had Octavian. He left her in the city of Sicyon, where she became ill and died.

Fulvia and Antony had two sons. The eldest, Antyllus, was executed on Octavian's orders after

Antony's defeat at Actium. The other, Iullus Antonius, was brought up in the household of Octavia, the emperor's sister and Antony's wife after divorcing Fulvia.

App., Bciv. 3.51; 4.29.32; 5.14, 19, 21, 33, 43, 50, 52, 55, 59.
Asc., Mil.
Cic., Phil. 2.44, 113; 5.4, 11; 6.2, 4.

Dio. 46.56.4; 47.8.2–5; 48.4.1–6; 5.1–5; 6.1–4; 10.2–4; 12.4; 15.2; 28.3–4.
Mart. 20.
Plut., Ant. 10.3–5.
Babcock, C., pp. 1–32.
Bauman, R. A., index.
Delia, D., pp. 197–217.
OCD, p. 614.
PW 113.
Syme, R., *Roman Revolution*, index.

G

GALERIA FUNDANA

(1st century C.E.)   Roman: Rome
Political player

Galeria Fundana both suffered poverty and en-joyed imperial wealth over the decades of a tumultus marriage with Aulus Vitellius, emperor for nine months before Vespasian in 69 C.E. She has been lauded in the sources for her probity and modesty in the face of both adversity and excess. Galeria's father had been a praetor, but little else is known of her family. She married Vitellius after he divorced his first wife, PETRONIA. They had two children, a girl and a boy.

By all accounts her husband was a spendthrift. By the time of their marriage, he had already gone through the money accumulated from an African command and had divorced his first wife when she refused to give him access to her fortune. His casualness with money was combined with lusty appetites. He was well known in Rome for his overindulgence in drink and food. The emperor Servius Sulpicius Galba offered him the command of troops in Lower Germany at a moment when he had no other apparent future and was hounded by debt collectors.

Vitellius raised the funds to equip himself with a mortgage on his house. He also took from his mother, SEXTILIA, some pearls to pawn or sell.

Galeria and their children remained in Rome in straitened circumstances living in the rather poor rented quarters of a tenement. She faced his un-happy creditors.

Vitellius was declared emperor by his forces in Lower Germany while Marcus Salvius Otho was declared emperor by the Praetorian Guard in Rome. Galeria and her mother-in-law were in danger as the opposing forces prepared to meet each other. Vitellius sought to protect them with a letter to the brother of Otho threatening to kill him and his children if his own family was harmed. After a tense period in which Galeria and Sextilia remained unharmed, Vitellius's army defeated Otho outside of Rome.

No happier in splendor than in poverty, Galeria moved into Nero's palace with Vitellius. Over the next months, Vitellius spent huge amounts on food, drink, and entertainment in which Galeria took as little part as possible. She, was not, however, without influence. As emper-ors go, Vitellius was far from among the most bloodthirsty, though he did kill some of Otho's supporters. The sources credit Galeria for protect-ing Trachalus, an adviser to Otho who may well have been her earlier protector.

The weaknesses of Vitellius were eventually his undoing, and the armed forces in varying parts of the empire revolted and rallied around

Vespasian. Vitellius was killed in December 69. Galeria's young son was also killed, but Galeria and her daughter were unharmed. Vespasian made a fine match for her daughter and even provided her with a dowry.

Suet., Ves. 14.
Suet., Vit. 6.
Tac., Hist. 2.60, 64.

⊡ GALLITTA

(1st century B.C.E.–1st century C.E.) Roman: Rome and Germany
Adulterer

Gallitta was caught in the paradox of the Julian laws. Intended to uphold traditional values, the *leges Juliae,* passed in 18 B.C.E. and expanded in 9 C.E., all but forced a husband to prosecute his wife, for adultery, since he would otherwise open himself to the charge of procuring.

Gallitta, the wife of a military tribune, had an affair with a centurion. Her husband had reported this to the legate of the consul, who in turn told the emperor Trajan. The centurion lover was banished. The husband, now satisfied and still in love with his wife, did not bring any charges against her. But in Roman legal logic, no husband could condone adultery by his wife unless he gained a financial return from her sexual activities. In that case he would be not her husband but her pimp and could be prosecuted by a third person under the charge of procuring. Gallitta's husband, therefore, faced a serious threat of prosecution.

Instead, Trajan only punished Gallitta. The emperor ruled that she should be banished to an island and forfeit half her dowry and one-third of her property. Her fate could have been worse. She could have been condemned to death and all of her property confiscated.

Plin., Ep. 6.31.
Berger, A., p. 352.
Gardner, J. F., pp. 127–31.

⊡ GLAPHYRA (1)

(1st century B.C.E.) Greek: Asia Minor
Political player

Glaphyra from Cappadocia, in Asia Minor, met the Roman general Mark Antony in 41 B.C.E. when she was in the court of the ruler of Commona. They had an affair. Sources credit her with his decision to appoint her son, Archelaus, ruler of Cappadocia in 36. She was the grandmother of GLAPHYRA (2).

App., Bciv. 5.7.
Dio. 49.32.3–4.
Mart. 11.20.

⊡ GLAPHYRA (2)

(1st century B.C.E.–1st century C.E.) Greek (probable Roman citizen): Cappadocia and Judaea
Adventurer

Glaphyra married three times into ruling families. She was a beautiful and smart woman, the daughter of Archelaus, ruler of Cappadocia, and the granddaughter of GLAPHYRA (1), who was said to have had an affair with the Roman general and triumvir Mark Antony. Her first husband was Alexander, the son of Mariamme I and Herod the Great. Her father-in-law was the ruler of Judaea and closely associated with the Roman Julio-Claudians. Glaphyra and Alexander had two sons, Alexander and Tigranes. The latter became ruler of Armenia (6–12 C.E.).

Glaphyra was not popular among the Jews. Proud of her elite birth, she flaunted her higher status in relation with the other women of the court. In 6 B.C.E., her father-in-law, Herod, executed her husband for conspiring against him. Herod returned Glaphyra's dowry and made clear that she was no longer welcome in Judaea. She returned to Cappadocia and married the learned king Juba II of Mauritania after the death of his wife, CLEOPATRA SELENE. They divorced, and she returned again to Cappadocia.

Her third husband was Archelaus II, the son of Malthace and Herod and the half brother of her first husband. They met after the death of Herod, when Archelaus visited her father in Cappadocia. He had inherited and ruled part of his father's kingdom. He divorced his wife in order to marry Glaphyra. The marriage created political problems for her new husband. He was a Jew, and it was considered an offense against the Torah for him to marry a woman who had been the wife of his half-brother and with whom she had had children. Glaphyra died soon after the marriage. Before her death, she was said to have dreamed that her first husband forgave her.

Jos., AJ 7.341, 345–53.
Jos., BJ 1.476, 552–53; 2.114.
Jones, A. H. M., index.
Perwone, S., pp. 22–23, 58.

▣ GLYCERA

(4th century B.C.E.)   Greek: Athens and Babylon
Self-made woman

Glycera was acknowledged as the most beautiful woman of Athens. She went to Babylon at the behest of Harpalus, a Macedonian, who was a lifelong friend of Alexander the Great. Harpalus was physically handicapped and could not serve as a foot soldier. Alexander appointed him as his treasurer headquartered in Babylon when he left to campaign in India. Harpalus, who was said to have believed that Alexander would never return, embezzled large sums of money to support an extravagant lifestyle. Prior to Glycera, he had lived with PYTHONICE, another Greek woman of great beauty, whom he treated well and for whom he gave a splendid funeral and erected a monument after she died. He did no less for Glycera who also lived in great splendor until Alexander returned and discovered Harpalus's misuse of funds. Harpalus fled with money and some soldiers. He bribed the Athenians, including Demosthenes, in an attempt to gain asylum in Athens. Refused, he fled to Crete, where he was murdered. Glycera's death is unrecorded.

Ath. 13.586c.
Diod. 17.108.4–8.

▣ GORGO

(5th century B.C.E.)   Greek: Sparta
Patriot

Gorgo has been portrayed in the sources as smarter and wiser than the men around her. She was the only child of Cleomenes I, ruler of Sparta (520–490 B.C.E.). After the death of her father, perhaps by suicide, she married Leonidas, a stepbrother of her father, who succeeded him as ruler in 490.

Gorgo was an astute and steadfast advocate of the Greek cause against the Persians at a time when their conflict dominated the future of the West. She was only eight years old when Aristagorus, tyrant of Meletus, came to Sparta in 499–498 to obtain Cleomenes' support, ostensibly to free the Greek settlements in western Asia Minor from Persian rule. In their final meeting, Aristagorus came to the house of Cleomenes and found him in a room with Gorgo. He asked to speak to Cleomenes privately, but Cleomenes told him to speak in front of his daughter. Aristagorus offered Cleomenes a bribe of 10 talents to betray his fellow Greeks and raised the offer as Cleomenes remained firm. Gorgo turned to her father and urged him to leave the room or he would certainly be corrupted by the ever-increasing amount of money. Cleomenes left the room.

Later, prior to the invasion by the Persian king Xerxes, Demaratus, a Greek exile living in the Persian city of Susa, discovered the Persian plan to invade Greece and sent a message of warning. He inscribed his message on wood and then laid it over with wax. When the tablet arrived in Sparta, Gorgo suggested removing the wax to see if a message lay beneath it. The Spartans sent word of the plan to the other cities in Greece.

It was Gorgo's husband, Leonidas, who held the pass at Thermopylae in one of history's most famous battles. He secured the retreat of the main body of his troops while he fiercely counterattacked with his small remaining force. He held off the Persians for two critical days before he was killed.

Hdt. 5.51; 6.75; 7.205, 239.
Burn, A. R., *Persian and the Greeks*, pp. 199, 394.

🔲 GRATILLA

(1st century C.E.)   Roman: Rome
Stoic

Gratilla followed the Stoic philosophy. Her husband, Junius Arulenus Rusticus, a well-known disciple of Stoicism, was executed by the emperor Titis Flavius Domitian in 93 C.E. after he had written in praise of two earlier Stoics: Thrasea Paetus, who had been condemned by the emperor Nero, and Helvidius Priscus, who had been executed by the emperor Titus Flavius Vespasian. Gratilla went into exile, following in the footsteps of the two praised Stoics' women: the younger ARRIA and FANNIA (2).

Plin., Ep. 3.11; 5.1.

🔲 GYGAEA

(5th century B.C.E.)   Greek: Macedonia
Political pawn

Gygaea was the daughter of Amyntas, ruler of Macedonia, and the sister of Alexander I (495–450 B.C.E.), with whom she lived. Bubares, a Persian, arrived to investigate the deaths of several Persian envoys said to have been murdered by the Macedonians on orders from Alexander for insulting Macedonian women at a banquet. Her brother sidetracked the investigation by arranging a marriage between Gygaea and Bubares, accompanied by a substantial dowry. Gygaea had a son, Amyntas, who governed the city of Alabanda in southwest Asia Minor.

Hdt. 5.21; 8.136.
Burn, A. R., *Persia and the Greeks*, p. 134.
Macurdy, G., p. 15.

HAGESICHORA

(7th century B.C.E.) Greek: Sparta
Choral leader

Hagesichora led a women's chorus in Sparta during the second half of the seventh century B.C.E. Described in the sources as beautiful with golden hair, she probably came from an elite family whose daughters took leadership positions in the religious festivals that marked the Spartan calendar.

Traditionally Spartan choruses of 10 women, accompanied by the flute and divided into 2 parts, sang poetic hymns to the gods. Hagesichora led one of the five-voice sections. It remains unclear if she sang or only performed other tasks of direction and production. Also uncertain were the relationships among the women. They appear to have been loving, sensual, and possibly erotic.

Bing, P. (Alcman, frag. 1.39–101).
Bowra, C. M., *Greek Lyric Poetry*, pp. 30–65.
Fantham, E., et al., pp. 12–15.
Page, D., *Alcman*.
Pomeroy, S. B., *Goddesses*, p. 55.

HEDYTO

(5th century B.C.E.) Greek: Athens
Mother of Isocrates

Hedyto married Theodorus, a very rich man living in Athens during the 430s or 420s B.C.E. Her husband owned a workshop in which slaves made flutes. She had five children, one of whom, Isocrates, became a famous philosopher and rhetorician. His system of teaching rhetoric profoundly influenced education in writing and speaking.

Davies, J. K., p. 246.

HEGESIPYLE

(6th–5th century B.C.E.) Thracian: Thrace and Athens
Mother of Cimon

Hegesipyle, the daughter of Olorus, a wealthy Thracian ruler, married Miltiades (c. 550–489 B.C.E.), a member of the aristocratic Athenian family of the Philaidae. Their marriage strengthened the family links between Athens and Thrace. Her husband's father and grandfather had ruled over Chersonesus (Gallipoli), on the Thracian peninsula, under the suzerainty of Athens. In 524, Hippias, the tyrant of Athens, sent her husband to rule in his family's tradition. Hegesipyle gave birth to Cimon, who became a famous Athenian statesman and soldier, and to ELPINICE.

Plut., Cim. 4.1.

HELENA FLAVIA JULIA

(?–327 C.E.) Roman: Italy, Germany, Judaea, Asia, and Syria

Augusta and early Christian

Helena lived during a period of significant religious change. The daughter of an innkeeper from Drepanum in Bithynia, an area in northwest Asia Minor, she was a convert to Christianity, a supporter of the Arian cause, and an influential actor at the court of her son Constantine. She has been credited with introducing her son to Christianity, influencing him to end Christian persecution, and acting as a mediator to achieve compromise at the Council of Nicaea.

The lover or perhaps an early wife of Constantius, she gave birth to the future emperor Constantine in the military city of Naissus on the Danube in 285 C.E. Constantius either divorced or simply left Helena to marry Flavia Maximiana THEODORA, the daughter or stepdaughter of Maximian. Constantius's new father-in-law became co-Augustus at the behest of the emperor Diocletian in 293 and appointed Constantius as his second-in-command with the title of Caesar in the West.

Thirteen years later, in 306 C.E., Constantine became emperor. She and her son had remained close as he followed his father to power. She grew wealthy with extensive properties in Rome. Over the course of decades, she generously supported the troops and friends around her son and helped finance the construction of Constantine's new capital, Constantinople. She assumed the title of Augusta along with Flavia Maxima FAUSTA, Constantine's wife, in 324.

She also became a devout Christian. At the time of Constantine's rise to power, the position of Christianity in the empire was still unclear, and its adherents were subject to periodic persecution. Some tradition has ascribed to Helena the conversion of her son, who was said to have marked his soldiers' armor with a cross to test the power of the new God at the battle of Milvian Bridge in 312. His victory was also the victory of Christianity. Helena, however, was influenced by the bishop Eusebius, as was Flavia Julia CONSTANTIA, Constantine's half sister. They were both Arians at a moment when the movement posed the most serious threat to the unity of the church. Helena not only used her wealth to support the Arian cause, but it was said that she played a critical role in the agreement at the Council of Nicaea, which averted a schism.

In 326 a scandal occurred, the details of which are obscured. Constantine authorized the execution of his 20-year old son, Crispus, who was the child of his lover, MINERVINA, born prior to his marriage with Fausta. He also had Fausta killed or compelled her to commit suicide. Tradition has implicated Helena in the deaths. There is no evidence that Fausta shared Helena's devotion to Christianity, and she may have challenged Helena's Christian coalition. Possibly, Helena suspected Fausta of trying to gather a basis of support to assure the succession of one of her own sons.

Immediately after the tragedy, Helena, probably now in her late 70s, made a pilgrimage to Jerusalem where she supported the building of

Helena Flavia Julia

churches and shrines. She died in 327 in Constantinople. She was buried in Rome.

Eus., Vit. Const.
Balsdon, J. P. V. D., pp. 165–70.
Barnes, T., *Constantine and Eusebius*, pp. 220–21.
Barnes, T., *New Empire of Diocletian.*
Lane Fox, R., pp. 309–11, 670–71.
PW 7.

▣ HELVIA

(2nd–1st century B.C.E.) Roman: Italy
Mother of Cicero

Helvia's famous child, Marcus Tullius Cicero, was an orator, a statesman, and consul in 63 B.C.E. Although he was a prolific letter writer who had no hesitation in praising those he admired, he never referred to his mother and only sparingly to his father. The reasons remain unclear. She came from a respectable family that had social and economic connections in Rome. She married Marcus Cicero, the son of Marcus Cicero and Gratidia. Her husband came from a well-to-do family based near the town of Arpinum about 70 miles from Rome. Marcus was not a well man, and he spent a great amount of his time in study.

In addition to Marcus, born on January 3, 106, their second son, Quintus, was born about two years later. The family moved to Rome while the children were still young with the intention of providing them the best possible education.

Plut., Cic. 1.1.
Shackleton Bailey, D. R., p. 4.

▣ HERODIAS

(1st century C.E.) Jewish: Judaea, Italy,
and Gaul
Loyal wife

Herodias was the sister of Agrippa I, ruler of Judaea. Her brother's friendship with the emperor Gaius Caligula saved her life and fortune. Her brother had grown up in Rome as a close friend of Drusus Julius Caesar, the son of the emperor Tiberius. He was also a friend and client of the future emperor Gaius Caligula, who made him ruler over part of the territory once ruled by his grandfather Herod the Great.

Herodias was the daughter of BERENICE (1) and Aristobulus IV, and the grandniece of Herod the Great. Herodias's first husband was her stepuncle Hero. Their daughter was named Salome. Widowed, she married Antipas, the stepbrother of her first husband and another of her stepuncles. She was his second wife. Her husband was attacked by John the Baptist, who claimed the marriage violated the Torah's kinship law for legal marriage. Antipas feared a revolt and had John killed. At Salome's request, he gave her John's head as a reward for dancing at a party.

Antipas ruled Galilee and Peraea (Transjordan) from 4 B.C.E. to 39 C.E. Herodias became furious that her brother, Agrippa, had received a higher status than her husband, who had served Rome longer. In 39 she persuaded her reluctant husband to go with her to Italy where he sought the same status as her brother from the emperor Caligula. Her brother sent a letter to Caligula accusing Antipas of plotting against the life of the former emperor Tiberius, among other treasonable actions. Caligula banished Antipas to Gaul but offered to allow Herodias to keep her property and avoid banishment when he found out that she was Agrippa's sister. Herodias, however, rejected the offer and went into exile with her husband.

Jos., AJ 18.109–11; 136.240–55.
Grant, M., p. 125.
Perowne, S., index.

▣ HERPYLLIS

(4th century B.C.E.) Greek: Greece
Companion of Aristotle

Herpyllis became the companion of the great philosopher Aristotle after the death of his wife, PYTHIAS. One of their sons was named

Nicomachus after Aristotle's father. Aristotle named his greatest work, the *Nicomachean Ethics,* after their son.

When Aristotle died, he left his property to Herpyllis and the two children. He appointed Nicanor, who served under Alexander the Great, executor. The executor was instructed to care for Herpyllis and, should she choose, to help her find a suitable husband. The will offered her a choice of one of the two houses that Aristotle owned plus a sum of money and five servants.

Ath. 13.589c.
Diog. Laert. 5.1, 12–14.
Flaceliere, R., p. 125.

☐ HIPPARCHIA

(4th–3rd century B.C.E.) Greek: Greece
Philosopher

Hipparchia was born in Maroneia, in the northeastern part of Greece. She and her brother, Metrocles, adopted the philosophy of the Cynics. She threatened suicide unless her parents allowed her to marry Crates of Thebes (c. 365–285 B.C.E.), the leading proponent of Cynicism. Her parents asked Crates to dissuade her. Crates was said to have removed his clothes and stood before her to ask her if she was prepared to choose a helpmate naked in body and without any worldly possessions. She married him. They traveled together and lived a life of Cynic poverty, exhorting others to renounce their possessions for a simple life free of entanglements. Only this way, they claimed, could one achieve independence, peace, happiness, and reconciliation in midst of troubled times, wars, and social chaos.

Hipparchia matched her wits with challengers. Theodorus, an atheist, challenged her in an argument at a banquet. She asserted that any act not considered wrong when undertaken by Theodorus, would also not be wrong when done by her. Thus, if Theodorus struck himself, then she did no wrong if she too struck him. When he asked whether she was a woman who gave up the loom, she was said to have replied that time spent weaving the threads of her mind and educating herself was more important than time spent weaving cloth.

Diog. Laert. 6.96–98
Pomeroy, S. B., *Goddesses,* p. 136.

☐ HIPPARETE (1)

(6th–5th century B.C.E.) Greek: Athens
Independent wife

Hipparete divorced the famous Athenian statesman Pericles by mutual consent after five years of marriage. Hipparete had two sons with Pericles, Xanthippus and Paralus. Her second husband, Hipponicus, was the son of the beautiful and maligned ELPINICE and the nephew of the renowned Cimon. Hipponicus was enormously wealthy after he inherited his father's silver mines. They had two children, HIPPARETE (2), and a son, Callias. The daughter married the general Alcibiades.

Contrary to some reports, Hipparete's divorce from Pericles had nothing to do with ASPASIA, who only became a part of Pericles' life five years later.

Plut., Per. 24.5
Davies, J. K., pp. 260–63.

☐ HIPPARETE (2)

(?–417/416 B.C.E.) Greek: Athens
Rich Athenian

Hipparete sought unsuccessfully to end her marriage with the Athenian statesman Alcibiades. Her father, Hipponicus, was the wealthiest man in Athens. After her grandfather died, her father inherited the family property, including silver mines. Hipparete's mother, HIPPARETE (1), was the divorced wife of Pericles, Athens's most famous ruler.

Hipparete married Alcibiades sometime in the late 420s B.C.E. and was said to have been a proper and affectionate wife to her brilliant and mercurial husband, who led the Athenian navy to victory at Cyzicus in

421. Both charming and handsome, her husband was notorious for his sexual exploits and pranks, some of which were incorporated into several of Plato's Socratic dialogues. Nonetheless, Hipparete had every reason to expect from her husband the respect due to a well-born wife and adherence to the expected social proprieties. After he repeatedly brought prostitutes into their home, she fled to her brother's house. On her own, in a show of public independence, she went to register her divorce. Alcibiades intercepted her en route and forcibly carried her across the public market back into his house.

Alcibiades' interest in maintaining his marriage may have had more to do with money than affection. Hipparete had a dowry of 20 talents. The sum was huge when one considers that the total revenue of Athens in 431 B.C.E. was estimated at 1,000 talents. Under Athenian law, Alcibiades would have been forced to return the money had they divorced. Half of the dowry had been given at their marriage, and the second half would come due upon the birth of a son. Hipparete died shortly after the birth of that son in 417 or 416 B.C.E.

And. 4.14.
Plut., Alc. 8.2–6.
Davies, J. K., pp. 19, 259–61.
Pomeroy, S. B., *Goddesses*, p. 90.

🔲 HISPALA FAECENIA

(2nd century B.C.E.) Roman: Rome
Patriot

Hispala Faecenia was a celebrated hero of Rome who provided the information that uncovered a major religious scandal in 186 B.C.E. She had taken a young man of means, Publius Aebutius, for a lover. He was the only son of DURONIA and ward of his stepfather, Titus Sempronius Rutilus, whom his mother adored. Duronia conspired to avoid the discovery of Rutilius's misuse of her son's inheritance.

Aebutius revealed to Hispala that his mother planned to have him become an initiate of the Bacchic cult. Hispala was horrified. While still a slave, Hispala had attended Bacchic rites with her mistress. The secret cult, in which membership was said to be limited to those under 20 years old who had sworn to engage in unusual sex, robbery, and even murder, was believed to include some 7,000 people in Italy. She warned Aebutius that his mother and stepfather were out to destroy his reputation and made him promise not to be initiated into the rites. When he told his parents that he refused to be initiated, they threw him out of their house.

Aebutius related the story to his aunt, who advised him to go to the consul. Taken seriously by the authorities, they turned to Hispala for details. Finally persuaded to reveal information about the rituals in exchange for protection from retributory violence, she moved into a safe space above the household of the consul's own mother-in-law.

When presented with the facts, the Senate voted to execute the men found guilty of participation in the rites. The women implicated in the scandal were turned over to their families for punishment. The Senate voted 100,000 sesterces as a reward to Hispala and Aebutius. In addition, she was given the right to alienate her property and to marry any man of free birth. Moreover, it was decreed that the consuls and other officials should protect her. She left her property to Aebutius when she died.

Livy 39.8–14, 19
Balsdon, J. P. V. D., pp. 37–43.
Bauman, R. A., pp. 35–37.

🔲 HISPULLA

(1st century C.E.) Roman: Italy
Affluent Woman

Hispulla was part of the well-to-do and educated circle of men and women who lived primarily on their estates as they struggled with the political uncertainties of the late Julio-Claudian period. She was the wife of Corellius Rufus, a close friend of Pliny the Younger. Her husband was afflicted with a progressively painful gout, evidently inherited from his father. He told Pliny that the only reason he chose to continue to live in great agony was to outlive the emperor Domitian, whose reign of terror lasted from 93 until 96 C.E. and left many of his friends dead or in exile.

In his 67th year, with Domitian dead, her husband could no longer endure the pain and decided to end his life by fasting. Hispulla and her daughter, CORELLIA HISPULLA, tried to dissuade him but to no avail. Hispulla then sent for Pliny as their last hope. As he ran to her house, a messenger met him with the news that Rufus could not be deterred, and his friend died shortly thereafter.

Plin., Ep. 1.12.

▣ HORATIA

(7th century B.C.E.) Roman: Rome
War victim

Horatia's story comes from the period of early Roman history when fact and myth are inexorably intertwined. As it is told, marriage between Horatia and a son of the Curiatii family from nearby Alba Longa, southwest of Rome, had been arranged. In a battle with the Curiatii, two of her three brothers died. Her remaining brother killed her fiancé. Horatia met her brother as he returned from battle and recognized the cloak he carried from the body of his slain opponent. She had made that cloak for her soon-to-be husband. She cried. Her brother drew his sword and killed her.

When her brother was brought to trial, her father, Publius Horatius, justified his son's actions and declared he would have killed Horatia had his son not already done so. No Roman woman who mourned for an enemy of Rome deserved to live. Her brother was acquitted but was forced to do penance.

Livy 1.26.
Val. Max. 6.3.6.
Pomeroy, S. B., *Goddesses*, pp. 152–53.

▣ HORTENSIA

(1st century B.C.E.) Roman: Rome
Orator

Hortensia was an orator. She was well educated and articulate. Her father was the famous Roman orator Quintus Hortensius (114–50 B.C.E.). She was also a wealthy woman and was the chosen spokesperson to argue against a special tax levied against women in 42 B.C.E.

The triumvirs Antony, Octavian, and Lepidus were hard-pressed for cash. Needing to overcome a shortfall of some 200 million drachmas for war preparations, they published an edict requiring 1,400 of the wealthiest women to make an evaluation of their property and to donate a portion to the triumvirs. In usual fashion, anyone found to be concealing information would be fined, and informers, whether free or slave, would be rewarded.

The women objected and successfully enlisted support from LIVIA DRUSILLA and OCTAVIA (2), respectively, the wealthy and independent wife and the stepsister of Octavian. They were repulsed, however, by FULVIA (2), the wife of Mark Antony and the woman most directly engaged by the military aspects of war. United, they marched into the Forum where Hortensia spoke for all of them.

She declared that the women had not been involved in any actions against the triumvirs and should therefore not be penalized. Why, she asked, should women pay taxes, since they could not be involved in politics or the military and therefore could not share in the honors and wealth that men acquired? If Rome were fighting a foreign enemy, the women would have no hesitation in supporting the government with all means in their power. But this was a civil war, and women should not be required to give aid in a conflict between Roman citizens that men had fomented. Hortensia pointed out that such an assessment had never before been demanded in the whole history of Rome.

The crowd supported them. Despite their evident anger, the triumvirs eliminated the tax for all but 400 of the women and in addition levied a tax on all men who owned more than 100,000 drachmas.

App., Biv. 4.32–34.
Val. Max. 8.3.3.
Bauman, R. A., pp. 81–83.
Pomeroy, S. B., *Goddesses*, pp. 175–76.

⬚ HYDNA

(5th century B.C.E.) Greek: Scione
Patriot

Hydna was a Greek heroine in the war against the Persians in 480 B.C.E. She was the daughter of Scyllis, from Scione, a city on a peninsula in the Thracian Sea controlled by Athens. She learned to swim and dive as a child alongside her father. When the Persians attacked the Greeks, Xerxes anchored the Persian fleet off Mount Oelion. During a storm, Hydna and her father swam to the fleet and, diving underwater, cut a number of the ships' anchor ropes. Many of the ships drifted and were tossed on the rocks and sank.

Statues of Hydna and her father were dedicated at Delphi. Her statue may have been plundered by the emperor Nero and carried off to Rome in the first century C.E.

Paus. 10.19.1–2.
Harris, H. A., pp. 112–13, 124–25.

ILIA

(2nd–1st century B.C.E.) Roman: Rome
Victim

Ilia was the first wife of the young Lucius Cornelius Sulla, the future dictator of Rome. Her husband married increasingly rich and well-connected women as his career soared. Ilia probably died after the birth of their only child, CORNELIA (4).

Plut., Sull. 6.10.

ISMENODORA

(1st century C.E.?) Greek: Thespiae
Self-made woman

Ismenodora snatched a much younger man for her husband. A wealthy and beautiful young widow who lived in Thespiae, a city in central Greece, she fell in love with Bacchon, the son of a relative and friend. The friend had asked Ismenodora to arrange a suitable marriage for the boy, but the friend was not enthusiastic about the idea of the much older and richer Ismenodora becoming the boy's wife.

Bacchon, shy and still a minor, sought advice. He found no consensus. Ismenodora, convinced that his hesitation was primarily embarrassment, took matters into her own hands. She invited to her house some of her women and men friends who favored the marriage. When Bacchon walked by, which he invariably did, they dragged him in, locked the doors, put on wedding garments, and the couple were married.

Plut., Mor., Amat. 749d–750a; 754e–755b.

ISODICE

(5th century B.C.E.) Greek: Athens
Loyal wife

Isodice was probably the second wife of Cimon, an Athenian statesman and soldier of renown. She came from the aristocratic Athenian family of the Alcmaeonidae. Her father was Euryptolemus, a son of Megacles. Isodice's husband was grief-stricken at her death. She had for certain one son, Callias, and possibly bore an additional three children, all boys.

Diod. 10.31.
Plut., Cim. 4.8–9; 16.1–2.

J

JULIA (1)
(?–68 B.C.E.) Roman: Rome
Brave woman

Julia was descended from a patrician family. When she died, her nephew Julius Caesar used the occasion to glorify himself by tracing her ancestry to the gods. Her mother was a Marcia from the family of the Marcii Reges, the ancient kings of Rome. Julia married Gaius Marius, a noted general and statesman. Her husband held seven consulships before he died in 86 B.C.E. She had one son, also named Gaius Marius, born in 110 B.C.E.

Julia's life was worthy of her lineage. She supported her husband in the tense and sometimes violent confrontations of his political career. She was often alone, honored by some and despised by others. She managed the difficult time of her husband's illness, and after Marius's death, she remained a symbol for the Marians. Julia opposed her son's consulship of 82 B.C.E. She was convinced he was being used for his name by the Marian forces. Events proved her fears well founded. Her son led an army against Lucius Cornelius Sulla and was defeated. He committed suicide.

After Sulla's victory Julia remained in Rome, both vulnerable and proud. She may have supported Caesar as he left the city after he refused Sulla's terms, which included that he divorce his young and even more vulnerable wife CORNELIA (5). It is also possible that she aided Cornelia, whose family had close ties to Marius. She survived Sulla's proscriptions of 81–80 and lived to see her nephew Caesar return from the East. She died in 68 B.C.E.

Suet., Caes. 6.1.
Balsdon, J. P. V. D., p. 46.
OCD, p. 776.
PW 541.

JULIA (2)
(1st century B.C.E.) Roman: Rome
Power broker

Julia lived amidst the maelstrom of civil war politics after Caesar's assassination and played a part in the diplomacy of the Second Triumvirate. Her father was Lucius Julius Caesar, consul in 90 B.C.E. and censor in 89. Her aunt was JULIA (1), wife and widow of Gaius Marius, and Julius Caesar was her cousin. Her mother was a Fulvia whose family had supported reform since the Gracchi. She married Marcus Antonius Creticus, praetor in 74 B.C.E., whom she dominated. Their eldest son, born in 83, grew up to become the famous triumvir Mark Antony. A younger son, Lucius Antonius, became his brother's ally. After the death of her husband in 72, Julia married Publius Cornelius Lentulus Sura, consul in 71. Her second husband was implicated in the conspiracy of Lucius Sergius Catilina and executed on the orders of Marcus Tullius Cicero in 63.

In November 43 the triumvirs undertook a proscription and issued death warrants for some 300 senators and 2,000 equestrians. Among them was Julia's brother, Lucius Julius Caesar, consul in 64 B.C.E. and the uncle of Antony, whom he had opposed after Caesar's murder. Faced with proscription, he took refuge in Julia's house. She secured his pardon from Antony and the restitution of his citizenship. Antony was said to have observed that Julia was a fine sister but a very difficult mother.

Julia remained a widow. She lived in Rome when Antony was in the East with CLEOPATRA VII. Her younger son, Lucius, consul in 41, and her daughter-in-law FULVIA (2) were defeated in Italy by Octavian in the Perusine War of 40 B.C.E. Fearing retribution, Julia left Rome and took refuge in Sicily where she was kindly treated by Sextus Pompeius, who controlled the island. Pompeius, who sought an alliance with Antony against Octavian, sent Julia with two of his envoys to Athens to meet Antony as he returned to Italy from the East.

With the alliance secured, Julia accompanied Antony from Athens to Brundisium in Italy in 39. He laid siege to the city when he was refused admittance. War with Octavian appeared imminent. However, the troops on both sides demanded a settlement. Julia took part in the subsequent negotiations. The result was the pact of Brundisium, sealed with the marriage of Antony and Octavian's sister, OCTAVIA (2). Julia was mollified with a letter from Octavian assuring her that she need not have fled Rome since she was his kinswoman, and that he would have seen to her safety.

App., Bciv. 2.143; 4.37; 5.52, 63.
Dio. 48.15.2; 48.27.4; 51.2, 5.
Plut., Ant. 1.1–3; 2.1–2; 22.3.
Balsdon, J. P. V. D., pp. 52–53.
PW 543.

▣ JULIA (3)

(1st century B.C.E.) Roman: Rome
Politically well connected

Julia was the daughter of AURELIA (1), who came from the family of the Aurelii Cottae, and Gaius Julius Caesar, who died in 85 B.C.E. She was the elder sister of Julius Caesar and JULIA (4). Her first husband was Lucius Pinarius of whom little is known except that they had a son, Lucius Pinarius Scarpus. She later married the equestrian Quintus Pedius and had another son, Quintus Pedius, consul in 43 B.C.E. In his will, Julius Caesar left a share of his fortune to her two sons. They gave their inheritance to Octavian, who had inherited three-quarters of the estate.

Suet., Caes. 83.2.
PW 545.
Syme, R., *Augustan Aristocracy.*
Syme, R., *Roman Revolution,* p. 128.

▣ JULIA (4)

(?–51 B.C.E.) Roman: Rome
Witness

Julia, along with her mother AURELIA (1), gave testimony against Publius Clodius in the notorious Bona Dea scandal of 62 B.C.E. Julia was the daughter of Gaius Julius Caesar, who died in 85 B.C.E. Her mother came from the illustrious Aurelii Cottae. Julia was the younger sister of Julius Caesar, with whom she remained close throughout her life. She married Marcus Atius Balbus from Aricia and had two daughters. The eldest, ATIA (1), married Gaius Octavius, and Julia became the grandmother of Octavian, the future emperor Augustus and the independent OCTAVIA (2).

In 62, Caesar was *pontifex maximus,* and his household was the site of the celebration of the Bona Dea rituals presided over by Julia and Aurelia. The religious rites, restricted to elite women, were a traditional part of the Roman *pax deorum,* which joined the well-being of the state with the proper performance of an annual cycle of religious ritual. Publius Clodius Pulcher, an aristocrat of the finest lineage, violated the sanctity of the female-only rite. He entered the household disguised as a woman. It was alleged that he had an assignation with Caesar's wife POMPEIA (1). Discovered and tried with testimony from Julia and her mother, he was acquitted with the help of large bribes. Caesar was said not to have taken the matter seriously, although he did divorce his wife in its wake.

After the death of her son-in-law Gaius Octavius, Julia's grandson Octavian lived with her for eight years from 58 B.C.E. until her death in 51. The 12-year-old Octavian delivered her funeral oration.

Suet., Aug. 4; 8.
Suet., Caes. 74.2.
PW 546.
Syme, R., *Roman Revolution*, p. 112.

▣ JULIA (5)

(83–54 B.C.E.) Roman: Rome
Political wife

Julia, born in 83 B.C.E., was the only child of Julius Caesar. Her mother was CORNELIA (5), the young first wife of Caesar. Julia was to marry Quintus Servilius Caepio until her father and Gnaeus Pompeius (Pompey the Great) established a political alliance (along with Marcus Licinius Crassus) in April 59 for which her marriage with Pompey formed the symbolic center.

The union did not appear promising. Julia was Pompey's fourth wife. He was some 23 years her senior and already had adolescent sons plus a daughter of marriageable age. Nonetheless it worked. Not only did Pompey and Caesar draw closer together, but the sources claim that Pompey handed over his provinces and armies to friendly legates so that he and Julia could spend time on his estates in Italy. The sources did not approve of what they considered to be this dereliction of his duty.

Julia had a miscarriage in 55, precipitated by the arrival of servants carrying her husband's clothes splattered with blood from an altercation to which she later learned he was a witness, not a participant. She died a year later in childbirth. Her child died a few days later. Her death in 54 distressed her husband, her father, and their followers, who felt that she was the bond that kept their alliance alive. Indeed, that alliance dissolved within a few years. At the demand of the populace her body was carried to the Campus Martius for final rites.

Plut., Caes. 23.5–7.
Plut., Pomp. 47.6; 53.1–5.
Val. Max. 4.6.4.
OCD, p. 776.
PW 547.

▣ JULIA (6)

(39 B.C.E.–15 C.E.) Roman: Italy, Gaul, and Pandateria
Political player

Julia held a unique position in the Augustan empire: She was the only child of the emperor. Born in 39 B.C.E., her mother was SCRIBONIA, whom her father divorced to marry LIVIA DRUSILLA. Her father ignored his own record of notorious divorce and second marriage to insist that Julia live with rules and strictures from an idealized vision of Rome's past. Brought up in the household of her stepmother, she was to be an example of women who lived lives dutifully devoted to father, children, husband, and kin. Her father insisted she be taught the ancient arts of spinning and weaving and discouraged friendships without his permission and approval.

Julia, however, was her father's daughter in more ways than Augustus may have foreseen, and the place she sought for herself was more than as a model and docile wife bringing forth strong sons. Educated and well read, she had a sharp and witty tongue that challenged her father's restrictive vision for her life. Julia, and possibly Augustus, suffered the unintended consequences of their different expectations. Beguiled by Julia's charm and wit, her father underestimated her determination to use fully her position as Caesar's daughter. She, on the other hand, may have lost sight of her father's ruthlessness.

Julia married Marcus Claudius Marcellus, the son of Augustus's independent-minded sister OCTAVIA (2), in 25 B.C.E. The marriage might have provided Augustus with a solution to his dynastic problems had Marcellus not died two years later. In 21 Julia married Marcus Vipsanius Agrippa, Augustus's confidant, supporter, and adviser. Some 21 years older than Julia, this was his third marriage. Moreover, to marry Julia, Agrippa divorced the elder MARCELLA, who was Julia's cousin and with whom he had had a harmonius marriage. Despite the inauspicious circumstances, Julia had five children over the next eight years: Gaius Caesar; Lucius Caesar; Agrippa Postumus, who was born after the death of his father; and two daughters, JULIA (7) and the elder AGRIPPINA. Augustus adopted her three sons and brought them up as members of his household to prepare for succession.

Again widowed in 12 B.C.E., Julia married her father's grown stepson, Tiberius. As with Agrippa, to marry Julia, Tiberius divorced his wife, VIPSANIA AGRIPPINA, with whom he had had an agreeable relationship. The new marriage initially promised success, and Julia traveled with Tiberius to northern Italy when he campaigned in the Balkans, but the relationship quickly deteriorated. The witty and outgoing Julia thrived in a world distasteful to her husband. He was stern and disciplined, little given to the hothouse of gossip, intrigue, and power politics that was the lifeblood of imperial Rome. Primarily a military man, he appeared most comfortable with more retiring women like his first wife. During her husband's self-imposed exile in 6 B.C.E., Julia remained in Rome. Secure in her position as Caesar's daughter, she surrounded herself with a set of friends more her own age and more in tune with her tastes.

She was alleged to have engaged in a series of love affairs, and in 2 B.C.E., her father created a public scandal with a letter to the Senate in which he described her transgressions and named her lovers. They made up a formidable group and included the poet Sempronius Gracchus; the consul of 9 B.C.E. Quinctius Crispinus; the patrician Appius Claudius Pulcher, and Cornelius Scipio, who was her stepbrother. Their names resonated with republican glory, and their probable leader was Iullus Antonius, the son of Mark Antony and FULVIA (2), who had married Julia's cousin, the elder Claudia MARCELLA, in 21 B.C.E. after her divorce from Agrippa.

Growing up in the households of Octavia, Livia, and the other elite women who raised the motherless or fatherless children left in the wake of civil wars, this first postwar generation of men and women had probably known one another since childhood. By 2 B.C.E. Julia and her circle were in their late 30s and early 40s. Like Julia, most had been married more than once. Many already had nearly grown children and honorable political careers. By then Julia's father was an old man. His power was unchallenged, and his plans for succession repeatedly frustrated. The viciousness with which he attacked Julia and her friends would possibly suggest a political motive hiding behind the cloak of sexual misbehavior.

The descriptions of Julia that have come down over time—soliciting in the Forum, indiscriminate lewdness, and multiple simultaneous relationships—strain credulity when compared with the evidence of an educated, proud, and witty 40-year old Roman woman who had had three marriages, was twice widowed, and had borne five children in eight years. The punishments meted out by her father were equally contradictory. He issued a decree divorcing Julia from Tiberius, who was still on Rhodes. When Tiberius wrote to ask that Julia be allowed to keep her personal property, Augustus refused and instead allowed her only a modest allowance. She was banished to the island of Pandateria off the coast of Naples. Her mother,

Scribonia, a woman renowned for her virtue, accompanied her. No man was allowed to visit her unless he was screened to determine that he was politically safe and physically unattractive. Her father further decreed that any illicit association with her, or for that matter with any woman of the Julian house, was henceforth high treason.

The banishment was not popular, and eventually Augustus allowed Julia to move to Reggio in southern Italy. The men said to have been involved with her were also exiled, with the exception of Antonius, who was executed. Of the other women in the circle, Augustus issued an edict that they should not be punished for indiscretions more than five years old.

Julia's father died without ending her exile. His will specified that she should not be buried in his tomb. Tiberius showed no pity or kindness to her when he became emperor. He stopped the allowance granted her by Augustus, since the emperor had made no provision for it in his will. He also restricted her to her house and allowed no visitors. She died in 15 C.E. at the age of 53.

Dio. 54.6.5; 55.10.12–16, 13.1; 56.32.4; 57.18.1a.
Macrob., Sat. 2, 5.
Plin., NH 21.9.
Sen., Ben. 6.32.1–2.
Suet., Aug. 63.1–2; 64.1–3; 65.1–4.
Suet., Tib. 7.2–3; 11.4; 50.1.
Tac., Ann. 1.53.
Balsdon, J. P. V. D., pp. 81–87.
Bauman, R. A., index.
Ferrill, A., "Augustus and His Daughters," pp. 332–46.
Hallett, J., "Perusinae Glande," pp. 151–71.
Levick, B., Tiberius, index.
OCD, pp. 776–77.
PW 550.
Richlin, A., "Julia's Jokes," pp. 65–91.
Syme, R., History in Ovid, pp. 193ff.
Syme, R., Roman Revolution, index.

JULIA (7)

(19 B.C.E.–28 C.E.) Roman: Italy
Political victim

Julia suffered the same tragic fate as her mother. Born in 19 B.C.E., the granddaughter of Augustus,

her birth was heralded with the promise of lifelong splendor. She was one of five children; her mother JULIA (6), was the only daughter of Augustus, and her father, Marcus Vipsanius Agrippa, was the famous general, statesman, and confidant of the emperor. At her father's death, when she about seven years old, she and her younger siblings—Gaius Caesar, Lucius Caesar, Agrippa Postumus, and the elder AGRIPPINA—came under the authority of her grandfather. He imposed on them traditions of virtue contradicted by the realities of the new empire. In the face of imperial wealth and status, the girls were taught spinning and weaving; their relationships were closely controlled; and their future was managed.

Augustus almost succeeded in his efforts to mold his granddaughter. In 4 B.C.E. Julia married Lucius Aemilius Paullus, consul in 1 C.E. and a distant relation through their respective grandmothers. Julia's mother-in-law, CORNELIA (8), whose virtue and glory was eulogized in the poetry of Propertius, came from a family that embodied the greatness of the Roman republic. Over the next decade, however, tragedies followed one after another. In 2 B.C.E. Julia's mother became part of a public scandal that resulted in her exile for adultery and conspiracy. Four years later her brother Lucius died, followed two years later by her brother Gaius. Her third brother, Agrippa Postumus, was accused of brutal rebellious behavior by the emperor and sent to Surrentum. The Senate later voted to exile him on the island of Planasia.

In 8 C.E., exactly 10 years after her mother's exile, Julia too was exiled. The nature of her crime remains unclear. She was sent to the island of Trimerus off the Apulian coast on grounds of adultery with Decimus Junius Silanus, a Roman aristocrat. At the same time, her husband, Aemilius Paullus, was accused of conspiracy against the aged emperor and executed. The poet Ovid also exiled was sent to Tomis on the Black Sea, a far outpost of the empire where he remained until his death. After the exile of her mother, Augustus had issued an edict that illicit behavior with any woman of the Julian clan would be considered high treason, yet to punish Silanus Augustus merely revoked his friendship with him. Silanus went into voluntary exile and was later allowed to return to Rome by the emperor Tiberius through the intervention of his influential brother Marcus Silanus.

In exile, Julia gave birth, but Augustus refused to allow the father to acknowledge the child, and it was exposed on the emperor's orders. After 20 years in exile, Julia died in 28 C.E.

Suet., Aug. 64.1–3; 65.1, 4.
Tac., Ann. 3.24; 4.71.
Bauman, R. A., pp. 120–21.
Levick, B., *Tiberiius*, index.
OCD, p. 777.
PW 551.
Syme, R., *Augustan Aristocracy*, index.
Syme, R., *History in Ovid*, pp. 206ff.
Syme, R., *Roman Revolution*, index.

JULIA (8)

(?–43 C.E.) Roman: Rome
Political victim

Julia shared the tragic fate of many women born with her name. She was both pawn and actor in the drama of succession to the emperor Tiberius who was her grandfather on her father's side. Through her mother, Livia Julia Claudia Livilla, she was directly descended from OCTAVIA (2), the independent-minded sister of the emperor Augustus. She married Nero Julius Caesar, the older son of the elder AGRIPPINA. The marriage joined the direct descendants of Augustus and of his wife LIVIA DRUSILLA in a line of succession through Julia's father Drusus Julius Caesar.

When her father died in 23 C.E., succession became an open hunting ground among the probable heirs. The battle for succession was dominated by women. Julia's mother, LIVILLA, was a willing player. Her opponent was the wily and ruthless Agrippina. Each sought to secure the place of emperor for her son. Livilla had one son, Julia's young brother, Tiberius Gemellus, the survivor of twin

sons born in 19 C.E. Agrippina had, in addition to Julia's husband, two other sons waiting in the wings.

The married Julia was apparently close to Livilla, but her husband was not Agrippina's favorite child. In addition, neither one of the couple appears to have been politically adroit. Julia's husband was brash and indiscreet, outspokenly looking forward to his own time of power. Julia rashly disclosed her husband's intemperate remarks to her mother.

Were not the wealth and power of the empire the prize, the couple's behavior would have been less noteworthy. However, Julia's mother had become the accomplice of Lucius Aelius Sejanus, the prefect of the Praetorian Guard. With Tiberius relatively secluded in Capri, Sejanus became the emperor's eyes and ears in Rome. His aspirations possibly expanded to include marriage with Julia's mother and even a regency over her small son.

The tales brought by Julia to her mother were used as evidence by Sejanus to convince Tiberius that Julia's husband Nero Julius Caesar was treacherous. In a letter to the Senate in 29 C.E., Tiberius denounced him and his mother, Agrippina, for plotting against the emperor. Agrippina was exiled to Pandateria, and Nero, to Pontia. He was put to death the following year.

Shortly thereafter, Tiberius turned on Sejanus and accused him before the Senate of treason. He was executed. Julia's mother was accused and convicted of being Sejanus's lover and of conspiring with him to poison her husband, Tiberius's son, eight years earlier. Released into the care of Julia's grandmother the younger ANTONIA her mother starved herself to death.

Still a widow in 33, Tiberius arranged that Julia marry Gaius Rubellius Blandus, consul suffectus in 18 C.E. He came from an equestrian background, which limited the threat any child of their marriage would pose to the existing aspirants for succession. Although Rubellius Blandus was close to 60, and Julia, about 30, they soon had a son, Rubellius Plautus. Julia however was still not safe.

By 43 Julia's uncle Claudius had succeeded Tiberius. Valeria MESSALLINA was his wife, and Julia posed a possible obstacle to her plans for the succession. Fearing a rival in anyone connected to the imperial family, even Julia's equestrian son, Messallina accused Julia of immoral conduct. She was put to death.

Dio. 58.8, 9; 21.1; 60.18.4.
Tac., Ann. 3.29.4; 6.27.1; 13.32.5; 13.43.4.
Bauman, R.A., index.
Levick, B., *Claudius*, pp. 56–57.
Levick, B., *Tiberius*, index.
Marsh, F. B., pp. 182, 192.
PW 552.
Syme., R., *Augustan Aristocracy*, index.
Syme, R., *Tacitus*, index.

Julia Avita Mamaea

JULIA AQUILIA SEVERA

(3rd century C.E.)   Roman: Rome
Vestal Virgin married to emperor

Julia Aquilia Severa was a Vestal Virgin pressed into marriage by the increasingly unstable emperor Elagabalus in 219 or 220 C.E. after he divorced JULIA CORNELIA PAULA. In a letter to the Senate, Elagabalus wrote that not only had he fallen in love with Julia, but it was fitting that he, the high priest, should marry a Vestal Virgin, a high priestess, to create godlike children. Subsequently, he divorced Julia Severa, married and divorced other women, and then again married her in 221. Elagabalus was murdered the following year.

Dio. 80.9.3–4.
Herodian 5.6.2.
Balsdon, J. P. V. D., p. 159.
PW 557.

JULIA AVITA MAMAEA

(?–235 C.E.)   Roman: Syria and Italy
Power broker

Julia Avita Mamaea successfully wielded power during difficult times in the third century C.E.

Born the younger daughter of JULIA MAESA and the consul Julius Avitus, she married Gessius Marcianus, a knight from Arca Caesarea in Syria. She was widowed after the birth of her son, Alexianus, who would become the emperor Severus Alexander. All sources agree that Julia ruled her son and through him the empire.

Like her mother and her aunt, JULIA DOMNA, Julia Mamaea was intelligent, strong willed, courageous, pragmatic, and power-loving. Interested in Christianity, she provided the theologian Origen with a military escort to come to Alexandria and deliver to her a sermon. Not surprisingly, her son, after he assumed power, kept statutes of Christ and Abraham along with the deified emperors of Rome in his private chapel.

Julia Mamaea's position as the dominant imperial force in the empire was won with blood. Her mother had successfully plotted with Julia's older sister, JULIA SOAEMIAS BASSIANA, to make Julia's nephew Elagabalus emperor of Rome. Once emperor, Elagabalus's behavior became increasingly scandalous and bizarre. Julia Soaemias not only failed to curb her son but appeared to revel in his extravagances. Julia Maesa feared that Elagabalus would be overthrown, bringing to an end her own position of power and influence. She then conspired with her younger daughter, Julia Mamaea, to replace Elagabalus with Alexianus.

Julia Maesa persuaded the 16-year-old Elagabalus to adopt the 12-year-old Alexianus. His name became Marcus Aurelius Alexander Caesar. Julia Mamaea declared to the army that late emperor Caracalla was the father of her son, just as her sister had earlier claimed the late emperor father of Elagabalus. Keeping her nephew appeased and the troops well bribed, she had the younger boy tutored in Latin and Greek and trained to behave as an emperor. Within the year Julia Mamaea and her mother arranged for the Praetorian Guard to kill Elagabalus and Julia Soaemias. Alexianus assumed the name Marcus Aurelius Severus Alexander and became emperor in 222 C.E.

Julia Mamaea and her mother took up the reins of government in the boy's name. They gained the support of the Senate, establishing an advisory council of 16 distinguished senators. They neither sought the right to sit in the Senate nor to sign decrees and they did not object when the Senate abolished the right that had been granted Julia Soaemias. They appointed Domitius Ulpian, a distinguished jurist, head of the Praetorian Guard and charged him to restore order and discipline in the army which had become lax and unruly under Elagabalus. With Ulpian's advice, they instituted financial reforms that increased the treasury and allowed them to ease the burden of taxation that had escalated under Caracalla and Elagabalus. Expenditures for the imperial household were modified. The corn supply was assured, and loans at low interest were made available from the treasury. In 223 the Praetorian Guard, angered at the strict discipline imposed by Ulpian, mutinied and pursued him into the palace. Ulpian was killed in spite of Severus's attempt to save him. The leader of the revolt was later executed.

After the death of her mother in 224, Julia Mamaea alone directed Severus Alexander. She instituted additional needed reforms and pushed her son toward behavior that was judicious and fair, avoiding mass executions or deportations. For 12 years, between 222 and 235, the empire was largely peaceful. During this period she may have ended a marriage between her son and Gnaea Seia Herennia Sallustia Barbia ORBIANA, whose name appeared on coins and inscriptions between 225 and 227. The daughter of Sallustius Macrinus, whom Severus Alexander had appointed Caesar, her father was executed for treason and Orbiana was sent back to Africa.

In 233 the Persian king Artaxerxes invaded Mesopotamia. Julia went with her son to Antioch to oversee the troops. The campaign was not a great success, but the Persians suffered enough casualties to allow the Romans to regain Mesopotamia. A greater threat now took place on the Rhine, were German tribes invaded. Severus again went to the front accompanied by Julia Mamaea. She tried to placate the Germans rather than fight. The Roman army regarded her behavior as cowardly. In addition, they coveted for themselves the bribe money that she used to buy off the Germans. In 235 they revolted under the leadership of Maximinus and murdered both Julia Mamaea and her son.

Dio. 79.30.2–4; 38.4; 80 (fragment)
Herodian 5.3.3, 7.1–5, 8.2–3, 10; 6.1–9.
SHA, Alex. Sev. 3.1; 14.7; 26.9–11; 59.8; 60.1–2; 63.5.
Balsdon, J. P. V. D., pp. 156–64.
OCD, p. 777.

JULIA CORNELIA PAULA

(3rd century C.E.) Roman: Italy
Augusta

Julia Cornelia Paula was the unfortunate first wife of the emperor Marcus Aurelius Antoninus Elagabalus. He was the son of JULIA SOAEMIAS BASSIANA and took his name from the sun-god of Emesa in Syria, for whom he was the hereditary priest. Julia Paula came from an aristocratic family in Rome. She married Elagabalus probably in the summer of 219 C.E., when he was about 16. Her marriage to the young emperor may well have been an effort to improve relations between the emperor and the Senate. The nuptials were accompanied by an expensive celebration with elaborate banquets, gladiatorial contests, and the slaughter of some 51 tigers.

Julia Paula was given the title Augusta, and her name appeared on coins. Elagabalus, whose behavior became increasingly bizarre, divorced her within a year. He claimed that she had a blemish of some sort on her body. She returned to private life; her successor, JULIA AQUILIA SEVERA, would be hardly more successful as the emperor's wife.

Dio. 80.9.1–4.
Herodian 5.6.1.
PW 564.

▣ JULIA DOMNA

(2nd century–218 C.E.)   Roman: Syria and Italy
Augusta

Julia Domna was ambitious, indomitable, and handsome. She came from Emesa in Syria, where her father, Julius Bassianus, was the priest in the Temple of the Sun. In 187 C.E. she married Lucius Septimius Severus, whom she had met earlier while he commanded a legion in Syria. He was said to have remembered that her horoscope matched his and sought her out after his wife died. North African, from an equestrian family, he was consul in 190 and became emperor in 193. They had two sons: Marcus Aurelius Antoninus Caracalla was born in 188, Septimius Geta, in 189.

After Septimius Severus became emperor, Julia, her sister JULIA MAESA, and the latter's two daughters, JULIA SOAEMIAS BASSIANA and JULIA AVITA MAMAEA, collected around them an interesting circle that included the Greek philosopher Philostratus, from whom Julia commissioned a biography of Apollonius; the physician and medical writer Galen; and possibly the historians Appian and Dio.

Early in her husband's reign, Julia traveled with him. She rebuilt the temple of Vesta in Rome and restored a meeting hall for women erected by Vibia SABINA in the Forum of Trajan. Her influence on her husband diminished after 197 when he appointed Plautianus, a fellow countryman from Africa, as prefect of the Praetorian Guard. A cruel and avaricious man, he perceived Julia as his enemy. In 201 he threatened her with the charge of adultery. The accusation, either dismissed or never pursued, nevertheless curtailed her power. In 202, Plautianus's daughter PLAUTILLA married her son Caracalla. Her son hated Plautilla as much as Julia hated Plautilla's father.

Julia Domna regained her former position when Caracalla convinced his father that Plautianus was a traitor. After Plautianus was murdered on January 22, 205, Caracalla divorced Plautilla and banished her to the island of Lipara. Once more secure, Julia Domna and her whole family accompanied her husband to Britain during his campaign of 208–211. She was named Augusta and was also given the title of Mater Castrorum (Mother of the Encampment).

After the death of her husband in 211, Julia Domna successfully opposed dividing the empire between her two sons. She worked to bridge their mutual hatred. In February 212, Caracalla requested a meeting with his brother with Julia present to resolve their differences. Caracalla, instead, sent centurions to murder Geta, who died in Julia's arms.

Julia Domna handled her unstable son Caracalla carefully, and as a result, her relationship with him remained excellent. She focused him on his responsibilities as emperor and sought to curb his excessive expenditures. She spent a great deal of time in Nicomedea on the Black Sea in Asia Minor in 214–215 while her son was in the East on military campaigns. There she received petitions and answered most of the official correspondence. Dispatches to the Senate were sent in her name as well as his. She held public receptions attended by prominent men who sought from her the services and benefits of an emperor. When

Caracalla became disabled by venereal disease, which increasingly affected his temper, she effectively governed in his name.

In April 217 Caracalla was murdered at the instigation of the Praetorian prefect Macrianus, who feared for his own life. Julia Domna received the news in Antioch where she was conducting the business of government. Initially, Macrianus allowed Julia to retain her guards and other honors. She began to lay plans to overthrow Macrianus and rule in his stead. He became suspicious and ordered her out of Antioch. Ill with breast cancer but unwilling to surrender power, she committed suicide by starvation in Antioch in 218.

Dio. 76.15.6–7; 78.2.1–6; 18.2–3; 79.23–24.
Herodian 3.15.6; 4.3, 4–5.
SHA, Sev. 18.8.
Balsdon., J. P. V. D., pp. 150–56.
Birley, A. R. *Septimius Severus*, index.
OCD, p. 777.
PW 566.

▣ JULIA DRUSILLA (1)
(16–38 C.E.) Roman: Rome
Deified

Julia Drusilla was born in 16 C.E. into an ill-omened family. Her mother, the elder AGRIPPINA, and her father, Germanicus Julius Caesar, were a popular couple and leading contenders in the politics of succession to Tiberius. Disaster struck when her father died suddenly at Antioch in 19 C.E. Convinced that he had been poisoned under orders from Tiberius, her mother returned to Rome and entered the fray of imperial politics. A decade later her mother and elder brother, Nero Julius Caesar, were accused of treason. Both exiled in 29, Nero was executed in 31, and her mother died by starvation in 33. Another brother, Drusus Julius Caesar, imprisoned in 30, died in 33.

In 33, as the reign of the ailing Tiberius was drawing to an end, Julia Drusilla married Lucius Cassius Longinus, consul in 30 C.E. After her brother, Gaius Caligula succeeded Tiberius, he dissolved her marriage. Her second husband was Marcus Aemilius Lepidus, the son of Marcus Aemilius Lepidus, consul in 6 C.E. Still clearly close with her brother, rumors of an incestuous relationship were fueled when Caligula named her his heir during an illness in 37. In the malicious gossip of the time, it was also rumored that her husband was her brother's lover.

When Julia Drusilla died in 38, Caligula could hardly contain his grief. He enforced public mourning throughout the empire. Although there was no precedent, Julia Drusilla was deified as Panthea, and the emperor had her statue placed alongside the temple statues of the traditional female deities.

Dio. 59.11.1–6.
Suet., Calig. 7; 24.1–2.
Tac., Ann. 6.15.4.
Balsdon, J. P. V. D., p. 250.
Bauman, R. A., pp. 159–63.
Ferrill, A., *Caligula*, index.
OCD, p. 777.
PW 567.
Syme R., *Augustan Aristocracy*, index.

▣ JULIA DRUSILLA (2)
(c. 40–January 24, 41 C.E.) Roman: Rome
Political victim

Julia Drusilla was born in 40 C.E., either on the day of her parents' marriage or a month before they wed. She was the daughter of the emperor Gaius Caligula and his fourth wife, MILONIA CAESONIA. Her father, who was probably mad, claimed that her birth was sudden and therefore supernatural. Supposedly, when she displayed her temper by scratching people's faces her father proudly claimed that by her temper he knew her to be his daughter.

Drusilla died after her head was dashed against a wall on January 24, 41, the same day on which her mother and father were murdered.

Dio. 59.28.8.
Suet., Calig. 25.3–4; 58.
PW 568.

🏛 JULIA FLAVIA

(65–91 C.E.) Roman: Rome
Augusta; deified

Born in 65 C.E., Julia was the daughter of the future emperor Titus Flavius Vespasianus by his second wife, MARCIA FURNILLA. Her parents divorced in 64. She was declared Augusta by her father during his short reign, 79–81.

Her father unsuccessfully sought to marry her with his brother, the future emperor Titus Flavius Domitian. Julia instead married her cousin Titus Flavius Sabinus, who was consul with Domitian in 82 and whom Domitian executed in 84. After her husband's death, Julia lived openly with Domitian. She died in 91, and Domitian deified her. Her death has been attributed to an abortion.

Dio. 67.3.2.
Plin., Ep. 4.11
Suet., Dom. 22.1.
Suet., Tit. 4.2–4.
Balsdon, J. P. V. D., p. 133.
OCD, p. 600.
PW 552.

🏛 JULIA LIVILLA

(18–41 C.E.) Roman: Italy, Germany, and Gaul
Political player

Julia Livilla came from a family plagued by misfortune. She was the youngest daughter of the popular elder Vipsania AGRIPPINA and Germanicus Julius Caesar. Born in 18 C.E., one year before her father's unexpected death, her life was burdened with her mother's suspicions. Bringing her husband's ashes back from Antioch where he had died, Agrippina was convinced that her husband's death had been orchestrated by the emperor Tiberius. Scarcely a decade later, her mother and brother, Nero Julius Caesar, were charged with treason by Tiberius and exiled to islands off the coast. The next year, he imprisoned another brother, Drusus Julius Caesar.

In 33, the same year in which her exiled mother starved herself to death and her brother Drusus died in prison, she married Marcus Vinicius, consul in 30 and 45. It was not a brilliant match, but it may have been a peaceful one. Her husband, a gentle person and a fine orator, came from an equestrian background outside the eternal imperial fray.

In 37 her brother Gaius Caligula became emperor. He honored all his living siblings. Although their sister JULIA DRUSILLA was Caligula's favorite, all the siblings were subject to malicious gossip about incestuous relations. In 39, Julia Livilla joined other family members and accompanied the emperor and the army to Mainz in Germany. On arrival, Caligula accused them of conspiracy, treason, and adultery in a plot that included Julia Livilla, the younger AGRIPPINA, Marcus Aemilius Lepidus, and the governor of Upper Germany Gnaeus Cornelius Lentulus Gaetulicus. Julia Livilla and her sister were banished to the Pontian islands. Lepidus was executed.

When her uncle Claudius became emperor in 41, he recalled both Julia Livilla and Agrippina from exile and restored their property. However, Valeria MESSALLINA, her uncle's wife, was fearful of Julia Livilla's beauty and jealous of both sisters' influence over Claudius. Julia Livilla was soon accused of adultery with Lucius Annaeus Seneca, a brilliant orator and philosopher. Again exiled, this time to the island of Pandateria, she was killed soon after.

Dio. 60.4.1; 8.4–5.
Suet., Calig. 24.3.
Tac., Ann. 6.15.
Ferrill, A., *Caligula*, index.
Levick, B., *Tiberius*, index.
OCD, p. 777.
PW 575.
Syme, R., *Augustan Aristocracy*, index.

Julia Maesa

▣ JULIA MAESA

(2nd century–224 C.E.) Roman: Syria, Asia, and Rome

Power broker

Julia Maesa was ambitious and thrived in a world of intrigue populated by strong women and weak men. She was the daughter of Julius Bassianus of Emesa in Syria and the sister of JULIA DOMNA. She married a Syrian, Julius Avitus, consul suffectus and proconsul of Asia under her brother-in-law, the emperor Lucius Septimius Severus. Avitus died during the reign of Marcus Aurelius Antoninus Caracalla, Julia Maesa's nephew. She had two daughters, JULIA SOAEMIAS BASSIANA and JULIA AVITA MAMAEA. After the murder of Caracalla and the suicide of his mother, Julia Domna, in 218 C.E., the emperor Marcus Opellius Macrinus ordered Julia Maesa to leave Rome and return to Emesa. She left with a great deal of wealth, amassed during the previous reigns.

Julia Maesa plotted with her daughter Julia Soaemias, a widow with a son, to have the boy declared the child of Caracalla and thereby challenge the legitimacy of the emperor Macrinus. The boy, Varius Avitus Bassianus, a very handsome 14-year-old, was priest of the sun-god at Emesa, a position that he inherited from his great-grandfather. Smuggled into the army camp along with enough of Julia Maesa's gold to smooth the way, the soldiers proclaimed him emperor.

When Macrinus attacked, she and her daughter leaped from their chariots and rallied the retreating troops. With the young boy leading the forces, they defeated Macrinus on June 8, 218. Macrinus was killed as he fled to Rome in disguise. The boy immediately assumed all of the titles and honors of the emperor without waiting for confirmation by the Senate and took the name Elagabalus, after the sun-god of Emesa.

The 15-year-old emperor, along with Julia Maesa, her daughters Julia Soaemias and Julia Mamaea, and their entourage, began the trip to Rome. Over a year later, in July 219, they arrived.

Elagabalus's behavior became increasingly erratic and bizarre. Julia Soaemias, who enjoyed the luxurious life, failed to restrain him. Concerned that his foolishness would result in the loss of her own power and position, Julia Maesa conspired with her second daughter, Julia Mamaea, to replace Elagabalus with her other grandson. They convinced Elagabalus to adopt his 12-year-old cousin Julia Mamaea's son Alexianus and let it be known to the army that Alexianus was also a son of Caracalla. The plot succeeded. Elagabalus and his mother were killed by the Praetorian Guard in 222, and Alexianus was declared emperor as Marcus Aurelius Severus Alexander.

His mother, Julia Mamaea, now received the title of Augusta and carefully supervised the education and upbringing of her son. Since he was only 13, Julia Maesa and Julia Mamaea were unimpeded. No action was taken without the approval of the two women. They ruled well. They improved relations with the Senate by establishing an advisory council of 16 senators. Julia Maesa died two years later in 224 and was deified by her grandson.

Dio. 79.30.2–4, 38.4.
Herodian 5.3.2–3, 9–12; 5.5–6; 6.1, 4; 7.1–3; 8.3–4.

SHA, Marc. 9.
Balsdon, J. P. V. D., index.
OCD, pp. 777–87.

▣ JULIA PHOEBE

(1st century B.C.E.–1st century C.E.) Roman: Rome

Loyal attendant

Julia Phoebe was a freedwoman of JULIA (6), the only child of the emperor Augustus and SCRIBONIA. When Julia was banished by Augustus in 2 B.C.E., Julia Phoebe, who was close to Julia, committed suicide.

Suet., Aug. 65.2–3.

▣ JULIA PROCILLA

(?–69 C.E.) Roman: Gallia Narbonensis and Rome

Honorable woman; murder victim

Julia Procilla died violently at the hands of marauding soldiers in 69 C.E. She had lived a principled life that sought to balance study and political engagement. Born in Narbonese Gaul, her father was an imperial official named Julius Proculus. She married Julius Graecinus, an equestrian and student of philosophy. Her husband became a senator under the emperor Tiberius and attained the office of praetor. In 40 C.E., already irritated with him because of his interest in philosophy, the emperor Gaius Caligula had Graecinus executed when he refused to accuse Marcus Junius Silanus of treason.

In the same year, Julia Procilla gave birth to a son, Gnaeus Julius Agricola. After the death of her husband, she returned with her son to Massilia (Marseilles), where she attended to his education. Later, Agricola's son-in-law, the great Roman historian Cornelius Tacitus, would write that Agricola would have immersed himself in philosophy had his mother not wisely tempered this inclination and arranged that he also study more practical arts.

Her son became quaestor of Asia, tribune, praetor, consul, and later legate of Britain. In 69 Julia Procilla was murdered on her estate by plundering sailors of the insurgent emperor Otho. The estate itself was looted and a good part of Agricola's inheritance was lost.

Tac., Agr. 4.7.

▣ JULIA SOAEMIAS BASSIANA

(2nd century–222 C.E.) Roman: Syria and Italy

Augusta

Julia Soaemias Bassiana successfully plotted to make her son emperor. She was the elder of JULIA MAESA's two daughters. Her father was Julius Avitus and her grandfather was Julius Bassianus, priest of the sun-god at Emesa in Syria. She married Sextus Varius Marcellus, an equestrian from Apamea in Syria who died leaving her with a son, Varius Avitus.

Julia Soaemias conspired with her mother to have her young son challenge the rule of Macrinus, who had supplanted Marcus Aurelius Antoninus Caracalla as emperor. Caracalla had been her cousin; his mother was her aunt, JULIA DOMNA. Julia Soaemias and her mother had lived with them in Rome. After Caracalla's death the women were expelled. Using the large fortune her mother had accumulated during the reigns of Septimius Severus and Caracalla, she gained support from the troops in Syria after she declared that her son was the child of Caracalla and the legitimate heir. Gannys, who was her lover and her son's tutor, and an army soldier named Comazon were her coconspirators in the army camp who rallied the troops to her cause. The defeated Macrinus fled and was murdered on the way to Rome.

Avitus, the hereditary priest of the sun-god Elagabalus at Emesa in Syria, became Emperor

Elagabalus in 218 C.E. He was 15 years old. Immediately he assumed all the titles of the office without regard for custom, which assigned to the Roman Senate the right to bestow the offices and titles of the emperor. Julia Soaemias, her son, her mother, her sister JULIA AVITA MAMAEA, Gannys and Comazon, and their supporters traveled to Rome. Elagabalus carried with him the black conical stone image of the sun-god. In Nicomedea, Elagabalus murdered Gannys after he attempted to temper the young emperor's behavior.

When the party reached Rome a year later, in July 219, Elagabalus heaped honors on his mother. She was named Augusta and called Mater Augustorum (Mother of Augustus) and Mater Castrorum (Mother of the Encampment). Elagabalus reputedly brought her into the Senate chamber. She also presided over a female senate that issued a set of rules of etiquette for women, including clothing to be worn in public and proper means of conveyance. Elagabalus's behavior became increasingly erratic and scandalous as he married and divorced a number of women including JULIA CORNELIA PAULA and the Vestal Virgin JULIA AQUILIA SEVERA. Julia Soaemias, who enjoyed her lifestyle, made no attempt to curb her son.

Her mother, Julia Maesa, determined that Elagabalus and her daughter must be removed before his troops revolted. She hatched a plot with her younger daughter, Julia Mamaea, to replace Elagabalus with Alexianus, Julia Mamaea's son. Julia Maesa first persuaded Elagabalus, who was 16, to adopt Alexianus, who was 12. When Elagabalus began to suspect a plot, Julia Maesa and Julia Mamaea had soldiers of the Praetorian Guard murder him and Julia Soaemias in Rome in 222. Their bodies were stripped naked and dragged all over Rome. Alexianus, who was 13, was proclaimed the new emperor, but power remained in the hands of the women, Julia Mamaea and her mother.

Dio. 79.30.2–4, 38.4; 80.3–6, 20.2.
Herodian 5.3.3, 8.8–10.

Balsdon., J. P. V. D., pp. 156–62.
OCD, p. 778.
PW 596.

JUNIA (1)

(1st century B.C.E.)   Roman: Rome
Conspirator

Junia was one of three daughters born to SERVILIA (1) and Decimus Junius Silanus, consul in 63 and 62 B.C.E. Her sisters were JUNIA (2) and JUNIA TERTIA. Her mother had been the lover of Julius Caesar, and her uncle was the republican Marcus Porcius Cato Uticensis. Her half brother was Marcus Junius Brutus, one of Caesar's assassins. Her father was dead by 57 B.C.E., and her forceful mother who wielded power by virtue of her personality and connections, arranged marriages for all three sisters. Shortly after 61, Junia married Marcus Aemilius Lepidus, consul in 46 and, along with Antony and Octavian, a member of the Second Triumvirate. She had two sons, Marcus and Quintus.

Her husband was removed from office by Octavian, and Octavian's general, Gaius Maecenas, prosecuted her son Marcus for plotting to assassinate Octavian on his return to Rome in 30 B.C.E. He sent Marcus to Octavian in Actium, where he was executed. Maecenas also charged Junia, claiming that she was aware of the plot. To spare her the trip to Actium, Maecenas demanded surety that she would appear before Octavian when he came to Rome. Her husband went to the consul suffectus, Lucius Saenius, to put himself up as security for his wife or else be allowed to accompany her to Actium. The consul released Junia. Whether she subsequently made peace with Octavian or died is unrecorded.

App., Bciv. 4.50.
PW 193.
Syme, R., *Augustan Aristocracy*, pp. 19, 35.

◻ JUNIA (2)

(1st century B.C.E.)   Roman: Rome
Political player

Junia was one of three daughters born to SERVILIA (1) and her second husband, Decimus Junius Silanus, consul in 63–62 B.C.E. The other two were JUNIA (1) and JUNIA TERTIA. Marcus Junius Brutus, the tyrannicide, was her half brother, and the republican Marcus Porcius Cato Uticensis, her uncle. Although her father died in 57, her mother was well able to care for her. One of the most politically astute women of her day, Servilia and Julius Caesar had been lovers, remained friends, and traded favors.

Junia married Publius Servilius Isauricus, consul in 48 B.C.E. and a supporter of Julius Caesar. He was a good choice. A careful man, he navigated a narrow course through the political conflicts after the death of Caesar. Marcus Tullius Cicero, who did not trust him, tried to win him over, but he claimed family obligations. Related to the tyrannicides not only through Junia's half brother Brutus but also through two brothers-in-law, Gaius Cassius Longinus and Marcus Aemilius Lepidus, he sought a conciliatory role. He might even have entertained the idea of serving as a mediator between Caesarians and the republicans, which his mother-in-law, Servilia, would have welcomed.

Junia gave birth to a son and a daughter. Her daughter, SERVILIA (3), was to have married the young Octavian in 43 B.C.E. when her uncle, Marcus Aemilius Lepidus, was part of the Second Triumvirate with Octavian and Antony. Octavian instead married CLAUDIA (5), the daughter of FULVIA (2) and the stepdaughter of Antony. To placate Junia's husband, Octavian supported him in his successful bid for the consulship for 41. Junia's daughter, Servilia, later married her cousin Marcus Aemilius Lepidus, the son of her sister Junia. Junia's son-in-law was prosecuted by Octavian's intimate friend and supporter Gaius Maecenas for plotting to kill Octavian in 30 B.C.E. and was sent to Actium, where he was executed.

Suet., Aug. 62.1.
PW 192.
Syme, R., *Augustan Aristocracy*, pp. 19, 35.

◻ JUNIA (3)

(1st–2nd century C.E.)   Roman: Rome
Priestess

Junia, a Vestal Virgin, became seriously ill with tuberculosis and had to be removed from the house of the Vestals. The Stoic FANNIA (2) was related to Junia and nursed her. Junia died of the disease. Fannia, who had suffered exile three times, became infected and also died.

Plin., Ep. 7.19.

◻ JUNIA CALVINA

(?–79 C.E.)   Roman: Italy
Long-lived woman

Junia Calvina was the only one of five siblings to die a natural death. Unconventional and beautiful, she was the last direct descendant of the emperor Augustus. Her great-grandmother was Augustus's only daughter, JULIA (6). Her mother was AEMILIA LEPIDA (3) and her father, Marcus Junius Silanus Torquatus, was consul in 19 C.E.

Junia's clear claim on succession by virtue of her ancestry simultaneously made her a desirable marriage partner and left her vulnerable. She married Lucius Vitellius, consul suffectus in 48 C.E., the younger son of a close ally of the emperor Claudius. Divorced for unknown reasons the same year, she was accused by her former father-in-law, Vitellius, of incest with her brother Lucius Junius Silanus Torquatus. The sources attributed the charge to the younger Julia AGRIPPINA, the emperor Claudius's niece, who would become his wife a year later, and who was assiduous in clearing the way for the succession of her son, Nero. Julia Calvina was sent into exile in 49, and her brother committed suicide on the day that Agrippina married Claudius.

Agrippina prevailed, and Nero became emperor. After his mother's death, Nero ended Junia's exile, and she returned to Rome. Her other siblings were not as fortunate. Nero forced her brother Decimus Junius Silanus to commit suicide. Her sister JUNIA LEPIDA was falsely accused of engaging in magical practices and having sexual relations with her nephew, Lucius Junius Silanus. In 79, when the emperor Vespasian was informed on his deathbed that a huge crevice had appeared in the mausoleum of Augustus, he was said to have quipped that it was for Julia Calvina, Augustus's long-lived last descendant.

Suet., Ves. 23.
Tac., Ann. 12.4.8; 14.12.
Balsdon, J. P. V. D., pp. 129–30.
OCD, p. 787.
PW 198.
Syme, R., *Augustan Aristocracy*, index.

JUNIA CLAUDILLA
(1st century C.E.) Roman: Rome
Political wife

Junia Claudilla was the daughter of Marcus Junius Silanus, a noted orator and consul suffectus in 15 C.E. Her sister was JUNIA SILANA. Her mother was unknown. The emperor Tiberius arranged her marriage to Gaius Caligula in 33. She died in childbirth a few years later, before her husband became emperor. In 38, Caligula forced her father to commit suicide.

Suet., Calig. 6.20.1; 12.1–2.
Levick, B., *Tiberius*, pp. 207, 215.
PW 199.

JUNIA LEPIDA
(1st century C.E.) Roman: Italy
Political player

Junia Lepida, one of five siblings, including JUNIA CALVINA, who were the last generation of direct descendants of the emperor Augustus, was a victim of the struggle for succession to the emperor Claudius. Her mother, AEMILIA LEPIDA (3), was the great-granddaughter of Augustus, and her father, Marcus Julius Silanus Torquatus, was an orator of note and consul in 19 C.E.

She married the eminent jurist Cassius Longinus, consul suffectus in 30 C.E. In 65 the emperor Nero accused her of engaging in magical practices and having sexual relations with her nephew Lucius Junius Silanus. He also charged her nephew and husband with treason.

Silanus was murdered before his exile took place, and her husband was exiled to Sardinia. He was later recalled by the emperor Vespasian. Nothing more is known about Junia.

Tac., Ann. 16.8.
PW 203.
Syme, R., *Augustan Aristocracy*, index.

JUNIA SILANA
(?–c. 59 C.E.) Roman: Italy
Political player

Junia Silana was both beautiful and of noble lineage. Under three different emperors she took part in the battles waged among the elite over power, prestige, and succession. She was the daughter of Marcus Junius Silanus, consul suffectus in 15 C.E. Her sister, JUNIA CLAUDILLA, married the young Gaius Caligula probably in 30 or 31 and died in childbirth a few years later. Caligula forced her father to commit suicide in 38. After Claudius became emperor in 48, she married Gaius Silius, consul designate and considered one of the handsomest men in Rome.

Her marriage was destroyed by the relationship between her husband and Valeria MESSALLINA, wife of the emperor. Messallina and Silius may have been allies in a conspiracy to supplant Claudius. The powerful freedmen around Claudius, led by Narcissus, convinced the emperor of their nefarious intent, and the lovers were seized and executed.

Junia was a close friend of the younger Julia AGRIPPINA who followed Messallina as the wife of

Claudius and who was intent upon her son Nero's succession to the emperor. She broke with Agrippina, however, when the latter told the young Sextius Africanus, whom the widowed Junia wanted to marry, that Junia was both immoral and too old. Gossip had it that Agrippina was not interested in Africanus but hoped to keep Junia a widow so that she might inherit her estate.

Junia found an opportunity for revenge. In 55, when Nero began to tire of his mother's domination, Junia arranged for Nero to suspect Agrippina of conspiracy. She had two of her clients tell Atimetus, a freedman of Nero's aunt DOMITIA, that Agrippina was plotting with Rubellius Plautus against Nero. Domitia had ample cause to share Junia's hated of Agrippina. Agrippina, the widow of Domitia's brother, had persuaded Domitia's husband, consul in 44 C.E., to divorce his wife so that he could marry her. She was also responsible for the execution of Domitia's sister, DOMITIA LEPIDA.

Junia's revenge failed. Nero was prepared to order his mother's death but was persuaded to allow Agrippina to defend herself. A delegation was sent to Agrippina, who convinced them of her innocence. The accusers, including Junia Silana, were exiled in 55. In 59 Nero lifted her exile, but she died in Tarentum (modern Taranto) before she could return to Rome.

Suet., Calig. 12.
Tac., Ann. 11.12; 13.19–21.
Balsdon, J. P. V. D., pp. 120–21.
Bauman, R. A., pp. 196–98.
PW 205.
Syme, R., *Augustan Aristocracy,* index.

🔲 JUNIA TERTIA

(73 B.C.E.–22 C.E.)   Roman: Italy
Political player

Junia Tertia outlived her enemies and supporters alike, dying at age 95 in the reign of the emperor Tiberius. The youngest of three sisters, her parents were SERVILIA (1) and Decimus Junius Silanus, consul in 62 B.C.E. Her father died by 57, but her mother played a significant part in the politics before and after the assassination of Julius Caesar. Her mother arranged her marriage with Gaius Cassius Longinus, later one of Caesar's assassins. They had a son who assumed the *toga virilis* on the Ides of March in 44 B.C.E.

Despite a recent miscarriage, Junia Tertia was present at a meeting at Antium on June 8, 44 B.C.E., called and presided over by her mother, who was acknowledged to have once been the lover and still a friend of the recently slain Caesar. Also present were Junia's husband, Cassius; Marcus Tullius Cicero; her half brother Brutus; and his wife PORCIA, the daughter of Marcus Porcius Cato Uticensis and a cousin of Junia. The meeting was called to decide on a response to the Senate's offer to appoint Brutus and Cassius supervisors for the collection of corn taxes in the provinces of Asia and Sicily. It provided an honorable way for them to escape the city in the aftermath of Caesar's assassination. Cicero argued that the offer should be accepted; Brutus was undecided and Cassius contemptuous. No decision was taken, but Servilia declared that she would see to it that the offer was withdrawn.

Junia's husband, Cassius, committed suicide in 42 B.C.E. after his camp was captured at Philippi by the troops of Antony and Octavian. She never remarried and died a very wealthy widow in 22 C.E. She left legacies to almost every important patrician. Although she did not mention the emperor Tiberius, he allowed a splendid celebration of her funeral. Emblems of 20 great republican houses were carried in the funeral procession.

Cic., Att. 14.20.2; 15.11.1.
Macrob., Sat. 2.2; 5.
Tac., Ann. 3.76.
PW 206.
Syme, R., *Augustan Aristocracy,* index.
Syme, R., *Roman Revolution,* pp. 69, 116, 492.

▣ JUNIA TORQUATA

(1st century B.C.E.–1st century C.E.)
Roman: Rome
Priestess

Junia Torquata was a Vestal Virgin for 64 years and served as the head of the Vestal college for much of that time. Considered a woman of exemplary virtue, she lived a more fortunate life than did her siblings. She was born into a noble family, probably the daughter of Appia Claudia and Junius Silanus, about whom little is known.

In 8 C.E., her brother Junius Silanus was charged with an adulterous relationship with JULIA (7), the granddaughter of the aging emperor Augustus. He went into voluntary exile. In 20, her brother Marcus used his influence with the emperor Tiberius to allow Junius's return to Rome. Two years later, her brother Gaius Silanus was accused of extortion and treason. Found guilty, he was exiled.

Junia intervened with the emperor. Tiberius requested of the Senate that Gaius Silanus be sent to the island of Cythnus rather than the bleak and uninhabited island of Gyaruss. The Senate acquiesced and also approved a motion supported by Tiberius that any property of Silanus that came from his mother should not be confiscated but given to his son.

Tac., Ann. 3.69.
Syme, R., *Augustan Aristocracy,* pp. 193, 196.

L

▣ LABDA

(7th century B.C.E.) Greek: Corinth
Heroine

Labda was said to have lived during the seventh century B.C.E. in Corinth, which had been captured by Dorian Greeks invading from the north during the previous century. Her father was Amphion from the clan of the Bacchiadae, the first Dorian rulers. She married Eetion, one of the conquered Lapithi.

Her husband consulted the oracle at Delphi since he had not yet fathered a son. The priestess foretold that Labda would have a son who would conquer Corinth. Her family saw the prophecy as a message of their downfall. They sent 10 men to kill the son Labda had delivered. Labda allowed them into the house to admire the child, who beguiled them. They returned with the intention of kidnapping the boy. Labda overheard their plans. She successfully hid the baby in a bin. The would-be assassins returned to Corinth and claimed that the child had been killed.

Her son Cypselus overthrew the Bacchiadae and became tyrant of Corinth (c.657–625 B.C.E.).

Hdt. 5.92.
OCD, p. 420–21.

▣ LAELIA

(2nd–1st century B.C.E.) Roman: Rome
Orator

Laelia was an elegant speaker. Her father was Gaius Laelius, consul in 140 B.C.E. and one of the greatest orators of his time. After the Punic Wars, the study of Greek literature and philosophy spread among the educated elite of Rome. Laelia's family became patrons of literature and art. Her father taught her rhetoric. Laelia married Quintus Mucius Scaevola, an outstanding orator and consul in 117 B.C.E. He taught Marcus Tullius Cicero who compared Laelia favorably with her father. Years later, the great rhetorician Quintilian also praised her.

Laelia's daughter, MUCIA and her granddaughters LICINIA (1) and LICINIA (2) were also elegant rhetoricians.

Cic., ad Brut. 58.211–12.
Quint., Inst. 1.1, 6.
Bauman, R. A., pp. 47–48.

◫ LAÏS

(5th–4th century B.C.E.) Greek: Sicily,
Corinth, and Thessaly
Self-made woman

Laïs was beautiful. Her mother was Lysandra, a
lover of Alcibiades, the Athenian statesman and
general. When she was seven years old, she and
her mother were brought to Corinth, Greece, as
prisoners after the fortified town of Hycarra in
Sicily fell during the Peloponnesian Wars.

Laïs was said to have been the lover of the famous painter Apelles, although her dates make
the claim improbable. More likely, she followed a
lover to Thessaly, in northern Greece, where she
was said to have died at the hands of women who
feared her beauty. The women were said to have
stoned her after they lured her into the temple of
Aphrodite.

Her tomb beside the river Peneus was said to
have an epitaph that recorded her power to en-
slave the invicible Greeks with her godlike
beauty.

Ath. 13.588c–89b.
Plut., Alc. 39.4–5.
Plut., Mor., Amat. 767f–68b.
Plut., Nicias 15.4.
Licht, H., p. 347.

◫ LAMIA

(4th–3rd century B.C.E.) Cyprian: Cyprus
and Egypt
Flute player

Lamia, a noted flute player, captivated the handsome Macedonian general Demetrius I when she
was taken prisoner in 306 B.C.E., after he defeated
Ptolemy I in a naval battle. No longer young herself, she was said to have been older than
Demetrius.

Plut., Demetr. 16.3–4; 20.4; 27.2–6.

◫ LANASSA

(4th–3rd century B.C.E.) Greek: Syracuse,
Corcyra, and Greece
Political player

Lanassa left her husband, took back her dowry,
and then offered herself in marriage to the ruler of
Macedonia. She was the daughter of Agathocles,
the tyrant of Syracuse, on the island of Sicily. She
married Pyrrhus, the great general and ruler of
Epirus in northwestern Greece. As her dowry, she
had been given the large island of Corcyra (modern Corfu) off the coast of Greece in the Ionian
Sea.

She became disenchanted with Pyrrhus, who
had taken another wife, and left Epirus for
Corcyra. In 292 or 291 B.C.E. she offered to marry
the handsome Demetrius I, ruler of Macedonia,
and to bring him Corcyra as a dowry. The offer
was too good to refuse. She became one of
Demetrius's wives. In 288, her new husband was
defeated by her former husband and the general
Lysimachus. Demetrius fled to Asia. He died five
years later, in 283 B.C.E.

Lanassa had a son, Alexander, by her first husband.

Plut., Pyrrh. 9.1; 10.5.
Macurdy, G., pp. 66–67.

◫ LAODICE I

(3rd century B.C.E.) Greek: Syria and
Asia Minor
Ruler

Laodice fought for power for herself and her sons
in the tumultuous generations following the
death of Alexander the Great in 323 B.C.E. Her
grandfather Seleucus founded the Seleucid Empire, encompassing Asia Minor and western Asia.
Her father was Achaeus, Seleucus's younger son.
The older son, Antiochus I, became ruler after her
grandfather's death. She married his son and her
cousin, Antiochus II. She had two sons, Seleucus

Callinicus and Antiochus Hierax, and two daughters, Stratonice and Laodice.

Her husband repudiated her in 252 B.C.E. to marry BERENICE SYRA, the daughter of Ptolemy II Philadelphus of Egypt. The match secured for him the friendship of Ptolemy, the return of previously lost territories, and Berenice's dower wealth. He named Berenice's son his heir. To appease Laodice, Antiochus gave her estates near the cities of Babylon and Borsippa. Laodice, who was very wealthy even before her former husband's settlement, moved herself and her children to Ephesus, which became a second royal center. In time, Laodice enticed Antiochus to Ephesus and persuaded him to abandon Berenice. The elderly Antiochus died in 246, possibly poisoned by Laodice, soon after he had named her son his successor.

Laodice and Berenice fought to control the empire. Berenice had supporters in Antioch and some of the towns of Syria. She requested aid from her father in Egypt. Laodice arranged to have Berenice's son kidnapped. Berenice pursued the kidnappers on a chariot and killed one with a stone. Faced with a hostile crowd, the kidnappers produced a child. Without relinquishing him, they claimed he was the son of Berenice. Berenice withdrew to a palace in Daphne, a suburb of Antioch, with a guard of Galatian troops. Laodice, afraid of the arrival of Egyptian forces, had her murdered despite the efforts of Berenice's women retainers to shield her with their bodies.

Ptolemy III Euergetes I, Berenice's brother, had in the meantime succeeded their father in Egypt. He arrived too late to save his sister, but the events precipitated the Third Syrian War (246–241). At this point, Laodice and her son moved their court to Sardis away from the coast of Asia Minor. They left Ephesus governed by Sophron, the lover of DANAE, Laodice's favorite woman retainer. For an unknown reason, Laodice became disenchanted with Sophron and summoned him to Sardis. Danae warned him, and he succeeded in winning enough time to escape. He offered himself to Ptolemy and became a com-

mander in the Egyptian fleet. Laodice killed Danae for her treachery.

Although Ptolemy made some important gains in Asia Minor, Laodice and her son Seleucus II successfully organized resistance to the invasion. While Seleucus fought to regain his territories in 245 B.C.E., he left his brother Antiochus Hierax, who was still a minor, in Sardis in Asia Minor. When Seleucus requested reinforcements, Laodice, who favored her younger son, had the troops sent on condition that Hierax became the coruler of the Seleucid Empire in Asia Minor.

Laodice's end is not recorded. Her two sons, however, became so weakened by fighting each other that they lost control of most of their territory.

App., Syr. 65.
Ath. 13.593c.
Just. 27.
Plin. NH 7.53.
Polyaenus, Strat. 8.50.
Val. Max. 9.10.1.
Bevan, E. B., pp. 181 ff.
Cary, M., pp. 86–88, 109, 369, 395–99.
Downey, G., pp. 87ff.
Macurdy, G., pp. 82–90.
OCD, p. 814.
CAH, pp. 715 ff.

LAODICE III

(3rd–2nd century B.C.E.) Persian: Asia Minor and Asia
Philanthropist

Laodice III was generous and supported worthy causes throughout the Seleucid Empire. Born the daughter of Mithradates II, the ruler of Pontus in northern Asia Minor, she was married with great pomp and ceremony in 221 B.C.E. to Antioch III. Her husband, a descendant of Seleucus I, who had fought under Alexander the Great, reigned over territory from Anatolia, Syria, and Babylonia into central Asia.

Laodice established dowries for the daughters of the poor. After her husband conquered the city of Caria in Asia Minor, she granted 10 years of corn to its inhabitants at a fixed price, which prevented profiteering. Her husband established a priesthood in her honor, and civic cults honoring her were founded in several cities. Her two sons were Seleucus IV and Antiochus IV, and her daughter, CLEOPATRA I (THE SYRIAN), married Ptolemy V Epiphanes of Egypt.

Poly. 5.43.1–4.
Macurdy, G., pp. 91–93.
OCD, pp. 814–15.
Pomeroy, S. B., *Women in Hellenistic Egypt*, pp. 15–16.

⌘ LASTHENEIA

(4th century B.C.E.) Greek: Greece
Philosopher

Lastheneia came from the city of Mantinea in the Peloponnese, the peninsula in southern Greece. She studied philosophy with Plato and his successor, Speusippus, at the Academy in Athens. She was reputed to have sometimes dressed like a man.

Diog. Laert. 3.46.
Hawley, R., pp. 74, 81–82.

⌘ LEAENA

(6th century B.C.E.) Greek: Athens
Brave woman

Leaena was the lover of Aristogeiton. In 514 B.C.E. Aristogeiton and Harmodius, both members of an ancient Athenian clan, attempted to murder Hippias, the tyrant of Athens, and his younger brother Hipparchus. Harmodius and Hipparchus were killed in the struggle. Hippias was unharmed, and his guards seized Aristogeiton.

Hippias tortured Leaena, but she refused to betray her lover. She died. Aristogeiton, also tortured, was executed. A bronze lioness was later erected in Leaena's honor at the entrance to the Acropolis.

Paus. 23.1–2.
Plin., NH 7.23, 87.

⌘ LEONTION

(4th–3rd century B.C.E.) Greek: Athens
Philosopher

Leontion was a philosopher and companion of the philosopher Epicurus at his school in Athens. Leontion's philosophical writings rivaled those of Theophrastus, the student, collaborator, and ultimately successor to Aristotle. She and Metrodorus (330–277 B.C.E.), another disciple of Epicurus, became lovers. They had a son named after Epicurus and a daughter, DANAE.

In his will, Epicurus ordered his trustees to provide for the children's maintenance, to give Danae a dowry, and when she came of age to find a member of the Epicurean school for her to marry.

Ath. 593c–d
Diog. Laert. 10.19–21, 23.
Sen., Ep. 52.3.
Hawley, R., pp. 74, 80–81.
Pomeroy, S. B., *Goddesses*, p. 141.

⌘ LICINIA (1)

(?–154 B.C.E.) Roman: Rome
Convicted murderer

Licinia and PUBLILIA (1) were convicted in 154 B.C.E. of poisoning their husbands, both of whom were ex-consuls. Licinia's husband was Claudius Asellus. Licinia assigned the property she owned to the praetor as surety for her presence in the city after she was charged. After her conviction, she was turned over to her family and put to death.

Livy 48.
Val. Max. 6.3.7.
Baumann, R. A., p. 39.
PW 178.

▣ LICINIA (2)

(2nd century B.C.E.)   Roman: Rome
Reformer

Licinia was the elder daughter of Publius Licinius Crassus Dives Mucianus, a wealthy expert in Roman law, a noted orator, and consul in 131 B.C.E. Her family was part of the circle around the Gracchi that demanded tax and land reform. Her sister LICINIA (3) married Gaius Sempronius Gracchus, strengthening the families' political ties.

Licinia married quite young in 143 B.C.E. Her husband was Gaius Sulpicius Galba, also a supporter of the Gracchi. From 121 to 119 he served on the land commission that Gaius Gracchus had established at Carthage. In 110 he was condemned for corruption during the Jugurthine War in Numidia, North Africa. Nothing more is known of Licinia.

Cic., Brut. 82, 85–90
OCD, p. 1454.
PW 179.
Richardson, K., pp. 41, 180.

▣ LICINIA (3)

(2nd century B.C.E.)   Roman: Rome
Reformer

Licinia, the younger daughter of Publius Licinius Crassus Dives Mucianus, a noted legal expert, orator, and consul in 131 B.C.E., participated in the violent struggle for land and tax reform. Her family was a political ally of the Gracchi, and her marriage with Gaius Sempronius Gracchus had probably been arranged since her childhood. Married to him in 133 B.C.E., she brought to the union a significant dowry from her wealthy family. She had an older sister, LICINIA (2).

Determined to carry forward the reforms of his brother Tiberius, her husband was elected tribune in 123 and 122. He passed a series of measures that included land distribution, subsidies for wheat, the establishment of new colonies for citi-

zens, and public works. The measures reflected efforts to address the simultaneous problems of an increasing class of landless citizens and the inflation that accompanied their settling in the city. Opposition to him and to the reforms he represented, however, was strong. His proposal to grant citizenship to people of Italy outside Rome was defeated, and he lost the election for tribune in 121.

As his opponents moved to overturn the most objectionable of the reforms, a skirmish occurred in which one person was killed. The Senate summoned Gaius to the Forum. Licinia was fearful he would be assassinated, as had been his brother before him. Her fears were well founded: Gaius was murdered in the Forum.

After Gaius's murder in 121, his enemies sought to destroy his allies. They pursued Licinia through attacks on her property. Her wealth was saved by the efforts of her uncle the eminent jurist Publius Mucius Scaevola. However, to recover her dowry, her uncle was forced to publicly disavow her husband and lay responsibility on him for the riot in which he was killed.

Plut., G. Gracch. 21.1–2; 15.2, 5; 17.5.
PW 180.
Richardson, K., pp. 114, 187–89.

▣ LICINIA (4)

(?–113 B.C.E.)   Roman: Rome
Priestess

Licinia, Vestal Virgin and daughter of Gaius Crassus, tribune in 145 B.C.E., challenged authority. In 123 she dedicated an altar, oratory, and sacred couch at the temple of the Bona Dea. The praetor, Sextus Julius Caesar, protested that she had no prior authorization to do such a thing. The Senate sent the case to the pontifices, who ruled the donations unsanctified and ordered them removed.

In 114, a slave charged three Vestal Virgins with illicit behavior. AEMILIA (1) was accused of having an affair with an equestrian, L. Veturius. Licinia and MARCIA (1) were said to have had relationships at Aemilia's instigation with her lover's friends. Aemilia was condemned, but the *pontifex maximus* Lucius Caecilius Metellus found the two others innocent. Then a special *quaestio* (investigation) was called, over which Lucius Cassius Longinus Ravilla presided. Licinia's cousin Lucius Licinius Crassus, an outstanding orator, defended them, but to no avail. Both were condemned to death.

Cic., Brut. 43.160.
Cic., Dom. 53.136.
Dio. 26.fr.87.
Livy 43.
Oros. 5.15, 20–22.
Plut., De fort. Rom. 83.
Bauman, R. A., pp. 52 ff.

▣ LICINIA (5)
(1st century B.C.E.) Roman: Rome
Elegant conversationalist

Licinia was noted for the elegance of her speech. She was part of a family for whom conversation was a practiced art. Her mother, MUCIA, and her grandmother LAELIA had also been regarded as elegant conversationalists. Her grandfather was the famous orator Gaius Laelius, and she was the elder daughter of Lucius Licinius Crassus, a well-known orator and consul in 95 B.C.E.

Licinia married Publius Scipio Nasica, praetor in 93. Her sister LICINIA (6) married the son of the general Gaius Marius. Cicero praised both women for the beauty and precision of their conversation.

Cic., Brut. 211–12.
PW 183.

▣ LICINIA (6)
(1st century B.C.E.) Roman: Rome
Elegant conversationalist

Licinia, the younger daughter of MUCIA and the famous orator Lucius Licinius Crassus, consul in 95 B.C.E., was born into a family whose members were famous for their elegant conversation.

Licinia and her sister LICINIA (5) were admired for their speaking abilities. They both took after their mother and grandmother LAELIA.

Licinia married Gaius Marius, the son of the great general Gaius Marius, consul seven times. Her husband was offered the consulship of 82 after his father's death. His mother, JULIA (1), urged him to reject the office. She feared he was being used by the Marians against the dictator Lucius Cornelius Sulla. Her fears were well founded. After a defeat by Sulla, he committed suicide.

Cic., Att. 12.49.1.
Cic., Brut. 211–12.
PW 184.

▣ LICINIA (7)
(1st century B.C.E.) Roman: Rome
Priestess

Licinia, a Vestal Virgin and a member of the aristocratic Licinii, was accused in 73 B.C.E. of immoral behavior with her cousin Marcus Licinius Crassus. Both were subsequently found innocent.

Crassus had spent time with Licinia in private to persuade her to sell him a villa she owned in the suburbs of Rome at a price less than its true value. The immensely wealthy Crassus, who had made a fortune buying property cheaply during the Sullan proscriptions, was renowned for his eagerness to acquire more. He eventually bought the land. The attack on Licinia was probably led by Crassus's enemies.

Plut., Crass. 1.4ff.
Balsdon, J. P. V. D., p. 239.
PW 185.

▣ LIVIA
(?–92 B.C.E.) Roman: Rome
Political wife

Livia married twice, and each marriage produced a child important in the history of the Roman revolution. She was the daughter of Marcus Livius

Drusus, consul in 112 B.C.E. In 104, she married Quintus Servilius Caepio, praetor in 91, and gave birth to two daughters, SERVILIA (1), who became the lover and friend of Julius Caesar, and SERVILIA (2), and a son, Gnaeus Servilius Caepio. Divorced around 98 B.C.E. because of a quarrel between her brother and her husband, she married Marcus Porcius Cato in 96. They had a daughter, Porcia, and a son, Marcus Porcius Cato Uticensis, who became one of the republican leaders against Caesar. Livia's second husband died just before the wars in Italy, and she died shortly thereafter in 92 B.C.E.

OCD, p. 1,394.
PW 35.
Syme, R., *Augustan Aristocracy*, p. 25.

🔲 LIVIA DRUSILLA

(January 30, 58 B.C.E.–29 C.E.) Roman: Italy
Power broker

Livia was the most important woman of her time. Her character, discretion, and intellect complemented her strategic skills and were enhanced by the advantage of a long life. She spanned the period before the onset of civil war, through the reign of her husband Augustus and much of that of her son Tiberius. In her household were nurtured many of the enmities and alliances that shaped the first 50 years of the empire, and her travels and correspondence with friends and clients spread her reach across the Roman world. Her reception rooms were always filled with visitors and petitioners. Her household, which sometimes encompassed 1,000 people or more, included multiple generations of children, grandchildren, nieces and nephews, more distant kin and clients of the extended Julio-Claudian families.

Born on January 30, 58 B.C.E., she was the daughter of Marcus Livius Drusus Claudianus, from the illustrius Claudian clan, and Alfidia, the daughter of a rich councillor from the Italian city of Fundi. Livia's father lived well into the years of the civil war and fought against Mark Antony and Octavian. He killed himself after the defeat of Marcus Brutus and Gaius Cassius at Philippi in 42 B.C.E.

Livia married twice. Her first husband, whom she married at the age of 15 or 16, in 43 or 42 B.C.E., was Tiberius Claudius Nero, quaestor in 48 and a distant relative. She gave birth on November 16, 42 B.C.E. to Tiberius, the future emperor. Her husband's political allegiance followed a not-too-unusual course for the times. A republican and a supporter of Caesar, he commanded Caesar's fleet in the Alexandrian War in 47 B.C.E. After Caesar's death, however, he called for special honors for the assassins. In 41, he sided with Antony against Octavian. In 40, as part of the Perusine war, he attempted to ignite a slave revolt in Campania. When the war failed, he fled from Rome and Octavian with Livia and their infant son. In Sicily he joined the friendly Sextus Pompeius. After a falling-out with Pompeius, he rejoined Antony in Achaea. He, along with Livia and their young son, returned to Rome in 39 after the Pact of Misenum secured peace under the Second Triumvirate. In that same year, Livia became pregnant with her second child.

She also began an affair with Octavian. How it started remains unclear. That it quickly became notorius, however, is well attested. In a society reeling with the social dislocations of civil war, it was still a flagrant violation of tradition for the pregnant Livia to live openly with Octavian while both were divorcing their respective spouses. Octavian divorced SCRIBONIA on the day she gave birth to his only child, JULIA (6). He sought an opinion from the college of pontifices about contracting a marriage with the still-pregnant Livia. They ruled in his favor. Perhaps there was little else they could do except to accept the new marriage but to establish that Tiberius Claudius Nero was the legitimate father of the unborn child. Gossip about the behavior of both Octavian and Livia reached epic proportions. On January 28, 38 B.C.E. Livia's first husband presided over the wedding feast.

After the birth of Livia's second son, Nero Claudius Drusus, both boys went to live with their father to avoid further scandal. Shortly thereafter, their father died and left Octavian guardian. The boys moved back into Livia's household. The three months between the birth, death, and the return of the boys to their mother kept tongues wagging. Again in 36 during a food shortage in Rome, the couple caused scandalous gossip when they tastelessly hosted a banquet for the gods. Subsequently they changed their image: Livia adopted a modest persona and her unconventional move from one husband to another faded into history, while Octavian's future sexual exploits never again exceeded what was considered acceptable among the aristocracy. The two became a model Roman husband and wife and remained married for 50 years, until the death of the emperor in 14 C.E. Over the course of the next decades the memory of their union's notorious beginning so faded that years later, when Augustus meted out harsh punishments to his daughter and granddaughter for their adulterous behavior, nary an eyebrow was raised in remembrance of the past.

After their marriage, even before Octavian became Augustus, Livia's elevated status was clear. In 35 B.C.E., Livia and Octavian's independent-minded sister OCTAVIA (2) were accorded the status of *tribunica sanctissima,* which made any assault upon their person as if an attack on the state. Never previously held by a woman nor ever again, it was probably Octavian's intention to protect Octavia from her husband Antony, and it would not have been politic to exclude Livia. The office also gave the women independent authority over property and wealth. Then in 18 and 9 B.C.E., with the passage of the Julian laws, which Livia supported, she was granted rights that released her from any form of even token male guardianship. In one of those ironies of history, had those same laws been in effect at the onset of their affair, both Livia and Octavian would have been sent into exile on different islands for adultery and much of their wealth confiscated. Moreover, instead of hosting their wedding, her first husband could have been prosecuted for pandering. No less ironic, these same laws were the basis for Augustus's later exile of his daughter and granddaughter.

A wealthy woman to begin with, Livia managed people and property well. Her alliances with other women, many of whom were also influential in the public and private affairs of the period, constituted a circle within which she did business and traded favors. Some were her peers, like her sister-in-law Octavia. Some were clients from abroad like SALOME, the sister of Herod the Great, who bequeathed to Livia the towns of Jamnia, Phasaelis, and Archelais. Still others were well-born women who sought her influence. She was instrumental in having the son of her close friend URGULANIA made consul in 2 B.C.E. She probably had a hand in the marriage of the future emperor Claudius to PLAUTIA URGULANILLA, granddaughter of Urgulania. In 16 C.E., when the senator Lucius Piso obtained a summons against Urgulania for money owed him and Urgulania refused to pay, it was to Livia's house she went and put herself under her friend's protection.

Livia invited into her house her extended family and clients from abroad. In addition to her own children, Tiberius and Drusus, there were Augustus's daughter Julia and Julia's chidren—twin sons, Gaius Caesar and Lucius Caesar, and two daughters, JULIA (7) and the elder Vipsania AGRIPPINA. After Livia's youngest son, Drusus died in 9 B.C.E., her daughter-in-law, the younger ANTONIA and her three children, Germanicus, Claudius, and Livia Julia Claudia LIVILLA, moved into the household. Gaius Caligula and two of his sisters, JULIA DRUSILLA and JULIA LIVILLA, also lived with Livia for a short time after their mother, the elder Agrippina, was exiled. Marcus Salvius Otho, grandfather of the later emperor Otho, was yet another later political figure who grew up in Livia's household.

Livia and Augustus's relationship joined both family and the affairs of state, and sometimes the two were indistinguishable. The events and arrangements in which she was central ranged from macro state decisions to micro private affairs. Augustus regularly asked her advice. Often he took it. After a plot was uncovered against him led by Gnaeus Cornelius, a descendant of Pompey the Great, she argued that he could coop the conspirators. It was Livia who persuaded Augustus and Tiberius to implement the arrangements for Claudius, the future emperor who was afflicted with some kind of palsy. In addition there was a steady stream of senators and other officials who came to consult and curry favor. Livia arranged for Marcus Salvius Otho to be made a senator. When Quintus Haterius, whose remarks offended the emperor and who had accidentally knocked down Tiberius, came to apologize, Livia saved him from being executed. She sometimes went beyond the bounds of Augustus's decisions. During his daughter Julia's 20 years of exile she helped Julia.

In all Livia worked unceasingly, especially, to enhance the interests of her family and particularly the future of her own sons. Although Augustus had adopted her children, she faced arrogant opposition from Augustus's Julian relatives who felt their family without peer, and succession to Augustus their birthright. Along with Livia, Octavia and Marcus Vipsanius Agrippa completed Augustus's most intimate circle. Her sister-in-law Octavia, whose household rivaled Livia's in its size and influence, had married her daughter the elder MARCELLA to Agrippa. The links by marriage were further extended through the marriage in 25 B.C.E. of Octavia's son Marcus Claudius Marcellus and Julia, Augustus's daughter.

Succession seemed assured with Agrippa as regent should anything happen too soon for the next generation to assume control. Barely two years later, in 23, Marcellus, the most likely heir, died. Agrippa then divorced Marcella and married Julia, and they had three sons in rapid succession: Lucius Caesar, Gaius Caesar, and Agrippa Postumus, all of them possible heirs to Augustus. Once more the line of succession seemed secure. Years earlier, Livia and Titus Pomponius Atticus,

the very wealthy father-in-law of Agrippa's first wife Caecilia ATTICA, had arranged for the marriage of Livia's son Tiberius with Attica and Agrippa's daughter VIPSANIA AGRIPPINA. They married in 20 or 19 B.C.E. At the time it appeared a desirous union. All during the civil war years there were problems with money, and Atticus had enormous wealth. Agrippa was in his prime, and clearly a family link between Livia and Agrippa could only be advantageous in strengthening both of their positions in the intimate circle around Augustus.

Agrippa died unexpectedly in 12 B.C.E. The three sons born of his second marriage with Julia were adopted by Augustus. The line of succession through the Julians still appeared in place. However, marriage to Julia appeared to be the way to succession, so Tiberius divorced Vipsania and married his stepsister Julia in 11 B.C.E. It seems likely that Livia and Augustus had both agreed to the arrangement, even though it was said that Augustus favored Livia's younger son, Nero Claudius Drusus. In 9 B.C.E. the younger son died from an infection after a fall off his horse.

Livia had successfully used unexpected deaths in the Julian family to place Tiberius in the most advantageous position for succession as regent over her husband's young grandsons, if not as emperor. In 6 B.C.E. Augustus granted Tiberius *tribunicia potestas* (powers of a tribune) for five years and asked him to go to the East on a diplomatic mission. Tiberius, however, had his own views and was not necessarily amenable to the plans of his mother and adoptive father.

Much to Livia's consternation and Augustus's anger, Tiberius insisted that he be allowed to retire to the island of Rhodes. For four days he refused food, and threatened to kill himself if they failed to agree. They agreed, and he left Rome. He walked away from his parents, his wife, and an empire. Tiberius's behavior was outside the bounds of acceptability. In 2 B.C.E., he changed his mind and asked to return to Rome. Augustus refused. Livia persuaded him to appoint Tiberius legate to Rhodes in an attempt to paint over his own involuntary stay on the island. It was, however, another four years, in 2 C.E., before she finally secured Augustus's agreement for Tiberius to return to Rome.

Fate took a hand. In the same year, the cherished grandson of Augustus, Lucius Caesar, died on his way to Spain. A second grandson, Gaius, was wounded and died two years later in 4 C.E. Augustus banished the third grandson, Agrippa Postumus, in the same year. Although a fine physical specimen, his cruelty and ungovernable temper made him clearly unfit to rule. Tiberius alone remained among the possible successors.

Livia's good fortune in her son Tiberius did not pass unnoticed among the elite whose lives were lived in the arena of imperial power. Rumors abounded that Livia was responsible for the deaths of the grandsons and later, even for the death of her partner and husband, Augustus. Augustus fell gravely ill during August 14 C.E. in Nola some 20 miles east of Naples. Livia sent an urgent message to Tiberius, who was on his way to Illyricum (the Balkans), to come to Nola. In the meantime, Livia admitted only a trusted few to Augustus's side. Optimistic bulletins were issued. It is not clear whether Tiberius arrived before or after Augustus's death, but only after his arrival was public notice given that Augustus was dead. His death occurred on August 19, just shy of his 76th birthday. Livia's son and Augustus's adopted son, Tiberius, was named successor.

Agrippa Postumus, the difficult grandson in exile on the island of Planasia, was immediately put to death. It is not known whether Augustus had given prior orders to his close adviser, Gaius Sullustius Crispus, or whether Livia had issued orders for the execution under Augustus's name. Tiberius knew nothing about the execution and decided that the Senate should look into it, but Crispus and Livia persuaded him to drop the matter. In her husband's will, Livia was named Julia Augusta and was adopted into the Julian gens. She was granted exemption from the *lex Voconia*, which limited women's rights to inheritance. Augustus left her one-third of his estate, and her son,

Tiberius, two-thirds. She also became the priestess of her husband's cult after his deification.

Livia had succeeded. She had lived to see her son succeed her husband, and he, anxious perhaps to demonstrate his independence from a mother who had herself become symbolic of the new imperial Rome, was embarrassed by the role she played. Livia assiduously coveted honors that Tiberius foiled. He refused to allow an altar to celebrate her adoption into the Julian clan. Members of the Senate proposed a number of possible titles for Livia, such as *parens patriae* (Parent of her Country) or *mater patriae* (Mother of her Country). Others wanted to add *Iuliae filius* (Son of Julia [Augusta]) to Tiberius's name. Tiberius claimed history had no such honors for women and added that he would also refuse similarly nontraditional honors for himself. He also refused requests that she be granted *lictores*, the traditional attendants who carried fasces, symbols of the legitimacy and inviolability of Roman magistrates.

In public Tiberius and Livia maintained correct relations. Gossip circulated, however, that their private relations were more difficult. Tiberius retired to Capri. Livia remained in Rome. In the next three years, he only visited her once and then only for a few hours. Still, her influence remained significant. She intervened and brought about the acquittal of her friend MUNATIA PLANCINA, who, along with her husband Gnaeus Calpurnius Piso, had been accused of treason after the death of Germanicus Julius Caesar, husband of the elder Agrippina. She also was responsible for advancing the career of Gaius Fufius Geminus, consul in 29 C.E. and the husband of her friend MUTILIA PRISCA, in spite of Tiberius's dislike for him. After Livia's death the two women and Fufius were forced to commit suicide.

Livia died in 29 at the age of 86. Tiberius did not attend her funeral and would not allow her to be deified. He also refused to execute her will in which her largest bequest was to the future emperor Galba, whom she had befriended. Her reach into the future, however, was long. Her eulogy was delivered by her grandson and future emperor, the young Gaius Caligula, who had lived for a short time in his grandmother's house. He called her *Ulixes stolatus*, "Ulysses in skirts." When he became emperor, he executed her will, and when Claudius, who also had lived in her household, became emperor, he deified her.

Dio. 48.15.3–4, 34.3, 44; 49.38.1; 53.33.4; 54.19.3–4; 55.2.5–6, 10a, 10, 14, 1 seq., 32.1–2; 56.30.5–32.1–2, 46.1–3, 47.1; 57.3, 5–6; 57.12; 58.2.1–6; 59.2.3; 60.5.2.
Suet., Aug. 62.2; 63.1; 84.2; 101.2.
Suet., Calig. 10.1; 16.3; 23.2.
Suet., Claud. 1.1; 4; 11.2.
Suet., Galb. 5.2
Suet., Tib. 4.3; 6.1–3; 10.2; 12.1; 13.2; 50.2–3; 51.
Tac., Ann. 1.3–7, 8, 10, 13–14, 33; 2.14, 34, 43, 77, 82; 3.15, 17, 34, 64, 71; 4.8, 12, 16, 21–22, 57, 71; 5.13; 6.5, 26, 29; 12.69.
Bauman, R., index.
Levick, B. *Tiberius*, index.
Marsh, F. B., index.
OCD, p. 876.
PW 37.
Syme, R., *Augustan Aristocracy*, index.
Syme, R., *Roman Revolution*, index.

LIVIA OCELLINA

(1st century C.E.) Roman: Rome
Political player

Livia Ocellina, a wealthy and beautiful woman, married Gaius Sulpicius Galba, consul suffectus in 5 B.C.E. She ignored his short stature and hunchback: After he removed his robe and displayed his body so that she should have no illusions about him, she was said to be even more anxious for the union.

Her husband had previously been married to MUMMIA ACHAICA, the mother of his two children, Gaius and Servius Sulpicius Galba. Livia Ocellina adopted Servius, who took her name and the surname Ocella. Her adopted son grew up to become a favorite of both Augustus and Tiberius. He ruled for a short while during the troubled year of the four emperors then was assassinated in January 69 C.E.

Suet., Galba 3.4; 5.1.

LIVIA ORESTILLA

(1st century C.E.) Roman: Rome
Political victim

Livia Orestilla suffered the consequences of her beauty. She attracted the attention of the emperor Gaius Caligula when she was the wife of the handsome, popular Gaius Calpurnius Piso, a member of a prominent family and an excellent orator. Caligula attended their wedding in 37 C.E., and the sources report that he had the bride taken to his own home. The next day he announced that he had taken a wife in the ancient way. The relationship ended within two months.

In 40, Caligula accused the reunited Livia and Piso of adultery and exiled them. Although there is no further mention of Livia, Piso returned to Rome during the reign of the emperor Claudius.

Dio. 59.8.7–8.
Suet., Calig. 25.1.
Ferrill, A., *Caligula*, p. 108.
PW 42.

LIVILLA, LIVIA JULIA CLAUDIA

(c. 13 B.C.E.–31 C.E.) Roman: Rome
Conspirator

Livilla, sometimes called Livia Julia, died in the struggle to secure succession of her son. Twice widowed by men who were the emperor Tiberius's likely successors, she was the daughter of the younger ANTONIA and Tiberius's brother Nero Claudius Drusus, consul in 9 B.C.E. Born in 13 B.C.E., her great-uncle was the emperor Augustus. One grandmother was the independent-minded OCTAVIA (2), Augustus's sister, and the other, LIVIA DRUSILLA, his wife.

After her father's death in 9, she lived with her mother and brothers in her grandmother Livia's household. In 1 B.C.E. she married Gaius Julius Caesar, the oldest grandson of Augustus, who also had spent part of his youth in Livia's household. Gaius died of battle wounds in 4 C.E. Livilla remarried. Her second husband was Drusus Julius

Caesar, the son of Tiberius. The marriage, which united the Julian and Claudian family lines, provided her husband with a privileged position for succession.

Livilla and Drusus had a daughter, JULIA (8), and years later twin sons, Germanicus and Tiberius Gemellus, born in 19 C.E. Despite her husband's vicious personality and dissolute lifestyle, Livilla expected him to succeed his 65-year-old father. Drusus, however, died in 23 C.E. In the same year one of the twins, Germanicus, also died, leaving Livilla with a grown daughter and a young son—and the issue of succession to Tiberius again unsettled.

Livilla set about to protect her own interests and especially those of her son. Two women opposed her: Her mother, Antonia, sided with Livilla's sister-in-law Agrippina in promoting Gaius Caligula, Agrippina's youngest son, as successor. Although Antonia was well regarded, Tiberius had no love for Agrippina, who was convinced that Tiberius had murdered her husband Germanicus, despite the absence of clear evidence. Devoted to the interest of her children and fearful of Agrippina, Livilla allied herself with Lucius Aelius Sejanus, prefect of the Praetorian Guard in Rome. Tiberius was a military man who had never liked the urban life of Rome. He may also have been tired of dynastic infighting, possibly distressed at his increasingly displeasing appearance, and ready to enjoy other pursuits. He retired to Capri in 26 C.E. and left Sejanus as his eyes and ears in the capital.

Livilla and Sejanus had good reason to join forces. Sejanus could not aspire to the position of emperor—it would be some decades more before a man born outside the charmed circle of the elite could rule. Livilla offered Sejanus the link with the imperial family that only birth could secure. While Tiberius did not view him as a threat, Sejanus already had control over the Praetorian Guard and unique access to the emperor. If not emperor, he could possibly aspire to become regent for the young Tiberius Gemellus, provided the way was clear of other contenders.

In 20 C.E. Livilla's daughter, Julia, had married Nero Julius Caesar, the eldest surviving son of her sister-in-law Agrippina. In 23 C.E., with the death of Livilla's husband, her grown son-in-law was a more likely successor than her still young child. Already quaestor, probably in 26, Nero was intemperate, made rash statements, and openly staked his claim to the empire. Whether with conscious intent to harm or simply the loose tongue of a lover, Livilla passed on to Sejanus information from conversations with her daughter about Nero, whom both mother and daughter disliked.

Sejanus convinced Tiberius that Nero and his mother, Agrippina, were conspiring against the emperor. Tiberius exiled them both. Deported in 29, Nero was executed in 31. Drusus Julius Caesar, Nero's brother and a second son of Agrippina, supported Sejanus's accusation. While Drusus's position had been enhanced with the banishment of his brother, it proved a short-lived advantage. Only a year later, he too was imprisoned.

Gaius Caligula, the remaining son of Agrippina, and Gemellus, the young son of Livilla, were now the two most probable heirs of Tiberius. Caligula was more favorably positioned since he was much older. In 30, however, Sejanus appears to have gained Tiberius's consent for his marriage. It is possible that the planned marriage was not with Livilla, who was about 43 years old, but with her widowed daughter Julia, now around 25. In any case, through either of the unions, he would have moved closer to the imperial family and perhaps Livilla's son would also have moved closer to becoming the heir.

Good fortune ended abruptly; Livilla's downfall followed that of Sejanus. Possibly Caligula convinced Livilla's mother, Antonia, that Sejanus was engaged in a conspiracy. Surely it was not a conspiracy aimed directly against Tiberius, since the latter's immediate death would only have endangered Sejanus's own position. Most likely it was a conspiracy aimed at Caligula, who was the last impediment to the son of Livilla. It remains unclear why Antonia supported Caligula when she must have been aware that the downfall of Sejanus would also bring down her daughter and probably her granddaughter Julia and her grandson Gemellus. Whatever the reasons, she informed Tiberius, and Sejanus was killed, as were his two children. APICATA, the divorced wife of Sejanus, killed herself two days after Sejanus's execution and left a letter for Tiberius in which she accused Sejanus and Livilla of eight years earlier having poisoned Drusus, Livilla's husband and Tiberius's son.

The slaves and attendants of Livilla and Sejanus were tortured. Their "confessions" allowed Tiberius to declare that Sejanus and Livilla had engaged in a conspiracy against the children of Agrippina and Germanicus. After Tiberius heard the case, Livilla was turned over to the custody of her mother, Antonia. She starved herself to death.

Dio. 57.22.1–2; 58.11.6–7.
Suet., Tib. 62.1.
Tac., Ann. 2.43, 84; 4.3, 12, 39–40, 60.
Baumann, R. A., p. 147.
Levick, B., *Tiberius*, index.
Marsh, F. B., index.
OCD, p. 876.
PW 38.
Syme, R., *Augustan Aristocracy*, index.

LOLLIA PAULINA

(1st century C.E.) Roman: Italy
Political player

Lollia Paulina was rich, smart, and beautiful. All three attributes shaped her life. Her father possibly was consul suffectus in 13 C.E., although the family enmity with Tiberius leaves his career open to question. Her mother was Volusia, also of a consular family. Lollia inherited enormous wealth from her grandfather Marcus Lollius, consul in 21 B.C.E., who made the family fortune in spoils from the provinces.

The emperor Caligula was determined to marry Lollia. Her husband, Memmius Regulus, consul in 31 C.E. was in Greece as governor of Moesia and was agreeable to a divorce. She and Caligula married in 38. Lollia had emeralds and pearls of enormous value and beautifully worked to cover her head, hair, ears, neck, and fingers.

She adorned the emperor with her beauty and her jewels, but her wealth and beauty were not sufficient. Caligula divorced her a year later in 39 and forbade her to remarry.

Ten years later, in 48, Lollia was again in the running to become the wife of an emperor. This time it was Claudius. She was supported by Gaius Julius Callistus, one of the influential freedmen of the emperor, on the grounds that she was childless, would remain so, and was therefore a possible stepmother for Claudius's offspring free of any competing claims.

The younger AGRIPPINA's success over Lollia in the competition for Claudius apparently did not sufficiently eliminate the threat Agrippina felt she posed. Moreover, she wanted Lollia's property and jewels. Agrippina charged her with consulting astrologers. Claudius condemned Lollia without a hearing. She was stripped of her vast wealth, except for 5 million sesterces to enable her to live, and was banished in 49 C.E. Agrippina sent a tribune to force Lollia to suicide. As a rebuke to his mother, Agrippina's son, the next emperor Nero, allowed Lollia Paulina's ashes to be brought back to Rome and erected a tomb to house her remains.

Dio. 59.12.1, 23.7; 61.32.4.
Plin., NH 9.57, 117–19.
Suet., Calig. 25.
Tac., Ann. 12.1–2; 14.12.
Bauman, R. A., pp. 181–82.
Levick, B., *Claudius*, pp. 70–71.
OCD, p. 883.
PW 30.
Syme, R., *Augustan Aristocracy*, index.

LUCILIA

(2nd–1st century B.C.E.) Roman: Rome
Mother of Gnaeus Pompeius (Pompey the Great)

Lucilia came from a rich aristocratic family. Her father was a senator, and her uncle Gaius Lucilius, a famous poet and satirist. She married Gnaeus Pompeius Strabo, consul in 89 B.C.E. He was a successful general but had a reputation for cruelty and corruption. He died in an epidemic, and his body was dragged through the streets by the people, who hated him. He and Lucilia had a son, Gnaeus Pompeius (Pompey the Great).

Vell. Pat. 2.29.1 ff.
Syme, R., *Roman Revolution*, p. 28.

▣ LUCILLA, ANNIA AURELIA GALERIA
(148–182 C.E.) Roman: Asia, Africa, Germany, and Rome
Augusta

Annia Aurelia Galeria Lucilla, the daughter of the emperor Marcus Aurelius, organized an unsuccessful conspiracy against her brother, the emperor Commodus. She was born in 148 C.E., the daughter of the younger Annia Galeria FAUSTINA and Marcus Aurelius. Had she been born a son rather than a daughter, she may well have been a worthy successor to her father. Her father became emperor in 161, succeeding Antoninus Pius. In 164 her father arranged her marriage with Lucius Verus, whom he had made co-emperor in 161. The marriage took place in Ephesus, and she was given the title Augusta. She was some 18 years younger then her weak and ineffectual husband who died in 169 on his way back to Rome from the Danube.

Against her will and the wishes of Faustina, Marcus Aurelius immediately had Lucilla marry the much older Tiberius Claudius Pompeianus, a native of Antioch. She was 21, and he was probably over 50. Her new husband was her father's trusted friend and had been a commander in all of his campaigns. His father had been prefect of Egypt, and the family was descended from rulers in the East. Lucilla undoubtedly considered the marriage beneath her and detested the sedentary country life that suited her ailing husband.

Marcus Aurelius died in 180, and was succeeded by his son Commodus, whom he had appointed joint ruler in 177. Commodus treated his

Annia Aurelia Galeria Lucilla

sister Lucilla respectfully. She sat on the imperial seat at the theater and retained other privileges. However, she hated her sister-in-law, CRISPINA BRUTTIA, and recognized her brother's limitations. In 182 Lucilla had uncovered sufficient discontent with her brother's rule to organize a conspiracy for his overthrow. Members of the group included her cousin Ummidius Quadratus; Paternus, who was head of the imperial guard; and, Claudius Pompeianus Quintianus, who was to do the actual stabbing. Pompeianus turned out to be an inept murderer. He was arrested while announcing to Commodus his intention to stab him. Lucilla was banished to Capri and soon afterward killed. Her son, Claudius Pompeianus, was later murdered by the emperor Caracalla.

Dio. 71.1, 3; 73.4.4–5.
Herodian 1.8.3–6, 8; 4.6.3.
SHA, Comm. 4.1, 4; 5.7.
SHA, Marc. 7.7; 9.4; 20.6.–7.6.
Balsdon, J. P. V. D., index.
OCD, p. 99.
PW 123.

🔲 LUCRETIA

(6th century B.C.E.) Roman: Rome
Heroine

Lucretia was a Roman heroine from the early years of the city-state when myth and history were inexorably intertwined. She was the wife of Lucius Tarquinius Collatinus. As the story goes, her husband was present at a dinner in which the men boasted about the virtue of their wives. Among them was Sextus, the son of Tarquinius Superbus, the last king of Rome. After Tarquinius Collatinus claimed no other wife could compare with his, the men agreed to go together to each of their houses to see what the women were doing. The wives were all found to be socializing until they came to Lucretia's residence. She was busily engaged in working with wool, and her servants were busy doing useful tasks, all signs of a virtuous Roman matron. The men agreed that she was the winner.

Sextus returned a few days later while Lucretia's husband was away. He raped her after she refused his advances. Afterward he demanded her silence by threatening to ruin her reputation. He promised he would kill her and place a naked dead slave in bed by her side.

Lucretia summoned her husband, her father, and her uncle Lucius Junius Brutus. She told them that her heart was pure, but her body had been desecrated. She made them swear that they would avenge her. Lucretia then stabbed herself and set an example for all future women of Rome.

According to Roman tradition, Tarquinius Collatius and Junius Brutus led a revolution in 510 B.C.E. that established the Roman republic. They became the first consuls. While the story may be apocryphal, Lucretia was revered, and Romans credited her for the end of the monarchy and the creation of the republic.

Livy 1.57.6–11, 58–60.
OCD, p. 888.
Pomeroy, S. B., *Goddesses*, pp. 160–61.

🔲 LYSANDRA

(4th–3rd century B.C.E.) Greek: Egypt, Macedonia, and Syria
Power broker

Lysandra was a fighting woman. She was the daughter of two Macedonian rulers of Egypt, EURYDICE (3) and Ptolemy I Soter. In 298 B.C.E. her father-in-law, Cassander I, ruler of Macedonia, died, and her sister-in-law THESSALONICE became regent. She divided rule between Alexander V, her younger favored son, and his brother Antipater. Lysandra married Alexander.

Enraged that Thessalonice had deprived him of rule over all of Macedonia, Antipater murdered his mother. Alexander asked the general Demetrius, called the Besieger, for help in avenging her death. Instead, Demetrius murdered Alexander, ousted Antipater, and made himself king of Macedonia in 295 B.C.E. Lysandra fled with her children to her father's court in Egypt.

Two years later, Lysandra married Agathocles, the son of Lysimachus of Thrace. Her father-in-law became ruler of Macedonia in 285 after defeating Demetrius. He married Lysandra's half sister ARSINOË II PHILADELPHUS. Arsinoë persuaded her elderly husband to have Lysandra's husband Agathocles murdered on suspicion of treason in 283. Lysandra fled with her children to Antioch seeking the protection of Seleucus, an enemy of her father-in-law. In 281, Lysimachus was defeated and killed in a battle with Seleucus.

Lysandra was so angry over the murder of Agathocles that it was difficult for members of her father-in-law's family to retrieve his body. Nothing more is known of Lysandra's saga.

Paus. 1.9, 10.3–5.
Plut., Demetr. 36.1–5.
Macurdy, G., pp. 55–58.

M

MAECIA FAUSTINA

(3rd century C.E.)   Roman: Italy and
North Africa
Ruler for son

Maecia Faustina was able, wealthy, noble and
lived during difficult times in the third century C.E.
Her family was old and honored. Her mother,
Fabia Orestilla, was the daughter of the consul
Annius Severus. Her father, Marcus Antonius
Gordianus, was a man of culture and wealth. A
follower of the Epicurian school, he traced his lineage back to the Gracchi on his father's side and
to the emperor Trajan on his mother's. Maecia
Faustina spent her childhood in a house built by
the great republican general Pompey whose previous owners also included the triumvir Mark Antony and the emperor Tiberius. She married
Junius Balbus, a man of consular rank, and gave
birth to a son, Antonius, who became emperor at
the age of 13.

Her father, while proconsul of Africa, was
asked to become emperor of Rome by a young
group of aristocrats in revolt against the emperor
Maximinus, whom they considered hostile to the
Senate. Reluctantly, he accepted. In 238 C.E., at
the age of 79, he was recognized by the Senate. He
took the title Gordian I and made Maecia
Faustina's brother, Gordian II, his colleague. Her

brother died soon after in battle, and her father
committed suicide, having ruled for only 22 days.

After the deaths of the two Gordians, the Senate appointed Decius Caelius Balbinus and
Pupienus Maximus joint emperors. They were a
part of a senatorial board of 20 that had led the
earlier opposition to Maximinus. To satisfy the
popular demand for imperial continuity, they elevated Maecia's son to Caesar. Three months later,
the two emperors were murdered by the Praetorian Guard. Maecia Faustina and her husband
had probably bribed the Praetorian Guard to act
quickly. The 13-year-old Antonius was declared
emperor on July 9, 238.

The new emperor, who took the name Gordian
III, followed a political course favored by the Senate. Maecia Faustina directed the affairs of state,
supported by the faction that had supported her
father and opposed Maximinus. Reform policies
were initiated in administration, fiscal affairs, and
the army. Efforts were taken to limit frivolous
charges against the rich and notable. Attention
was paid to strengthening defenses at the frontiers, and gross abuses of power in the provinces
were prosecuted. Despite efforts of reform, however, it was a period of financial difficulty and political instability.

In 241, Gaius Furius Timesitheus was appointed prefect of the Praetorian Guard and as-

sumed effective control over the young emperor. Gordian III married Timesitheus's daughter, Furia Sabina Tranquillina in the same year. The able Timesitheus died in 243. Gordian appointed Philippus from Arabia to take his place. Gordian III died of battle wounds in 244, and Philippus took the title of emperor.

Nothing is known of the final fate of Maecia Faustina.

SHA, Gord. 22.4; 23.6–7; 25.3–4.
Townsend, P. W., "The Administration of Gordian III," pp. 59–132.
Townsend, P. W., "The Revolution of A.D. 238," pp. 49–97.

🔲 MAESIA

(1st century B.C.E.)   Roman: Umbria and Rome
Lawyer

Maesia was a native of Sentium from Umbria, in Italy. Tried on a criminal charge, she conducted her own defense before the praetor Lucius Titus. She was acquitted by the jury. Praised for her skill in successfully pleading her case, she was also denigrated with the epithet "androgyne" for stepping beyond the traditional female role.

Val. Max. 8.3.1.
Bauman, R. A., p. 50.
Marshall, A. J., "Ladies at Law," pp. 41, 47.

🔲 MAGIA

(1st century B.C.E.)   Roman: Italy
Mother of Virgil

Magia was the mother of Virgil, Rome's greatest poet. She lived near Mantua in northern Italy and was married to a man who may have begun his career as a potter. Her husband may have been employed by her father as an assistant to the magistrates before their fortunes improved, and he became a landowner able to provide Virgil with a good education.

Virgil was probably born on October 15, 70 B.C.E. According to legend, Magia gave birth in a ditch on the side of the road while traveling with her husband in the country.

Suet., Virg. 1–3.
OCD, p. 1602.

🔲 MALLONIA

(1st century C.E.)   Roman: Rome
Political victim

Mallonia is the only name we know of a woman reputed to be of high rank. She was said to have attracted the attentions of the emperor Tiberius around 26 C.E. The emperor was already old, emaciated and bald with a face disfigured by blotches. He repelled Mallonia, who may have been a good deal younger, and she refused his advances. Tiberius supposedly gathered derogatory information about her, which resulted in a trial. Tiberius pressed her to regret her behavior toward him. After leaving the court, she returned home and stabbed herself. A rude joke about Tiberius and Mallonia became current in the next street-corner Atellan farce, a popular entertainment of the day.

Suet., Tib. 45.

🔲 MARCELLA THE ELDER, CLAUDIA

(43 B.C.E.–? B.C.E./C.E.)   Roman: Rome
Political player

The elder Cluadia Marcella belonged to the generation whose childhood was marred by the violence of civil wars. Born in 43 B.C.E., Marcella was one of three siblings: a brother, Marcus Claudius Marcellus, born in 42, and a sister, the younger Claudia MARCELLA, born in 39. Her father, Gaius Claudius Marcellus, consul in 50 B.C.E., died by the time she was three years old and she grew up under the care of her mother, OCTAVIA (2). As intermittent civil war took its toll, her mother collected in her household children from her own two marriages and the orphaned children from the marriages of her ex-husband Mark Antony with FULVIA (2) and with CLEOPATRA VII. Octavia educated, dowered, and married the children of this extended family, assuring republican family lines into the next generation.

Marcella married Marcus Vipsanius Agrippa in 28 B.C.E. She was about 15; he was 36 years old. She was his second wife. Agrippa was a military man loyal to Octavian throughout the civil war. She brought Agrippa a tie to an elite republican house and to Octavian himself since not only was Octavian Marcella's uncle but her great-grandmother was JULIA (4), the favorite sister of Julius Caesar.

Although austere and older, Agrippa appears to have been a good husband. A daughter may have been born to them. Seven years later, however, the marriage succumbed to new political realities. Marcella's brother had died two years earlier. He had been the husband of JULIA (6), Augustus's only child, and favored for succession. In 21 B.C.E., when there was unrest in Rome and Augustus was obliged to leave the city, he sought someone of unquestioned loyalty. Who better qualified than Agrippa, and how better to assure his already tested loyalty than a marriage with his daughter Julia. Marcella was divorced with Octavia's concurrence.

Marcella almost immediately married again. Her new husband was her childhood playmate, Iullus Antonius, consul in 10 B.C.E. He was the handsome, cultured second son of Fulvia and Mark Antony, and he was some 20 years Agrippa's junior. With Antonius she became part of the most visible group of post–civil war aristocrats in public life with ties to the republican past. They were a part of the group around the emperor's daughter, Julia.

Augustus had made clear on many occasions that his daughter and her friends lived a lifestyle he found objectionable. In 2 B.C.E. Augustus provoked a public scandal with a letter to the Senate detailing the adulterous behavior of his daughter and her friends. It seems probable that more than illicit sex was involved. Julia was exiled. We have no evidence to what part, if any, Marcella played in the scandal. However, her husband was identified as the group's ringleader and condemned to death for adultery and conspiracy against Augustus. He was either executed or forced to commit suicide.

Marcella and Antonius had a son, Lucius, and perhaps a daughter. Nothing is known of the end Marcella's life.

Dio. 54.6.5.
Plut., Ant. 87.2–3.
Sen., Ad Marciam con. 2.3–4.
Suet., Aug. 63.1.
Balsdon, J. P. V. D., p. 208.
PW 422.
Syme, R., *Augustan Aristocracy*, index.

▣ MARCELLA THE YOUNGER, CLAUDIA
(39 B.C.E.–? C.E.) Roman: Rome
Political wife

Claudia Marcella was born in 39 B.C.E. and grew up part of the first post-Actium generation. Her father, Claudius Marcellus, was consul in 50 B.C.E. and died in 40. She spent her youth in the household of her mother, OCTAVIA (2), with her siblings, the children of her mother's marriage with Mark Antony, and the orphaned children of Mark Antony and his two wives, FULVIA (2) and CLEOPATRA VII. Marcella, tphe descendant of a great republican house, was the great-granddaughter of JULIA (4), the favorite sister of Julius Caesar. She and her siblings provided a critical link between the republican past and the new empire.

About 15 B.C.E. when she was 24, she married Paullus Aemilius Lepidus, consul suffectus in 34 B.C.E. and censor in 22. Possibly there had been an earlier marriage. The marriage linked two honored republican houses and tied them closely to the imperial circle. Before her husband died, Marcella gave birth to a son, Paullus Aemilius Regulus.

After her husband's death she married Marcus Valerius Messalla Barbatus Appianus, consul in 12 B.C. She outlived him. They had a daughter, CLAUDIA PULCHRA, and a son, Messalla Barbatus. Her son married DOMITIA LEPIDA, and their child, Valeria MESSALLINA, would become the wife of the emperor Claudius. Marcella would have been about 64 when Messallina was born; it is not known if she was still alive.

Balsdon, J. P. V. D., pp. 71, 73, 74.
PW 423.
Syme, R., *Augustan Aristocracy*, index.

🔲 MARCIA (1)

(?–113 B.C.E.) Roman: Rome
Priestess

Marcia was one of three Vestal Virgins charged with illicit relations in 114 B.C.E. It was believed an ill omen for Rome for three out of the six Vestals, who protected the sacred flame in one of the city's oldest temples on the Forum, to be charged with the most serious crime they could commit.

Of the three, only one, AEMILIA (1), was found guilty and condemned. Her partner was identified as L. Veturius, an equestrian. Although Marcia and the third Vestal, LICINIA (4), were declared innocent by the *pontifex maximus,* popular protest resulted in the establishment of a special tribunal to reexamine the case. Lucius Cassius Longinus Ravilla conducted the investigation. Both Marcia and Licinia were found guilty and condemned to death in 113.

Marcia was accused of having had only one man, a companion of Veturius. Her sister Vestal, Aemilia, was said to have made the arrangements. The evidence was given by a slave.

Dio. 26, 87.
Livy 43.
Oros. 5.15, 20–22.
Plut., Quaest. Rom. 83 (284).
Bauman, R. A., pp. 53–55, 57–58.

🔲 MARCIA (2)

(1st century B.C.E.) Roman: Rome
Political wife

Marcia divorced her husband to marry another man, who died and left her a wealthy widow. She then remarried her first husband. Other than the obvious financial benefit, any reason for her remarriage remains obscure. Marcia was one of three siblings. Her father was Lucius Marcius Philippus, consul in 56 B.C.E., and her stepmother was ATIA (1), the mother of the future emperor Augustus and his sister OCTAVIA (2) by her first husband. Her father's marriage, probably sometime around 58 B.C.E., was followed by her brother's marriage to her stepmother's sister, ATIA (2). In consequence, there was a double relationship between Marcia and her siblings and Augustus and his sister.

Marcia became the second wife of the younger Marcus Porcius Cato. Her husband, attracted to the Stoic philosophy, was a stubborn man of rigid principles and somewhat unpleasant personality. He believed that he alone lived in accordance with the traditions of the ancients. He also believed that one should only engage in sex to produce children. He had two children by his first wife and three daughters with Marcia.

A close friend of her husband, Quintus Hortensius, consul in 69 B.C.E., was a famous orator and, like Cato, one of the leaders of the conservative oligarchy. When he was in his early 60s and already had grown children, he sought to marry PORCIA, Cato's eldest daughter by his first wife, ATILIA. Porcia was already married and had two sons. Undeterred, Hortensius asked Cato to divorce Marcia so that he could marry her. Cato agreed if it was amenable all around. Neither Marcia nor her father objected. The divorce and new marriage took place in 56 B.C.E. Cato hosted the wedding. No children resulted, and Hortensius died leaving Marcia a much richer woman. She then remarried Cato.

During the five remaining years of Cato's life, he was said to have refrained from sex with Marcia since he felt that they already had enough children and Marcia had experienced a sufficient burden in bearing them. Marcia might well have concurred with their abstinence, given the high death rate for women bearing children. Abstinence was abetted by Cato's absence. He spent most of these years fighting with Gnaeus Pompeius (Pompey the Great) against Caesar. In 46, he died by his own hand in Africa after Caesar defeated the remaining core of senatorial opposition. Her stepdaughter Porcia also killed herself a year before the defeat of Brutus and Cassius at the battle of Philippi in 42. Marcia's life after Cato is unrecorded.

Lucan Phar. 2.326–89.
Plut., Cat. Min. 25.1–5; 52.
Balsdon, J. P. V. D., p. 190.
Pomeroy, S. B., *Goddesses*, pp. 158, 160–61.
Gordon, H., pp. 574–78.
PW 115.

⊞ MARCIA (3)

(1st century B.C.E.–1st century C.E.) Roman: Italy, Cyprus, Asia, and Spain
Patron of the arts

Marcia was born into an ancient and honored republican family with close ties to the nascent empire through Octavian, later the emperor Augustus, and his sister OCTAVIA (2). Part of the circle that included some of the greatest of the Latin poets, she was on the periphery of the scandals in 8 C.E. that rocked the Roman elite and resulted in the banishment by Augustus of his granddaughter JULIA (7) and the exile of the poet Ovid.

Marcia's immediate family relationships were complicated. Her father was Lucius Marcius Philippus, tribune in 49 B.C.E., consul suffectus in 38 and governor of Spain in 34–33?; her mother, ATIA (2), was the younger sister of her grandfather's second wife. The older ATIA (1) had already been married once before she married Marcia's grandfather. During her earlier marriage the older

Atia had had two children, Octavian and Octavia. Marcia, therefore, had Augustus and Octavia as a stepuncle and -aunt. Their children were her stepcousins.

To further complicate the relationships, after Marcia's father died, her mother married Quintus Fabius Maximus, the father of Paullus Fabius Maximus, whom Marcia married in 16 B.C.E. Her husband had an illustrious career. A close associate of Augustus, he was appointed quaestor in 22 or 21, elected consul in 11, was proconsul in Asia in 10–9, and then governor in northwest Spain in 3–2 B.C.E.

Her husband was also known as an orator and a patron of poets. Horace, whose principal benefactor was Gaius Maecenas, wrote an ode in honor of her marriage in 16 B.C.E. Marcia followed her husband and was honored by a dedication at Paphos in Cyprus. A close friend of Marcia and her mother was Ovid's third wife, whose name remains unknown. Marcia appears in Ovid's poetry. He composed a wedding ode to Marcia and her husband in 12 or 13 C.E. In a poem of 4 C.E., he wrote that her beauty matched her noble birth.

In 8 C.E., Augustus banished Ovid to Tomis on the Black Sea for reasons that are still obscure. Ovid used his poetry and the friendship of Marcia and his wife in an attempt to have the banishment rescinded. In a poem written about 13 C.E., he admonished his wife to affirm her devotion to Marcia. Whatever may have been Marcia's efforts on Ovid's behalf, however, they were unsuccessful.

Her husband died in 14. Rumors arose that Fabius Maximus had committed suicide and at the funeral that Marcia had blamed her indiscretion for his death. Her husband had accompanied Augustus on a secret trip to Planasia where Agrippa Postumus, the third son of the great general Marcus Vipsanius Agrippa and Augustus's daughter JULIA (6), had been exiled. Still without a firm designation of his heir, Augustus was exploring the possibility that the boy's personality disorders had mitigated, and perhaps of pardoning him. Marcia, a friend of Augustus's wife LIVIA DRUSILLA, purportedly told her of the trip, and the resulting anger of the emperor caused her husband to kill himself.

Marcia and Maximus had a son, Paullus Fabius Persicus, consul in 34 C.E., and a daughter, Fabia NUMANTINA.

Dio. 56.30, 1–2.
Tac., Ann. 1.5.1 ff.
Levick, B., *Tiberius*, p. 64.
OCD, p. 582.
PW 120.
Syme, R., *Augustan Aristocracy*, index.
Syme, R., *History in Ovid*, index.

▣ MARCIA (4)

(?–193 C.E.) Roman: Rome
Conspirator

Marcia, probably a freedwoman of the co-emperor Lucius Verus, protected herself and her own interests at a time when imperial power, always arbitrary, had become increasingly unbounded. As a young woman and the lover of Ummidius Quadratus, she was persuaded by Annia Aurelia Galeria LUCILLA, sister of the emperor Commodus, to join in a plot to kill the emperor. The plot was discovered. Quadratus and Lucilla were executed in 182 C.E. Marcia, however, escaped charges and punishment and became companion and lover of Commodus, whom she greatly influenced. She favored Christianity and persuaded Commodus to adopt a benign policy toward Christians. She asked Victor, the bishop of Rome, for a list of Christians who had been deported to Sardinia and persuaded Commodus to allow them to return to Rome.

Commodus's behavior became increasingly bizarre until in 192, he decided to present himself to the Roman people on the first day of the new year in a gladiator's costume instead of the traditional purple worn by Romans with the power of *imperium*. Marcia could not dissuade him, nor could his servant Eclectus or Aemilius Laetus, the prefect of the Praetorian Guard. In fact, their efforts to control the emperor almost led to their execution: A slave boy of the emperor found a list of proscribed names. Marcia discovered that the list contained the names of many prominent senators and that her name, as well as Eclectus and Laetus, headed the list.

Marcia, Eclectus, and Laetus decided to kill Commodus. Marcia poisoned a cup of wine. Commodus, already made very ill, was strangled. They sent the body to the edge of the city and spread a rumor that Commodus had died of apoplexy. They chose a distinguished senator, Publius Helvius Pertinax, to replace Commoodus and revealed their plot to him. He was declared emperor by the Praetorian Guard on January 1, 193. Marcia married Eclectus. Six months later, Pertinax was executed by members of the Praetorian Guard who were angered by his strict discipline, and Marcia and her husband were also killed.

Dio. 73.4, 6–7, 22.4–6; 74.16.5.
Herodian 1.8.4–5, 8, 16.4, 17.4–11; 2.1.3.
SHA, Comm. 11.9; 17.1–2.
SHA, Did. Jul. 6.2.
SHA, Pert. 4.5–2.
Balsdon, J. P. V. D., pp. 148–50.
OCD, p. 922.

▣ MARCIA FURNILLA

(1st century C.E.) Roman: Rome
Political wife

Marcia Furnilla, the daughter of Antonia Furnilla and the senator Marcius Barea Sura, married Titus Flavius Vespasianus after his first wife, ARRECINA TERTULLA, died. They had one child, JULIA FLAVIA. Titus divorced Marcia Furnilla in 64 C.E., before he became emperor.

Suet., Tit. 4.2–3.

▣ MARCIANA, ULPIA

(?–112 C.E.) Roman: Spain, Germany, Italy, and Asia
Augusta; deified

Ulpia Marciana lived with her brother, the emperor Trajan, most of her adult life. Their parents

157

Ulpia Marciana

Marciana and Plotina initially refused the Senate's request to honor them with the title Augusta. Both, however, accepted in 105. Marciana was the first woman to receive this honor who was not either the wife or the daughter of an emperor. In 112 Marciana and Plotina were given the right of coinage. Marciana died that same year. When Plotina died in 122, Hadrian consecrated both of them.

Plin., Pan. 84.
Balsdon, J. P. V. D., pp. 133–36.
OCD, p. 1570.
Syme, R., *Tacitus*, pp. 231, 233, 246, 603.

MARTINA

(? B.C.E.–19/20 C.E.)   Syrian: Syria and Italy
Poisoner

Martina, well known for her skill with poisons, became a suspect in 19 C.E. after the sudden death of Germanicus Julius Caesar, the popular general and probable heir to Tiberius. Martina was a client and possibly even a friend of MUNATIA PLANCINA, the wife of Gnaeus Calpurnius Piso, consul in 7 B.C.E. and political opponent of Germanicus. She appears to have been with Munatia, who had accompanied her husband to the East, when he was sent by Tiberius to temper Germanicus's aggressive policies. Piso and Germanicus were soon at odds. So too were Munatia and the elder AGRIPPINA, Germanicus's wife. After Germanicus's death, Agrippina carried his ashes back to Rome convinced that her husband had died from poison in a plot supported, if not arranged, by the emperor.

In Rome charges were brought against Munatia and Piso, who returned under guard after soldiers friendly to Germanicus had seized them in the East. Martina was also sent back to Rome to testify at the trial. She died on her arrival in Italy. Her death further inflamed passions on both sides. Although no poison was found on her body, some claimed that she had hidden the poison in her hair.

were Marcus Ulpius Traianus and a woman named Marcia who probably came from Spain. Before she moved in with her brother, she had married Matidius, a little-known senator from Vicetia in northern Italy. Her husband came from the heartland of Antonine support that flourished with her brother's rise to imperial power. After being widowed, Marciana joined Trajan and his wife Pompeia PLOTINA in Cologne, where Trajan commanded the troops on the Rhine before he became emperor. It was a large household and also included MATIDIA (1), Marciana's daughter and a favorite of Trajan and his wife, and Matidia's two daughters, the half-sisters Vibia SABINA and MATIDIA (2).

In 99 C.E. Marciana and her family settled in Rome with Trajan and Plotina. Trajan spent much of the early years of his reign away campaigning, leaving Plotina and Marciana in Rome sometimes for as long as three years at a time. In his absence they patronized the leading figures of the day to encourage the arts and the study of literature and philosophy. The future emperor Hadrian, adopted by Trajan, was brought up by the women and married Marciana's granddaughter Vibia Sabina in 100.

Dio. 57.18.6–10.
Tac., Ann. 2.74; 3.7.
Levick, B., pp. 96–97, 103–4.

🔲 MATIDIA (1)

(68–119 C.E.)   Roman: Italy, Asia, and Germany
Augusta; deified

Matidia lived in the multigenerational household of the emperor Trajan. Born no later than 68 C.E., she was the only child of Trajan's older sister Ulpia MARCIANA and Matidius, an obscure senator from northern Italy. Her first marriage seems to have been to a man named MINDIUS of whom nothing is known. She gave birth to a daughter named MATIDIA (2). She then married Lucius Vibius Sabinus, consul in 97 C.E., and they had a daughter, Vibia SABINA. Her husband died shortly after his consulship, and she moved with her daughters and her mother into the household of Trajan and Pompeia PLOTINA.

Matidia was honored with the title Augusta by Trajan. While her daughter Sabina, who had married the future emperor Hadrian in 100 C.E., remained in Rome, Matidia and Hadrian accompanied Trajan and Plotina on the campaign to the East in 114. Three years later, in 117, Trajan became ill and died in Syria. A letter of Trajan's named Hadrian his adopted son and heir. Rumors circulated about the authenticity of the letter. Plotina and Matidia, however, supported the soldiers' acclamation of Hadrian as the new emperor. Hadrian, who was campaigning in Syria, met them in Antioch and sent Plotina and Matidia to Rome with Trajan's ashes.

Although Hadrian's marriage was difficult, he remained close with his mother-in-law. When she died in 119, Hadrian gave the funeral oration and deified her. He also issued coins in her honor with the epithet "Diva Augusta Matidia." She was probably the first woman deified by the emperors to have a temple in Rome.

Dio. 69.1.
SHA, Hadr. 5.9; 9.9; 19.5.
Balsdon, J. P. V. D., pp. 133–39.
Birley, A. R., *Marcus Aurelius*, p. 241.
OCD, p. 937.
PW 28.

🔲 MATIDIA (2)

(1st–2nd century C.E.)   Roman: Italy, Asia, Germany, and Egypt
Never married

Matidia was an extremely unusual woman in a society where nearly everyone, man and woman, married at least once: She never married. Matidia grew up with her mother, half sister, and grandmother in the household of Pompeia PLOTINA and the emperor Marcus Ulpius Trajan. She was the daughter of MATIDIA (1) and an obscure man named Mindius. Her mother was the only child of Ulpia MARCIANA, the eldest sister of the Trajan. Matidia's half sister, Vibia SABINA, became the wife of the emperor Hadrian.

Matidia shared a taste for cultured life with her mother, Marciana, and Plotina. In latter life she

Matidia (1)

was close to her great-nephew Marcus Aurelius and when he was emperor, his daughters sometimes stayed with her. At her death, she left bequests of a million sesterces to some members of her family and associates. The money was to be administered by the younger Annia Galeria FAUSTINA, the wife of the emperor, and distributed at the rate of 50,000 sesterces a year.

Like many wealthy women who remained childless, she attracted a number of hangers-on who hoped to be remembered in her will. They persuaded her to include a number of codicils. As she lay unconscious, on her deathbed some took the opportunity to seal the codicils, thereby assuring their validity. Over half of her estate became encumbered and was assigned to nonfamily members, an illegal condition under the provisions of *Lex Falcidia*.

The bequests grew into a contentious issue. Marcus Cornelius Fronto, orator, former tutor, and close friend of Marcus Aurelius, sought a solution. He expressed particular concern about the jewels, especially Matidia's valuable pearls. Faustina, the emperor's wife, refused to buy the pearls or any of the other jewelry. Fronto surmised that she feared being accused of buying them cheaply. Finally, Aurelius washed his hands of the matter and turned over the problem of the will and jewels to his co-emperor, Lucius Verus.

Fronto, Ep., pp. 95–99.
Birley, A. R., *Marcus Aurelius*, pp. 132, 241.

▣ MELINNO

(2nd century B.C.E.) Greek: Italy
Poet

Melinno was a Greek poet who wrote in a Doric dialect most probably during the first half of the second century B.C.E. Possibly she lived in one of the Greek cities in southern Italy, all of which came under Roman control after the defeat of Pyrrhus in the middle of the third century.

She composed a hymn to the power of Rome in five Sapphic stanzas. In it she depicted warlike Rome, the conqueror of the world, as a goddess who was the daughter of Ares, father of the Amazons. Nothing is known about her personal life.

Bowra, C. M., "Melinno's Hymn to Rome," pp. 21–28.
OCD, p. 953.

▣ MELISSA

(Late 7th century B.C.E.) Greek: Greece
Murder victim

Melissa was the daughter of Proclus, the ruler of Epidaurus in Greece. She married Periander, the tyrant of Corinth. He fell in love with her after seeing her body revealed through her dress while she was pouring wine for workmen in a field. He murdered her in a fit of jealously and in despair made love to her dead body.

Periander sent a messenger to Thesprotia to consult the oracle of the dead on Acheron, presumed to be the entrance to Hades. He sought the whereabouts of a pledge given to him by a stranger. Melissa was said to have appeared and refused to reveal information about the pledge. She claimed to be cold in the clothing with which she was buried that had not been burned. As proof of who she was, she sent a message to Periander revealing knowledge that he had had sex with her dead body.

Periander ordered all the married women of Corinth, including slaves, to go to the temple of Hera and remove their clothing. The garments were then burned in a pit while he called out the name of Melissa. He then sent a second messenger to the oracle, and Melissa's ghost was assuaged.

Ath. 589 ff.
Hdt. 3.50; 5.92.
Blundell, S., p. 68.
Pomeroy, S. B., *Goddesses*, p. 35.

🎜 MESSALLINA, VALERIA

(c. 20–48 C.E.) Roman: Rome
Power broker

Valeria Messallina died condemned and notorious. Smart, beautiful, arrogant, ruthless, even cruel, and certainly seductive, she sought to secure her position in the face of a disapproving Senate and a powerful group of imperial freedmen who dominated the reign of her husband, the emperor Claudius. Her parents DOMITIA LEPIDA and Messalla Barbatus linked her with the greatest houses of the old republic, and on both sides she was a Julian, a descendant of OCTAVIA (2) and a descendant of the emperor Augustus. Messallina was somewhere between 14 and 20 years old in 38 or 39 C.E. when she married the 48-year-old Claudius, after he divorced his second wife, AELIA PAETINA. In a society that prized above all men's military prowess and idealized the male body, the young and beautiful Messallina's future was linked with her far-from-ideal second cousin who since birth had suffered from a form of palsy that affected his walk and caused a speech impairment.

Claudius had not been expected to become emperor. The many legitimate candidates seemed to assure that there would be no problems of succession after the death of his uncle Tiberius. Claudius's physical condition was perceived as an unalterable barrier by Augustus, his grandmother LIVIA DRUSILLA, and Tiberius. Livia persuaded her husband to consult with Tiberius as to the part Claudius should play in public life. A decision was made to carefully circumscribe his public appearances so as to protect Claudius and themselves from possible ridicule. One by one, however, possible successors to Tiberius died, leaving only the young Gaius Caligula and the infant Nero. Caligula succeeded Tiberius, but after Caligula was murdered, the unanticipated happened. Amid the general disorder and looting, Claudius was found by a soldier hiding in the palace in fear for his life. He was taken to the praetorian camp and declared emperor by the Praetorian Guard, even as the Senate sat in debate over the restoration of the republic.

Claudius became emperor in January 41, three years after his marriage with Messallina. They already had a daughter, Claudia OCTAVIA, and Messallina was some seven or eight months' pregnant with a son, Britannicus. In an uncertain world, the less-than-perfect Claudius and Messallina were raised to power by the troops and the myths of their lineage, but without the support of many, if not most, of the Senate. Claudius ruled through a small and increasingly powerful clique of freedmen—Narcissus, Polybius, Pallas, and Callistus. In concert with her husband and alone, Messallina used these men to rid herself of real or perceived threats to herself, her son, and her husband. To this end she also used the skillful politician Lucius Vitellius, a man from the equestrian order and a close confidant of Claudius, and Publius Suillius Rufus, a senator with a reputation as a ruthless prosecutor.

Danger to Claudius and Messallina came from many sides, most especially from those who could also claim the legitimate mantle of the Julio-Claudian family. JULIA LIVILLA was the sister of the murdered Caligula, a child of the elder AGRIPPINA. Like Messallina, she could claim descent from Octavia. She had been exiled by her brother Caligula for adultery. Julia Livilla's husband Marcus Vinicius had offered himself as a possible candidate to succeed Caligula after the latter's murder. One of his claims was the lineage of his wife. Although Claudius allowed her to return to Rome in 41 C.E., Julia Livilla was accused of adultery and again exiled. This time, she was also killed. Her alleged lover, Lucius Annaeus Seneca, a well-known orator and writer, was also exiled.

Gaius Appius Junius Silanus, consul in 28 C.E., was the descendant of several august republican houses, a popular leader of soldiers, and a favorite with the Senate. He was governor of Hispania Tarraconensis when Claudius recalled him to Rome in 41. Removed from immediate access to an army and the rights of *imperium,* he appeared less of a direct threat. Claudius honored him and arranged that he and Domitia Lepida marry. Domitia, Messallina's mother, was no less a contender for power than her daughter. Widowed, her marriage to Silanus was mutually advantageous. He gained a direct connection to the imperial family, and she, a husband of high repute.

By the following year, the effort to integrate Silanus into the imperial family and regime had failed. Charged with plotting to kill the emperor, he was executed without trial on Claudius's orders. The tale of his condemnation reads like a French farce and reflects poorly on Claudius, Narcissus, and Messallina. Supposedly, Narcissus broke into Claudius's bedroom before daybreak to inform the emperor that he had had a dream in which Silanus had attacked Claudius. Messallina appeared immediately and told Claudius that she had had a similar dream. The two of them had previously arranged for Silanus to come to the emperor's bedchamber. When he arrived, Claudius thought he was forcing his way into his room to assassinate him and ordered him executed. Whatever the reasons—Messallina may well have suspected Silanus's loyalty—by siding with the freedman she violated the code of kin and class, angering her mother. Like her daughter, Domitia Lepida was beautiful, arrogant, wealthy, and accustomed to power. She was also more politically astute than Messallina. Her mother was an ally Messallina could ill afford to lose, both for her political connections and for the advice she might have given over the years that followed.

The death of Silanus sparked an abortive revolution by the Senate in 42. Since the death of Tiberius, tension between the emperor and the Senate had heightened. The senators were led in Rome by Lucius Annius Vinicianus, who had been involved in a plot against Caligula, and Lucius Arruntius Camillus Scribonianus, consul in 32 and now the governor of Dalmatia with an army under his command. Arruntius called on Claudius to resign. The soldiers, however, did not back him, and the revolt ended four days later. The leaders committed suicide. Messallina, Claudius, and his loyal

freedmen had others executed. The sources claim that the victors were merciless and included men and women among the condemned. The numbers of condemned, however, suggest no more bloody an end than was traditional, and in fact less extreme than some earlier proscriptions.

For the already suspicious Claudius and Messallina, the revolt strengthened their focus on possible plots. They found evidence of intrigue everywhere. In 43 Suillius Rufus accused JULIA (8), the wife of Rubelius Blandus and the daughter of Livia Julia Claudia LIVILLA and Tiberius's son Drusus Julius Caesar, of immoral conduct. She was found guilty and killed. The climate of suspicion increased the imperial reliance on freedmen, further infuriated the elite, and fed popular gossip with tales of imperial excess, especially about Messallina.

As in all of Roman history, the gossip about women focused on sexual promiscuity, and Messallina was a perfect subject. Beautiful, young, and seductive, she had no hesitation in using her charms for her own interests. It was not hard for whispers to suggest that she had had sex with 25 men in 24 hours and that she had used false names to entertain men in brothels. The tales about Messallina's sexual misconduct steadily expanded in number and outrageousness. There were accounts of her forcing innocent wives and daughters into sex games in the imperial household while being watched by their loving and distraught husbands and brothers.

Nor was Claudius exempt from sexual attacks. Messallina was accused of supplying him with women and of assuring her own safety from his anger by exciting his appetites. The link between sex and blood, never far separated in Roman prurient literature, placed a long list of killings at the door of Messallina, with and without the aid of Claudius and the imperial freedmen. Messallina was said to have had the prefect of the Praetorian Guard, Catonius Justus, killed before he could reveal her sexual misconduct to Claudius. In 46 C.E., when Marcus Vinicius, the husband of Agrippina's daughter Julia Livilla, died and was given a state funeral, Messallina was said to have poisoned him because he refused to succumb to her charms and might have sought vengeance for the earlier death of his wife.

Later in 46 or early 47, the death of Gnaeus Pompeius Magnus, bearer of a great republican name, had serious political overtones. He was the husband of ANTONIA (4), the daughter of Claudius and his divorced second wife AELIA PAETINA. Messallina was said to have wanted him killed to prevent any possible future son who would present an alternative in succession to her son Britannicus. The sources attributed his death, however, to Claudius, not Messallina, and add that Claudius also killed some 35 senators and more than 300 equestrians. Among these were Pompeius's parents, Marcus Licinius Crassus Frugi and Scribonia. Their two younger sons were exiled. After the bloodbath, Antonia was married to an unthreatening husband, Faustus Cornelius Sulla Felix, the half brother of Messallina.

Messallina was said to have arranged the death of Claudius's freedman Polybius for his opposition to further purges by Messallina, particularly that of Decimus Valerius Asiaticus. Polybius's death in 46 marked the first break in solidarity between Messallina and the powerful freedmen clique. Without the support of the senators, and handicapped by her image of sexual promiscuity, sowing uncertainty among the freedmen would prove a fatal error for Messallina, but not before the successful prosecution of Decimus Valerius Asiaticus.

In 47 Asiaticus was accused of adultery with POPPAEA SABINA (1) and of bribery of the troops. Asiaticus, consul in 35 and 46 C.E., was a native of Vienne, a city on the Rhone in Gaul. He was immensely wealthy and proud and lived in great splendor. He owned the famous gardens of Lucullus, which had belonged to Lucius Licinius Lucullus in the republican era. The package of accusations against him, attributed to Messallina, mixed the trivial and banal with the threat of revolt. Messallina was said to have wanted Asiaticus's gardens. She implicated Poppaea, an extremely beautiful, wealthy, and independent-minded woman whom she believed to be his lover and knew to be a rival for

the attention of Mnester, a well-known actor of the day. Messallina used Publius Suillius Rufus to lodge the charge of adultery while her son's tutor, Sosibius, told Claudius that Asiaticus was about to travel to Germany where he planned to foment trouble among the troops.

In a tale reminiscent of the earlier condemnation of Silanus, on orders of Claudius, Asiaticus was brought to the palace in chains from the city of Baiae, a fashionable resort on an inlet of the Bay of Naples. At an informal hearing in the emperor's bedchamber with Messallina present, Suillius presented the charges that Asiaticus had corrupted the military and committed adultery with Poppaea. The sources record that Asiaticus's defense moved the listeners to tears. Nonetheless, Messallina instructed Lucius Vitellius, consul in 34, 43, and 47, that Asiaticus was to be indicted. When Claudius asked Vitellius whether Asiaticus should be acquitted, Vitellius, after praising the latter's past service, proposed suicide. Asiaticus committed suicide, and Messallina forced Poppaea Sabina to kill herself rather than face imprisonment.

Asiaticus had been among the key instigators in the destruction of Caligula, and he had put his name forward as a possible replacement. His enormous wealth and influence in Gaul could well have been used to influence and aid forces opposed to Claudius. Desire for the gardens of Lucullus or jealousy over Mnester, even if true, could in this case have covered the ongoing fear of conspiracy that marked Claudius's and Messallina's reign. However, the death of an exconsul without a trial aroused further resentment among senators and others opposed to Messallina and Claudius. Conversely, it further pushed Messallina's and Claudius' dependence on the imperial freedmen.

In 48 Messallina fatally mistook the degree of support she had among the clique of freedmen. She fell in love with Gaius Silius, a senator and one of the most handsome men in Rome. Silius was already married to JUNIA SILANA. Messallina persuaded him to divorce her. She appeared everywhere in public with Silius, openly showed her infatuation, and showered him with gifts from the imperial household. It was a dangerous situation, in part because Claudius was rapidly aging, and once more talk of succession was in the air.

Silius personified the kind of senator that Claudius and the imperial freedmen had most often feared and killed. Possibly, he may have already begun to array the forces in the Senate that needed only support from Messallina to change the advisers around the emperor and the tone of his reign. The powerful freedmen probably sensed the potential of Silius and Messallina's partnership. For Messalina's part, in the face of an increasingly debilitated Claudius, whose health and susceptibility to youthful female charms were an apparent danger, there was more to be said for an alliance with Silius, who was her contemporary, than with Claudius and the freedmen, especially after Silius promised to adopt her son Britannicus. Ardor overbalanced caution. With Claudius in Ostia, she and Silius sealed their bargain and acted out a marriage ceremony, without any attempt at concealment.

Her allies among the freedmen deserted her. Narcissus persuaded Callistus and Pallas that action had to be taken to destroy Messallina. Silius, consul designate in 48, was young, ambitious, well connected, and a danger to all of them. He would use his influence with Messallina to undermine their positions under Claudius, and if something happened to the emperor, their lives would be in danger. Narcissus took the lead. His position was the most precarious. Lucius Vitellius took a more ambivalent position so that he would emerge unscathed no matter what happened.

The senario was analogous to one that had been played before. Narcissus had CALPURNIA (2) and CLEOPATRA (4), lovers of Claudius, tell the emperor about the marriage. Narcissus then told him that all of Rome was aware of the wedding and urged Claudius to act before he was deposed by Silius. Claudius gave orders for the couple's apprehension. Narcissus took Claudius to Silius's house to see the valuables Messallina had given

him. Fearing that Claudius would still forgive Messallina if she confronted him, Narcissus kept Messallina and their children away from Claudius. He turned aside the Vestal Virgin VIBIDIA, who demanded that Messallina be allowed to defend herself.

On word of what happened, Silius went to the Forum, and Messallina retired to the garden that once had belonged to Asiaticus. Silius offered no defense and was executed along with a number of senators and knights. Domitia Lepida hurried to her daughter's side and told her the only honorable way out was to kill herself. Messallina still felt that she could persuade Claudius to forgive her if she could only see him alone. Narcissus had made it impossible. Messallina tried to stab herself but failed, and she was killed by one of the men sent by Narcissus. Her body was turned over to her mother.

The ultimate irony was that Claudius replaced his wife Messallina with the younger AGRIPPINA, a more ruthless and devious woman than Messallina and surely as intelligent. Agrippina succeeded where Messallina had failed and skillfully maneuvered the elevation of her son Nero to become emperor, perhaps poisoning Claudius to make it possible

Dio. 60.8.4–5, 12.5, 14.1–4, 18.1–4; 61.30.8, 31.1–5.
Juv. 6.115–32; 10.329–45.
Suet., Claud. 26.2; 27.1; 29.3; 36; 37.2; 39.1.
Tac., Ann. 11.1–5; 12.26–38.
Balsdon, J. P. V. D., pp. 97–107.
Bauman, R. A., index.
Grimal, P., pp. 277–88.
Levick, B., Claudius, index.
OCD, pp. 1,576–77.
PW 403.
Syme, R., Augustan Aristocracy, index.

▣ MILONIA CAESONIA

(c. 5–41 C.E.) Roman: Rome
Political player

Milonia Caesonia, born about 5 C.E., joined with her husband, the emperor Gaius Caligula, in the imaginative and extravagant productions that characterized the emperor's last years. Condemned in the sources as promiscuous, she was murdered at the same time as the emperor.

Milonia was the youngest child of VISTILIA, a woman from Umbria, who was notable for having married six men and having borne children with all of them. By the time Milonia married Caligula, she already had three children from a previous marriage. Neither young nor beautiful, she was Caligula's fourth wife. They married about the time she gave birth to a daughter, JULIA DRUSILLA (2). Caligula loved her and was more faithful to her than to any other woman with whom he consorted.

Milonia, dressed in helmet, cloak, and shield, was reputed to have accompanied her husband to review the troops and was said to have sometimes paraded nude among friends. She probably became very wealthy. Caligula appointed her, along with other wealthy individuals, to priesthoods and collected 10 million sesterces from each of them for the honor. On January 24, 41, Caligula, Milonia Caesonia, and their daughter where murdered.

Dio. 59.23.7–8; 28.5–7.
Plin., NH 7.39.
Suet., Calig. 25.3–4; 59.
Syme., R. "Domitius Corbulo," p. 31.

MINERVINA

(3rd–4th century C.E.)   Roman: Asia
Lover of Constantine

Minervina was the lover of the future emperor Constantine. Their relationship ended when Constantine married Flavia Maxima FAUSTA in 307 C.E. Minervina had a son, Crispus, who grew up in the palace. In a scandal whose details are obscure, Constantine had the 20-year-old Crispus poisoned and his own wife, Fausta, killed in 326.

Balsdon, J. P. V. D., p. 167.

MINUCIA

(?–337 B.C.E.)   Roman: Rome
Priestess

Minucia came from a plebeian family that had once been patrician. She was the first plebeian Vestal Virgin, one of the guardians of the sacred flame of Rome in the temple of Vesta in the Forum. In 337 B.C.E. she was convicted of adultery on the testimony of her slave. She suffered the traditional punishment of being buried alive.

Livy 8.15.8.
Bauman, R. A., pp. 17, 223, footnote 18.

MUCIA

(2nd–1st century B.C.E.)   Roman: Italy
Elegant speaker

Mucia was born into a family renowned for rhetorical skill. She was the daughter of LAELIA, well known for her elegant speaking. Her father, Quintus Mucius Scaevola, consul in 117 B.C.E., was admired as an orator, as was her grandfather, Gaius Laelius.

Mucia married Lucius Licinius Crassus, consul in 95 B.C.E., who was himself a remarkable orator. Mucia had two daughters, LICINIA (5) and LICINIA (6), who carried on the family tradition of eloquence.

Cic., Brut. 211–12.
Quint., Inst. 1.1, 6.
Bauman, R. A., pp. 47–48.

MUCIA TERTIA

(1st century B.C.E.)   Roman: Italy
Power broker

Mucia Tertia helped mediate the pact of Misenum in 39 B.C.E. between her son, Sextus Pompeius Magnus, and Mark Antony and Octavian. A woman of independent spirit, she was one of several Roman women who negotiated among the warring factions on several occasion during the civil wars.

Daughter of Quintus Mucius Scaevola, consul in 95 B.C.E., she was the third wife of Gnaeus Pompeius (Pompey the Great), Roman general and leader of the republicans at the outbreak of civil war in 49 B.C.E. She married him after the death of his second wife, AEMILIA (2). They had two sons, Gnaeus Pompeius Magnus and Sextus Pompeius, and a daughter, POMPEIA (2). She and Pompey divorced in 62. There were rumors of lovers and tales of salacious propositions, common for all divorces among the elite, who were always subject to insistent gossip, both true and false. Mucia's second husband was Marcus Aemilius Scaurus, a quaestor under Pompey and praetor in 56. They had a son, Marcus Aemilius Scaurus. Her husband was charged with bribery during the consular elections in 53. Her former husband contributed to his conviction and exile. Mucia did not accompany her husband out of Italy.

After Pompey's defeat at Pharsalus in 48 and his murder in Egypt, Sextus took up his father's mantle. Sextus controlled the sea and made Sicily a friendly retreat for the Roman elite escaping the proscriptions. Mucia had been in Rome, at least for much of this period. When Octavian became alarmed at Sextus's overtures to Antony, he sent Mucia to placate Sextus. In a further gesture of reconciliation, Octavian also married SCRIBONIA, the sister of Sextus's father-in-law, Lucius Scribonius Libo. These efforts failed. In 40 B.C.E. Antony and Octavian were reconciled with the signing of the Treaty of Brundisium, and Antony married the latter's sister, OCTAVIA (2). Sextus, however, still controlled the sea lanes and cut off the corn supply to Italy. Faced with possible famine, the people demanded a settlement between the triumvirs and Sextus. A mob sent Mucia, who strongly favored an agreement, to her son in search of peace after threatening to burn her and her house. The protagonists met on the coast at Puteoli, north of Naples. The troops on both sides demanded an accord. The result was the treaty of Misenum in which Sextus became reconciled with the triumvirate. The agreement soon fell apart, and Sextus was defeated and exe-

cuted in 36 B.C.E. In consideration of Mucia's efforts, Octavian spared her other son, Marcus Aemilius Scaurus, who had faced the death penalty after the battle of Actium.

App., Bciv. 5.69, 72.
Cic., Att. 1.12.
Dio. 51.5.
Suet., Caes. 50.
Suet., Gram. 14.
Balsdon, J. P. V. D., p. 53.
OCD, p. 999.
PW 28.
Syme., R., *Augustan Aristocracy*, pp. 255, 264.
Syme., R., *Roman Revolution*, pp. 32, 33.

▣ MUMMIA ACHAICA

(1st century B.C.E.–1st century C.E.) Roman: Rome
Mother of emperor Servius Sulpicius Galba

Mummia Achaica was the great-great-granddaughter of Lucius Mummius, consul in 146 B.C.E. Her father's probable name was Lucius Mummius Achaica. Her mother was Lutatia, the daughter of Lutatius Catullus, consul in 78 B.C.E. She married Gaius Sulpicius Galba, a squat ugly man who had a hunchback. They had two sons: Gaius, who later committed suicide, and Servius Sulpicius Galba, born December 24, 3 B.C.E., who later succeeded Nero as emperor.

Suet., Galba. 3–4.
Syme, R., *Augustan Aristocracy*, pp. 75, 77.

▣ MUNATIA PLANCINA

(?–33 C.E.) Roman: Italy, Asia, and Syria
Political player

Munatia Plancina was the aristocratic, wealthy, arrogant daughter or possibly granddaughter of Lucius Munatius Plancus, consul in 42 B.C.E. and censor in 22. Her paternal family was on the winning side of the civil wars. Plancus had served under Julius Caesar, supported Marcus Junius Brutus, and switched first to Mark Antony and then to Octavian. It was he who proposed the name Augustus for Octavian.

Munatia, a friend of LIVIA DRUSILLA, married Gnaeus Calpurnius Piso, a friend of the emperor Tiberius. In 17 C.E. she accompanied her husband to the East after Tiberius appointed him governor of Syria at least in part to restrain the impetuous adventurism of Germanicus Julius Caesar headquartered in Syria and accompanied by his wife, the elder AGRIPPINA.

Germanicus, the favored heir of Tiberius, and Agrippina were well regarded by the troops. Munatia and Piso curried favor with the troops to counter the popular couple. Munatia attended military exercises and maneuvers, as did Agrippina. Conflicts soon arose between Germanicus and Piso, and they came to dislike each other, as did their wives. Munatia made disparaging remarks about Germanicus and Agrippina before the troops, and Agrippina, every bit her match, did the same to support Germanicus.

Tensions escalated after Piso refused Germanicus's request for troops to take to Armenia. Germanicus ordered Piso to leave Syria. Munatia and her husband went to the island of Cos off the southern coast of Asia Minor. Germanicus suddenly fell seriously ill in Antioch and died on October 10, 19 C.E. Before dying, he declared himself poisoned by Piso and Munatia. Munatia and Piso made no secret that they regarded the death as good news. Piso set out to take Syria by force from Gnaeus Sentius Saturninus, who had become temporary governor appointed by the officers until Tiberius could send a new appointment. However, the troops failed to support Piso. Defeated, Piso and Munatia were taken to Rome to be tried on charges of treason.

In Rome neither Tiberius nor Livia nor Germanicus's own mother, the younger ANTONIA, attended the ceremony when Agrippina returned with her husband's ashes in 19 C.E. Rumors were rife that Tiberius and Livia had colluded in Germanicus's death so that Tiberius's son, Drusus Julius Caesar would succeed his father. Agrippina formally accused Munatia and Piso of poisoning her husband. Piso was tried in the Senate with Tiberius presiding. Munatia first supported her husband, but she soon distanced herself, and Livia intervened on her behalf to separate her trial from that of her husband. Unable to prove that Piso poisoned Germanicus, he was convicted of trying to regain Syria by force. He killed himself before the trial ended and sent a letter to Tiberius protesting his loyalty and asking that his two sons be spared. He made no mention of Munatia.

Tiberius sought support for Munatia from her sons, who refused. Munatia was freed when Tiberius told the Senate that Livia asked that the charges against her be dropped. The death of Livia in 29 deprived Munatia of her protector, but no harm immediately followed. In 33, however, she was again accused and convicted, and she killed herself. The charges are not clear, but it is known that her death quickly followed on the heels of that of her chief enemy, Agrippina.

Dio. 57.18.9–10; 58.22.5.
Tac., Ann. 2.43, 55, 57, 71, 74, 82; 3.9, 13, 15–18; 6.26.
Balsdon, J. P. V. D., p. 95.
Bauman, R. A., pp. 140–43.
Levick, B., *Tiberius*, pp. 157, 210.
Marsh, F. B., pp. 85–104.
OCD, p. 1,000. PW 44.
Syme, R., *Augustan Aristocracy*, pp. 369, 374.

▥ MUSA, THEA URANIA

(1st century B.C.E.–1st century C.E.) Italian: Italy and Parthia
Ruler

Musa was a slave woman from Italy who became the wife of the ruler of Parthia. In 20 B.C.E. Musa was part of a gift Augustus gave to the king of Parthia, which lay south of the Caspian Sea in Asia. It was a client kingdom of Rome ruled by Phraates IV from 38 to 2 B.C.E. Phraates married Musa and gave her the name Thea Urania Musa after she had borne him a son.

Musa persuaded her husband to send his older sons, along with their wives and children, to Rome. In 10 or 9 B.C.E. Phraates IV turned them

Thea Urania Musa and Phraates V

over to the Roman governor of Syria, Marcus Titius, who arranged their trip. In 2 B.C.E. Musa and her son, also named Phraates, poisoned her husband. Her son took control of the kingdom and married Musa in the same year. Despite the notoriety of the marriage, Phraates V reached an accord with Augustus, and the heads of Musa and Phraates V appeared on coins. In 4 C.E. Phraates V was either overthrown or killed in a revolt. Nothing more is known about Musa.

Debevoise, N. C., *Political History of Parthia*, pp. 143, 147–49, 151–52.
OCD, p. 1,175.

▣ MUTILIA PRISCA
(? B.C.E.–30 C.E.) Roman: Rome
Political victim

Mutilia Prisca and her husband, Gaius Fufius Geminus, consul in 29 C.E., were both favorites of the powerful and influential LIVIA DRUSILLA. Livia was instrumental in advancing the career of Geminus, who became an ally of the powerful Lucius Aelius Sejanus in the political battles of the late 20s.

Geminus used his stinging wit against Tiberius. In 30, a year after Livia died, Tiberius forced both Mutilia Prisca and Geminus to commit suicide, after he charged Geminus with treason for being impious and disrespectful. Before he died Geminus went to the Senate and read his will in which he left his estate in equal amounts to his children and the emperor. Mutilia Prisca, furious about the charges and distraught over her husband and his behavior, went to the Senate armed with a dagger and stabbed herself.

Dio. 58.5–6.
Tac., Ann. 4.12; 5.2.
Levick, B., *Tiberius*, pp. 176–77.

▣ MYRRHINE
(6th–5th century B.C.E.) Greek: Athens and Asia Minor
Loyal wife

Myrrhine was the daughter of the well-born Athenian Callias and the granddaughter of Hyperochides. She married Hippias, the eldest son of Pisistratus, tyrant of Athens (546–527 B.C.E.). Hippias succeeded his father and ruled from 527 to 510 B.C.E. Initially, he was an enlightened ruler like his father, but threats from Persia and later Sparta resulted in a harsher rule. During these years Myrrhine had five sons and a daughter, Archedice. Her daughter married Aeantides, the son of Hippoclus, tyrant of Lampsacus at the eastern entrance to the Hellespont. Hippocles was favored by the Persian king Darius, and Hippias sought to gain Persian support against his domestic enemies.

In 510, Hippias surrendered to a Spartan force supported by Athenians who wanted to free the city. Myrrhine went with her husband and family to Sigeum near Troy in Asia Minor and then to her son-in-law in Lampsacus. Her husband later went to the court of Darius and fought alongside the Persians at the battle of Marathon in 490 in a vain attempt to regain control of Athens. Nothing is known of Myrrhine's death.

Thuc. 6.55, 59.

MYRTIS

(5th?-century B.C.E.) Greek: Greece
Poet

Myrtis was a Greek lyric poet from Anthedon in Boeotia, in central Greece. She was said to have composed a poem about the tragic hero Eunostus, who was killed after a false accusation by a woman he rejected. None of her work survives. Some sources claim that she was also the teacher of the poets Pindar and CORINNA, a lyric poet from Tanagra in Boeotia. In one fragment by Corinna she appears to criticize Myrtis for competing against Pindar. However, Corinna most probably lived in the third century B.C.E., some 200 years after Pindar and Myrtis.

Plut., Quaest. Graec. 40.
Campbell, D. A., v. 4, pp. 2, 15–17.
Edmonds, J. M., v. 3, pp. 3, 15.
OCD, p. 1,017.
Page, D. L., *Corinna*, p. 31.

MYRTO

(5th–4th century B.C.E.) Greek: Athens
Wife of Socrates

Myrto was the first wife of Socrates and with him had two sons, Sophroniscus and Menexenus. The children were still young in 399 B.C.E. when Socrates committed suicide after being found guilty of corrupting youth and introducing strange gods. Although there is no record that Myrto and Socrates divorced, at some point Socrates had a second wife, XANTHIPPE.

Ath. 13.555d–56.
Aul. Gell. 15.20.6.
Diog. Laert. 2.26.
Fitton, J. W., pp. 56–66.

N

NEAERA

(4th century B.C.E.) Greek: Corinth and Athens
Self-made woman

Neaera began life as a slave in a Corinthian brothel. Her struggle to move across the social and legal boundaries from slave to free and gain the position of legal wife dominated her life. That her daughter and her grandson may have become Athenian citizens was her crowning achievement. She first gained her freedom after two wealthy young men purchased her from the brothel. The young men allowed her to buy her way out of slavery on the condition that she leave and never return to Corinth. There is no record of what influence she brought to bear for them to agree to free her.

Neaera raised the money she needed from her admirers. One of them, Phrynion, an Athenian citizen, took Neaera and her three children, all born during her time of slavery, to Athens. Dissatisfied with her treatment by Phrynion, Neaera joined with Stephanus, another admirer and an Athenian citizen. She claimed to be Stephanus's wife. At the same time, her relationships with other men provided sufficient income for her to care for her family.

Stephanus claimed Neaera's daughter, Phano, as his legitimate child and arranged marriage for her with a man named Phraestor. She had a respectable dowry of one-half talent. After the marriage, when Phano was already pregnant, Phraestor discovered her background. He threw her out of the house. Phano moved back into her mother's house. Phraestor also refused to return her dowry, claiming to have been deceived.

The ensuing scandal opened the way for Stephanus's enemies to attack him. Two men, Appolodorus and his brother-in-law Theomnestus, brought suit against Neaera for not being a citizen and claiming to be legally wed to a citizen. Although the suit was against Neaera, the attack was directed against Stephanus in revenge for an earlier injury. If convicted, Neaera could have been sold back into slavery and Stephanus fined 1,000 drachmas.

Whatever the decision, no harm came to Neaera, who continued to live as before. When the angry Phraestor became seriously ill, Neaera and Phano moved into his house and nursed him. He agreed to acknowledge his paternity of Phano's son, especially since he was otherwise childless and at odds with his family. Property was now at stake; serious business in ancient Athens. Phraestor's clansmen challenged Phano's citizenship on the basis that her mother was not an Athenian citizen. Phraestor countersued. However, he refused to testify under oath that Phano was an Athenian citizen and that they had been married under the Athenian law.

Neaera and Phano did not give up. Some time later, Phraestor married Phano to Theogenes of Erchia, again without revealing her origins in order to try to obtain Athenian citizenship for Phano's son. Eventually, Phano married a highly placed religious magistrate, and it is possible that she finally gained the citizenship so dearly sought by her mother for her and her son.

Dem. 59.30–32.
Fantham, E., et al., pp. 114–5.
Pomeroy, S. B., *Goddesses*, pp. 67–68.
Walters, K. R., pp. 204–5.

▣ NICAEA (1)

(4th century B.C.E.) Greek: Macedonia and Thrace
Political pawn

Nicaea was the daughter of Alexander the Great's trusted general Antipater. When Alexander departed for his last expedition to the East, he left Antipater behind to govern Macedonia and the cities of Greece. After Alexander's unexpected death in 323 B.C.E., Antipater was one of three generals who jockeyed to rule Alexander's empire. It became advantageous for Nicaea to marry one or another of her father's colleagues. Perdiccas sought her out, and a match was agreed upon. However, in the fluid world of post-Alexander politics, OLYMPIAS (1), the mother of Alexander the Great, was a force to reckon with, and she hated Antipater, who had denied her authority in Macedonia while Alexander was alive and in the East.

To thwart Antipater, Olympias offered Perdiccas the hand of her daughter, CLEOPATRA (3). Marriage with Cleopatra offered Perdiccas an alliance with the Macedonian ruling house. Caught between the two choices, he promised Cleopatra to marry her, although he would first marry Nicaea and later divorce her. It is not clear whether he married Nicaea, but the sources agree that Antipater discovered the plan and broke with Perdiccas. Cleopatra also turned him down. The only victor was Olympias, who had succeeded in creating a breech between Antipater and Perdiccas.

Antipater instead formed an alliance with Craterus and Ptolemy I Soter of Egypt, also Macedonian colleagues under Alexander. To assure these alliances, Antipater used his three daughters as surety. PHILA (1) and Craterus married, as did EURYDICE (3) and Ptolemy. Nicaea married Lysimachus, a close companion of Alexander who governed Thrace, to ensure his continued neutrality. Lysimachus named a city in Bithynia in Asia Minor after his wife, who had three children. One daughter, ARSINOË I, became for a time coruler of Egypt. Another daughter, EURYDICE (4), married her cousin Antipater. She was killed in the wars over Macedonia. Her son, Agathocles, should have succeeded his father, but he was killed to eliminate any chance of his succession through the machination of Lysimachus's later wife, ARSINOË II PHILADELPHUS.

Diod. 18.23.1–3.
Cary, M., pp. 12–13, 55–57.
Macurdy, G., pp. 37, 59, 102, 109, 113.

▣ NICAEA (2)

(3rd century B.C.E.) Greek: Corinth
Ruler

Nicaea ruled Corinth for a short time after the death of her husband, Alexander (290–245 B.C.E.). He had succeeded his father, who had ruled Corinth and the surrounding areas under the suzerainty of Demetrius I. He repudiated Demetrius and left Nicaea as his heir.

Nicaea set about finding another husband amid the quicksands of Greek political alliances during the third century B.C.E. Antigonus Gonatus, the son of Demetrius I and PHILA (1) who had once controlled Corinth, sought to reassert his control. He offered her marriage with his son, Demetrius II, and arranged to celebrate the wedding in Corinth. On arrival, he immediately sent a group of soldiers to the fort and bluffed the troops there into surrendering. Nothing more is heard of Nicaea.

Just., Epit. 28.
Plut., Arat. 17.1–3.
Cary, M., p. 140.

▣ NICOPOLIS

(2nd century B.C.E.)   Roman: Rome
Self-made woman

Nicopolis was a wealthy woman who took the relatively impoverished, young, and nobly born Lucius Cornelius Sulla for her lover. She appointed Sulla her heir before she died. It was not the only time that Sulla, future dictator of Rome, would financially benefit from his relationships with women.

Plut., Sull. 2.4.

▣ NOSSIS

(3rd century B.C.E.)   Greek: Locri
Poet

Nossis was a Greek poet from Locri, a city in southern Italy. Influenced by the poetry of SAPPHO, she wrote dedications, mostly to the gods, and epigrams, only 12 of which survive. Nossis was probably well born. She was the daughter of Theophilis, and she paid tribute to her mother and grandmother in the dedication of a valuable linen wrap to the goddess Hera.

Nossis explored new possibilities in the very formulaic and conventional form of a dedication. She added a personal voice that spoke to women and about women. She praised the beauty of women's bodies and celebrated the sweetness of desire as the greatest of all pleasures, even sweeter than the sweetest honey. Speaking as if from the grave, Nossis asked any passing stranger to remember her. The conceit and the lament were characteristic of the ancients, but her language carried the passion that raises poetry above the trite and sentimental.

Fantham, E., et al., pp. 165–66.
Gow, A S., and Page, D. L., v. 2, pp. 434 ff.
OCD, p. 1,049.
Skinner, M. B., "Nossis Thelyglossos," pp. 20–47.

▣ NUMANTINA, FABIA

(1st century C.E.)   Roman: Rome
Litigant

Fabia Numantina successfully withstood a trial on charges brought by her not-completely-sane second husband. She had family ties with the emperor Augustus. Her grandmother ATIA (2) and the emperor's mother, ATIA (1), were sisters. Her mother, MARCIA (3), was Augustus's young stepcousin, and her father, Paullus Fabius Maximus, consul in 11 B.C.E., was his friend. Numantina's first husband was Sextus Appuleius, consul in 14 C.E. They had a son who died while young. She noted on his gravestone that he was the last of the illustrious house of the Appuleii.

Widowed, Numantina remarried. Her second husband was Plautius Silvanus, praetor in 24 C.E. Silvanus may have been a fortune hunter who married the rich Numantina in order to divorce her after securing some part of her wealth and a settlement.

He may have succeeded, at least in part. After they were divorced, Silvanus married APRONIA, the daughter of Lucius Apronius, and brought a suit against Numantina. He charged her with the use of spells and drugs to drive him insane while they had been married. Before the conclusion of the suit, Silvanus threw Apronia out of a window and killed her. He was forced to take his own life. Numantina was acquitted of all charges.

Tac., Ann. 4.22.
Syme, R., *Augustan Aristocracy*, pp. 59, 418.

O

▣ OCCIA

(? B.C.E.–19 C.E.) Roman: Rome
Priestess

Occia was a Vestal Virgin with an unblemished record of dedication for 57 years, from 38 B.C.E. until her death in 19 C.E. One of six women devoted to the protection of the sacred flame in the temple of Vesta in the Forum, the purity of the Vestals was associated with the well-being of the city. Usually the women served for a term of 30 years and retired well endowed. Occia's length of service was unusually long and successful through difficult decades of civil war.

Tac., Ann. 2.86.1.
Balsdon., J. P. V. D., p. 236.

▣ OCTAVIA (1)

(1st century B.C.E.) Roman: Rome
Half sister to Augustus and Octavia

Octavia was the half sister of the emperor Augustus and OCTAVIA (2). They all shared the same father, Gaius Octavius, who came from a wealthy equestrian family. Her mother was ANCHARIA, her father's first wife. Octavia married Sextus Appuleius and bore him two sons: Sextus Appuleius, consul in 29 B.C.E., and Marcus Appuleius, consul in 20 B.C.E.

Suet., Aug. 4.1.
OCD, p. 1,059.
PW 95.
Singer, M. W., pp. 268–74.
Syme, R., *Augustan Aristocracy,* index.
Syme, R., *Roman Revolution,* pp. 112, 378, 421.

▣ OCTAVIA (2)

(69–11 B.C.E.) Roman: Italy and Greece
Power broker

Octavia was dignified, intelligent, and attractive; she was held in high regard as a woman of virtue and principle. She played an important role in the shifting political realities of the civil war and the early empire. She acted to promote the best interests of her husbands and of her brother, the emperor Augustus. In the aftermath of civil war, she led the way in nurturing the children of the republican elite to assure the continuity of the great houses of the past.

Born in 69 B.C.E., she died in 11 B.C.E., having married twice, borne five children and been a close adviser to her husbands and her brother. She was the daughter of Gaius Octavius, praetor in 61 B.C.E., and the niece of Gaius Julius Caesar on the side of her mother, ATIA (1). Around 54 B.C.E., Octavia married Gaius Claudius Marcellus, who was more than 20 years her senior. Consul in 50 B.C.E., he initially supported Gnaeus Pompeius (Pompey the Great) and tried to bring about Caesar's recall, for which Caesar later forgave him.

Marcellus died in 40 B.C.E. With him Octavia had three children: the elder Claudia MARCELLA, born in 43; Marcus Claudius Marcellus, born in 42; and the younger Claudia MARCELLA, born in 39, after her father's death. Octavia married Mark Antony in the autumn of 40, so quickly after her first husband's death that she needed a special dispensation from the Senate. The new marriage sealed the treaty of Brundisium, which divided the empire between her brother Octavian, her husband Antony, and Marcus Aemilius Lepidus.

Octavia and Antony settled in Athens during the winters of 39–38 and 38–37. In 37, she brokered the treaty of Tarentum, in which Antony agreed not to support Sextus Pompeius Magnus, the younger son of Pompey the Great and to turn over two squadrons, consisting of 120 ships, to Octavian for use against Sextus. In return Octavian promised him four legions. Octavia persuaded Antony to furnish her brother with an additional 10 ships. She also persuaded her brother to supply Antony with a bodyguard of 1,000 soldiers of his choosing. Antony then went east to deal with the client states and to fight the Parthians. Octavia, who had just given birth to a second daughter by Antony, the younger ANTONIA, accompanied him as far as Corcyra in the Ionian Sea. Her health deteriorated, and she returned to Rome.

Antony summoned CLEOPATRA VII to Antioch and resumed their relationship. They agreed that she would rule over Coele-Syria, Cyprus, and a part of Cilicia, and he acknowledged her twins, CLEOPATRA SELENE and Alexander Helios as his sons. She provided him with significant material and financial support. In the face of Antony's alliance with Cleopatra, Octavia persuaded Octavian in 35 B.C.E. to allow her to bring

Antony additional troops and equipment. Octavian, however, only sent one-tenth of the promised troops and a furious Antony told Octavia she need go no further than Athens. Sadly Octavia returned to Rome. Despite the urging of her brother, Octavia refused to leave Antony's house and claimed that under Roman law she was his wife.

In 35 Octavia and Octavian's wife, LIVIA DRUSILLA, were accorded the privilege of *tribunica sanctissima*, a status neither previously nor ever again held by a woman. The office made any assault on their persons an attack on the state. It also gave the women independent authority over their property and wealth. It was probably Octavian's intention to protect his sister from Antony, and given the context, impossible to exclude his wife in the honor. So long as Octavia remained Antony's putative wife, she was the visible symbol of the Treaty of Brundisium, and Octavian was constrained in his behavior toward Antony, who remained in the East. In 32, however, Antony officially divorced Octavia and thereby removed for Octavian his major impediment to war. Even so, Octavian was careful to declare war against Cleopatra, rather than Antony. Antony not only had support among the troops, but few found palatable the prospect of yet another openly declared war between two Roman generals.

After Cleopatra's and Antony's death in 30 B.C.E., Octavia brought up the children of her first and second marriages, as well as Iullus Antonius, Antony's son with FULVIA (2), and Cleopatra Selene, Antony's daughter with Cleopatra. She brought in Nestor of Tarsus, a philosopher and teacher, for Marcellus. She had her brother assign money from Antony's estate to the two Antonias, and probably for his son, to ensure that they were well educated.

She married them all well. The elder Marcella married Marcus Vipsanius Agrippa, the great general and close confidant of Augustus, in 28 B.C.E. The younger Marcella married Marcus Valerius Messalla Appianus, consul in 12 B.C.E. The elder

ANTONIA was betrothed to Lucius Domitius Ahenobarbus, consul in 16 B.C.E., the younger Antonia, to Livia's son Nero Claudius Drusus, consul in 9 B.C.E. Octavia's son Claudius Marcellus and Livia's son Tiberius were regarded as Augustus's most likely successors, and he took both of them when he went campaigning in Spain in 27 B.C.E. In 25, Augustus and Octavia arranged a marriage between Augustus's only child, JULIA (6), and her son Marcellus, which marked him as the most probable heir apparent.

Two years later Marcellus fell ill and died. Octavia never completely recovered from the loss. She spent a good deal of time alone, dressed in mourning clothes, and for the remaining 12 years of her life did not allow her son's name mentioned in her presence. Her relationship with her sister-in-law, Livia, deteriorated. Livia's son Tiberius remained alive and healthy, a constant reminder of Octavia's loss. Her sadness, however, did not prevent her from continuing to oversee the marriages of the children of her household: In 20 B.C.E. Cleopatra Selene married Juba II, king of Mauritania, a man of culture, who had been granted Roman citizenship by Augustus.

In the same year, Augustus had a crisis. He needed someone trustworthy in Rome, which faced food shortages, while he traveled to the provinces. Octavia convinced her brother that Agrippa, his closest military ally and friend, should marry his daughter Julia, who was also Octavia's widowed daughter-in-law. The two men would then be linked through the living symbol of Julia, as Octavian and Antony had been joined through Octavia decades before. The new marriage required Agrippa to divorce Octavia's daughter the elder Marcella. Octavia immediately married Marcella to the handsome, young, and dashing Iullus Antonius, who also had grown up in her household. Everyone seemed to benefit. Marcella exchanged Agrippa, who all concur was a good husband, for a much more handsome man with a seemingly bright future, who was her contemporary and childhood mate. The widowed Julia had a new husband with a standing at least equal to that of her first husband, and Augustus had a reliable man in Rome. Finally, the intimate threesome surrounding Augustus of Livia, Octavia, and Agrippa was strengthened.

In 15 Octavia became a grandmother when the younger Antonia and Nero Claudius Drusus, the younger son of Livia, gave birth to Germanicus Julius Caesar. Octavia died in 11 B.C.E. and was given a state funeral. Augustus and the popular Nero Claudius Drusus, at that moment the more likely heir to the emperor, delivered funeral orations. She was widely esteemed by the people for her virtue, nobility, loyalty, and humanity. In her honor, Augustus erected the Porticus Octaviae, which contained a building housing a fine library.

App., Bciv. 5.64, 76, 93, 95.
Dio. 48.31.3; 49.43.8; 54.6.4–5, 35.4–5.
Plut., Ant. 31.1–5; 53.1–5; 54.1–2; 87.1–3.
Suet., Aug. 61.2; 63.1.
Balsdon, J. P. V. D., index.
Bauman, R. A., index.
OCD, p. 1,059.
PW 96.
Syme, R., *Augustan Aristocracy*, index.
Syme, R., *Roman Revolution*, index.

OCTAVIA, CLAUDIA

(39/40–62 C.E.) Roman: Italy
Faultless wife; banished

Claudia Octavia was an emperor's daughter and subject to the dangerous intrigues of those closest to imperial power. Born in 39 or 40 C.E., her mother was Valeria MESSALLINA, and her father, the emperor Claudius. Her life was transformed when her father ordered the death of her mother and chose the younger AGRIPPINA for his next wife. Even before her own marriage to Claudius, Agrippina sought to marry Octavia and her son, Nero. There was, however, a standing arrangement between Octavia and Lucius Junius Silanus, praetor in 48 C.E. This obstacle was overcome when Lucius Vitellius, consul in 47 C.E., one of the emperor's closest advisers, and an ally of Agrippina, charged JUNIA CALVINA, who was his former daughter-in-law, of incest with her brother, Silanus. The engagement was dissolved, and Silanus committed suicide on the day that Agrippina married Claudius. Junia Calvina was exiled.

In 53 C.E. Octavia, who was 13 or 14, married the 16-year-old Nero. The next year, her husband became emperor. His affections were soon transferred to a freewoman, ACTE, despite Agrippina's strong disapproval. He then fell in love with the beautiful and wealthy POPPAEA SABINA (2). In 59 Nero arranged to have his mother murdered, and three years later, he divorced Octavia, claiming her sterile after he failed to prove her adultery with a slave. He exiled her to Campania, where she was kept under military guard.

Octavia kept her dowry, and her popularity was undiminished. She received the house of the deceased Burrus, a freedman of Claudius and Nero, and the estate of Rubellius Plautus, who had been forced to suicide by Nero. But rumors of her return led to demonstrations of approval, and her statues were hung with flowers while those of Poppaea were destroyed. Nero and Poppaea became alarmed. He bribed Anicetus, prefect of the fleet at Misenum and the murderer of his mother Agrippina, to testify that Octavia had committed adultery with him. Octavia was banished to the island of Pandateria where she was murdered on June 9, 62 C.E.

Dio. 61.7.1–3, 31.7–8; 62.13.1–2.
Suet., Claud. 27.1–2.
Suet., Ner. 7.2; 35.1–3.
Tac., Ann. 11.32, 34; 12.1–5, 8, 9, 58; 13.18; 14.1, 59–64.
Balsdon, J. P. V. D., pp. 124, 126–27.
Bauman, R. A., pp. 205–8.
OCD, pp. 336.
PW 428.

▣ OCULATA

(1st century C.E.) Roman: Rome
Priestesses

Oculata and her sister, also named Oculata, were Vestal Virgins. In 83 C.E. the sisters and a third colleague, VARRONILLA, were convicted of incest by the pontifical college as part of a campaign against immorality launched by the emperor Domitian. The Vestal Virgins, six in number, served to protect the eternal flame of Rome in one of the oldest temples in the Forum. Historically, any kind of illicit behavior was considered an ill omen for the city and was punished by entombment. In this case, however, the three women were allowed to commit suicide. Their supposed lovers were sent into exile.

Dio. 67.3.3(2)–4(1).
Suet., Dom. 8.4.
Balsdon, J. P. V. D., p. 241.

▣ OENANTHE

(3rd century B.C.E.) Greek: Samos and Egypt
Conspirator; murderer

Oenanthe left the island of Samos and went to Egypt with her two children, AGATHOCLEIA and Agathocles. She was a tambourine player and her daughter was a dancer. Oenanthe and her son became lovers of Ptolemy III Euergetes. Her daughter, Agathocleia, became the lover of Eugertes' son, Ptolemy IV Philopator.

Oenanthe joined the conspiracy to overthrow Ptolemy IV and ARSINOË III PHILOPATOR in 205 B.C.E. Her son proclaimed himself regent of the murdered rulers' five-year-old boy, and he placed the child under the guardianship of Oenanthe and Agathocleia. However, Arsinoë III, more than her husband, had been widely admired, and her murder aroused the anger of the army and the populace. The conspirators were seized. Oenanthe and her daughter were driven through the streets naked before being killed by the mob.

Ath. 13.577.
Poly. 14.11.1; 15.25.3–33.
Pomeroy, S. B., *Women in Hellenistic Egypt,* index.

OLYMPIAS (1)

(4th century B.C.E.) Greek: Epirus and
Macedonia
Ruler

Olympias was the most remarkable woman of her
day. Both revered and feared, she was proud, imperious, and passionate, as well as beautiful, tempestuous, and ruthless. She sought and used
political power fearlessly with the charisma of a se-
ductress and the skill of a sorcerer. Born into a
family that claimed ancestry back to Achilles, her
father, Neoptolemus, was ruler of Molossia in
Epirus, a part of northwestern Greece. From
youth onward Olympias zealously practiced mystery rites (later identified with Demeter and
Dionysius) that used snakes, with which she became expert and terrorized friend and foe. She
met her husband, Philip, the future king of Macedonia, when she was quite young. He was about
20 years old. They had both traveled to the island
of Samothrace in the northeast Aegean to be initiated into religious rites for the worship of the
Cabiri gods, who promoted fertility in women and
the land and also protected seafarers.

Olympias married Philip II in 357 B.C.E. She
gave birth to a son, the future Alexander the
Great, in 356, and to a daughter, CLEOPATRA (3),
two years later. Philip had already been married
probably more than once. With her husband away
on military campaigns, Olympias solidified her position of leadership in his household and developed close relations with her children that lasted
over the course of her lifetime. She supervised the
children's education and made sure that her
daughter followed her example and learned to
hunt, ride, and use weapons.

Olympias had a ready wit as well as a sharp
tongue and a violent temper. When Philip
claimed that a young and beautiful woman had
cast a spell over him, Olympias looked at the
woman and noted that witchcraft was not necessary. When Alexander claimed that his father was
Zeus, Olympias laughed and responded that her
son slandered her if he compared her with Zeus's
wife, Hera.

After almost 20 years of marriage, Philip unexpectedly married a much younger woman, CLEO-
PATRA (2), the niece of Attalos, one of his most
prominent generals. The reasons may have been
passion or demands of his supporters that he
marry a Macedonian woman. Olympias and Alexander withdrew to Epirus. In 336 Philip was murdered during a celebration of their daughter
Cleopatra's marriage. Ancient rumors implied
that Olympias had a hand in the murder. There is
no question that her husband's death and the
ascendency of her son, Alexander, vastly improved her position. No woman was her peer.

Murder was a feature of Macedonian politics,
and Olympias had no hesitation in using it to protect her position. She was responsible for the
death of the widowed Cleopatra and her small
son, killed while Alexander was away campaigning. Alexander was said to have felt that the punishment was too harsh, but to preclude any future
threat, he had Attalos and all of his kinsmen killed
as well.

When Alexander set out in 334, Olympias presided over the court of Macedonia and vied for
power with Antipater the general whom Alexander left behind as overseer of Greece and Macedonia. Olympias and Antipater wrote many latters
to Alexander complaining bitterly about each
other's conduct. In 331, furious, she left Macedonia for her inherited lands in Epirus, which she
ruled along with her daughter Cleopatra after the
death of the latter's husband in 330. As was her
way, she ruled despotically with little regard for
popular support and in 325 Olympias sent Cleopatra back to Macedonia to stir up trouble against
Antipater. Alexander expressed little fear of his
mother's plans, since he believed the Macedonians would never accept rule by a woman. Alexander's unexpected death in 323, however,
altered the political realities and posed new possibilities for Olympias's unceasing struggle to gain
control over Macedonia. Cognizant of Alexander's view about female rule, Olympias invited the

young and handsome Leonnatus, a general under Alexander and distant kin, to marry her daughter Cleopatra and become titular ruler over Macedonia. He accepted but was soon killed in battle.

At the same time other claimants came forth. EURYDICE (2), a granddaughter of Philip II and the Illyrian princess Audata, married her cousin Philip Arrhidaeus, the weak son of Philip II and PHILINNA. The rival generals agreed to recognize as joint kings Philip Arrhidaeus and Alexander IV, the infant son of ROXANE and Alexander the Great. In 322, Olympias, whose hatred for Antipater was unappeased, sent her daughter Cleopatra to Asia to offer marriage to Perdiccas, one of Antipater's two major opponents. Marriage into the family of Alexander with its ties to the rulers of Macedonia was a prize that Perdiccas could not turn down. When Antipater discovered the possible liaison he and his allies put Cleopatra under guard in Sardis.

In 319 Antipater died, and the dissolution of Alexander's empire accelerated. Polyperchon, whom Antipater had named as his successor, Antigonus, and Antipater's son Cassander engaged in a three-way struggle that opened space for Olympias to maneuver for power. Polyperchon invited Olympias to return to Macedonia from Epirus and take charge of her grandson Alexander IV. Olympias hesitated and was advised by her closest ally, the general Eumenes, to wait until the struggle between Polyperchon and Cassander produced a clear victor. In 317 Cassander landed in Macedonia. Eurydice, pulling the strings behind her husband and always opposed to Olympias, had her husband recognize Cassander. With the legitimacy accorded by Philip Arrhidaeus, Cassander was acknowledged the strongest contender for rule over Macedonia.

Polyperchon fled to Epirus with Roxane and her son, Alexander IV, and begged help from Olympias. With Polyperchon's support Olympias had found the moment to confront Eurydice and Philip Arrhidaeus, regain the throne for the young Alexander IV, and make herself regent. She led her army into Macedonia in 317. Instead of wait-

ing for the return of Cassander, who was in southern Greece, Eurydice and her husband met Olympias at the border. At the appearance of Olympias, whom they regarded as sacred, the Macedonian army refused to fight, and Olympias won the day without any bloodshed.

Olympias executed Philip Arrhidaeus and had Eurydice commit suicide. She ordered the execution of 100 of Cassander's closest Macedonian supporters, including his brother. She had achieved her long-sought goal—rule over Macedon through her barely six-year-old grandson, Alexander IV. Cassander, however, was still very much alive. Moving north, he slipped his army into Macedonia, catching Olympias by surprise. She withdrew with a small force to Pydna, the capital, where she was besieged. With her were Roxane and Alexander IV. Her collaborator Polyperchon failed to break the siege. The city faced starvation. She allowed some soldiers to leave the city, possibly to ease the pressure on diminishing supplies. They fled to Cassander, who directed them to various parts of Macedonia to undermine support for Olympias. In 316 Olympias surrendered to Cassander after he promised to spare her life.

Cassander sought to honor his pledge and succeed in killing Olympias simultaneously. He sent friends who offered her a ship to Athens. Olympias refused, recognizing a ruse. Since she refused to leave the country, Cassander arranged for the relatives of those she killed to accuse her in the assembly. No one was allowed to speak on her behalf. She was condemned. Cassander refused her request to appear before the assembly, fearing her power. He sent 200 soldiers to murder her. When they came into her presence, however, they did not kill her. Cassander then sent relatives of her victims, who did kill her. Olympias faced death as she had lived and asked no mercy. For generations, the Macedonians continued to revere her grave at Pydna.

Dio. 16.91.4; 18.57.2, 58.2–3, 65.1–2; 19.11.1–9; 35–36; 49–51.

Paus. 1.9.1–4; 8.7.5.
Plut., Alex. 2.1–9; 31–34; 5.7; 9.5–11; 10.6–8; 39.7–8;
   68.4–5; 77.8.
Carney, E. D., "The Career of Adea-Eurydice,"
   pp. 496–502.
Carney, E. D., "Olympias," pp. 35–62.
Carney, E. D., "What's in a Name?" pp. 154–57, 163.
Heckel, W., "Philip and Olympias," pp. 51–57.
Macurdy, G., pp. 22 ff.
OCD, p. 1,066.
PW 5.

▣ OLYMPIAS (2)

(3rd century B.C.E.)   Greek: Epirus
Ruler

Olympias ruled Epirus in northwestern Greece after the death of her husband. She was the daughter of Pyrrhus, the general and ruler of Epirus. Her father was succeeded by his son Alexander II, who married Olympias. They were probably stepsiblings. They had two sons, Pyrrhus and Ptolemy, and three daughters, PHTHIA (nicknamed Chryseis), Nereis, and Deidamia.

After the death of her husband in 240 or 239 B.C.E., Olympias became regent for her son Pyrrhus II. When the Aetolians threatened to annex the northern half of Acarnania, which had been assigned by treaty to Epirus, Olympias offered her daughter Phthia in marriage to Demetrius II, who in 239, had just become ruler of Macedonia. Demetrius accepted the alliance and divorced his wife STRATONICE (3). In the war that followed, Demetrius saved Acarnania. However, Olympias's son Pyrrhus died. She relinquished rule to her second son, Ptolemy, who also died. Shortly thereafter, she too died.

Just. 28.1, 3.
Macurdy, G., p. 79.
Walbank, F., p. 9.

▣ OPIMIA

(?–216 B.C.E.)   Roman: Rome
Priestess

Opimia was a Vestal Virgin accused of violating her vow of chastity in 216 B.C.E. One of six Vestals, she was responsible for maintaining the eternal flame in the temple of Vesta, one of the oldest temples in the Forum. She was charged together with a colleague, FLORONIA. It was considered an extremely serious ill omen for the state when the Vestal Virgins trangressed. Opimia was either entombed or committed suicide.

Livy 22.57.2–5.
Bauman, R. A., pp. 23–24.

▣ ORBIANA

(3rd century C.E.)   Roman: Italy
Possible Augusta

Gnaea Seia Herennia Sallustia Barbia Orbiana was 15 years old when she married the 17-year-old emperor Severus Alexander in 225 C.E. She may have immediately been declared Augusta. The marriage was recorded with a run of celebratory coins struck in gold, silver, and bronze. Orbiana was on the obverse and, with probably unintentional irony, *Concordia* (harmonious agreement) on the reverse.

Orbiana's new mother-in-law, JULIA AVITA MAMAEA, who had dominated the reign since her son had become emperor at 13, did not welcome the intrusion of Orbiana or her father, Sallustius Macrinus, or Macrinianus. Possibly, the father was elevated to the position of Caesar, and the marriage may have been part of plot to overthrow the emperor or to eliminate Julia Mamaea. Whatever the intention, it failed. Julia Mamaea emerged unscathed. Orbiana's father was executed; Orbiana was divorced and exiled to Libya in 227 C.E.

Herodian 6.1, 9–10.
SHA, Alex. Sev. 20.3; 49.4–5.
Balsdon, J. P. V. D., p. 163.
Gibbon, E., p. 117.

P

▣ PAPIRIA

(3rd–2nd century B.C.E.) Roman: Rome
Financially strapped well-born woman

Papiria was divorced and left financially strapped. She was the daughter of Caius Papirius Maso, consul in 231 B.C.E. She married Lucius Aemilius Paullus Macedonius, general and statesman, who was twice consul. She had two sons, Quintus Fabius and Publius Cornelius. When her husband divorced her, he was criticized in the Senate. Her virtues were enumerated: She was beautiful and virtuous and had borne sons. It was said that her husband held his shoe high and commented that it too was new and good-looking, but that only he knew where it pinched.

Papiria ceased to participate in women's rites to which her birth and status admitted her since her divorce left her poor. Publius Cornelius however was adopted by Publius Cornelius Scipio, son of the Publius Cornelius Scipio Africanus Major who conquered Hannibal. He inherited a large fortune from his adoptive grandmother AEMILIA TERTIA, who was the wife of Scipio Africanus. Papiria's son gave her all of his grandmother's servants, ornaments, and utensils used in religious ceremonies. Her son's generosity was noted, and many women offered prayers for such a son. It was observed that the son's gift was exceptional, especially in Rome, few ever willingly parted with anything they had gained.

Plut., Aem. 5.2–3.
Balsdon, J. P. V. D., pp. 43, 211–12.
PW 78.

▣ PAULINA

(1st century C.E.) Roman: Rome
Victim of deception

Paulina was a devotee of Isis. Isis worship had been brought from Egypt to Rome, where it attracted a wide following. The underlying sensuality and sexuality in the worship of a figure who was simultaneously wife, mother, and prostitute affirmed female sexual potency and was especially attractive to women. Paulina became the center of a scandal that rested on the naïveté of some Isis followers and that had serious political consequences.

She had rejected the advances of one Decius Mundus. Undeterred, he was said to have bribed a priest in the temple of Isis to inform Paulina that she was desired by the Egyptian god Anubis. Paulina made no secret of her appointment in the temple with the god, even telling her husband of the assignation. Later Mundus bragged of his deception. Paulina learned of his duplicity and her husband went to the authorities. After an inquiry Mundus was exiled.

The emperor Tiberius had the priests of Isis crucified and deported thousands of worshipers to Sardinia.

Jos. AJ 18.65–80.
Tac., Ann. 2.85.5.
Balsdon, J. P. V. D., p. 247.

🔲 PAXAEA

(1st century C.E.) Roman: Italy and the Balkans
Charged with treason and extortion

Paxaea and her husband, Pomponius Labeo, the former governor of the Roman province of Moesia in what is now Serbia, were tried in the Senate on charges that probably included treason and extortion. The emperor Tiberius had turned against Labeo in 34 C.E., the same year as the trial. The precise nature of the treason of which Labeo was accused is not known. It is also uncertain if Paxaea was charged with both crimes or just one.

Paxaea and her husband committed suicide before the Senate reached a verdict. After her death, the emperor Tiberius declared that Paxaea had been in no danger despite the fact that she was guilty.

Tac., Ann. 6.29.
Levick, B., *Tiberius*, pp. 197, 213 ff.
Marshall, A. J., "Women on Trial," p. 347.

🔲 PERICTIONE

(5th century B.C.E.) Greek: Athens
Mother of Plato

Perictione, an Athenian from a distinguished family that traced its ancestry back to Solon, was notable for being the mother of the great philosopher Plato. She was born in the early 440s. Her father was Glaucon, and her brother Charmides was the protagonist in a Socratic dialogue named after him. Perictione married Ariston, a man from a similar background, and in addition to Plato, they had two other sons, Adeimantus and Glaucon, and a daughter, POTONE. After the death of her husband, she married her maternal uncle, Pyrilampes. He served as an ambassador in Persia and was noted for his breeding of Persian peacocks.

Diog. Laert. 3.1.3–4.
Pl., Chrm. 158a.
Davies, J. K., pp. 330, 332–33.

🔲 PETRONIA

(1st century C.E.) Roman: Rome
Political player

Petronia was the daughter of a wealthy consul and had a large personal fortune. She married Aulus Vitellius, the future emperor. She made a will naming their son, Petronianus, her heir on condition that Vitellius renounce his paternal rights. Vitellius agreed, but their son died. Vitellius said the young man had had suicidal leanings and had mistakenly taken poison that was intended for him. It was generally believed that Vitellius had murdered his son to obtain the inheritance.

Petronia divorced Vitellius. She married Cornelius Dolabella. Dolabella supported the emperor Servius Sulpicius Galba and was banished by the emperor Marcus Salvius Otho, who supplanted Galba in 69 C.E. After Otho's death, Dolabella returned. When Vitellius became emperor later in 69, he ordered Dolabella killed. Nothing more is known of Petronia.

Suet., Vit. 6.
Tac., Hist. 2.64.

🔲 PHAENARETE

(5th century B.C.E.) Greek: Athens
Mother of Socrates

Phaenarete was the mother of the great philosopher Socrates. Her husband, Sophroniscus, was an Athenian sculptor or stonemason. Phaenarete was a midwife. She belonged to the Alopece clan.

Diog. Laert. 2.18.

🔲 PHILA (1)

(c. 351–283 B.C.E.) Greek: Macedonia
Wise, loyal, and influential wife

Phila was a woman of exceptional character who used the circumstances in which she found herself to exert influence and exercise power. She was said to have been close to her father and his confidant since her childhood. Her father, Antipater, the Macedonian general whom Alexander the Great left with oversight of the Greek city-states and Macedonia when he went east on campaign, was generally regarded as a wise ruler, and Phila learned well. Her mother was Stratonice, daughter of a Macedonian named Corrhagus.

After Alexander's unexpected death, his generals divided the empire. Antipater and Craterus became convinced that a third general, Perdiccas, was plotting to make himself dominant. They formed an alliance with Ptolemy I Soter, the Macedonian general who had made himself ruler of Egypt. To cement the alliance, Phila married Craterus in 322 B.C.E., and another daughter of Antipater, EURYDICE (3), married Ptolemy I Soter. A third daughter, NICAEA (1), married Lysimachus, the former companion and bodyguard of Alexander who ruled Thrace, to assure his neutrality to the pact. Phila had a son also named Craterus. Her husband was killed leading his troops in 321.

Before she was even able to bury her husband, her father arranged a marriage with the 18-year-old Demetrius who was the son of his longtime fighting companion, Antigonus. He was some 12 years her junior and an extraordinarily handsome man. A notorious womanizer, he was frequently engaged in multiple sexual adventures and married several women. Once his wife, however, Phila remained steadfastly loyal. Demetrius

recognized her political sagacity, and she was undoubtedly the most important and influential woman in his life.

In 319, Antipater died and Antigonus, with the aid of Demetrius, attempted to reunite Alexander's empire. Left behind, Phila sent a ship filled with letters, bedding, and clothing to Demetrius when he besieged Rhodes in 305. Unfortunately for her husband, it was intercepted by the Rhodians. She also quelled troublemakers on the home front. She was said to have arranged marriages and given dowries to settle many women and to have protected many suffering from false allegations. She also resolved disputes among the soldiers whose camps she visited and was regarded by them as a fair arbitrator.

In 298, Phila accompanied Demetrius when he set sail for Syria to marry their daughter, STRATONICE (2), to Seleucus I. They stopped at Cilicia, in southern Asia Minor, which was ruled by Pleistarchus, a brother of Phila. Pleistarchus was furious at the landing and further angered by any alliance with Seleucus, for Demetrius had been the common enemy of both Pleistarchus and Seleucus. After the wedding, Demetrius seized Cilicia. Phila went to Macedonia where her other brother, Cassander, was king to convince him not to side with Pleistarchus.

In 294 the Macedonian army invited Demetrius I to become king because he was related to Antipater through his marriage to Phila. For Phila it was a great moment of success that was short-lived. The alliance with Seleucus I fell apart. Demetrius was defeated and captured by Seleucus in 285. Seleucus kept him in luxurious confinement, and he drank himself to death in 283. Phila committed suicide by taking poison. In addition to Stratonice, Phila and Demetrius had a son, Antigonus Gonatus, who reestablished control over Macedonia.

Plut., Demetr. 14.2–3; 22.1; 31.3; 32.1–3; 37.3; 45.1; 53.3.
Diod. 18.18.7; 19.59.3–6; 20.93.4.
Cary, M.
Macurdy, G., pp. 58–69.

⊡ PHILA (2)

(3rd century B.C.E.) Greek: Asia, Asia Minor, and Macedonia
Power broker

Phila grew up living with her father, Seleucus I, whose rule extended from Asia Minor into central Asia. Her mother, STRATONICE (2), had gone to the eastern part of the empire as the wife of Antiochus I, her father's son by APAMA (1) and coruler. When Antiochus succeeded her father, Phila was about 21. Her mother arranged for her to marry her uncle Antigonus Gonatus, who had become ruler of Macedonia. The marriage sealed a compact in which Antiochus I surrendered any claim to Macedonia and renounced his claim to what is now called the Gallipoli Peninsula.

Phila's husband was a fine man, a sound general, and a prudent ruler. He was educated in philosophy and had philosophers, poets, and historians as friends. Among the guests at Phila's elaborate wedding was the noted poet Aratus, who wrote a hymn and poems for the occasion. Her marriage appears to have been successful and was remarkable for its longevity. She had been married for 37 years when her husband died in 239 B.C.E.

Phila's son Demetrius II succeeded his father as ruler of Macedonia. He married STRATONICE (3), who was both a half sister and niece of his mother, but later divorced her.

Plut., Demetr. 31.3; 38.
Bevan, E. B., v. 1, pp. 145, 173.
Macurdy, G., pp. 69–70.

⊡ PHILESIA

(5th–4th century B.C.E.) Greek: Athens and Sparta
Wife of Xenophon

Philesia, an Athenian woman, married Xenophon, who came from a wealthy family and was a follower of Socrates. Xenophon, known for his work on household management, asserted that a man should marry a woman sufficiently young and pliable to bend to his ways.

Xenophon, however, was rarely at home. He spent most of his life in the military. In 401 B.C.E. he left Athens and joined Greek mercenaries in Asia Minor under Cyrus II to gain control over Persia. The expedition was a failure, and Xenophon, with the rank of general, led the Greek forces to safety. In 399 he enlisted his troops in the services of Sparta in Asia Minor and was exiled by Athens. From 396 to 394 he served with Agesilaus, ruler of Sparta, campaigning in Asia Minor. When Agesilaus returned to Sparta, Xenophon went with him and fought against Athens. In honor of his service, the Spartans gave him an estate at Scillus near the city of Olympia. Philesia and their two sons went there with him. Later, the area came under attack, and the family moved to Corinth.

Athens rescinded his exile in 366 after relations with Sparta improved. Xenophon returned to Athens in that year and lived there until his death in 354. Philesia, if still living, would have returned with him. Both their sons served with the Athenians against Sparta. One son was killed in battle in 362 B.C.E.

Diog. Laert. 2.48–59.

⊡ PHILINNA

(4th century B.C.E.) Greek: Thessaly and Macedonia
Cowife of Phillip II

Philinna was especially vulnerable in the household of Philip II, ruler of Macedonia. With the exception of OLYMPIAS (1), she was the only wife of Philip II to have a son. She came from Larissa in northwest Thessaly. Larissa had called on Philip to help overthrow the tyrant of Phaere who threatened them. Philip complied and married Philinna in 356 B.C.E. to solidify his ties with the aristocratic families of Larissa. Their son Philip Arrhidaeus was born in the 350s. The child was born with some impairment, which could have been epilepsy or a limited mental capacity. Alternatively, as one of the sources contends, he may have been debilitated with poison fed him by Olympias.

Philip had married Olympias the year before his marriage with Philinna, and she bore him the future Alexander the Great and CLEOPATRA (3) thereafter. Olympias was formidable, and determined that Alexander would be her husband's heir. She succeeded, and Alexander became king after the death of his father. After the unexpected death of Alexander in 323, however, Alexander's infant son was declared joint ruler with Philinna's son, Philip Arrhidaeus. There is no mention of Philinna in the subsequent struggles for power. Possibly, even probably, she was already dead.

Philinna had another son, Amphimachus Triparadeisus, who was born before she married Philip and not a part of the post-Alexander struggles.

Diod. 16.14.2.
Just. 13.2, 11.
Greenwalt, W. S., pp. 69–77.
Hammond, N. G. L., *History of Greece*, pp. 539, 573.
Macurdy, G., pp. 26–27.

▣ PHRYNE

(5th century B.C.E.) Greek: Greece
Self-made woman

Phryne, renowned for her beauty, lived in Athens and became very wealthy. Her father was Epicles from Thespiae in southern Greece. Phryne modeled for the great sculptor Praxiteles who inscribed an epigram on the nude Cnidian Aphrodite expressing his passion for her. She also modeled for the painter Apelles who portrayed her as Aphrodite rising from the sea.

Praxiteles was said to have offered her the gift of one of his works. Desiring the piece he most valued, she was said to have told a slave to run and tell Praxiteles that his studio was on fire. Praxiteles ran to his studio crying that all of his

work was in vain if he lost his sculptures of Eros and Satyr. Phryne chose Eros which she donated to the temple of Eros at Thespiae. It is also said that a group of friends paid Praxiteles to sculpt a golden statue of Phryne, which she dedicated at Delphi.

In contentious Athens, it was not surprising that a suit was brought against Phryne, who chose her friends, lovers, and patrons from among the artistic and public men of the day. She was charged by Euthius with corrupting young women by organizing them to worship the Thracian god Isodaetes. If convicted, she could have been put to death. One of her presumed lovers, the orator Hyperides, successfully defended her. To counter the prejudice against her on the part of the judge, he was said to have torn off Phryne's clothes and exposed her breasts. The judge, it was said, feared that Phryne was a ministrant of the goddess Aphrodite and declared her innocent. It was also reported that the Athenians later passed a law prohibiting women from removing their clothes during a trial.

Ath. 13.567d–e, 590e–591f.
Paus. 1.20.1–2; 9.27.5; 10.15.1.
Plut., Mor., Amat. 753.
Fantham, E., et al., pp. 175–76.
Licht, H., pp. 311, 348 ff.
Pomeroy, S. B., *Goddesses*, p. 141.

▣ PHTHIA

(3rd century B.C.E.) Greek: Epirus
and Macedonia
Coruler

Phthia, who was often called Chryseis, no doubt in reference to her golden hair, lived with her mother, OLYMPIAS (2), who ruled Epirus as regent for her young son after the death of her husband, Alexander II. To prevent the Aetolian League from annexing the northern half of Acarnania, which by treaty had been assigned to Epirus, Olympias established an alliance with Demetrius II, who became ruler of Macedonia in 239 B.C.E.

Phthia and Demetrius married to solidify the relationship after he divorced his wife, STRATONICE (3), who had borne him no male heirs. Demetrius prevented the takeover of Acarnania and won territory from the Aetolian League.

Demetrius, however, was a rather weak ruler. He suffered a series of defeats and died in 229. Phthia's son Philip, who was born in 238 B.C.E., succeeded his father. Since he was only nine years old at the time, his uncle Antigonus Doson was regent. Antigonus Doson took full control, married Phthia, and adopted Philip.

During the earthquake of 227 in Rhodes, Phthia sent corn and lead to help the inhabitants. In 221 her son became Philip V, ruler of Macedonia.

Just. 28.1.
Poly. 5.89.7.
Tarn, W. W., "Phthia-Chryseis," pp. 483 ff.
Walbank, F., pp. 5, 9–10, 258.

▣ PILIA

(?–c. 44/43 B.C.E.) Roman: Rome and Italy
Loyal wife and friend

Pilia lived a protected life during the tumultuous decades that led to civil war in the second half of the first century B.C.E. Her husband, Titus Pomponius Atticus, was one of the wealthiest men of Rome. In a period when fortunes were lost through confiscation, wantonness, and inflation, Atticus's wealth only increased. Careful to maintain good relations all across the political spectrum, Atticus was banker to many, including Marcus Tullius Cicero and Octavian. He and Pilia, however, always had time for their private life. From the time they married in February 56 B.C.E. until her probable death in 44 or 43 B.C.E., Atticus loved her, and she would seem to have returned the feeling. They often traveled together and entertained on estates spread through southern and central Italy. They had one child, Caecilia ATTICA, who was born in 51 and was cherished by both of them.

Atticus was already 53 when he married the much younger Pilia. It appeared to be a first marriage for both of them. Atticus was Cicero's closest friend and ally, and in their frequent correspondence, there is no indication that either Atticus or Pilia had extended families. The demands on Atticus called him to Rome and sometimes left Pilia free to travel in Italy to visit friends in resort towns or to attend weddings and funerals. The close friendship with Cicero was strengthened by the marriage of Atticus's sister and Cicero's brother. An unhappy marriage, it provided all the members of the family with a constant source of comment, gossip, and advice. Atticus and Pilia were frequent visitors with Cicero and his wife TERENTIA (1). It was TULLIA (2), Cicero's daughter, with whom Pilia was friends, and they were probably close in age. Tullia stayed with Pilia a number of times when she was at a crossroads in her own life.

Illness loomed large in ancient life. On August 19, 44 B.C.E., a greatly perturbed Cicero was on his way to Pompeii by ship when he wrote Atticus about the news from Marcus Junius Brutus that Pilia had suffered some form of paralysis. That was the last letter between the men that mentioned Pilia.

In 37 their daughter Attica was betrothed to Marcus Vipsanius Agrippa, the great general and supporter of Octavian, the new emperor Augustus. She brought with her a huge dowry.

Cic., Att. 4.16; 5.11; 8.7; 10.13.47a, 15; 14.17, 19; 15.1a; 16.7, 11.

▣ PIPA (PIPARA)

(3rd century C.E.) German: Germany and Italy
Young lover

Pipa, who was also called Pipara, was the daughter of Attalus Publius Licinius, leader of the Marcomani, a west German tribe. In 253 C.E. Publius Licinius Egnatius Gallienus, who was co-Augustus with his father the emperor Valerian, fell in love with Pipa while he was married to Cornelia SALONINA, a highly cultured Greek woman from Bithynia in Asia Minor. Although Pipa's feelings are unrecorded, she became his lover. Her father received a large portion of Pannonia, territory lying west of the Danube, either in return for his daughter or for his help in repelling Germanic invasions, or perhaps for both. It is not known what happened to Pipa, but Salonina remained Augusta and accompanied Gallienus on his campaigns.

SHA, Gallien. 21.3.

PLANGON

(404–? B.C.E.) Greek: Athens
Self-made woman

Plangon's life was made difficult by the perfidious behavior of her husband and the criminal behavior of her father. Her father was Pamphilus, a wealthy and prominent citizen of Athens. Born around 404 B.C.E., shortly before the end of the Peloponnesian War, she married Mantias with a substantial dowry of 100 minas.

In 388 her father, who held the rank of general, was dismissed from service, convicted of embezzlement, and his property confiscated. The family was ruined. Her husband promptly divorced her, while she either was still pregnant or had just given birth to a son. Plangon did not succeed in recovering her dowry from Mantias, or possibly her dowry had also been confiscated as part of her father's estate. In any event, she was without the means to arrange another marriage. In addition, Mantias refused to acknowledge her child, named Boiotus, and introduce him into his phratry.

Mantias later married another woman with a dowry. Plangon, however, was beautiful, and Mantias remained sexually attracted to her. They continued a relationship, even after he remarried. She had another son, this one named after Pamphilus, whom Mantias also refused to ac-

knowledge. With two sons who were without the legal recognition that would entitle them to citizenship and the right to inherit from their father, Plangon initiated a suit against Mantias.

Plangon was very clear on her goals and offered her ex-husband a settlement. If he would give her 30 minas, a reasonably substantial sum at the time, her brother would adopt the two boys. She assured him if the arbiter in the suit asked her to swear to the fact that Mantias was the father of the boys, she would refuse. Mantias accepted Plangon's offer. When the arbiter asked her if Mantias was the father of the boys, however, she answered in the affirmative. Mantias, fearing attack by his political foes if he engaged in a protracted suit, gave in and agreed that he was the father. He then enrolled both sons in his phratry. Her sons assumed their rightful citizenship and became heirs of a wealthy estate.

Dem. 39.40.
Walters, K. R., pp. 205–8.

PLATHANE

(5th–4th century B.C.E.) Greek: Athens
Wife of Isocrates

Plathane lived during the Pelopennesian Wars between Athens and Sparta. Her first husband was Hippias, an obscure Athenian. She had three sons before she was widowed. Her second husband was the famous sophist Isocrates. His family lost their wealth during the war. In the contentious and litigious society of Athens, however, Isocrates successfully supported them through teaching and speechwriting.

Isocrates adopted her youngest son, who became a poet and also a speechwriter.

Plut., Mor., Vit. dec. orat. 838a, c; 839b.
Davies, J. K., p. 247.

▣ PLAUTIA URGULANILLA

(1st century B.C.E.–1st century C.E.)   Roman:
Italy
Political player

Plautia Urgulanilla was the first wife of the future
emperor Claudius. They married in about 10 C.E.
She was the daughter of Marcus Plautius
Silvanus, consul in 2 B.C.E., and the granddaughter of URGULANIA, a close friend of the powerful
LIVIA DRUSILLA. No doubt the two older women
had a central role in arranging the marriage. On
the one hand, Claudius, while of the finest ancestry, suffered from an impairment that affected his
speech and walk. Plautia, on the other hand, had
some odd relatives. For example, her only brother,
Marcus Plautius Silvanus, praetor in 24 C.E., murdered his wife, APRONIA, by throwing her from a
window. He committed suicide before he could be
tried.

Plautia and Claudius had two children, a boy,
Drusus, who choked to death when he tossed a
pear and caught it in his mouth, and a daughter,
Claudia. Claudius divorced Plautia and rejected
Claudia as his daughter. He claimed that his
freedman Bota was Plautia's lover and the father
of the child.

Suet., Claud. 26–27.
Balsdon, J. P. V. D., p. 122.
Levick, B., *Claudius*, pp. 16, 23–25.
PW 66.

▣ PLAUTILLA

(2nd–3rd century C.E.)   Roman: Rome
Augusta

Plautilla was her father's ally in a bitter struggle for
power during the reign of Septimius Severus. Her
father was Gaius Fulvius Plautianus, the prefect of
the Praetorian Guard under Severus. Between
197 and 205 C.E., Plautianus exercised de facto
power. During these years he worked to secure
Plautilla's future. Hostile stories about him during
this period claim that he was obsessed with

Plautilla and that he had grown men castrated so
only eunuchs would attend and instruct her. In
202 Plautilla married Marcus Aurelius Antoninus
Caracalla, the son of the emperor. She received
the title Augusta at the time of her marriage. Her
dowry was said to be equal to the wealth of 50 elite
women.

JULIA DOMNA, the powerful wife of Severus
and mother of Caracalla, opposed the marriage.
She was an impacable enemy of Plautianus, whose
authority had diminished hers and who had attacked her with charges of adultery. Her strong influence on her son, not surprisingly, led him to
hate Plautilla. He refused to eat or sleep with her
and swore to kill her and her father when he became emperor. Despite the formal marriage,
Plautilla lived in her father's house.

In 205, Caracalla orchestrated the downfall of
Plautianus by convincing his father that the latter
was about to assassinate him. Caracalla formally
divorced Plautilla, and Severus banished her to
Lipara, an island north of Sicily. She was killed by
Caracalla after he became emperor, as he had
promised.

Dio. 76.14.4–5, 15.2; 77.1.2, 2.4–5, 3.1, 4.4, 6.3.
Herodian 3.10.5–7, 13.2–3; 4.6.3.
Balsdon, J. P. V. D., pp. 152–53.
OCD, p. 614.
PW 117.

▣ PLOTINA, POMPEIA

(1st–2nd century C.E.)   Roman: Gaul, Italy,
Asia, Egypt, Germany, Syria, and Greece
Augusta

Pompeia Plotina has been depicted as a plain and
virtuous woman with high moral standards and
sound judgment. The portrayal does not do her
justice. She was a close adviser on policy to her
husband, the emperor Trajan, and her views
shaped his policies in such diverse areas as provincial taxes and political appointments. In contrast
with her husband, she was interested in the arts
and was attracted to philosophy, especially

Pompeia Plotina

accompanied her husband to Rome early in 99. Her multigenerational household followed. With her husband away for long periods of time campaigning, she assumed responsibility for the running of the household and the affairs of the emperor in Rome. The Senate sought to honor Plotina and Marciana with the title of Augusta in 100 C.E., but both women refused. It was her proud boast that the woman she was before her husband became emperor, was the woman she remained. Five years later, in 105, they relented. In 112, coins were issued depicting Plotina on the obverse and the goddess Vesta on the reverse.

In 113 Plotina, Matidia, and Hadrian accompanied Trajan to the East where he was to begin a military campaign against the Parthians. It was an ill-fated trip. First they barely escaped death from a terrible earthquake in Antioch in 115, and then Trajan suffered a stroke. On August 9, 117, Hadrian received a dispatch that he had been adopted by Trajan. Two days later, he learned that Trajan had died in Selinus in southern Asia Minor and that the army had declared him emperor. Plotina and Matidia were with Trajan in his final days, and rumors arose that Plotina had signed the adoption decree after Trajan's death. Certainly, she would have chosen Hadrian as the successor to her husband.

Plotina remained close with Hadrian after he became emperor. She became a patron to the Epicurean school in Athens and urged Hadrian to open the selection of the school's head beyond the limit of those who held Roman citizenship. Hadrian honored Plotina on coins with Divus Trajan on the obverse and her portrait as Diva Plotina on the reverse. When she died sometime between 121 and 123, he had her consecrated and built two temples, one in the Campus Marius in Rome and the other in Nimes. In his funeral oration, he praised Plotina for her modesty and reasonableness.

Epicureanism. The future emperor Hadrian, who had been left fatherless, lived with her as a child and was part of a family circle that also included Trajan's sisters and nieces. Plotina arranged for Hadrian to marry Vibia SABINA. When Trajan's life ended, Plotina saw to it that there was a peaceful transition to the new regime.

Plotina came from the new aristocracy that dominated the Antonine period. Her father was Lucius Pompeius from Nemausus (Nimes) in the Roman province of Narbonensis. She married Marcus Ulpius Trajan before he became emperor. She had no children with her husband, who was born in Spain of an Italian father and Spanish mother. All his life a military man, in 88 C.E. Trajan went to stem a revolt in Upper Germany. He was appointed governor of the province 10 years later in 97. Plotina accompanied him. Living with them in Cologne were Ulpia MARCIANA, Trajan's widowed sister, and her daughter, MATIDIA (1), as well as her two granddaughters, Vibia Sabina and MATIDIA (2).

Trajan was adopted by the emperor Nerva and succeeded him at the end of January 98. Plotina

Dio. 68.5.5; 69.1.3–4, 10.3–3a.
Plin., Pan. 83; 84.
SHA, Hadr. 2.10; 4.1, 4, 10; 5.9; 12.2.

Balsdon, J. P. V. D., pp. 133–39.
Fantham, E., et al., pp. 349–53.
OCD, p. 1,214.
PW 131.
Syme, R., *Tacitus.*

▣ POMPEIA (1)

(1st century B.C.E.)   Roman: Rome
Political wife

Pompeia is remembered for her divorce from Gaius Julius Caesar in the aftermath of a scandal during celebration of the rites of the Bona Dea. She was the granddaughter of Lucius Cornelius Sulla, the Roman general and dictator, and ILIA, one of his early wives, through her mother CORNELIA (4). Her father, Quintus Pompeius Rufus was the son of Quintus Pompeius Rufus, consul in 88 B.C.E. She married Julius Caesar in 67 B.C.E. after the death of his first wife, CORNELIA (5). Five years later, in December of 62 when her husband was *pontifex maximus* and head of the priestly college, his house was the setting for the annual Bona Dea celebration. Restricted to elite women, the celebration of the goddess was an annual nocturnal event held under the supervision of the wife of the *pontifex maximus* with the assistance of the Vestal Virgins.

During the ceremony in 62, Publius Clodius Pulcher, a brash young aristocrat, disguised himself as a woman slave lute player and gained admittance to the house. Rumor had it that he had an assignation with Pompeia. Caesar's mother, AURELIA (1), recognized the culprit, and he was ousted. Caesar divorced Pompeia without the accusation of adultery but with the assertion that the wife of the *pontifex maximus* must be above suspicion. Clodius was accused of sacrilege and put on trial in 61. He was acquitted when Marcus Licinius Crassus bribed the jury. Crassus probably hoped to use Clodius's popularity with the masses for his own ends. Caesar was not perturbed by what had happened, remained on friendly terms with Clodius, and refused to give a deposition against him. Nothing more is heard of Pompeia.

Cic., Att. 1.12; 13.16.
Plut., Caes. 9.1–8; 10.1–10.
Plut., Cic. 28.1–4; 29.9.
Balsdon, J. P. V. D., pp. 244 ff.
OCD, p. 1,214.
PW 52.

▣ POMPEIA (2)

(1st century B.C.E.)   Roman: Rome
Political wife

Pompeia was the daughter of Gnaeus Pompeius Magnus (Pompey the Great). Her father was three times consul, a much-loved general, and leader of the republicans during the civil war of 49–48 B.C.E. He was also a man who married well and often. Her mother, MUCIA TERTIA, was from a consular family and had been her father's third wife.

Pompeia and Faustus Cornelius Sulla, quaestor in 54, were to marry. He was the son of Lucius Cornelius Sulla, who had been dictator of Rome in 81 B.C.E. and was a former father-in-law to Pompey. The planned marriage was temporarily derailed when Gaius Julius Caesar formed an alliance with Pompey in 59 B.C.E. Caesar also had a daughter, JULIA (5). She was to have married Servilius Caepio but instead married Pompey to cement the alliance between the two men. It was proposed that Pompeia marry Caepio.

Nothing came of the planned marriage with Caepio, and Pompeia married Faustus Sulla as originally planned. Her husband inherited substantial wealth from his father. He spent a great portion of it on living lavishly. He served under Pompey in the East and was killed in 46 fighting with Pompey in the civil war. Pompeia gave birth to CORNELIA (7), whose son became consul in 11 C.E. Pompeia married a second time to Lucius Cornelius Cinna, consul suffectus in 32 B.C.E. They had two children: Gnaeus Cornelius Cinna, consul in 5 C.E., and Pompeia Magna.

Plut., Caes. 14.7.
Syme, R., *Augustan Aristocracy,* index.

▣ POMPEIA MACRINA

(1st century C.E.) Roman Greek: Lesbos
and Sparta
Conspirator

Pompeia Macrina was exiled, and the members of
her family were killed in a conflict with the emperor Tiberius for reasons that remain obscure but
are probably related to the exercise of power in
Greece. Her father, Pompeius Macer, a friend of
both Augustus and Tiberius, was a member of an
important Greek family from Mytilene on the island of Lesbos. He became a high-ranking Roman
equestrian, and Augustus appointed him procurator of Asia. Pompeia Macrina's brother, Quintus
Pompeius Macer, praetor in 15 C.E., was the first
senator from the eastern part of the empire and
one of the few provincials Augustus admitted to
the Senate.

Pompeia Macrina married Iulius Argolicus, a
member of the Euryclad dynasty of Sparta. Her
husband and his father, Iulius Laco, the most
prominent men in Sparta, had held Roman citizenship since her husband's grandfather had been
made ruler of Sparta by the future emperor Augustus as a reward for participating in the battle of
Actium against Mark Antony 31 B.C.E. Shortly
before 2 B.C.E., however, the same grandfather
had been banished by Augustus for fomenting discord in Greece. After Tiberius became emperor,
the dynasty was restored and her husband appointed ruler. In 33 C.E. her husband and his father were removed and punished on orders of
Tiberius. Perhaps their reach had begun again to
upset the balance of power.

Shortly thereafter, the ire of the emperor
shifted from Pompeia Macrina's husband to herself, her father, and her brother. They were accused of supporting the cult of Theophanes of
Mytilene, the great-grandfather of Pompeia
Macrina. Theophanes had been very close to
Pompey the Great, to whom he owed his Roman
citizenship; he had served as his secretary and
written a life of the general. As a favor to
Theophanes, Pompey declared Mytilene a free

city, and after Theophanes died he was deified at
Mytilene. Pompeia's father and brother commit-
ted suicide, rather than wait to be condemned.
Pompeia Macrina was exiled.

Tac., Ann. 6.18.
Levick, B., *Tiberius*, pp. 211–12.
Marsh, F. B., pp. 207, 294.
PW 128.

▣ POMPEIA PAULINA

(1st century C.E.) Roman: Rome
Political victim

Pompeia Paulina exhibited the classic virtue of a
true Roman woman: a willingness to die with her
husband. The wife of the philosopher, orator, and
statesman Lucius Annaeus Seneca, she was part
of a circle of educated Romans who sought to lead
a principled life under the emperor Nero. Her
husband was the tutor of the emperor and later
became his political adviser and minister. In 65
C.E. Nero demanded that he commit suicide. He
accused Seneca of taking part in the Pisonian conspiracy against him.

Pompeia planned to kill herself at the same
time. Both cut veins in their arms, but Seneca also
cut arteries in his legs. In the meantime, fearing
that he would be attacked for cruelty, Nero ordered that Pompeia not die and sent soldiers to be
sure that her slaves and freedmen bandaged her.
She lived, but from that point on she was said to
have been very frail, her face unusually pale. She
died a few years later.

Tac., Ann. 15.63, 64.
Balsdon, J. P. V. D., p. 57
PW 130.

▣ POMPONIA (1)

(3rd–2nd century B.C.E.) Roman: Rome
Mother of Publius Cornelius Scipio Africanus

Pomponia was honored as the mother of Publius
Cornelius Scipio Africanus, the general who con-

quered Hannibal. Born of an ancient family, she married Publius Cornelius Scipio, consul in 218 B.C.E. She had two sons. The eldest, Publius Cornelius Scipio Africanus, was victorious over Hannibal at Zama in 202 B.C.E. and successfully ended the Punic Wars. Her younger son, Lucius Cornelius Scipio Asiageus, served as consul in 190 B.C.E. The legend that Pomponia died in childbirth when Scipio Africanus was born is false.

Poly. 10.4.3–9; 5.1–5.
PW 28.
Scullard, H. H., *Scipio Africanus,* pp. 28, 30.

⊞ POMPONIA (2)

(1st century B.C.E.)   Roman: Italy
Angry wife

Pomponia suffered life with a hot-tempered and irritable husband with whom she was often angry. She and her brother Titus Pomponius Atticus had been friends since childhood with the brothers Marcus Tullius and Quintus Tullius Cicero. In 70 B.C.E. when she and Quintus married, the alliance strengthened friendship with kinship, and the best wishes of all accompanied the marriage.

The marriage was a failure, although it lasted for some 25 years. Pomponia was several years older than her husband and much wealthier. Quintus was neither an insightful nor an especially talented man. He lived in the shadows of his brother's fame and his wife's money. Moreover, both her brother, Atticus, and her brother-in-law, Marcus, interfered in the relationship.

The letters between Cicero and Atticus provide an unusually intimate look at the marriage. They also record the annual cycles of visiting and traveling that included Cicero's wife, TERENTIA (1), and later Atticus's wife, PILIA, as well as the childhoods of their respective children, Quintus, Marcus, TULLIA (2) and Caecilia ATTICA. Time and again Pomponia demanded that Quintus recognize her position and her authority over the household, and he, either from insensitivity, ignorance, or perversity, chose to make household ar-

rangements through his freedmen and slaves, instead of his wife. She was not a silent sufferer and railed against him to her brother and her brother-in law. Marcus Cicero, whose pomposity slips through many of his letters, regarded her as a shrew. Angered still more by her brother-in-law's support for her inept husband, she would refuse to sleep with her husband or to be his hostess, which led to further estrangement and fury all around.

The marriage finally ended in divorce in 44 B.C.E. They had one son, Quintus Cicero, whom each parent tried to turn against the other. Quintus and his son were killed in the proscriptions in 43. Pomponia outlived both of them.

Cic., Att. 5.I.3 ff.; 14.13.5.
Balsdon, J. P. V. D., pp. 46, 212.
Johnson, W. H., pp. 160–65.
Shackleton Bailey, D. R., index.

⊞ POMPONIA GALLA

(1st century C.E.)   Roman: Italy
Friend of Pliny the Younger; disinherited her son

Pomponia Galla, a Roman matron and friend of Pliny the Younger, had disinherited her worthless son Asudius Curianus and made Pliny, along with several other eminent Romans, her coheirs. Although it remains unclear what exactly constituted "worthlessness" in Pomponia's eyes, her assessment of her son was largely affirmed after her death.

After her death, Curianus asked Pliny to agree to give him Pliny's share of the inheritance, which he would secretly return. The son hoped that this would set a precedent for the other coheirs to renounce their shares in his favor. Pliny proposed an alternative. He would waive his share if, Curianus could prove that his mother should not have disinherited him. Curianus asked Pliny to investigate the case himself. Pliny held a hearing with two eminent advisers who listened to Curianus. They ruled in favor of Pomponia's decision to disinherit.

Despite the ruling, the son brought suit in the Centumviral court against all the coheirs except Pliny. Since the outcome of a suit was never certain, Pliny acted as a mediator and settled the suit with the assignment of a fourth part of the estate to Curianus. Pliny voluntarily added his portion.

Plin., Ep. 5.1.

▣ POMPONIA GRAECINA

(?–c. 83 C.E.)   Roman: Italy
Political player

The aristocratic Pomponia Graecina was the wife of Aulus Plautius, who was consul suffectus in 29 C.E. and led the successful Roman attack to secure southern Britain in 43. Pomponia was devoted to JULIA (8), to whom she was related. When Julia, who had once been the daughter-in-law of the elder AGRIPPINA, was executed on orders of Valeria MESSALLINA in 43, Pomponia put on mourning clothes, which she wore until her death around 83. In 57, Pomponia was charged with immorality for becoming a believer in an alien superstition, possibly one of the monotheistic religions. She was turned over to the jurisdiction of her husband, and a family council declared her innocent.

Tac., Ann. 13.32.3–5.
Balsdon, J. P. V. D., p. 248.
PW 83.
Syme, R., *Tacitus*, p. 532.

▣ POMPONIA RUFINA

(?–213 C.E.)   Roman: Rome
Condemned priestess

Pomponia Rufina was one of four Vestal Virgins accused in 213 C.E. by the emperor Marcus Aurelius Antoninus Caracalla of unchaste behavior. Pomponia, along with AURELIA SEVERA and CLODIA LAETA, were buried alive. The fourth Vestal, CANNUTIA CRESCENTINA, killed herself.

Vestals served the goddess Vesta and were responsible for keeping the sacred flame burning. In an earlier age, the condemnation of four of the six Vestals would have been taken as an omen of calamitous times for Rome, but by the third century C.E. few appeared to have feared such a consequence.

Dio. 78.16.1–3k.
Herodian 4.6.4.
PW 86.

▣ POPILIA

(?–102 B.C.E.)   Roman: Rome
Loyal wife

Popilia was said to have been the first Roman woman honored with a public funeral oration. Her son Quintus Lutatius Catullus delivered the oration in her honor in 102 B.C.E., the year he became consul.

Cic., De. or. 2.44.
Balsdon, J. P. V. D., p. 46.

▣ POPPAEA SABINA (1)

(?–47 C.E.)   Roman: Italy
Political player

Poppaea Sabina was beautiful, rich, and arrogant. Born during the early empire when many women competed for power and wealth, she was forced to suicide by her opponent, Valeria MESSALLINA. Her father was Poppaeus Sabinus, consul in 9 C.E., who was said to have gained his position more through friendship than merit. She married Titus Ollius from Picenum, a relative unknown in imperial politics. Her daughter, POPPAEA SABINA (2), later became the wife of the emperor Nero. In 31 her husband died, probably in Tiberius's purge of Lucius Aelius Sejanus and his supporters. Poppaea emerged unscathed from the debacle. She remarried; her new husband was Publius Lentulus Scipio, consul suffectus in 24 C.E. Their son, Publius Scipio Asiaticus, became consul suffectus in 68.

Her conflict with Valeria Messallina began over the attractive Mnester, the leading pantomimist and pop culture idol in Rome, who became lover to both women. Although both were beautiful and very rich, Messalina was not only younger and more powerful, she was the emperor's wife. In 47 Messallina attacked Poppaea through Decimus Valerius Asiaticus, one of the leading political figures of the day and an opponent of Messallina's marriage with Claudius.

Asiaticus and Poppaea were accused of adultery, and in addition, he was charged with plotting against the emperor. Consul in 46 and a native of the city of Vienne on the Rhone, Asiaticus was an impressive man with a following. He was not only wealthy but owner of a house and gardens in Rome that were the envy of many, including Messallina. Although Claudius may not have thought Asiaticus was himself a threat, Asiaticus had voiced approval of the earlier assassination of the emperor Gaius Caligula. It was certainly possible to imagine that should there be a conspiracy, Asiaticus would throw his political weight and wealth on the side of the conspirators.

Claudius ordered Asiaticus's arrest, and he was brought to Rome in chains. Publius Suillius and Lucius Vitellius were the prosecutors. Suillius owed Claudius for his recall after having been banished for corruption by Tiberius and he had again become a notorious prosecutor, growing richer every day on the percentage of property gained with each conviction. Vitellius, one of the most successful politicians of the day and easily moved by Messallina, was another of Claudius's sycophants. With Messallina present, Asiaticus was judged at a mock trial in a bedroom of the emperor. Vitellius recommended that Asiaticus commit suicide. Without any official verdict, Asiaticus took his own life.

Poppaea was not tried but also committed suicide after being threatened with prison by supporters of Messallina. Claudius may not have known of her death since he was reputed to have asked her husband about her whereabouts at a dinner soon after.

Tac., Ann. 11.1–4.
Balsdon, J. P. V. D., pp. 124 ff.
Bauman, R. A., pp. 172 ff.
Levick, B., *Claudius*, pp. 62, 64.
PW 3.
Syme, R., *Augustan Aristocracy*, pp. 178, 184, 299.

▣ POPPAEA SABINA (2)

(31?–65 C.E.) Roman: Italy
Augusta

Poppaea Sabina followed in the footsteps of her mother, POPPAEA SABINA (1), and she avenged her downfall at the hands of Valeria MESSALLINA. She has been accused of duplicity, promiscuity, and sundry other vile acts as she moved through two marriages prior to her marriage with the emperor, which occurred after the death of his powerful mother, the younger Julia AGRIPPINA, and his divorce from his popular wife. Endowed with wit, beauty, and intelligence, she successfully usurped Messallina's daughter, Claudia OCTAVIA, as the wife of Nero and became Augusta. Along the way, she made a fool of her first husband, Rufius Crispinus, the man who had accused her mother of adultery.

Poppaea's father, Titus Ollius, came from Picenum, was relatively unknown, and died in 31 C.E., the same year she was born. Possibly her father's death was tied to the downfall of Lucius Aelius Sejanus, the prefect of the Praetorian Guard accused of treason in the same year. In any case, Poppaea was not given his name, but that of her maternal grandfather, the more illustrious Poppaeus Sabinus, consul in 9 C.E.

Her first marriage, around 44, was with Rufius Crispinus, prefect of the Praetorian Guard under the emperor Claudius. Her husband had grown rich and gained the office of praetor through Messallina. Among the services he performed for her was to bring a charge of adultery against Poppaea's mother, which had led to her suicide. The younger Poppaea repaid him in kind. After she gave birth to a son, she became the lover of the young senator Marcus Salvius Otho, whose reputation as a spendthrift is better remembered than his rule as emperor for a few months in 69. For seven years after her husband lost his position of influence in 51 when the younger Agrippina supplanted Messallina as the wife of Claudius, she remained married. She also continued her open liaison with Otho.

In 58 Poppaea and Crispinus divorced, and she married Otho. She was one year older than her 27-year-old second husband who was a friend of the new emperor, the young Nero. A boastful and not very subtle man, Poppaea's beauty and accomplishments were often her husband's chosen subject. Nero's appetites were whetted. The emperor sent Otho to govern the province of Lusitania in western Spain and became her lover before the year was out.

Poppaea, six years Nero's senior, threatened to end their relationship unless he divorced his wife, Octavia and married her. Not only was Nero faced with the prospect of divorce from a popular and loyal wife, but his mother, the powerful Agrippina, was also against the new marriage. There is no clear evidence that Poppaea urged Nero to murder his mother or knew of his plans to do so. Nonetheless, it was to Poppaea's advantage that Nero had her killed in 59. Poppaea, however, still had three years to wait before Nero divorced Octavia. Between 59 and 62, Nero eliminated several potential rivals, around whom a conspiracy could gather in support of Octavia. Finally with the death in 62 of Sextus Afranius Burrus, who was the head of the Praetorian Guard, Octavia lost her last serious political supporter. Nero appointed Gaius Tigellinus the new head of the guard. It was reported that Poppaea, abetted by Tigellinus, tried unsuccessfully to use Octavia's slaves and charge her with adultery. In the end, Nero divorced her on grounds of sterility. He returned her dowry in the form of the confiscated house of Burrus and the estates of Rebellius Plautus, whom he had exiled and murdered. Octavia was soon banished under an armed guard to the Campania region of Italy.

Poppaea married Nero 12 days after his divorce despite public protests. A false rumor that Nero had repented and recalled Octavia led joyous crowds to surge into the streets, destroying statues of Poppaea and carrying likenesses of Octavia covered with flowers. Some even came to the palace but were repelled by the guards. The statues of Poppaea were replaced, and the fear that Octavia could be the center of an uprising sealed her doom. Octavia was exiled to the island of Pandateria and executed. In 63 Poppaea gave birth to a daughter named Claudia. Although the daughter died after a few months, the title of Augusta was bestowed upon them both. Poppaea had reached the pinnacle of her ambitions.

There is evidence that Poppaea was religious and interested in some of the mysticism of the East. She also showed some sympathy for the Jews. In 64, the Jewish priest Josephus came to Rome as part of a delegation to secure the release of some Jewish priests who had been sent to Rome in chains by the Roman governor of Judaea. Josephus became friends with Aliturus, an actor who was a favorite of the emperor. Through him, he was introduced to Poppaea, who not only obtained the release of the priests but sent Josephus home laden with gifts. She later persuaded Nero to accede to a Jewish request to prevent the tearing down of a wall that had been erected in the Jewish temple in Jerusalem.

Poppaea's remedies to preserve her beauty became fashionable among the women in Rome. They adopted her practice of washing her face with ass's milk several times a day as a way of whitening the skin and keeping it free of wrinkles. Nero wrote a poem praising Poppaea's amber-colored hair, and it became a popular hair dye color for women. Poppaea had once expressed a desire to die before her beauty started to fade. Her wish was granted. In 65 she was again pregnant when a kick from Nero whom she had angered for some unknown reason killed her. In remorse, he did not cremate the body but had it embalmed and stuffed with spices. She was then placed in a mausoleum of the Julian clan and deified. A public funeral was held, and Nero eulogized her beauty. After her death he ordered that her son by her first husband be drowned and, in 68, her ex-husband be executed.

Dio. 62.11.2–3, 12.1, 13.1–2, 28.1–2; 63.26.4.
Jos. AJ 20.195.
Jos., Vit. 13–16.
Juv. 6.462.
Plin., NH 28.183; 33.140; 37.50.
Plut., Galb. 19.2–5.
Suet., Ner. 35.1–3.
Suet., Oth. 3.1–2.
Tac., Ann. 13.45–46; 14.1–2, 59–65; 15.23; 16.6, 7.
Tac., Hist. 1.13, 22, 78.
Balsdon, J. P. V. D., index.
Bauman, R. A., pp. 199–209.
Griffin, M. T., pp. 75–76, 98–104.
OCD, p. 1,221.
PW 4.
Smallwood, E. M., pp. 329–35.
Syme, R., *Tacitus*, v. 1, pp. 290, 316–17, 353, 376.
Townsend, G. B., 227–48.
Walter, Gerard, pp. 109–27.
Warmington, B. H., pp. 47, 50, 139–40.

PORCIA

(?–43 B.C.E.) Roman: Italy
Political player and victim

Porcia was a passionate woman as devoted to the cause of republican Rome as her father, Marcus Porcius Cato Uticensis, a leader among the optimates opposing Gaius Julius Caesar. She lived and died by her father's code of honor. Her mother, ATILIA, and her father were divorced. Porcia's first husband was Marcus Calpurnius Bibulus, coconsul with Caesar in 59 B.C.E. His election had been arranged by her father with large scale bribes. Bibulus opposed the agrarian law supported by Caesar and Gnaeus Pompeius (Pompey the Great). Prevented from using his consular veto, he withdrew to his home, and tried to prevent a meeting of the Senate. On each day there was to be a meeting for the rest of the year, he observed the heavens for omens and declared the day in auspices.

Porcia gave birth to two sons during her marriage with Bibulus. They accompanied her husband in 51 B.C.E. when she remained in Rome and he went as proconsul to Syria. She never saw any of them again. After the outbreak of civil war her husband sided with the optimates and died in 48 as he attempted to prevent Caesar from reaching Epirus. By 45, her father, her brother, and one of her sons were also dead.

Also in 45, she married Marcus Junius Brutus. It was a strange union. She bore the mantle of her father, who in many ways, both good and bad, was the last great voice of the republic and at the same time she was a victim of the war. Brutus was a complex man and no less a victim. He admired Porcia's father and had fought on the side of Pompey against Caesar, even though Pompey had earlier been responsible for the death of his own father. Caesar pardoned Brutus after the battle of Pharsalus in 48 and appointed him praetor. Again in Rome, holding office and beholden to Caesar, Brutus divorced his wife to marry Porcia. Brutus's mother, SERVILIA (1), who was Cato's half sister, had once been the lover of Caesar, remained his friend, and opposed Bruutus and Porcia's marriage.

Porcia was said to have sensed that Brutus was engaged in a secret undertaking. She sought to convince him that whatever he might plan, she was a worthy confidant. She made a deep gash in her thigh that bled freely. Violent pains, chills, and fever followed. Brutus was distressed. She claimed that her ability to inflict the cut and withstand the pain was evidence of her ability to keep confidences. She was her father's daughter and her husband's partner. Brutus revealed to her the plot against Caesar. After Brutus left for the Forum, Porcia fainted and for a while lost the power of speech. A messenger ran to tell Brutus that his wife was dead, and even as Porcia regained consciousness, Brutus participated in the assassination of Caesar.

Porcia attended meetings after the assassination to assess her husband's future. She was present at a meeting at Antium on June 8, 44, that included JUNIA TERTIA, the wife of Gaius Cassius Longinus; Marcus Favonius, an admirer of Cato; Brutus; Cassius; and Marcus Tullius Cicero. Her mother-in-law, Servilia, presided over the discussion to consider an offer made by the Senate at the instigation of Mark Antony for Brutus and Cassius to supervise the collection of corn taxes in the provinces of Sicily and Asia until the end of the year. In reality, it was an honorable way for them to leave Rome in the wake of the passions raised by the assassination. Brutus and Cassius were uncertain whether or not to accept. Finally, Servilia took it upon herself to try to arrange for the Senate to rescind the offer.

Brutus did leave Italy for the East in August 44. Porcia, who had been with him outside Rome, returned to Rome. Porcia was ill and despondent, and her friends were worried that she might kill herself. Despite their efforts, Porcia took her own life in the summer of 43. Brutus committed suicide in October 42 after his defeat at Philippi.

Cic., Att. 13.9.2; 15.11, 22.4.
Cic., Brut. 17.7.
Dio. 44.13.2–14.1; 47.49.4.
Plut., Brut. 13.1–11; 15.5–9; 53.5–6.
Val. Max. 4.6.5.
Balsdon, J. P. V. D., pp. 50–51.
Bauman, R. A., p. 75.
OCD, p. 1,224.
PW 28.
Syme, R., Roman Revolution, pp. 22, 58, 116.

▣ POTONE

(5th–4th century B.C.E.) Greek: Athens
Sister of Plato

Potone was the sister of the philosopher Plato and mother of Speusippus, his successor. The daughter of PERICTIONE and Ariston, she came from distinguished Athenian families. She married Eurymedon, and their son became a famous philosopher who succeeded Plato as head of the Academy, the school in Athens that Plato had founded.

Diog. Laert. 4.4.
OCD, p. 1,434.

▣ PRAECIA

(1st century B.C.E.) Roman: Rome
Self-made woman; political player

Praecia was of obscure origin but beautiful, witty, and engaging. Her lover was Publius Cornelius Cethegus, a patrician and master of political intrigue, who was said to have wielded as much power as a consul during the 70s B.C.E. He was regularly accused of taking his orders from Praecia, and the evidence offered was the successful advancement of those who curried her favor.

She was specifically associated with the advancement of Lucius Licinius Lucullus, consul in 74, and his brothers Marcus Licinius Lucullus and Marcus Antonius Creticus. Lucius Lucullus, an able soldier and fine administrator, was beholden to Praecia for his appointment as governor of the province of Cilicia in Asia Minor and, later, to the command of the campaign against Mithridates the Great.

Plut., Luc. 6.2.2–4.
Balsdon, J. P. V. D., p. 53.
Bauman, R. A., pp. 65–66.

▣ PRAXILLA

(5th century B.C.E.) Greek: Sicyon
Poet

Praxilla, a poet from Sicyon in Greece, wrote short poems, drinking songs, and hymns of which only a few fragments survive. Her innovation in meter, the praxilleion, was named in her honor. She juxtaposed the conventional and the unconventional, a characteristic that was mocked by some critics. In one poem, Adonis is asked on his arrival in Hades what he will miss most. His list is headed with sunlight, followed by the shining stars and the moon, and then ripe cucumbers, apples, and pears. In another fragment, she linked the parts of the body with two different stages of life. The viewer was described as the possessor of a virgin's head and a married woman's body. Lysippus of Sicyon, a famous sculptor, caste a bronze statue of her.

Campbell, D. A., v. 4, pp. 371–81.
Edmonds, J. M., pp. 73–79.
OCD, p. 1,242.

▣ PRISCA

(3rd century–c. 316 C.E.) Roman: Balkans, Syria, Italy, Asia, and Greece
Early Christian sympathizer

Prisca's life was intertwined with that of her daughter, VALERIA (2), and both suffered the same tragic fate. Prisca and her husband, the future emperor Diocletian, came from Dalmatia on the Adriatic coast. Both were of lowly birth. Diocletian, commander of the guard, was chosen emperor by the army after the death of the emperor Numerian in 284 C.E. Embattled in the East, he did not reach Rome until 303. Prisca traveled with him.

After Diocletian resigned on May 1, 306, Prisca appears to have gone to live with her daughter. Both she and her daughter sympathized with Christianity, although they were probably not converts. Her son-in-law, Galerius, who followed Diocletian as emperor and initially persecuted Christians, issued the Edict of Toleration before his death in 311, which may have reflected the women's influence.

After his death, Galerius was succeeded by Valerius Licinius, whom the women mistrusted. Prisca and Valeria went to live under the protection of Maximin Daia, who was then Augustus of the East. Valeria rejected his proposal of marriage.

He put to death some of their friends and banished both of them to a remote area of Syria. Prisca wrote Diocletian for help, but he no longer had the power or physical stamina to come to her aid. When Maximin was killed in 313, Prisca and her daughter spent some 15 months in disguise

trying to return to Dalmatia and Diocletian. His death in 316 put an end to their hopes. They were recognized in the Macedonian city of Thessalonica. Their heads were cut off, and their bodies thrown into the sea. Why the two women were so vigorously pursued remains a mystery.

Lact., MP 15, 39, 50–51.
Balsdon, J. P. V. D., pp. 165–69.
Gibbon, E., pp. 333–34.

▣ PUBLILIA (1)

(2nd century B.C.E.) Roman: Rome
Convicted murderer

Publilia (or Publicia) and LICINIA (1) were accused of poisoning their respective husbands for reasons that are obscure. Both of the men were ex-consuls. Publilia's husband was Postumius Albinus. Publilia used her property as surety for her person. Found guilty, she was strangled by decree of her own family.

Livy 48.
Val. Max. 6.3.8.
Bauman, R. A., p. 39.

▣ PUBLILIA (2)

(1st century B.C.E.) Roman: Italy
Ill-used young heiress

Publilia was a young and wealthy heiress, ill used by the orator and statesman Marcus Tullius Cicero, who was a trustee of her estate. They married shortly after Cicero divorced TERENTIA (1), his wife of long standing, in 46 B.C.E. It could not have been an easy situation for Publilia. The marriage caused a good deal of gossip. He was a 60-year-old man, and she, a young woman of means. Some claimed he had been seduced by her beauty, but his freedman made no bones about what he wanted: her money. Cicero was in dire need of funds, including the next payment on the dowry of his daughter TULLIA (2).

As it happened, Cicero's unhappy daughter Tullia divorced her husband around the same time and died in childbirth only months later, in February 45 B.C.E. Cicero was inconsolable and retreated to his estate in Astura on the coast south of Rome. He also no longer needed Publilia's money. He claimed Publilia had not concealed her feeling of relief over Tullia's death. In the spring of 45, Cicero avoided Publilia and members of her family by escaping to the estate of his friend, Titus Pomponius Atticus. A divorce soon followed. After the divorce, Publilia's family sent an emissary to Cicero to explore the possibility of a remarriage. Cicero wrote Atticus that he found the offer repugnant.

Publilia then married her guardian, Gaius Vibius Rufus. It was a more successful relationship. Her husband, who had acquired the chair on which Julius Caesar used to sit, quipped that with Caesar's chair and Cicero's wife, he might become either a Caesar or a Cicero. He did become consul suffectus in 16 C.E.

Cic., Att. 12.32.1.
Dio. 57.15.6–7.
Plut., Cic. 41.3–4.
Shackleton Bailey, D. R., pp. 202–3, 210–11.
Syme, R., *Augustan Aristocracy*, p. 225.

▣ PUDENTILLA, AEMILIA

(2nd century C.E.) Roman: North Africa
Independent woman

Aemilia Pudentilla of Oea (Tripoli) used all her intelligence and skill to maintain a life over which she could exercise control and so chose her own husband. Widowed by Sicinius Amieus while still young and attractive, she had two sons, Sicinius Pontianus and Sicinius Pudens. Threatening to withhold her husband's estate from her if she refused, her father-in-law pressed her to marry her brother-in-law Sicinius Clarus. Pudentilla agreed to an engagement but successfully postponed the marriage for some 13 years until the old man died.

Then, at age 40 she announced to her sons that a husband would improve her failing health. Her son Sicinius Pontianus waited anxious lest a new husband deprive him and his brother of their inheritance. In 156 C.E. the author of the *Golden Ass*, Apuleius, who was a rhetorican and poet from a wealthy family in Madaura, North Africa, with whom Pontianus had become friends earlier in Athens, fell ill in Oea. Pontianus invited him to recover in his mother's house. Some 15 years younger than Pudentilla, Apuleius enjoyed her intelligence and admired her character. With the sons' approval, they married.

Sicinius Aemilianus, the brother of the suitor she had held off for 13 years, and Herennius Rufinus, the father-in-law of Pontianus, opened a suit against Apuleius on the grounds that he had used magic to win Pudentilla. Initially the sons backed the suit. Pontianus later recanted, although he died before the trial took place in late 158 or early 159. Apuleius spoke in his own defense and easily discredited his accusers. He pointed out that Pudentilla, despite her wealth, had made over a small dowry to him, which was put in trust. If she died without having any children, the dowry would revert to her sons. If she gave birth to a son or daughter, half would go to the children of the second marriage, and half to those of the first. He later published his defense, entitled *The Apologia*. After the trial, Pudentilla and her husband moved to Carthage where her health improved and he enhanced his reputation as rhetorician, philosopher, and poet.

Apul., Apol.
OCD, p. 131.

▣ PYTHIAS

(?–c. 335 B.C.E.) Greek: Asia Minor
Wife of Aristotle

Pythias was the wife of Aristotle. They met in Atarneus on the west coast of Asia Minor opposite the island of Lesbos. Her uncle and adopted father who ruled Atarneus had an interest in philosophy. He had gone to Athens and studied at the famous Academy. After Plato died, he invited Aristotle to teach in Atarneus.

Aristotle and Pythias had one daughter before she died sometime after 335 B.C.E. Aristotle requested that his executor, Nicanor, who had served under Alexander the Great, marry his daughter when she came of age. He did.

Diog. Laert. 5.1, 12.
OCD, p. 166.

▣ PYTHODORIS

(1st century B.C.E.–1st century C.E.)   Roman: Asia Minor and Pontus
Roman client ruler

Pythodoris married Polemon, and after his death she ruled Pontus. The granddaughter of Mark Antony, in about 34 B.C.E., her mother ANTONIA (3) had married Pythodorus from Tralles in Caria, Asia Minor. Her father, an ally of her grandfather, was immensely wealthy and influential throughout Asia at a time when Antony had extended his rule in the East.

Polemon was much older than Pythodoris. He too had fought with Antony against the Parthians. The son of the wealthy rhetorician Zeno, from Laodicea in Asia Minor, he and his father were rewarded by Antony with Roman citizenship and control over Pontus and lesser Armenia. Her husband stood between the Romans and the Parthians. Subsequently, Augustus confirmed his rule over Pontus but removed Lesser Armenia from his control.

In 15 B.C.E. Polemon fought alongside Marcus Vipsanius Agrippa in support of Augustus and Rome. He was rewarded with rule over Bosporus. In 8 B.C.E. he was killed fighting. Although Polemon and Pythodoris had a son, the young man was uninterested in ruling, and Rome recognized Pythodoris as her husband's successor. She pursued her husband's policy of support for Rome

in eastern Asia Minor. The coins she issued bearing the heads of LIVIA DRUSILLA and other members of the imperial family make clear her client status.

Pythodoris married Archelaus, the ruler of Cappadocia, with the approval of Rome since the marriage established a powerful bulwark against invasions. Her husband, however, fell out of favor with Augustus's successor Tiberius, and was lured to Rome with a letter from Livia Drusilla. On Archelaus's arrival, Tiberius requested the Senate to try him for treason. Old and infirm, Archelaus died before a decision was reached.

Pythodoris was allowed to retain rule over Pontus, but the other portions of her domain became a Roman province. It is not known how long she reigned or when she died. Two of her children by her first husband, however, were very successful. Her daughter ANTONIA TRYPHAENA married Cotys of Thrace and ruled Pontus as regent for her son after the death of her mother. Her youngest son, Zeno, ruled Armenia for 17 years.

Strabo 12.29.
Macurdy, G., pp. 10–11.
Magie, D., pp. 486–87.
OCD, p. 113.

▣ PYTHONICE

(4th century B.C.E.)   Greek: Greece, Asia Minor, and Babylon
Self-made woman

Pythonice became the companion of Harpalus, a friend of Alexander the Great. Originally from Corinth, Pythonice had moved to Athens where she met Harpalus, a Macedonian of high birth. She accompanied him to Babylon.

Although Harpalus had a deformity that made him unable to fight in Alexander's army, his skill with accounts led Alexander to assign him charge of the treasury deposited in Babylon in 331 B.C.E. Harpalus, like many others, believed that Alexander would never return from India. He raided the treasury to support a luxurious lifestyle that he enjoyed with Pythonice. During this period she bore a girl, whom Harpalus acknowledged as his daughter.

Pythonice died, probably before Alexander confounded expectations, returned alive and discovered Harpalus's embezzlement. Harpalus not only privately mourned her, but provided a magnificent funeral accompanied by songs and music. He built a tomb to her memory in Babylon and commissioned Charicles, the son-in-law of Phocion, a great Athenian general and statesman, to erect a costly monument over her grave in Hermus on the road from Athens to Eleusis, which later sources still noted as well worth a visit.

Harpalus made his escape from Alexander and Babylon with a fleet of ships and troops, but he was killed in Crete in 323 B.C.E. The Athenians Phocion and Charicles, provided for the education of Pythonice's daughter.

Ath. 13.586c.
Diod. 17.108.4–6.
Paus. 1.37.5.
Plut., Phoc. 22.1–3.
Licht, H., pp. 401–2.

QUARTA HOSTILIA

(?–c. 179 B.C.E.) Roman: Rome
Convicted murderer

Quarta Hostilia's second husband, the consul Gaius Calpurnius Piso, died in 180 B.C.E. and rumors circulated that Hostilia had poisoned him. Her motive was said to have been a desire for the advancement of Quintus Fulvius Flaccus, the son of her first husband, also Quintus Fulvius Flaccus, who had been consul four times. Twice the younger Quintus Fulvius Flaccus had failed to be elected consul. Witnesses came forward to testify that Hostilia had upbraided him for his failure and pressed him to try again. She assured him that the next time he would succeed. Her son became consul in 179, succeeding his deceased stepfather. Hostilia was convicted of poisoning her husband.

Livy 40.37.1–7.

R

⊡ RHEA

(2nd–1st century B.C.E.) Roman: Italy
Devoted mother

Rhea was a devoted mother and she had an equally devoted son. Her family was from Nursia, northeast of Rome. Widowed, alone she raised her son, Quintus Sertorius who became a successful army commander and led one of the divisions when Lucius Cornelius Cinna captured Rome in 87 B.C.E. Along with Cinna, Sertorius became praetor in 83 B.C.E. The following year he took command of Spain. He opposed Lucius Cornelius Sulla and fought successfully to maintain his authority over the province.

Sertorius received news of Rhea's death while in Spain. His pain was obvious. He withdrew into his tent and for several days refused to see anyone. His fellow officers finally forced him to emerge.

Plut., Sert. 2; 22.6–7.

⊡ RHODOPIS

(6th century B.C.E.) Thracian: Samos
and Egypt
Self-made woman

Rhodopis successfully used her beauty to achieve fame and wealth. Said to be of Thracian back-

ground, she and Aesop, the famous writer of fables, were fellow slaves of Iadmon on the island of Samos. She was brought to Egypt by Xantheus, also of Samos, during the time of the pharaoh Amasis (569–525 B.C.E.).

Charaxus of Lesbos, the brother of the poet SAPPHO, purchased her freedom. She remained in Egypt and amassed a considerable fortune. As a memorial to herself, in the temple at Delphi, she spent 10 percent of her wealth to purchase a number of iron spits used for roasting whole oxen. Sappho satirized Charaxus and Rhodopis in a poem, and thus Rhodopis's name became familiar throughout Greece.

Herodian 2.134–36.

⊡ ROXANE

(?–313 B.C.E.) Persian: Asia Minor
and Greece
Political player

Roxane's fate was determined by her father, her husband, and finally her son. A Persian by birth, she married Alexander the Great and was mother of his only son. For six war-filled years after Alexander's death, she successfully maneuvered to protect the child's future. In the end, she and her son were victims of the power that the very name of Alexander evoked.

Her father, Oxyartes, was a nobleman from Bactria who led the Sogdians against the invasion of Alexander in the eastern provinces of Persia after Alexander's defeat of Darius, the Persian king. Roxane, her mother, and her sisters had been sent for safety to the Sogdian Rock, which had so precipitous a drop that it was considered impregnable. In heavy snows, some 300 volunteers, promised significant rewards from Alexander, scaled the heights and conquered the citadel. Roxane was among the daughters of Oxyartes captured. She was immediately acknowledged the most beautiful woman in Persia, with the exception of the wife of the ruler Darius. Alexander married her in 327 B.C.E., and her father became his ally.

Roxane gave birth to Alexander IV in August 323, soon after her husband's unexpected death. Alexander's senior generals agreed that the new born son and the weak Philip Arrhidaeus, the last living son of Alexander's father Philip II, were Alexander's legitimate heirs. Roxane and her son became both actors and hostages in the subsequent struggle for control over the disintegrating empire. Conflict intensified after 319 and the death of Antipater, whose authority in Greece and Macedonia had assured a degree of stability. In the struggle that ensued among the next generation of leaders, possession of Roxane and her son became one of the critical conditions for asserting legitimacy.

Roxane was not the only woman with a stake in the future of Macedonia and a claim to rule. OLYMPIAS (1), Roxane's mother-in-law and the mother of Alexander the Great, was equally determined that only the son of Alexander should rule; EURYDICE (2), wife and regent for the impaired Philip Arrhidaeus, was no less determined that her candidate maintain control over Macedonia. With Eurydice in Macedonia under the protection of Antipater, Olympias had made a strategic retreat to Epirus, where she ruled. After Antipater's death, one of the major claimants,

Polyperchon, fled to Epirus with Roxane and her son and sought support from Olympias to help regain Macedonia from Eurydice and Polyperchon's opponent, Cassander.

Olympias, regarded as sacred by the people of Macedonia, seized the opportunity to ally herself with Roxane and her grandson. She marched into Macedonia in 317 to eliminate Eurydice and Philip Arrhidaeus and their supporters. At the sight of Olympias, the army joined her ranks en masse. Olympias won without a fight. She executed Philip and forced Eurydice to commit suicide. Olympias ruled Macedonia with Roxane and Alexander IV, who was barely six years old.

However, Cassander, Polyperchon's opponent, returned from the Peloponnesus and slipped his forces into Macedonia, catching Olympias by surprise. Unable to raise more troops in Macedonia, Olympias withdrew to Pydna. Although Polyperchon tried to free her, he failed, and in 316 Olympias surrendered to Cassander and delivered to him Roxane and Alexander IV. Cassander killed Olympias, despite a promise to spare her life. Roxane and Alexander IV remained alive for some six years during which Alexander was nominally ruler, but in reality a captive. He and Roxane were killed when the boy was 12 years old, just about the time he might have become an independent political force.

Arr., Anab. 4.19.5, 20.4; 7.4.4.
Diod. 18.3.3; 19.35.5, 52.4, 61.1, 105.1–4.
Cary, M., pp. 2, 20, 29.
OCD, p. 1,336.

RUBRIA

(1st century C.E.)   Roman: Rome
Priestess

Rubria was a Vestal Virgin, dedicated to chastity. According to the sources, she was raped by the emperor Nero.

Suet., Ner. 28.1.

S

▣ SABINA, VIBIA

(c. 87/88–136 C.E.) Roman: Rome, Greece,
Italy, Britain, Asia, Syria, Palestine,
and Egypt
Augusta

Vibia Sabina was a cultured woman who traveled extensively. She married the future emperor Hadrian, whom she had known since childhood. Their marital relationship appears to have been distant and formal. She was childless and spent her time largely separated from her husband among a circle of women. Her mother, MATIDIA (1), was the daughter of Ulpia MARCIANA, the sister of the emperor Trajan. Her father, Matidia's second husband, was Lucius Vibius Sabinus, consul in 97 C.E., who died shortly after his consulship. Her mother and grandmother accompanied Trajan and his wife, Pompeia PLOTINA, to Rome after he became emperor and lived with them during Sabina's childhood.

Plotina, along with Sabina's grandmother and mother, shaped the intellectual life of imperial Rome during Trajan's reign. It was Plotina who instigated Sabina's marriage with Hadrian. Sabina

Vibia Sabina

married the future emperor in 100 C.E., when she was 12 or 13 years old and he was 25.

Sabina probably remained in Rome when Hadrian campaigned against the Dacians between 101 and 106. She was not with her husband in Syria when he received word from Plotina and Matidia at Selinus in Cilicia, on August 8, 117 that Trajan had died. The women clearly controlled the always delicate transition between emperors, and Hadrian, adopted by Trajan immediately before his death, was successfully acclaimed the new emperor. Sabina, however, did accompany her husband to Britain when he campaigned there in 122.

It was not until 128 that Hadrian proclaimed Sabina Augusta. Differences in temperament and Hadrian's decided preference for boys may have hindered the marriage. However, the marriage, although childless, endured. In 121 and 122 Hadrian dismissed several men from his service—including one of his secretaries, the historian Gaius Suetonius, and Septicius Clarus, the prefect of the Praetorian Guard—for being too close with Sabina, although there was no evidence of anything more than friendship.

In 128 Sabina accompanied Hadrian on his trip to the Near East and visited Athens, Corinth, and other cities in Greece. They traveled to Ephesus, Smyrna, and Antioch and through Syria, Palestine, and Egypt. They returned to Rome sometime in 132. It was on this journey that Sabina was accompanied by the Greek poet Julia BALBILLA, who carved five epigrams on the foot of the Colossus of Memnon in Thebes. Sabina died some four years later in 136 or 137. Hadrian consecrated her, and she was commemorated on posthumous coins.

SHA, Hadr. 1.2; 2.10; 11.3; 23.9.
Balsdon, J. P. V. D., pp. 139–40.
OCD, pp. 1,341–42.
Perowne, S., Hadrian.

SALOME

(1st century B.C.E.–1st century C.E.) Jewish: Judaea
Client of Livia Drusilla

Salome was a client and friend of LIVIA DRUSILLA. The daughter of Antipater, an Idumaean from the area south of Judaea, her father had received Roman citizenship and became procurator in Judaea as a reward for aid to Julius Caesar. Her brother was the future Herod the Great, king of Judaea, over whom she exercised a great deal of influence. Salome cor-

responded with Livia and on occasion sought her intervention. Salome wanted Livia to support her marriage with Syllaeus, an influential Nabataean Arab who governed Arabia under the indolent ruler Obades. The sources differ as to Livia's response, and in the end Salome did not marry him. On her brother's death Salome inherited three towns, Jamnia, Azotus, and Phasaelis. When she died, she bequeathed the three towns to Livia.

She had a daughter, BERENICE (1), and a grandson Agrippa I who grew up in Livia's household in Rome together with the future emperor Gaius Caligula. Caligula later appointed him king of Judaea.

Jos. AJ 17.10.
Jos., B.J. 1.566.
Perowne, S., The Later Herods, p. 41.

SALONINA, CORNELIA

(3rd century C.E.) Greek: Asia Minor, Italy, and Rome
Augusta

Cornelia Salonina, a cultured neo-Platonist, was Augusta during the troubled decades of the mid-third century C.E. She was the wife of the emperor Publius Licinius Gallienus. Her husband became sole ruler after his father was captured by the Persians in 260 C.E. Salonina was Greek speaking and came from Bithynia, in northwest Asia Minor.

Neo-Platonic idealism stood in sharp contrast with the steadily deteriorating economic situation of the period and the unending struggle to maintain the integrity of the empire's borders. Salonina accompanied Gallienus on his campaigns and was with him in the military camp when he was assassinated in 268. Salonina and Gallienus had two sons. The eldest, Valerian, died in 258, and the younger son, Publius Licinius Cornelius Saloninus Valerianus, became Caesar after the death of his brother and died shortly thereafter in 260 or 261. When Salonina died, a coin celebrating peace was issued in her honor.

SHA, Gallien. 21.3–5.

⬚ SANCIA

(? B.C.E.–33 C.E.) Roman: Rome
Convicted of treason

Sancia was either an innocent victim of a vendetta against her brother, or his accomplice. Her brother, Considius Proculus, had risen to the rank of praetor. He accused Publius Pomponius Secundus of treason in 31 C.E. The accusation against Pomponius was one of a spate of charges for conspiracy and treason pressed against alleged accomplices of Lucius Aelius Sejanus, treasonous former head of the Praetorian Guard. Pomponius was not brought to trial but was kept under house arrest until after the death of Tiberius in 37 C.E.

Two years after Considius's charge and while Pomponius was under house arrest, in 33, Quintus Pomponius Secundus, a brother of the accused, entered a countercharge against Considius. Sancia's brother was seized while celebrating his birthday, brought to the Senate, tried for treason, and executed on the same day. Sancia was also charged, convicted, and exiled without delay. The charges and countercharges were matters of life and death, frequently driven by financial reward: a successful prosecution generally resulted in the prosecutor receiving a portion of the confiscated estate. There is a suggestion in the sources that Sancia might have been an innocent victim of greed.

Tac., Ann. 6.18.
Levick, B., *Tiberius*, p. 205.
Marsh, F. B., pp. 206–7.
Marshall, A. J., "Women on Trial," p. 346.

⬚ SAPPHO

(c. 612 B.C.E.–?) Greek: Lesbos
Poet

Sappho was ranked with the greatest poets of antiquity. Called "the tenth muse" by the philosopher Plato, her poetry was read and recited by Greeks and Romans across the Mediterranean. She composed nine books of lyric poetry. Some were love poems addressed to individual women; others were women's wedding songs. Still others address the goddesses of music, poetry, literature, and dance. Only one complete poem, "Hymn to Aphrodite," and a number of fragments have survived. There is enough extant, however, to suggest her union of the spiritual and the physically passionate, always with women as her subject.

Sappho taught a group of young women music and poetry and probably led rites in celebration of Aphrodite. Possibly she belonged to a formal school where women lived together until marriage. Alternatively the arrangements may have been a less formal sharing of poetry, music, and mutual affection.

Born about 612 B.C.E. in Eresus, on the west coast of the island of Lesbos, her parents, Cleis and Scamandronymus, were well-to-do landowners. She was orphaned at about age 6, and about 14, exiled to Sicily. She later returned to Mytilene, on the east coast of Lesbos, where she lived for the remainder of her life.

Sappho married Cercylas, a wealthy man from Andrus. She had a daughter named Cleis. One of her brothers, Charaxus, sold wine from Lesbos to the Egyptians. From an extant lampoon in her poetry, we know that in Egypt her brother met RHODOPIS, a famous beauty of her day, and was sufficiently enthralled to purchase her freedom.

Blundell, S., pp. 82–91.
Bowra, C. M., *Greek Lyric*, pp. 176 ff.
Edmonds, J. M., v. 2, pp. 140–307.
OCD, p. 1, 355.
Snyder, J. M., pp. 1–19.

⬚ SASSIA

(1st century B.C.E.) Roman: Italy
Victim in a celebrated trial

Sassia was caught up in a vicious family quarrel that resulted in charges and countercharges of murder and attempted murder. She had three husbands. With the first she had a son, Cluentius Habitus, and a daughter, Cluentia. Widowed, she married Aulus Aurieus Melinus and gave birth to a daughter. He was killed in the proscriptions following the victory of Lucius Cornelius Sulla in 81 B.C.E. Her third husband was Statius Albius Oppianicus, who was said to have been responsible for her second husband's death. Oppianicus had three children from a previous marriage. His son, named Oppianicus, married Sassia's daughter by her second husband. The children of the first and third marriage did not get along, and therein lies the tangled tale of two trials.

In 74 B.C.E. Sassia's son Cluentius charged his stepfather, Statius Albius Oppianicus, with attempted murder. The elder Oppianicus was convicted of an attempt to poison his stepson. Subsequently, the presiding arbiter of the court and some members of the jury were themselves convicted of various offenses, including bribery. A consensus emerged that the elder Oppianicus had been a victim of corrupt testimony. Subsequently, the elder Oppianicus died, and the younger Oppianicus charged Cluentius with murder. At the trial in 66 B.C.E., Marcus Tullius Cicero was one of Cluentius's defenders. In his statement, Cicero painted Sassia and the younger Oppianicus as the villains, not Sassia's son Cluentius. He portrayed Sassia as an odious person who controlled those around her and would stop at nothing, not even murder, to have her own way. It was she, not her stepson, who was the true instigator of the trial.

He alledged that Sassia, a wealthy widow after the death of her first husband, had fallen in love with Melinus when he was married to her daughter Cluentia. After her daughter and Melinus divorced, Sassia married him. Her son Cluentius disapproved. Sassia hated him for his disapproval. Her new husband, Melinus, was about to charge the elder Oppianicus with the murder of a kinsman, when Oppianicus left Larinum, a city on the Adriatic side of Italy where they all lived, to join the victorious forces of Sulla. Appointed the chief magistrate at Larinum, he arranged to have Melinus proscribed and killed.

The elder Oppianicus then asked Sassia to marry him, but she refused unless he agreed to kill two of his three sons, because she did not want to be the stepmother of his three sons. The elder Oppianicus complied, and she married him. Cicero charged that Oppianicus later left Sassia after she had an affair with a plebeian, Sextus Albius, and that Oppianicus died from a fever contracted after being thrown from a horse. Cicero made no effort to support this gruesome tale with independent evidence or witnesses. He did, however, succeed in securing the acquittal of Cluentius and later boasted that he had won the case with dust thrown into the eyes of the jury.

Cluentius was most likely guilty of bribery and the murder of his stepfather in an attempt to secure his inheritance. The younger Oppianicus, on the other hand, was also motivated by a desire to reinstate his inheritance, which had probably disappeared with his father's conviction. Sassia, the ostensible villain of Cicero's defense, lost her reputation, no small factor in Roman life, but held tight to her money and her freedom.

Cic., Clu. 175–90.
Hoenigswald, G. S., pp. 109–23.

▣ SATRIA GALLA
(1st century C.E.) Roman: Rome
Political player

Satria Galla had no family of note, but she was very beautiful. Her first husband was Domitius Silius, whom she divorced to marry his close friend, the eminent Gaius Calpurnius Piso. Piso was well born and very rich. In Rome of the mid-first century C.E., newly adorned with imperial munificence, he lived in a grand style. They were a popular couple. In 65 he was accused of leading a plot to overthrow the emperor Nero. Urged to rally his supporters, he instead, chose suicide, possibly to protect Satria and his estate.

Tac., Ann. 15.59.

🔲 SCRIBONIA

(70 B.C.E.–? C.E.) Roman: Italy and
Pandateria
Political player

Scribonia valiantly stood her ground and fought
against forces far stronger than her own in political battles that stretched from the end of the republic into the reign of Tiberius. She married
three times, watched her sons die, and voluntarily
accompanied her daughter into exile. Until the
end of her life she stood ready to use her voice on
behalf of her kin and possibly, to support conspiracies against the emperor.

Born about 70 B.C.E., her mother was Sentia,
and her father, Lucius Scribonius Libo. She had a
brother, Lucius, who was consul in 34 B.C.E. Her
first husband was Gnaeus Cornelius Lentulus
Marcellinus, consul in 56 B.C.E. She was either
widowed or divorced, and their son, Cornelius
Marcellinus, probably died before he reached
manhood. Her second husband, a man of about
her own age, was Publius Cornelius Scipio, consul
suffectus in 35 B.C.E. They had two children:
Publius Cornelius, consul in 16 B.C.E., and
CORNELIA (8). Her daughter died after she had
married and borne children. She was eulogized in
a poem by Propertius in which she spoke as if from
the grave, praising her mother's lineage and ad-
dressing her with tender and affectionate words.

Probably divorced from her second husband in
40 B.C.E., Scribonia married Octavian, who was
about seven years her junior. She was the aunt of
Sextus Pompeius Magnus, the younger son of
Gnaeus Pompeius Magnus (Pompey the Great),
and his closest unmarried female relative. The
marriage was part of an effort to strengthen relations between Octavian and Sextus Pompeius.
Octavian, however, was a problematic husband.
Intent on securing control over Italy, the future of
the marriage was inseparable from the fortunes of
the civil war. Octavian's forces had been victorious in the Perusine War, but Sextus's fleet controlled the seas, and Antony was about to invade
Italy. The demands of the army, facilitated by a

small group of influential women, led the opposing leaders to forge the Treaty of Brundisium in
40. The treaty affirmed the Second Triumvirate
and recognized Sextus.

Although the marriage between Scribonia and
Octavian had been politically useful, at least for
Scribonia it was never satisfactory and quickly
outlived its initial purpose. It ended in divorce in
39 on the very day Scribonia gave birth to JULIA
(6). It was anything but a friendly parting. Octavian gave as his reason for divorce Scribonia's
continuous opposition and arguments. He had, in
fact, flagrantly insulted her by publicly flaunting
his affair with LIVIA DRUSILLA. He made no attempt to conceal his passion for the 18-year-old
Livia, who was married, the mother of one child,
and pregnant with another.

Scribonia's daughter Julia was the only child
Octavian ever fathered. Although divorced,
Scribonia's link with her daughter remained
strong during the years that Julia grew up primarily in her stepmother's household. Thirty-seven
years later, in 2 B.C.E., Julia, now the wife of the future emperor Tiberius and the mother of JULIA (7),
was exiled to Pandateria, charged by her father,
now emperor Augustus, with multiple adulteries.
Scribonia voluntarily went with her daughter into
a bleak exile. Five years later, the two women were
allowed to go to Rhegium at the tip of Italy, where
they remained for 10 more years until Julia died.
While Scribonia was in voluntary exile, her
granddaughter was also banished by Augustus for
adultery. Her granddaughter had married a first
cousin, Lucius Aemilius Paullus. He was the son
of Scribonia's daughter Cornelia, and was executed for conspiring against the emperor.

In 16 C.E. her great-nephew Marcus Scribonius
Libo Drusus, praetor in that year, was accused of
plotting against Tiberius. The charge was based
on a list he had compiled with mysterious marks
against names of the members of the imperial family and a number of senators. Many viewed Libo as
a ridiculous and rather stupid young man; nonetheless, Tiberius took the charges seriously. He
may have considered Libo's connection to

Scribonia a potential threat. Libo, accompanied by a number of aristocratic women, went to his wife's relatives to plead with them to intervene on his behalf. Most feared to do so. Scribonia was possibly among his supporters. If there was truth to the conspiracy charged, it was possible that she played a part since she surely had no love for the emperor. She urged Libo to face execution rather than commit suicide. Despite Scribonia's plea, Libo committed suicide. Nothing more is heard of Scribonia.

Propertius 55–57.
Sen., Ep. 70.10
Suet., Aug. 62.2; 63.1.
Suet., Tib. 25.1–3.
Tac., Ann. 2.27–31.
Leon, E. F., pp. 168 ff.
Levick, Tiberius.
OCD, p. 1,370.
PW 32.
Syme, R., Augustan Aristocracy, index.
Syme R., Roman Revolution, pp. 213, 229.

▣ SEMPRONIA (1)

(2nd century B.C.E.) Roman: Italy
Political player

Sempronia was rich in family and unfortunate in marriage. She was the granddaughter of Publius Scipio Aemilianus Africanus, who defeated Hannibal in 202 B.C.E. Her grandfather had been attracted to Greek learning and had educated his daughters as well as his sons. Her mother, CORNELIA (2), married the upstanding but much older Tiberius Sempronius Gracchus, twice consul and once censor, who valued an educated wife. He died when Sempronia was young. Widowed her mother raised her and her two famous brothers, Tiberius and Gaius, with the same education in Greek philosophy, the arts, rhetoric, and mathematics that she had received.

Between 152 and 147, Sempronia married her cousin Publius Cornelius Scipio Aemilianus, a distinguished soldier and cultured statesman, consul in 147 and 134. Their relationship was not harmonious. Sempronia may have had some kind of deformity that inhibited her from bearing children, and in addition, her husband was politically opposed to her brothers. Tiberius and Gaius championed proposals for reform in the use of public lands for the benefit of the growing landless, especially veterans. They were opposed by a wealthy conservative faction to which her husband belonged. When he returned to Rome after a victorious campaign in Spain, he led the fight to prevent the organization of an agrarian commission for distributing public land in accordance with the new Gracchi laws. In the explosive atmosphere generated by the Gracchi proposals, living with a husband who was her brother's political opponent must have been both taxing and wrenching for Sempronia. Unpopular with the urban mob, her husband died unexpectedly in bed in 129 B.C.E. after the assassination of Tiberius in 133 and before that of Gaius. In the heated political situation, rumors circulated that Sempronia and her mother were responsible for Aemillianus's death.

Sempronia may have joined her mother in the country outside Rome after the deaths of both her brothers and husband. The women lived a cultured life and welcomed visitors. They also remained very much current with affairs in Rome. In 101 Sempronia testified in a criminal trial when tribune, Lucius Appuleius Saturninus, brought action against the censor Metellus Numidicus, who had refused to inscribe Lucius Equitius as a citizen. Equitius claimed that he was the illegitimate son of Sempronia's brother Tiberius Gracchus. He sought to use his claim to win popular support for election to the office of tribune. Despite the hostile questioning of Saturninus and the demands of Equitius's supporters, Sempronia adamantly denied that Equitius was her brother's son. The suit against Numidicus was dismissed. We hear no more of Sempronia after the trial.

App., Bciv. 1.20.
Val. Max. 3.8.6; 9.7.1, 15.1.
Balsdon, J. P. V. D., pp. 194, 214.

Bauman, R. A., pp. 48–49.
PW 99.
Richardson, K., pp. 26, 29, 115.
Stockton, D., p. 24–26.

🔲 SEMPRONIA (2)

(1st century B.C.E.) Roman: Rome
Possible conspirator

Sempronia chose her lovers and squandered her fortune. She was smart, fun, fearless, and dangerous to be around. Her father was probably Sempronius Tuditanus, consul in 129 B.C.E. Accomplished in Greek and Latin, she was said to have been adept at the seductive use of the lyre and dance. Sempronia was accused of supporting Lucius Sergius Catilina, who had incurred large debts and organized a conspiracy that included destitute soldiers and the impoverished wellborn, both men and women.

The conspirators, who intended to enact relief from debt, planned a coup against the elected officials. The women were supposed to render slaves impotent to protect their masters, to set fires, and to persuade husbands to join the conspirators or to kill them. The conspirators allegedly met in Sempronia's house while her husband, an opponent of any such movement, was away.

The conspiracy failed, and Catiline was killed. Nothing happened to Sempronia. It is possible that she never had any association with the conspiracy. Marcus Tullius Cicero, who rarely missed an opportunity to denigrate the women involved with the men he attacked, never mentioned Sempronia in his speech against Catiline. The accusations against her could well be yet another attack on any woman who was smart, somewhat unconventional, and visible.

Sall., Cat. 25.1–5; 40.5.
Balsdon, J. P. V. D., pp. 47–49.
Bauman, R. A., pp. 67–68.
Hillard, T., pp. 47–49.
PW 103.
Syme, R., *Augustan Aristocracy*, pp. 26, 198 ff.
Syme, R., *Sallust*, pp. 25–26, 135.

🔲 SERVILIA (1)

(1st century B.C.E.) Roman: Rome
Power broker

Servilia worked to enhance the position and fortunes of herself and her kin. A formidable woman with personal charm and intelligence, she influenced powerful men, including her friend and lover, Gaius Julius Caesar. With a wide range of friends, clients, and family connections, she participated openly and covertly in the traffic in favors that was the political medium of exchange among the elite of the late republic. In the complicated and tense times after the death of Caesar in 44 B.C.E. she proved more realistic and practical than her son Marcus Junius Brutus, her half brother Marcus Porcius Cato Uticensis, and her son-in-law Gaius Cassius Longinus.

Servilia was the daughter of Quintus Servilius Caepio, quaestor in 100 B.C.E., and LIVIA, the sister of Marcus Livius Drusus, tribune in 91 B.C.E. Servilia's father quarreled with his brother-in-law, Marcus Drusus, and divorced her mother about 96 B.C.E. Her mother then married Marcus Porcius Cato; their son Cato, born in 95, was Servilia's half brother. Servilia's father died in battle in 89, and her mother and stepfather died shortly before the outbreak of civil war. Servilia, some six years older than her half brother, looked after her siblings from the two marriages and had enormous influence over them.

She married Marcus Junius Brutus, tribune in 83 B.C.E. Her husband was executed by Gnaeus Pompeius Magnus (Pompey the Great) in 77. They had a son, the tyrannicide Marcus Junius Brutus. She then married Decimus Junius Silanus, consul in 62 B.C.E. and had three daughters whose advantageous marriages she later arranged. JUNIA (1) married Marcus Aemilius Lepidus, the triumvir. JUNIA (2) married Publius Servilius Isauricus, consul in 48 B.C.E. JUNIA TERTIA married Cassius, praetor in 44 B.C.E.

Servilla and Julius Caesar became lovers before 64 B.C.E., during Caesar's first consulship when he was said to have given her a pearl costing 6 million sesterces. She sent Caesar an intimate letter during the debate in the Senate over Sergius Catilina in 63. Cato and Caesar were on opposing sides in the debate; Cato demanded to see the letter, claiming it was from enemies of the Senate. Caesar handed it to him. The liaison between Caesar and Servilia was among the reasons Cato hated Caesar with a passion that only civil war assuaged. Servilia, occasionally restrained Cato. In 62 Caesar supported Servilia's husband Silanus in his successful bid for the consulship. Cato brought a suit of bribery against the second consul, but refrained from similar action against Silanus.

In 59 B.C.E., when Servilia's husband was already dead, Caesar divorced POMPEIA (1), and marriage with Caesar became possible for Servilia. However, she was as practical in love as in her life in general. An alliance between Caesar and Pompey was clearly more desirable and of greater importance at the moment. JULIA (5), Caesar's daughter, married Pompey, and rather than marry Servilia, Caesar married CALPURNIA, the daughter of Lucius Calpurnius Piso, whose election to consul in 58 B.C.E. Caesar and Pompey jointly supported. No doubt the young Calpurnia was also more likely than Servilia to have the son Caesar so dearly sought. Servilia's friendship with Caesar continued over the next decade and through the outbreak of hostilities. She purchased several confiscated estates at very low prices after Caesar's defeat of Pompey in 48. Gossip in Rome recognized the relationship between the two and maliciously speculated that Caesar's liaison with Servilia's daughter Junia Tertia was part payment for the estates.

The unforeseen consequence of their passion and friendship contributed to Caesar's death. Despite Servilia's alliance with Caesar, her son Brutus and her half brother Cato sided with Pompey against Caesar once war became unavoidable. For Brutus, his uncle's rhetoric of republican rectitude overcame Pompey's earlier treachery toward his father. Fortunately for Brutus, Servilia's own relationship with Caesar also protected him after Pompey's defeat at

Pharsalus in 48 B.C.E. Caesar not only issued orders to spare Brutus's life but spared many of the latter's friends and appointed Brutus praetor. As he was about to leave for Africa in pursuit of Cato, he put Brutus in charge of Cisalpine Gaul.

Brutus was unable to accept the fortunes of war and the benefits of his mother's friendship with Caesar. He was tortured by feelings of betrayal to the republican cause and all that his uncle Cato claimed as good. Possibly, shame over public knowledge of his mother and Caesar's affair also violated his romantic vision of a virtuous republic. To Servilia's dismay, Brutus divorced his wife in 45 in order to marry PORCIA, the no less tortured daughter of Cato.

After Caesar's murder Servilia concentrated her efforts on doing everything in her power to protect the interests of her family and to support the assassins, including Brutus and her son-in-law Cassius. Servilia presided in a meeting at Antium on the coast south of Rome on June 8, 44. Those present included Brutus and his wife, Porcia, Cassius and his wife, Junia Tertia, Marcus Tullius Cicero, and Marcus Favonius, an admirer of Cato. The family conference was to consider an offer made by the Senate at the instigation of Mark Antony to appoint Brutus and Cassius to supervise the collection of corn taxes in the provinces of Sicily and Asia until the end of the year. It offered them an honorary exile in the face of unrest in Rome after the assassination. Brutus and Cassius were uncertain whether or not to accept. When Cicero went into a long-winded speech of opportunities lost, Servilia cut him short and took it upon herself to try to have the corn commission removed from the senate decree.

By 43 events were moving quickly, and the breakup of the old order was increasingly evident. On May 29, 43, Marcus Aemilius Lepidus, the husband of Servilia's daughter Junia, defected to Mark Antony and was declared a public enemy by the Senate. Servilia, worried about her daughter and her two grandsons, appealed to Cicero to protect the boys. Brutus supported her with a letter to

Cicero. Cicero, after some ambivalence, said he would do what he could.

On July 25, 43 B.C.E., Servilia called another meeting in Rome. Present were Cicero, Publius Servilius Casca and Antistius Labeo, both participants in the assassination of Caesar, and Brutus's agent Marcus Scaptius. Servilia asked whether it would be advisable for Brutus to bring his forces to Italy or better that he remain away for the time being. Cicero gave his opinion that Brutus should return. In the end, however, Brutus and Cassius were too busy consolidating their gains in the East. After Brutus was killed, Antony sent his ashes back to Servilia in Rome as a mark of respect. Little more is known of Servilia, except that the astute Titus Pomponius Atticus, who maintained good relations with the powerful people on both sides of the civil war, continued his friendship with her and aided her after Brutus's death.

Cic., Att. 13.9.2, 22.4; 14.13; 15.11, 17.
Cic., Brut. 22.12.1–2; 26.18.
Nep., Att. 11.
Plut., Brut. 1.5; 2.1; 5.1–4; 6.10
Plut., Caes. 62.3–6.
Plut., Cat. Min. 21.2–3; 24.1–2.
Suet., Caes. 50.2.
Balsdon, J. P. V. D., pp. 51–52, 216–17.
Bauman, R. A., pp. 73–76.
Hillard, T., pp. 53–55.
OCD, p. 1,394.
PW 1,394
Shackleton Bailey, D. R., pp. 242–23.
Syme, R., Augustan Aristocracy, p. 25.
Syme, R., Roman Revolution, index.

▣ SERVILIA (2)

(1st century B.C.E.) Roman: Italy and Asia
Political wife

Servilia was the daughter of Quintus Servilius Caepio, praetor in 91 B.C.E., and LIVIA. Her grandfather was Marcus Livius Drusus, consul in 112 B.C.E. Her parents divorced in about 96, after a quarrel between her father and grandfather. Her mother married Marcus Porcius Cato; both of them died before the civil war.

Servilia made an apparently advantageous marriage with the wealthy soldier and administrator, Lucius Licinius Lucullus, consul in 74. Lucullus, a man of culture and an Epicurian, was a member of the powerful Metelli family. He had divorced his first wife, CLODIA (3), after her brother had led a rebellion among his troops while in Asia. Servilia had a son with Lucullus; the marriage ended in divorce. Lucullus always a difficult man, later died insane.

Servilia took her son and went to live with her half brother, Marcus Porcius Cato Uticensis. She traveled with him to Asia. He left her in Rhodes when he went to join Gnaeus Pompeius Magnus (Pompey the Great). Her son, Marcus Licinius Lucullus, fought with his cousin Marcus Junius Brutus against Octavian and Mark Antony. He killed himself, along with Brutus, in 42 B.C.E., after the defeat at Philippi. Servilia's death is unrecorded.

Plut., Cat. Min. 54.1–2.
Plut., Luc. 38.1.

▣ SERVILIA (3)

(1st century B.C.E.) Roman: Italy
Political wife

Servilia was the last member of an ancient republican family with roots in Alba Longa, southeast of Rome, and said to have been founded by Aenas. Her father was Publius Servilius Isauricus, consul in 48 B.C.E. and an ally of Gaius Julius Caesar. Her mother was JUNIA (2). In 43, she was to marry Octavian, the future emperor Augustus. The engagement ended when Octavian married the stepdaughter of Mark Antony, to cement the Second Triumvirate. Servilia married instead the son and namesake of the triumvir Marcus Aemilius Lepidus. Her husband became part of a plot to assassinate Octavian. The plot was discovered, and in 30 B.C.E. he was executed for treason. Servilia committed suicide by swallowing burning coals.

App., Bciv. 4.50.
Livy, Per. 133.
Suet., Aug. 62,1.
Vell. Pat, 2.88.4.
Syme R., *Roman Revolution*, pp. 182, 189, 230, 298.

▣ SERVILIA (4)

(c. 46–66 C.E.) Roman: Rome
Victim

Servilia was young and condemned unreasonably in 66 C.E. She died bravely with her father, Quintus Marcus Barea Soranus, consul suffectus in 52. Her husband, Annius Pollio, had been forced into exile by the emperor Nero for his participation in the Pisonian conspiracy in 65. In 66 her father was accused of conspiring with Rubellius Plautus, the philosophically inclined senator who had refused to take up arms against the emperor, even though he knew it was only time until he too would be killed by Nero. It was assumed that the charge against her father, who was an honorable man, was retribution for his having refused to allow the emperor's freedmen to loot the city of Pergamum of its statues and paintings when he was proconsul in Asia.

Servilia, who was not yet 20 years old, was called before the Senate with her father. She was accused of selling her bridal ornaments, including a necklace, to pay magicians. She explained that she had not asked the magicians to cast any spells against the emperor Nero but to preserve the safety of her father. Servilia declared that her father had known nothing of what she had done, and if there was any fault, it was hers alone. Her father interrupted to add that in addition, she had not gone with him to Asia and had not been implicated in the charges against her husband. His plea that she be tried separately from him was refused. However, the harshness of the sentence was mitigated to allow Barea Soranus and Servilia the choice as to the manner of their death.

Tac., Ann. 16.30–33.

▣ SEXTIA (1)

(? B.C.E.–34 C.E.) Roman: Rome
Committed suicide; political victim

Sextia urged her husband to kill himself rather than be executed for treason. She came from a distinguished family. Her first husband, who died in 21 C.E., was Cornelius Sulla, a descendant of Lucius Cornelius Sulla, the dictator of Rome in 81 B.C.E. With him she had two sons, Faustus Sulla, consul suffectus in 31 C.E., and Lucius Sulla Felix, consul in 33. Sextia's second husband was Mamercus Aemilius Scaurus, consul suffectus in 21 C.E. He was a cultured man and a noted orator and advocate, disliked by the emperor Tiberius. In 32, he was accused of treason. The trial was adjourned.

In 34, he was again charged with treason at the instigation of Quintus Naevius Cordus Sutorius Macro, prefect of the Praetorian Guard. Scaurus was alleged to be the lover of Livia Julia Claudia, LIVILLA, a relative of Tiberius. Livilla had been condemned for her close association with the treasonous Lucius Aelius Sejanus and starved herself to death in 31. As evidence against Scaurus, the prosecution put forth lines extracted from a tragedy written by Scaurus that could suggest references to Tiberius. Sextia urged her husband to commit suicide and both killed themselves before a trial took place. Their suicide gave an honorable end to their lives since they could be buried with due respect, their estates would not be confiscated, and their wills would remain valid.

Tac., Ann. 6.29.
Levick, B., *Tiberius*, p. 213.

▣ SEXTIA (2)

(?–65 C.E.) Roman: Italy
Political victim

Sextia died bravely. She was confronted with unanswerable charges by the emperor Nero. Sextia had watched helplessly as Rubellius Plautus, the husband of her granddaughter ANTISTIA

POLLITTA, was pushed to suicide in 62 C.E. Plautus had refused to take up arms against the emperor, although there was some indication that he would have found support had he chosen to do so.

Nero was still not satisfied. Three years later, in 65, Sextia, her granddaughter Antistia, and her son-in-law Lucius Antistius Vetus, consul with Nero 10 years earlier in 55, again were threatened. The three withdrew to Vetus's estate in Formiae. They then severed their veins and had themselves transported to the baths, where they died.

Tac., Ann. 16.10–11.

SEXTILIA

(?–c. 69 C.E.) Roman: Rome
Independent woman, Augusta

Sextilia rightly feared that disaster would follow after her son became emperor. A woman of fine character and from a distinguished family, she lived intimately with imperial intrigue. Sextilia married the successful politician and friend of the emperor Claudius, Lucius Vitellius. Her husband supported the younger Julia AGRIPPINA after her marriage with the emperor and was partner in her cleansing of enemies. Placed in charge of Rome while Claudius traveled to Britain, Vitellius died in 52 C.E., leaving Sextilia with two sons, Aulus Vitellius and the younger Lucius Vitellius.

Her eldest son, Aulus, also a friend of Claudius and his successor Gaius Caligula, amassed a considerable fortune as proconsul in Africa. He married a wealthy woman, PETRONIA, divorced her, and married GALERIA FUNDANA, the daughter of a former praetor. He lived extravagantly, gambled, and drank. When the emperor Servius Sulpicius Galba gave him command of the troops in Lower Germany, he was broke. To raise funds and finance his trip, he mortgaged his house, and Sextilia sold some jewels.

Sextilia and Galeria Fundana remained in Rome after Aulus Vitellius went to Germany. Although he left Galeria in straitened financial circumstances with creditors at her door, Sextilia retained a firm control over her own wealth and distanced herself from her son's financial debacle. After the death of Galba, on January 2, 69 C.E., the troops in Lower Germany declared Vitellius emperor. Probably more in response to Vitellius's loose regard for discipline than as a measure of his leadership qualities, the troops hailed him a second Germanicus, in reference to the able soldier and son of the younger ANTONIA who was Tiberius's probable heir. When Sextilia first learned of her son's rise to power, she was said to have responded that she had borne a libertine Vitellius, not a Germanicus.

In Rome Sextilia and Galeria Fundana were in some danger as Marcus Salvius Otho challenged Vitellius. Vitellius wrote Otho's brother and threatened to kill him and his family if the women were harmed. As it turned out, Sextilia may have had her own avenues of access to the camp of Otho, and neither of them were injured. Vitellius defeated Otho, and on his arrival in Rome, he embraced Sextilia and declared her Augusta. He also spent huge sums of money on food, drink, and entertainment. Troops in other parts of the empire deserted to Titus Flavius Vespasian. Vitellius was defeated in battle. Sextilia died shortly before both her sons were killed in December 69.

Suet., Vit. 3.1.
Tac., Hist. 1.75; 2.64, 89.3.

SILIA

(1st century C.E.) Roman: Rome and Italy
Exile

Silia, the wife of a senator, was involved in a scandal with the emperor Nero. A close friend of Titus Petronius, the probable author of the *Satyricon*, she most likely took part in the notorious entertainments he arranged for the emperor. When Nero turned against Petronius and Petronius committed suicide, a letter attached to his will described the orgies. Nero decided that Silia was guilty of spreading rumors, and he banished her.

Tac., Ann. 16.18, 20.

▣ SOSIA GALLIA

(? B.C.E.–c. 24 C.E.) Roman: Italy, Asia, and Germany(?)
Exile

Sosia Galla was a friend and ally of the elder Vipsania AGRIPPINA and was exiled for her allegiance to her. Sosia's husband, Gaius Silius, consul in 13 C.E., had served under Germanicus Julius Caesar, Agrippina's popular husband. Bad blood between the emperor Tiberius and Agrippina reached back to at least 19 C.E. when Germanicus unexpectedly died in Syria and Agrippina became convinced that Tiberius had arranged to have him poisoned.

Subsequently, Agrippina became the center of a powerful anti-Tiberius faction of which Sosia was a part. Lucius Aelius Sejanus, prefect of the Praetorian Guard and confidant of the emperor, launched a series of treason trials against those close to Agrippina, and in 24 Sosia and Silius were charged with treason and extortion. Silius committed suicide before he was condemned. Sosia was exiled and half of her estate was to be confiscated. Marcus Aemilius Lepidus, a friend of Tiberius, intervened and the confiscated amount was reduced to one-quarter, with the rest left for her children.

Tac., Ann., IV 18–20.
Bauman, R. A., pp. 145–46.
Levick, B., *Tiberius*, p. 163.
Marsh, F. B., pp. 169–70.
Marshall, A. J., "Women on Trial," pp. 343–44.

▣ STATILIA

(26 B.C.E.–? C.E.) Roman: Rome, Italy, Asia, and Samos
Political survivor

Statilia was very wealthy, widely traveled, and successfully avoided the politics that forced many of her contemporaries to exile or suicide. Her father was Titus Statilius Taurus, a noted military man, a general under Augustus, and twice consul. He died around 16 B.C.E., some 10 years after Statilia's birth in 26 B.C.E. She married Lucius Calpurnius Piso, consul in 1 B.C.E. Inscriptions honoring Statilia

and Piso found in Pergamum and on the island of Samos suggest that she accompanied him to Asia Minor where he was proconsul.

Piso was a cantankerous man who spoke his mind regardless of the circumstances or people involved. Not surprisingly, in 24 C.E. he was accused of treason for private conversations against the emperor. There may also have been charges stemming from his tenure in Asia Minor. However, he died before the trial began. A year later, in 25, Statilia's son died. Statilia not only survived but thrived. She was said to have established a second family. Very wealthy in her own right, she was the great-grandmother of STATILIA MESSALLINA, the last wife of the emperor Nero and the only one who managed to survive him.

Tac., Ann., IV 21
Marsh, F. B., pp. 172–73.
Syme., R., *Augustan Aristocracy*, pp. 376–77.

▣ STATILIA MESSALLINA

(1st century C.E.) Roman: Italy
Political player

Statilia Messallina managed her life well. She was renowned for her intelligence, beauty, charm, wealth, and culture. On both her mother's and her father's side, she was descended from consular families affiliated closely with Augustus. The fourth wife of the emperor Nero, she outlived him.

In her father's family were military men whose loyalty to Augustus was well rewarded. They also married well. Her grandfather married Valeria, the daughter of Marcus Valerius Messalla Corvinus, who was the patron of the poet Tibullus. In the literary circle around her grandmother was also the poet SULPICIA (1), whose poems are among the few extant writings by a Roman woman. Statilia's father was either Titus Statilius Taurus, consul in 44 C.E., or Taurus Statilius Corvinus, consul in 45, with the former the more likely candidate.

Her family knew the dangers of great wealth and imperial greed. When the younger Julia AGRIPPINA was the wife of the emperor Claudius, Agrippina persuaded Tarquitius Priscus, a legate of Statilia's father, to charge him with addiction to magical superstitions, among other things, as a means to force his beautiful gardens onto the market. Statilia's father committed suicide before the charges were heard by the Senate. The senators expelled the legate Priscus, despite Agrippina's efforts to save him.

After Statilia became the lover of the emperor Nero, she married Marcus Vestinus Atticus, consul in 65. He was her fourth husband and was aware of her liaison with Nero. Acquiescence was not sufficient, however, to save his life. Perhaps his tongue had been too quick. Nero accused him of mockery and sent soldiers to Vestinus's house while the latter was giving a dinner party. Vestinus had a doctor cut his arteries, and he bled to death.

After the death of Nero's wife POPPAEA SABINA (2), Statilia became the emperor's fourth wife. In 69, the year following Nero's suicide, she was in communication with Marcus Salvius Otho, who hoped to succeed Galba as emperor and evidently had some thoughts of marrying her. One of his last two letters was written to Statilia to bury him and preserve his memory. Her death is not recorded.

Suet., Ner. 35.1.
Suet., Otho 10.2.
Tac., Ann. 15.68, 69.
OCD, p. 1,438.
PW 45.
Syme, R., *Augustan Aristocracy*, index.

STRATONICE (1)

(5th century B.C.E.) Greek: Macedonia and Thrace
Political wife

Stratonice, from the Macedonian ruling house, married Sitacles, nephew and heir of his uncle the ruler of Thrace, in 429 B.C.E. Her brother Perdiccas II, who succeeded their father Alexander I as ruler of Macedonia, secretly made arrangements with Sitacles to marry Stratonice with a substantial dowry, if he convinced his uncle to withdraw from Macedonia. Sitacles persuaded his uncle to withdraw, and the marriage took place.

Thuc. 2.100–101.
Macurdy, G., p. 14.

STRATONICE (2)

(?–254 B.C.E.) Greek: Macedonia and Asia
Political wife and player

Stratonice was the much younger second wife of Seleucus I, who founded the Seleucid Empire after the death of the Alexander the Great. Her marriage in 298 B.C.E. was advantageous for all concerned. Stratonice was the granddaughter of Antipater, whom Alexander had left to govern Greece and Macedonia when he embarked on his final campaign. Her father, Demetrius I, became ruler of Macedonia in 294, in some measure because her mother, PHILA (1), gave Demetrius the legitimacy of Antipater's lineage. Stratonice carried the same gift to Seleucus. Since her father had lost most of his territory, his position was enhanced by an alliance with the powerful Seleucus, even as Seleucus gained a new claim on Macedonia.

Although Seleucus took his new bride back to his capital, Antioch, he did not divorce his first wife, APAMA (1). He founded a city in Asia Minor that he named after Stratonice, and she was worshiped as Aphrodite in the city of Smyrna. She gave birth to a daughter, PHILA (2). Her father and Seleucus later became enemies when Demetrius refused to sell Cilicia to Seleucus or give him Tyre and Sidon. In 293 Seleucus married Stratonice to his son Antiochus. There is a tale that Antiochus fell madly in love with her and was pining away. Seleucus's physician, Arasistratus, revealed his son's passion, and Seleucus arranged for the marriage. More likely, Seleucus was growing old and found it difficult to administer his vast empire, which now include Asia Minor. He made his son Antiochus I coregent of his eastern empire in Asia, married him to Statonice, and sent them off to rule.

There is some indication that Stratonice resisted the arrangement. Nonetheless, Stratonice had two sons with Antiochus. Seleucus, the eldest, became coregent in the East in 280 but was not successful and may have been executed for treason. The younger son, Antiochus II, succeeded his father. Stratonice outlived her husband by seven years and died in 254 B.C.E.

App., Syr. 59–61.
Plut., Demetr. 38.1–8.
Bevan, E. B., v. 1, pp. 62–64, 69, 121.
Cary, M., pp. 43, 54.
Macurdy, G.
OCD, p. 1,449.

STRATONICE (3)

(3rd century B.C.E.)   Greek: Asia
and Macedonia
Political leader

Stratonice was willing to face death in defense of the status and honors that she believed were her due. Her father was Antiochus I, who ruled the Seleucid Empire in Asia after 281 B.C.E., and her mother was STRATONICE (2). Around 225 Stratonice married Demetrius II of Macedonia, who was younger than she. Stratonice left him in 239, before he divorced her, obstensibly on account of infertility; however, his immediate marriage to PHTHIA—which cemented an alliance with OLYMPIAS (2) and strengthened his claim over Macedonia—suggests a stronger reason.

Stratonice approached her nephew Seleucus II, who succeeded her father as ruler of the Seleucid Empire, with an offer of marriage, which he rebuffed. She joined forces with another nephew, Antiochus Hierax, to overthrow his older brother, Seleucus. Stratonice led the revolt in Antioch, while Hierax launched an attack in Mesopotamia when Antiochus was campaigning against the Parthians. Antiochus hurried back, defeated Hierax, and captured Antioch. Stratonice, who had taken refuge at Seleuceia Pieria, a port city on the Mediterranean Sea west of Antioch, was executed.

App., Syr. XI 59,1.22.
Bevan, E. B., 1, pp. 173–74.
Cary, M., pp. 111–12, 147.

Downey, G., p. 91.
Macurdy, G., pp. 71–72.

SULPICIA (1)

(1st century B.C.E.)   Roman: Italy
Poet

Sulpicia is the only Roman woman whose poetry has survived from the tumultuous years at the end of the republic and the beginning of the empire. Although little is known of her life other than what appears in the poems, she fits the description of a *docta puella,* a well-born and well-educated woman who participated in the most elite intellectual and literary social circles.

She was the daughter or granddaughter of Servius Sulpicius Rufus, a renowned jurist and friend of Marcus Tullius Cicero, and a ward of Valerius Messalla Corvinus, a close political ally and friend of the emperor Augustus since Philippi in 42 B.C.E. Messalla had an illustrious military record, was a historian and orator, and was a patron of the arts. The poet Albius Tibullus was among his circle. At the end of the collected works of Tibullus are some 40 lines organized into 6 short elegiac poems that tradition has ascribed to Sulpicia.

Sometimes called the Garland of Sulpicia, the poems describe Sulpicia's love for Cerinthus, a man whose historical identity remains unknown but who seems to have been part of her social circle. The poems are quite conventional in form, and they have a youthful feel, more like that of a first infatuation than of experienced passion. However, many of the poems succeed in reconfiguring the coventional motifs to project a woman's own voice. Whether she impatiently speaks about Messalla taking her into the country away from Cerinthus, or speaks directly about her longing for Cerinthus, she is the subject of her poem, and Cerinthus, the object of her desire.

Some of the poems use stronger images of passion. They also take a more conventional perspective. Losing the ingenuous and personal qualities of her writing, they describe her love and her lover sympathetically, but from outside the actual experience. In those verses, Sulpicia and Cerinthus assume more of the character of idealized lovers conventional in Latin love poetry.

Tib. 3.13–18.
Creekmore, H., pp. 105–25.
Fantham, E., et al., pp. 323–25.
Nuck, G., pp. 100–102.
OCD, p. 1,454.
Pomeroy, S. B., *Goddesses*, pp. 173–74.
PW 114.

⊞ SULPICIA (2)

(?–c. 94/98 C.E.)   Roman: Rome
Poet

Sulpicia wrote love poems to her husband, Calenus. Of these poems only one fragment still exists. She was happily married for more than 15 years, and the text of her poetry seems to have combined fidelity and sensuality with a frankness unusual in the Latin poetry that lauded marriage. She probably died between 94 and 98 C.E.

Mart. 10.35, 38.12–14.
OCD, p. 1,454.
PW 4A.
PW supplement p. 9.

TANAQUIL

(7th–6th century B.C.E.) Etruscan: Rome
Heroine

Tanaquil's story forms part of the earliest history of Rome, in which fact and legend are inextricably interwoven. She was said to have been Etruscan and to have come from a noble family of the Tarquinii. She married Lucius Tarquinius Priscus, who had an Etruscan mother and whose father was Demaratus from Corinth. Her husband's mixed birth limited his opportunities in Tarquinii, and Tanaquil was said to have persuaded him to move to Rome.

In Rome, he became influential and established close relations with King Ancus. When the latter died, Priscus was elected king by the Comitia, the assembly of the Roman people. According to Roman tradition, he became the fifth king of Rome, reigning from 616 to 579 B.C.E. It was during his reign that the Circus Maximus was laid out, and the Forum, drained.

Tanaquil took great interest in the career of Servius Tullius, who was brought up and educated in her household. Possibly, the boy's mother had been captured after the death of his father, who was a prominent citizen of Corniculum, a city northeast of Rome. He married Tanaquil's daughter.

Tanaquil was instrumental in making Servius Tullius her husband's successor. After her husband was killed, she leaned out of her window and assured the concerned crowd below that her husband had designated Servius Tullius to carry out the affairs of state while he recuperated. When Servius Tullius had acted as king for a short time and seemed to be accepted by the people, Tanaquil and Servius Tullius announced that Priscus was dead. Tanaquil had two sons, Lucius Tarquinius and Arruns Tarquinius. They both married daughters of Servius Tullius.

Dio. 2, 7, 9.
Livy 1.34.1–12, 39.3–4, 41.1–7.
Zonar. 7.8, 9.
OCD, p. 1,473.

TELESILLA

(5th century B.C.E.) Greek: Greece
Poet and military leader

Telesilla was a renowned poet. She also organized and led a successful defense of her native city, Argos, against an invading army of Spartans. She was honored for both service to the muses and military victory. Sickly as a youth, her passion for poetry was a source of strength. Nine fragments from larger hymns survive. Her poetry was said to have been addressed to women, and women were her greatest admirers. The Greek meter telesilleion, or acephalous glyconic, was named after her.

At one point in her life, Cleomenes of Sparta defeated the Argive army, which suffered an unusually large number of causalities. He then attacked the city, which was filled with noncombatants. Telesilla organized a defense of the city's walls by the male slaves and any other available men, some too old and some too young to have been a part of the army. She also armed the women with weapons that had been left in the city. She led the women to a confined area through which the Spartans would have to travel. The women fought fiercely, and the Spartans retreated. The sources excuse the Spartan withdrawal with the observation that the Spartans feared the odium of either defeat or victory over an army of women.

The women who fell in battle against the Spartans were buried along the Argive Way. In a temple of Aphrodite in Argos, in front of a seated statue of the goddess, was a slab engraved with the figure of Telesilla holding a helmet. The victory was celebrated once a year by the people of Argos in the Hybristica, or Feast of Outrage. For hundreds of years after the event, on that day women dressed in the shirts and cloaks of men, and men, in the robes of women.

Paus. 2.20
Plut., Mor. 245–46.
Polyaenus, Strat. 8.33.
Edmonds, J. M., v. 2, pp. 237–45.
OCD, p. 1,480.

▣ TERENTIA (1)

(1st century B.C.E.–? C.E.) Roman: Italy
Financial manager; occasional head of household

Terentia was strong, even courageous in the face of adversity. She was ambitious and thought herself a partner with her husband during times of great political danger. As her 30-year marriage disintegrated under the stresses of civil war, she assumed responsibilities for the financial welfare of her children that extended beyond the law or the expectations of traditional Roman society. Terentia came from a Roman family of ancient lineage and noble status, the Fabii. Her only known relative, however, was her half sister FABIA, a Vestal Virgin. Although her age and the date of their marriage are unknown, Terentia married Marcus Tullius Cicero when both were relatively young. Terentia had two children: TULLIA (2), born in 79 B.C.E. shortly after their marriage began, and Marcus, born in 65. She was close to her daughter, and as her daughter grew into adulthood, they were friends and allies in the stressful period of civil war.

Her husband Cicero, who came from Arpinum, was a gifted orator and set on a public career. Terentia's family name enhanced his status as a newcomer in the most elite circles of Roman politics. Her substantial dowry of 400,000 denarii was no less critical for his career. In 63 her husband was elected consul. Her position as wife of a consul assured her place in the social hierarchy. Moreover, her husband's consulship was crowned with the successful defense of the state against a conspiracy led by Lucius Sergius Catilina. Her husband was hailed as a savior of the republic and the acclaim reflected upon Terentia.

Despite the opportunities of his position, Terentia remained wealthier than Cicero and was far more interested than he in the management and growth of her estate. She oversaw her own financial affairs and often managed her husband's finances as well. She was a close friend of the very wealthy Titus Pomponius Atticus, her husband's closest adviser, supporter, and boyhood friend. Their mutual interest in finance and his tie with Cicero were a source of solace and a lifeline in the difficult years when Cicero was exiled and in the negotiations that ended her marriage.

What little is known suggests that Terentia was a generally conservative woman with regard to both economics and religion. During the period of her husband's consulship, there was a serious problem of liquidity compounded by inflation. The roots of the Catiline conspiracy rested in some part on the lack of cash suffered by the rich. Among the issues was a tax on the use of public lands. Terentia was on the side of the conservatives, who sought to preserve free use of the public land and refused to pay the tax. Similarly conservative in religion, her sister was a Vestal Virgin, and with women of her own class, Terentia shared religious ceremonies that marked the annual calendar of Roman life. As the wife of a consul, Terentia participated in the rites of the Bona Dea traditionally restricted to women from families of high officials.

In December 62 B.C.E. the celebration of the rites at the house of Gaius Julius Caesar, the *pontifex maximus,* was disrupted when a man was found to have infiltrated the household disguised as a female flute player. Cicero became a key witness against the brash, brilliant, and dissolute Publius Clodius Pulcher, who was accused of the sacrilegious act. Clodius claimed that he had not been in Rome that day. Cicero, however, testified that Clodius had visited him in Rome on the day in question. The jurors were bribed. Clodius was not convicted, and Cicero made a bitter enemy. Speculation has assigned Terentia a role in Cicero's decision to go forward with his testimony. She was said to have been jealous of CLODIA (2), Clodius's sister, who may have at one time approached Cicero as a possible lover and even a husband. Possibly, Terentia simply regarded Clodius and Clodia as unacceptable by virtue of their lifestyle. Women, no less than men, had divisions and cliques, and Terentia's circle may well have held conservative social, as well as economic, and religious views.

Whatever Terentia's role, the consequences of alienating Clodius became evident within a few years. In 58 Clodius became a tribune and forced Cicero into exile. Clodius's weapon was handed him by Cicero himself. Clodius called for the banishment of anyone who had been responsible for having a Roman citizen killed without trial. Cicero had executed the ringleaders of the Cati-

line conspiracy without a full trial before the Senate, a violation of Roman tradition and against the advice of Julius Caesar. Cicero chose again to ignore the advice of Caesar and to heed that of Gnaeus Pompeius Magnus (Pompey the Great) and fled to Greece. Clodius won the day. Once the decision to flee was made, Terentia sought to accompany Cicero. He was adamant, however, that she remain behind to look after their daughter, Tullia, and work on his behalf.

Although Terentia was invisible in the political struggle that preceded her husband's decision to flee to Greece, the consequences affected the remaining years of her marriage. She faced a difficult situation on all sides. Clodius succeeded in having passed a decree of exile that confiscated Cicero's property and specified penalties for those who came to his aid. A mob burned his house. She was forced to seek refuge in the temple of Vesta in the Forum with her half sister Fabia, whose position as a Vestal Virgin probably protected her from the mob and from the immediate pursuit of officialdom. Nonetheless, she suffered the public humiliation of being taken before the tribunes and possibly the moneylenders on account of her husband's business affairs.

Cicero's advice to Terentia about money was largely gratuitous. Terentia successfully safeguarded her own wealth and possibly her dowry, which was comingled with Cicero's own funds, even as he was still writing to his friend Atticus that she might well have her estates confiscated. It was she in Rome who arranged for the salvage of Cicero's assets and saw to the well-being of Tullia and Marcus. She took counsel and possibly loans from her sister and Atticus, and had developed some plans for raising more cash through the sale of her own properties. Meanwhile Cicero, not one to hide his sufferings, bemoaned his fate, expressed his devotion, and wallowed in his despair at the state of affairs in which he had left her.

In the political sphere Terentia and Tullia did what they could with support from Tullia's husband, Gaius Calpurnius Piso, who had become quaestor. The situation, however, changed only with the successful election of the new consuls and tribunes, and a break between Cicero's sometime friend Pompey and inimical enemy Clodius. Finally, in 57, Cicero's exile was lifted, and he returned to Rome in triumph. Although Terentia undertook all of her husband's commissions and clearly worked on his behalf, she had also distanced herself from him during his exile. On his return, Cicero was neither grateful nor even understanding of the difficulties with which she successfully coped. His immediate concern was to restore his prestige and public standing, which entailed rebuilding the house that had been burned by the mob, as well as reconstructing and repairing his other properties.

Cicero needed a great deal of money to carry out his plans, and Terentia may have been unhappy with his expenditures, especially since they outstripped the compensation he received from the state. Cicero acknowledged to his friend Atticus that he was spending far more than he had before his exile and challenged Terentia's management of the finances.

Nothing is known about Terentia over the next several years, although her absence from Cicero's letters suggests that their estrangement intensified. However, in 51 Cicero went to Cilicia as proconsul, and Terentia was once more on her own in Rome with Tullia. The two women appear to have been close and allied in Tullia's choice of a third husband.

Tullia's first husband had died in 57 B.C.E. She next had married Furius Crassipes, whom she was in the process of divorcing. While Cicero pondered who would be his next son-in-law, Terentia and Tullia selected Publius Cornelius Dolabella. Recently divorced from a much older woman whom he had married for money, Dolabella was charming, sexy, and a scoundrel with regard to women. He was also rich and a supporter of Caesar.

The smoldering estrangement between Terentia and Cicero flared in 50, when Cicero accused her of falsified accounts. He claimed that the goods of his estate had sold for far more than

Terentia reported: Terentia had shortchanged him by more than half. Atticus, not Terentia, was henceforth to care for his finances.

The year of Cicero's return, 49 B.C.E., marked the outbreak of civil war. At first events moved slowly, and Terentia remained in Rome while Cicero went to his estate in Formiae on the coast southeast of Rome to decide with whom to cast his lot. Once more it fell to Terentia to organize their finances, since cash was again a problem and the promise of war a further complication. Terentia conferred with Atticus and used her land as surety with the moneylenders to obtain cash. Terentia, Tullia, and other members of his family joined Cicero at Formiae, and Tullia gave birth to a boy who evidently died shortly thereafter. After Terentia and her daughter returned to Rome, Cicero, a fervent supporter of the republic, arranged to leave Italy for Macedonia where for the third critical time in his life he would not side with Caesar.

With Caesar's army approaching, Terentia and Tullia faced the issue of their own safety. Cicero suggested by letter that they consult other women, and if others were staying in Rome, it might be improper for them to leave. More concrete support came from Terentia's son-in-law Dolabella, who was with Caesar and who would be able to protect them provided that fighting did not erupt in the city. They decided to remain in Rome.

Terentia's marriage was approaching its end. The distance, the uncertainties, and Cicero's penchant for misunderstanding the financial realities of Rome under Caesar's rule contributed to his growing certainty that Terentia had defrauded him. A crisis came with a payment of Tullia's dowry to Dolabella. Cicero simultaneously learned that Tullia was without income, despite the arrangements he had made before he left Italy, and that 60,000 sesterces had been deducted without his authorization from the payment of Tullia's dowry.

Cicero had reached the point in a failing relationship when only his understanding of the situation could possibly be true. He simply asserted that Terentia handled his funds fraudulently, on evidence from her freedman business manager Philotimus. The accusation made no obvious sense nor was the accuser fully creditable (he was the same person whom Cicero had accused of dishonesty two and a half years earlier) and Philotimus may have had a recent falling-out with Terentia.

Terentia was the richer one of the couple when they wed and remained so. Although Cicero was responsible for the children, he was not responsible for her nor she for him. In the nature of Roman marital finances, she lived off her money, not his. Her dowry was the only part of her estate comingled with his, and her claim on those funds was only valid in the case of divorce. That she handled his finances and contributed to the children from her personal wealth was a mark of the emotional unit they formed as a family and not any expectation of law or custom.

Their mutual friend Atticus maintained a delicate balance, respecting his friendship, admiration, and support of Cicero and at the same time maintaining sufficiently cordial relations with Terentia to remain an effective go-between. As Cicero requested and as would be quite proper under Roman law and social mores, Atticus took up the responsibility for Tullia's affairs. Terentia, however, still bore the burden of securing all the necessary funds to pay Tullia's dowry installment even after she had reported to Cicero that the war and his position made it impossible at the moment to sell any of his properties.

Despite the dispute over money with Terentia and Tullia's deteriorating relationship with Dolabella, all three worked to secure Cicero a pardon from Caesar. Dolabella succeeded in arranging that Cicero be allowed to return to Italy as far as Brundisium. While in Brundisium and the limbo between pardon and nonpardon, Cicero discovered what he believed to be additional evidence of Terentia's perfidiousness. He also considered ending Tullia's marriage. He refrained from acting against Dolabella for fear Dolabella

would turn the mobs against Tullia. He also expressed his concern that Terentia might face the confiscation of her property. However, in Rome Terentia and Tullia appeared to have the situation as well in hand as was possible. Terentia secured her estate. Tullia and she were harmonious collaborators, and they remained in close touch with Atticus, who was always their supporter.

Cicero was pardoned in 47. Aside from the necessary formal relationships, Terentia had no more to do with him. In 46 they divorced. Atticus became the intermediary who fashioned their financial separation. With no more grace than he had shown in his treatment of Terentia when in exile or later waiting for a pardon from Caesar, he accused her of shortchanging the children in her will. After Tullia died in 45 B.C.E. only two issues remained: their son, Marcus, and the return of Terentia's dowry. Cicero was killed in 43, and he may never have repaid all that was due her.

Terentia outlived Cicero by many years. She was said to have been 103 when she died. A wealthy widow, she may well have again married. However, reports that she married Marcus Valerius Messalla or the historian Sallust are false.

Att. 2.4, 15.3; 4.1.5, 2.5; 7.1.6, 3.12; 11.1.2, 2.16, 5.24.2–3; 12.19.3, 37.3; 16.15.4.
Cic., Fam. 14.1–24.
Plin., NH 7.158.
Plut., Cic. 20.3; 29.2–4.
Dixon, S., pp. 93–120.
OCD, pp. 1,484–85.
PW 95.
Shackleton Baily, D. R., index.

▣ TERENTIA (2)

(1st century B.C.E.–? C.E.) Roman: Rome
Literary patron

Terentia was part of the most exciting literary era in the history of Rome. At a moment when the republic was becoming an empire, Roman artists were writing the greatest works of Latin poetry. From Catullus through Virgil and Ovid, Roman civil wars produced two generations of literary genius. During part of this time Gaius Maecenas was one of the two most important patrons who encouraged and supported the literary outburst. Terentia was his spirited wife. She was smart, fun, and beautiful. The poet Horace, a client of Maecenas, who wrote wicked satire with observations about women that were sometimes dour, other times misogynistic, and always amusing, once even praised Terentia. He called her Licymnia, possibly a reference to the third-century-B.C.E. poet and rhetorician, and praised her singing and dancing with other women at a religious celebration for the goddess Diana.

Terentia came from the family of the Terenti Varrones and was the sister of Aulus Terentius Varro Murena, who was consul with Augustus in 23 B.C.E. She married Maecenas, a descendant of ancient Etruscan aristocracy. Despite their quarrels, they remained married until his death. Along with Marcus Vipsanius Agrippa, Maecenas was the emperor's key military adviser. For some period of time beginning before the end of the civil war, Octavian was Terentia's lover.

Their affair was far from secret. Mark Antony, well away from Rome in Egypt, was said to have written to Octavian that he married CLEOPATRA VII while Octavian played around with a number of women including Terentilla (Terentia), despite his marriage to the pregnant LIVIA DRUSILLA. Gossip about Terentia and Augustus was said to have peaked in 16 B.C.E, when it was rumored that his trip to Gaul on military matters was in some part motivated by his relationship with Terentia. The rumors, however, were contradictory. Either the trip was meant to end the affair or Terentia was to join Augustus.

If the gossip is to be believed, Terentia's affair with Augustus outlived his friendship with her husband. Terentia's brother Varro Murena, became involved in a conspiracy with Fannius Caepio against Augustus around 23 B.C.E. The conspirators were captured and killed. Not much is known about the conspiracy, and Murena may have died simply because of his outspoken views.

The times were still unsettled, and Augustus was far from certain that the Senate could be fully controlled. Maecenas, however, had angered Augustus when he revealed to Terentia that her brother was in danger. It was an unacceptable breach of confidence. Although Maecenas was not brought to trial, he lost his power and influence.

Maecenas died in 8 B.C.E., when gossip about Terentia and Augustus had long ended. Maecenas left his vast property to Augustus. Nothing more is heard of Terentia.

Dio. 54.19.3.
Horace, Odes 2, 12.
Sen., Ep. 114.6.
Suet., Aug. 66.3; 69.2.
Balsdon, J. P. V. D., pp. 91, 272, 273.
Syme, R., *Roman Revolution*, pp. 277, 334, 342, 452.

TETTIA ETRUSC

(?–c. 60 C.E.)   Roman: Italy and Asia(?)
Virtuous wife

Tettia Etrusc was praised for her virtue and beauty by the poet Publius Papinius Statius. Probably of senatorial rank, her mother's name and status were unrecorded. Tettia most likely married between 48 and 50 C.E. and had two children, one of whom, Claudius Etruscus, became a patron of the poets Martial and Statius.

Her husband, Tiberius Claudius, was an ambitious and talented freedman originally from Smyrna on the west coast of Asia Minor. He gained his freedom from the emperor Tiberius and lived a long and honored life. He served as a senior administrator to emperors from Tiberius to Domitian. Appointed procurator by Claudius, he was in charge of imperial finances under Vespasian, who elevated him to equestrian status. Tettia may well have accompanied her husband when he served as procurator in an eastern province. However, Tettia did not live as long as her husband. She probably died around 60 C.E. at no more than 30 years old.

Stat., Silv. 3.3, 111–37.
Pomeroy, S. B., *Goddesses*, p. 195.
Weaver, P. R., pp. 284–94.

▣ TEUTA

(3rd century B.C.E.)   Greek: Illyricum
Ruler

Teuta established an empire in the northern reaches of Greece. She gained control over the sea lanes used by Greek and Italian trading ships and grew rich on booty. An Illyrian by birth, she served as regent for her young stepson, Pinnes, after the death of her husband, Agron, in 231 B.C.E. Eager to build upon her husband's successful expansion of his empire, she sent a large armada of ships and men to Elis and Messenia on the Peloponnesus in southern Greece. En route her troops occupied Epirus in the northwest. Faced with an insurrection in Illyria, Teuta recalled the troops in exchange for a large ransom and a great deal of booty.

Epirus and Acarnania, situated south of Epirus, abandoned their alliances with Aetolia and Achaea to ally themselves with Teuta. She gained control over Atintania and the passes of Antigoneia through which forces could attack central Greece. She further extended her control and plundered Italian as well as Greek trading vessels. When her Illyrian forces killed Italian traders and took others as prisoners, an outraged Roman Senate sent envoys to end her disruption of trade. Teuta received the envoys in autumn of 230. She claimed that she could restrain her own forces but could not prevent others from attacking Italian traders. Her response left open the question of whether she intentionally had challenged the Romans or simply had insufficient authority to control the pirates that plagued the Adriatic.

The Romans, however, chose to view her response as a deliberate provocation, to which they responded with the threat of force. Enraged, Teuta broke off negotiations. Illyrian pirates attacked the envoys on their return voyage, and one or more of the Romans died. Teuta sent no regrets to the Senate, which convinced them that she had authorized the attack. She continued her expansionist policy and led an expedition that besieged the island of Issa off the Dalmatian coast in the Adriatic Sea, where she captured the island of Corcyra (Corfu) off the coast of Illyricum in the spring of 229. Teuta was close to controlling the mouth of the Adriatic and the Ionian Gulf, which would endanger all Italian shipping from the south of Italy.

The Roman Senate could not countenance this threat, and a surprise attack was launched with a fleet of 200 ships and a force of 20,000 infantry with 2,000 cavalry. Demetrius, Teuta's commander in Corcyra, treacherously turned the island over to the Romans. The Roman forces attacked Illyricum, and Teuta fled with a small force to the inland fortress of Rhizon. She capitulated early in 228 B.C.E., having surrendered most of her territory and, agreed to pay an annual indemnity and to restrict the operations of her ships so that they no longer threatened trade between Italy and Greece.

Dio. 12.49.3–7.
Poly. 2.4.7, 6.4, 9; 8.4; 11.4, 16; 12.3.
Hammond, N. G. L., "Illyris, Rome and Macedon," pp. 4–8.
OCD, pp. 1,488–89.

▣ THAÏS

(4th century B.C.E.)   Greek: Athens, Asia, and Egypt
Self-made woman

Thaïs was renowned in the ancient world for her beauty, her wit, and her good fortune. Born in Athens, she was the lover of Ptolemy, a friend of Alexander the Great and a general in his army. She was part of the inner circle around Alexander and accompanied Ptolemy and Alexander in the conquest of Persia. There was even some rumor, probably incorrect, that she and Alexander were lovers. Thaïs was also said to have been a part of

Alexander's single act of wanton revenge, which was to set fire to Xerxes' palace after the capture of Persepolis in return for Xerxes' desecration of the Acropolis at Athens decades earlier.

Thaïs was with Ptolemy after Alexander's unexpected death. She was at his side when he went to Egypt and became Ptolemy I Soter, the first Greek ruler. They had three children, one of whom was named Lagos after Ptolemy's father.

So widespread was her renown that the fourth-century comic playwright Menander named one of his plays after her. The Roman poet Propertius made reference to the play some three centuries later, at the end of the first century B.C.E. when he held up Thaïs as the model of a successful lover.

Arr., Anab. 3.18.11.
Ath. 11.484d; 13.566e, 576e.
Diod. 8.17.1–6.
Plut. Alex. 7.38.1–8.
Propertius 2.6.3; 4.5, 43–4.
Pomeroy, S. B., *Women in Hellenistic Egypt*, pp. 13, 53, 99.
Tarn, W. W., *Alexander the Great*, p. 54.

THEBE

(4th century B.C.E.) Greek: Pherae
and Thessaly
Avenger

Thebe hated her husband. She convinced her brothers to kill him and arranged for the deed. Her father was Jason, who ruled Pherae, a city in the northern Greek area of Thessaly. He was assassinated in 370 B.C.E. after 15 years of rule. Thebe married Alexander, her father's successor. Alexander was cruel and faithless, and he abused boys. Her brother may have been one of those he abused. Alexander also may have threatened to marry Thebe's mother, since Thebe had not borne him children.

In 358 or 357, Alexander was murdered by Thebe and her brothers Lycophron, Tisiphonus, and Peitholaus (or Pytholaus). Thebe instigated the assassination and made the arrangements. Telling her brothers that Alexander planned to murder them, she hid them in her house to wait for her husband's return. Alexander returned drunk and feel asleep. She brought out his sword, and when the brothers hesitated, she threatened to wake Alexander unless they did the deed. Some say that Thebe was the one who held the door shut until her husband was dead. The eldest brother, Tisiphonus, succeeded Alexander as tyrant of Pherae. Nothing more is heard of Thebe.

Plut., Pel. 28.4–5; 35.3–7.
Diod. 16.14.1.
Xen. 6.4, 25–37.

THEMISTA

(4th–3rd century B.C.E.) Greek: Athens
Philosopher

Themista was a philosopher. She and her husband Leontius were disciples of the philosopher Epicurus. At age 34, Epicurus returned to Athens and bought a house and garden on the outskirts of the city. Themista and her husband lived with him and his other disciples, who valued a rather austere, simple life and took no part in the public affairs of Athens. They pursued an ideal of self-containment and engagement that was the essential center of the Epicurean philosophy.

Diog. Laert. 10.5.

THEODORA, FLAVA MAXIMIANA

(3rd–4th century C.E.) Roman: Italy and the
western Roman Empire
Augusta

Flavia Maximiana Theodora disappeared from the historical record in 306 C.E. when her husband, the emperor Constantius, died. At the time of his death they were both at York in Britain to suppress a rebellion. Theodora may have been the daughter of Galeria Valeria EUTROPIA, before her mother married Maximian, Caesar in the West under Diocletian. Alternatively, she may have been the daughter of Maximian and an early unknown wife. She married Flavius Valerius Constantius sometime before 289. Her husband became Caesar in the West under Maximian in 293 and became emperor after Maximian abdicated in 305. The couple traveled throughout the empire. She had three sons and three daughters, including Flavia Julia CONSTANTIA.

Balsdon, J. P. V. D., pp. 165–66.
Barnes, T., *The New Empire*, pp. 33, 37.
Der Kleine Pauly v. 5, p. 687.

▣ THEOXENA

(3rd–2nd century B.C.E.)   Greek: Thessaly
Heroine

Theoxena's life was linked with that of her sister ARCHO. It was filled with hard choices. They were the daughters of Herodicus, a leading citizen of Thessaly, a region in northern Greece. Their father was killed during an invasion by King Philip V of Macedonia. The husbands of both sisters died opposing him. Widowed, each with a small child, Theoxena and Archo were forced to move in response to Philip's efforts of consolidation over his newly won territory. Her sister remarried. Theoxena, however, remained a widow. After having several children with her second husband, Poris, a well-respected man from Anea in northeastern Greece, Archo died. Theoxena, concerned about the children, married her former brother-in-law. At this time Philip, who was increasingly convinced that his safety would be threatened by the children of the men he had killed, issued a proclamation for their arrest.

Theoxena was determined that the children not fall into the hands of Philip's soldiers. She believed that they would not only suffer death, but their deaths would be preceded by abuse and sexual assault. She had the full support of Poris who arranged for the family to flee to Athens, where he had friends. They traveled from Thessalonica, stopping in Anea to take part in the annual sacrificial festival to Aeneas, the founder of the city, and

boarded a ship under cover of darkness. Winds came up and the ship was pushed back into the harbor. Observed by the army, a ship was sent to capture them. When it became obvious that the family could not outrun the pursuing ship, Theoxena offered the children a choice of death by poison or the sword. The sources capture the frenzied final minutes when Theoxena urged the family on to death, while Poris cried out to the gods. When Philip's men finally boarded the ship, they found no one.

Livy 40.3–4.

▣ THESSALONICE

(c. 346/340–298/294 B.C.E.)   Greek: Thessaly and Macedonia
Ruler

Thessalonice made the mistake of dividing rule over Macedonia between her two sons. War ensued. She and both sons died. Thessalonice was probably the daughter of Nicesipolis, who came from Thessaly, and Philip II, ruler of Macedonia. Her mother died when she was about three weeks old, and she probably grew up with her half brother, Alexander the Great, under the care of his mother OLYMPIAS (1). Thessalonice retreated with Olympias to Pydna when Olympias was besieged by Cassander in 317 B.C.E. As soon as possible after his final victory, Cassander had Olympias killed, followed by the wife and 12-year-old son of Alexander the Great. He spared Thessalonice and married her in 316, thereby establishing a link to the family of Philip II and legitimacy for his claim to rule Macedonia.

In 305, Cassander took the title of king. Cassander named Thessalonica, a city he built at the head of the Thermaic Gulf, in his wife's honor. They had three sons, Philip, Antipater, and Alexander. Cassander died in 298. After the death of her husband, her son Philip ruled for a brief time before he died of consumption. Antipater, the next eldest, should have succeeded Philip, but Alexander, the younger of the two boys, was Thessalonice's favorite. She assigned western Macedonia and Thessaly to Antipater and the rest to Alexander. Antipater murdered Thessalonice and launched a campaign against Alexander. The latter asked Pyrrhus, ruler of nearby Epirus, and the general Demetrius for aid. Pyrrhus came to his aid, but Alexander was later murdered by Demetrius, who became ruler of all Macedonia in 294 B.C.E.

Diod. 21.7.
Just. 16.1.1.
Plut., Demetr. 36.1–5.
Cary, M., p. 46.
Macurdy, G., pp. 52–54.

🔲 TIMAEA

(5th century B.C.E.) Greek: Sparta
Lover of Alcibiades

Timaea took the notorious Athenian general and statesman Alcibiades for a lover when he visited Sparta while her husband, the ruler Agis II (427–399 B.C.E.), was away on a military campaign. She conceived a child, Leotychides, whom her husband recognized only when he lay dying.

Leotychides failed to succeed Agis as ruler. He was banished by the successor Agesilaus who seized Agis's estate, kept one-half, and returned the other half to Timaea's family. She may well have died before her husband.

Plut., Agis 3.1–2; 4.1.
Plut., Alc. 23.7–8.

🔲 TIMANDRA

(5th–4th century B.C.E.) Greek: Sicily
and Greece
Faithful lover

Timandra was taken prisoner in the capture of Hyccara, a fortified town in Sicily, during the Peloponnesian War. She went to Corinth as a slave of the Cytheran poet Philoxenos, who had

been in Sicily at the court of the tyrant Dionysius I in Syracuse. She became the lover of Alcibiades, the noted Athenian general and politician who had many lovers and was faithful to none. It was Timandra who arranged his funeral after he was murdered in 404 or 403 B.C.E., while in exile in Phrygia, in Asia Minor. She covered his body with her own garments and gave him the finest funeral she could afford.

Timandra was the mother of LAÏS, called the Corinthian, who was one of the most famous beauties of her day.

Plut., Alc. 39.2–5.
Plut., Nicias 15.4.
Der Kleine Pauly p. 837.
Pomeroy, S. B., *Goddesses*, p. 90.

🔲 TIMO

(6th–5th century B.C.E.) Greek: Greek
Islands
Heroine

Timo held a modest position in the temple of Demeter during the 490s B.C.E. Located near Paros on the second largest island of the Cyclades off the southeast coast of Greece, the temple was a well-known center of worship for the goddess of the underworld, Demeter. Timo was captured by the Athenians led by Miltiades in the spring of 489. After the Greeks had won a decisive victory at Marathon and were on the offensive, they laid siege to Paros. The high walls held firm and Timo offered a plan to Miltiades for access to the city.

She told him to jump over the wall enclosing the sacred precinct of Demeter on the hill in front of the city. He approached the sanctuary and suddenly was overcome with horror. He quickly retreated. As he jumped back over the outer wall he injured himself so severely that he was forced to return to Athens, where he was assessed a large fine. He was charged with deception, since he had brought back none of the wealth he had promised. Soon after he died from a gangrene infection as a result of his fall.

Meanwhile the Parians discovered the treachery of Timo. They sought to punish her and sent a messenger to Delphi to query the oracle about a suitable punishment. The priestess at Delphi ruled that gods had decreed that Miltiades would die and Timo had simply been the instrument they used.

Hdt. 6.134–35.

▥ TIMOCLEIA

(4th century B.C.E.)   Greek: Thebes
Avenger

Timocleia was from Thebes in southeastern Greece. When the forces of Alexander the Great attacked the city in 335 B.C.E., a group of Thracians invaded and plundered her property. She was raped by Hipparchus, the leader of the group, who demanded any gold or silver hidden on the premises. Timocleia claimed that she had hidden her valuables in her well. She led him there. He looked over the edge, and she pushed him in. She threw stones down on his head until he was dead.

The Thracians bound her hands and took her to Alexander. He asked her who she was, and she replied that she was the sister of Theagenes, a Theban general who had led Greek forces against Alexander's father Philip II and died in the battle of Chaeroneia in 338 B.C.E. Alexander, impressed by her demeanor and what she had done, freed her and her children.

Plut., Alex. 121–6.
Polyaenus, Strat. 8.40.

▥ TRIARIA

(1st century C.E.)   Roman: Italy
Political player

Triaria was ruthless. In 69 C.E., when Rome had four emperors in one year, Triaria was the wife of Lucius Vitellius, whose brother Aulus Vitellius became emperor for a short while. She curried favor, and unlike her sister-in-law or her mother-in-law she encouraged the emperor in his excesses. As Vespasian's forces were advancing on Rome to challenge him, the emperor sent Triaria's husband to capture Tarracina some 65 miles south of Rome. Triaria accompanied him. Some accused her of engaging in the battle and participating in the massacre of soldiers and townspeople.

Soldiers of Vespasian murdered Aulus Vitellius in Rome on December 20, 69. Triaria's husband surrendered in return for his life; however, he was killed. Nothing is heard of Triaria's end.

Tac., Hist. 2.63–64; 3.77.

▥ TULLIA (1)

(6th century B.C.E.)   Roman: Rome
Political player

In early Rome, where history and legend join in narratives of good and evil, Tullia was the utterly ruthless daughter of Servius Tullius, the sixth king of Rome, traditionally dated 578–535 B.C.E. She married Arruns Tarquinius, the younger son of TANAQUIL and Lucius Tarquinius Priscus, the fifth king of Rome. Tullia's husband lacked ambition and failed to heed her advice. She conspired with her brother-in-law Lucius Tarquinius to murder her husband and Lucius's wife. They succeeded, and they married each other. She badgered her new husband to kill her father and ordered her charioteer to drive over her father's body to show support for her husband.

Her second husband, Lucius Tarquinius Superbus, ruled for five years. While his rule was oppressive, he did build the temples of Jupiter Capitolinus and the Cloaca Maxima and the sewage system of Rome, and extended Roman influence in neighboring Latium. In 510 he was driven from the throne. He was the last king of Rome, and his fall marked the end of Etruscan rule and the birth of the republic. Tullia fled Rome with her husband. He died around 495 B.C.E. The date of her death is unrecorded.

Livy 1.46.3–9, 47–48.7, 59.13.
Alfoldi, A., pp. 152 ff.
Balsdon, J. P. V. D., pp. 26–27.
OCD, pp. 1,557–58.
Scullard, H. H., *History of the Roman World*, pp. 55, 76.

▣ TULLIA (2)

(c. 79–45 B.C.E.) Roman: Italy
Victim

Tullia lived a sad life: three unsatisfactory marriages, a child who died soon after birth, and a second child whose birth resulted in her own death. As an adult, she had constant money problems, and her parents' divorce after 30 years of marriage left her father emotionally dependent on her. Tullia was born soon after her parents' marriage in about 79 B.C.E. She was the daughter of TERENTIA (1) and Marcus Tullius Cicero. Her childhood promised so much. Her father was a rising political star, praetor in 66 B.C.E. and consul in 63. Her mother was an independently wealthy woman proud of her husband and child. She was surrounded in childhood with loving relationships, especially her parents' friend Titus Pomponius Atticus and his young wife PILIA, with whom she was close. Her aunt, uncle, and cousin on her father's side, and a younger brother, Marcus, completed her immediate family circle.

She married young. Affianced when she was 12 years old, she was 16 in 63 B.C.E., about the time she married her first husband, Gaius Calpurnius Piso Frugi. He was the son of Lucius Calpurnius Frugi, praetor in 74, and his great-grandfather had been consul in 133. While married she maintained close relations with her parents and friends. She traveled with her father to his estates in Italy and regularly visited with Atticus, Pilia, and her other relations.

Politics had always been the leitmotiv of her family life, but it was in 58 that the violent side of Roman politics invaded her intimate family. A mob incited by the tribune Publius Clodius Pulcher, who was her father's sworn enemy, attacked her father. Faced with an enmity that was all but implacable, Cicero left for Greece shortly before Clodius succeeded in having passed a formal decree of exile. Her mother sought to accompany him, but he insisted that she remain in Rome to be with Tullia and to work on his behalf.

Although Tullia was a married woman, she faced a sharp change in her status and in her finances after her father's departure. She no longer was the daughter of an honored consul who had been acclaimed a savior of the republic. Their family house in the city was burned, and her mother fled to her sister in the Temple of Vesta. The final exile decree confiscated all her father's property, including the properties he had assigned for her support and the next payments of her dowry. Since in Roman law and custom a woman's father, not her husband or even her mother, was responsible for her dowry and upkeep, Tullia faced seriously straitened circumstances.

Her father suffered a severe depression after his arrival in Greece. As he mulled over the most dire possibilities, it fell to Tullia and her mother to listen to his posted lamentations and to encourage him about a better future. He beseeched Terentia to look after his dearest Tullia and do all she could to settle the latter's dowry and preserve her reputation. The responsibility for what was best, was, of necessity, always left to Terentia and Tullia with counsel from the unfailingly attentive Atticus.

Tullia and Terentia did what they could in the political sphere, aided by Tullia's husband, who had become quaestor. The election of new consuls and tribunes, and Gnaeus Pompeius's (Pompey the Great) break with Cicero's nemesis Clodius, however, radically changed the situation. In the same year as her husband's early death, Cicero's exile was lifted, and Tullia greeted him on her birthday, August 5, 57, as he disembarked at Brundisium. Only recently widowed, she shared his triumphant return.

On her father's return, he became suspicious of her mother's handling of their finances. As he became disenchanted with his wife, it was Tullia who increasingly was his emotional mainstay. Although he had always been an affectionate father, his closer relationship in these later years provided Tullia with the opportunity to influence his behavior. She was especially valuable when his friend Atticus was absent. They discussed political events, and as he reported to Atticus, on occasion he followed her advice.

In December 54, Tullia, who was almost 23, married Furius Crassipes from a minor patrician family. The marriage lasted only two or three years. The reasons for the divorce are not known. Cicero was again away, this time serving as proconsul in Cilicia, when in 50 Tullia and her mother chose Publius Cornelius Dolabella for her third husband. He was an extravagant and dissolute young patrician who had recently divorced his elderly wife Fabia, whom he had married for her money. He was also handsome, charming, and attractive. Cicero was not thrilled with the marriage. Reluctantly he assented even though embarrassed by the fact that Dolabella was prosecuting for bribery Appius Claudius Pulcher, the brother of Publius Clodius Pulcher, at a time when he, Cicero, was making every effort to establish better relations. To smooth troubled feelings, Cicero assured Claudius that Terentia and Tullia, not he, had chosen Dolabella.

Not long after her marriage, her father returned from Asia. Shortly after, in 49, civil war erupted. Her husband, a Caesarian, joined Caesar's army with the onset of hostilities. She gave her father the good advice to wait for developments to unfold. Possibly, she had gained information about Caesar from her husband. It was advice also echoed by Atticus, who was a model of caution about burning bridges with either side.

Cicero, who after much thought had sided with Pompey and the republicans, recognized Tullia's caring and concern for him at a time when she too was burdened with personal concerns. In May of 49, Tullia gave birth to a boy. The baby was premature, born in the seventh month. Her delivery was safe, but the infant died soon after. She was with her mother and father at her father's estate in Formiae. Her husband was not present. Not only had her child died, but she, like Cicero, was having marital problems. Dolabella's philandering and extravagant ways had not changed.

In June, a month or so after Tullia's delivery, Cicero left Italy to join Pompey in Thessalonica. He asked Tullia and Terentia to forgive him for causing them so much unhappiness and to take care of their health. With husband and father on opposite sides, Tullia and her mother were once again alone in Rome. Safety was always an issue. The question of whether or not they should leave the city and if so, where they should go engaged father, daughter, mother, and son-in-law. As earlier when her father was exiled or abroad as a proconsul, the distance and the difficulties in communication simply made it impossible for anyone other than Tullia and Terentia to decide on their own course of action. Cicero offered any of his villas that were furthest from possible conflict. If prices went up in Rome because of the war, he suggested his farm in Arpinum, in the interior southeast of Italy, where inflation would be less severe.

Despite increasing marital difficulties, Terentia still handled much of the family's money. Ready cash was a problem throughout the period, and the war added even further complications, as the threat of confiscation by whoever was the victor was always in the background. Terentia, on at least one occasion, had to resort to the services of moneylenders. At the same time, Tullia's relations with her husband continued to deteriorate as the second installment of her dowry was coming due. Before her father left, he had made careful arrangements for Tullia's income and her next dowry payment. However her mother had deducted some 60,000 sesterces from the sum that he had set aside and the income from the properties her father had assigned to her was not being paid. Without adequate funds from her father Tullia borrowed money from her mother.

Cicero expressed astonishment at the turn in her affairs and arranged for aid from Atticus. He became convinced that in some fashion Terentia had defrauded him of the money that was to have gone to Tullia. He also questioned the wisdom of payment for the second installment of Tullia's dowry. Tullia, however, decided not to divorce Dolabella at this time and the dowry payment went ahead. It was a sensible decision on her part since whatever Dolabella's faults, he did obtain Caesar's permission for Cicero to return to Italy after Pompey's defeat in Greece. Tullia with Atticus and her friend Pilia met Cicero when he landed at Brundisium in October. Tullia was also again short of money, and again requested help from Atticus.

In June 47 Tullia visited her father in Brundisium where he still waited for Caesar's pardon. The visit was not a happy one. Tullia showered him with affection, but they were both downcast by their respective problems. Tullia left to go to her mother. There was another family discussion about a divorce between Tullia and Dolabella. Again nothing happened. In September 47, Caesar landed at Brundisium; Cicero went to meet him and received a friendly reception. The restoration of his rights followed. With his citizenship no longer in question and his properties secured, her father divorced her mother not a year later, in August 46. He was probably even firmer in his pressure on Tullia to divorce Dolabella. Tullia divorced in the autumn or early winter of the same year.

She was, however, pregnant. In January 45 B.C.E. Cicero wrote Atticus both that he was trying to get Dolabella to return the first installment of Tullia's dowry and that Tullia was about to give birth. Tullia and the baby went to Tusculum with Cicero, where she died of childbirth complications in February. Her infant son died shortly thereafter.

Cic., Att. 1.3; 1.8.2; 1.10.5; 2.8.3; 3.19.2; 4.1.3, 5; 4.2.5; 4.4a; 4.15.4; 7.3.8; 7.13.2; 9.6.4; 10.18.1; 11.1.2; 11.2.2; 11.6.2; 11.7.4; 11.9.2; 11.1; 11.17a.1; 11.23.3; 11.24.2–3; 12.3; 12.5c.
Cic., Fam. 3.12.2–4; 5.6.2; 6.18.5; 14.1.5; 14.4; 14.6; 14.8; 14.13; 14.14.
Cic., Q. Fr. 2.4.3–4; 2.5.1.
Balsdon, J. P. V. D., pp. 179, 187–8.
Dixon, S., pp. 93–120.
Fantham, E., et al., pp. 275–76.
OCD, p. 1,558.
Shackleton Bailey, D. R., index.

U

URGULANIA

(1st century B.C.E.–1st century C.E.) Roman: Italy

Political player

Urgulania who was of Etruscan descent was a close friend of the powerful LIVIA DRUSILLA. She supported Livia and, in turn, enhanced her own power and promoted the position of her family members. Her husband Marcus Plautius was also of Etruscan background, and it was due in large measure to her influence that their son, Marcus Plautius Silvanus, became consul along with Augustus in 2 C.E. Urgulania was the grandmother of PLAUTIA URGULANILLA, the first wife of the future emperor Claudius. The marriage was probably arranged by Livia and Urgulania.

Urgulania was not an easy woman. It might even be said that she used her position to behave in a manner others thought outrageous. In 16 C.E. the augur Lucius Piso, an outspoken member of the aristocracy who had been consul in 1 B.C.E., brought suit against Urgulania to recover money that she owed him. When she was ordered to appear before the praetor, she went instead to Livia's house pursued by Piso. Livia, furious, persuaded Tiberius to intervene as Urgulania's advocate. Tiberius's journey to the tribunal was so deliberately slow that Livia paid the money owed Piso and the case was dismissed. Urgulania also refused to appear as a witness in another case before the Senate and a praetor had to be sent to her house to take evidence, although Roman custom had always been that even Vestal Virgins had to give evidence in the Forum or the courts.

In 24 Urgulania's grandson, the praetor Plautius Silvanus, threw his wife APRONIA out of the window of their house. Before the trial in the Senate opened, Urgulania sent him a dagger. Coming from a close friend of Livia, it meant that Silvanus should commit suicide, which he did.

Tac., Ann. 2.34.1; 4.22.1.
Bauman, R. A., p. 135.
Der Kleine Pauly p. 1,036.
Levick, B., *Tiberius*, p. 182.
OCD p. 1,574.
Syme R., *Augustan Aristocracy*, pp. 88, 376, 430.

V

▣ VALERIA (1)
(1st century B.C.E.) Roman: Rome
Self-made woman

Valeria enhanced the fortunes of her family through marriage with Lucius Cornelius Sulla when he was dictator of Rome. She was the niece of the famous orator Quintus Hortensius Hortales, consul in 69 B.C.E., who supported Sulla.

It is reported that the recently divorced Valeria deliberately leaned over and picked off a piece of lint from Sulla's cloak during a gladatorial game. Having drawn his attention, she noted her desire to secure for herself a piece of his good luck. Subsequently, Sulla was widowed and Valeria became his fifth wife.

Plut., Sull. 35.
Balsdon, J. P. V. D., p. 279.
Pomeroy, S. B., *Goddesses*, p. 157.

▣ VALERIA (2)
(3rd–4th century C.E.) Roman: Germany, Dalmatia, Syria, Asia(?), and Italy
Augusta

Valeria came to a tragic end. Her parents were PRISCA and the emperor Diocletian. She married Galerius after her father had established a system of shared power in 293 C.E. and appointed her husband Caesar to control the Danube region. Although the marriage lasted until her husband's death, she had no children. She evidently was a good mother to her husband's son Candidianus.

Valeria and her mother, Prisca, were sympathetic to the Christians, although there is no evidence that they were members of the church. Diocletian tolerated the followers of Christianity for some 19 years while he expended his energies restoring and shoring up the Roman Empire; however, he was a firm believer that the old Roman traditions of religion, order, and discipline were the foundations for preserving the unity of the empire. Christianity, which had become a growing and unsettling force, undermined this sense of order. Valeria and her mother conformed and burned incense to Jupiter as part of a program to promote ancient religious practices.

In 303 Diocletian allowed Galerius to issue edicts authorizing the persecution of Christians, including the destruction of their buildings. In 304 Diocletian suffered an almost fatal illness and retired the following year. He persuaded Maximian, the Augustus of the East, to step down at the same time and Constantius became the Augustus of the West. Valeria's husband Galerius, became Augustus of the East and Valeria was named Augusta. She lived with her mother in the

palace at Nicomedia in Asia Minor. For the remainder of Galerius life, Valeria and her mother
were honored.

Galerius suffered a fatal illness in 311 but before he died, he issued the Edict of Toleration toward the Christians. It is unknown what, if any,
part Valeria played in this, but she undoubtedly
approved.

Galerius also committed his wife and son to the
care of Licinius, who had been co-Augustus with
him since 308. For unknown reasons, Valeria mistrusted Licinius. She and her mother took refuge
with Maximin Daia, who had become Caesar in
305 and who was a son of her husband's sister.
Daia saw political advantage in a marriage with
Valeria. The marriage would link him closely with
the aged Diocletian and also give him access to
her extensive properties and other wealth.

Valeria refused and offered several reasons:
She was still in deep mourning for her husband;
moreover, her husband had adopted Daia and he
was her son as much as he was the son of her husband, therefore marriage with him would be incestuous; and last but not least, it would be
shameful for him to divorce his own faithful wife.
His response was to put to death many friends of
Valeria and Prisca, and he exiled them to a remote
area of Syria.

Valeria sought her father's help. Diocletian
sent some letters from his retirement palace protesting the treatment of Valeria and her mother,
but he was too old and lacked the energy to do
more. Valeria's position did not improve after
Daia was defeated and killed by Licinius in 313.
Licinius regarded the two women as enemies.
They escaped Licinius and wandered in disguise
for some 15 months in an effort to reach the Dalmatian coast and Diocletian. During that period
Diocletian died. His death ended their hopes of
finding a protected situation. They were recognized in Thessalonica, in Macedonia. Their heads
were cut off in public, and their bodies were
thrown into the sea as part of Licinius's purge of all
relatives of Galerius and Daia.

Lact., MP 15, 39, 50–51.
Balsdon. J. P. V. D., pp. 165–69.
Gibbon, E., pp. 333–34.
PW 7.
Williams, S., pp. 173, 199–200.

▣ VARRONILLA

(?–83 C.E.) Roman: Rome
Priestess

Varronilla, with the two sisters OCULATA, was one
of three Vestal Virgins condemned in 83 C.E. for
committing incest. (A fourth Vestal, CORNELIA
(12), head of the college, was accused but found innocent.) They were accused in the campaign by
the emperor Domitian against immorality in
Rome. He claimed that the Vestal Virgins and the
temple of Vesta had been a hotbed of sexual immorality since the reigns of his father and his
brother. The usual punishment was being buried
alive, but Domitian, in what he regarded as a magnanimous gesture, allowed them to commit suicide. Their alleged lovers were sent into exile.

Suet., Dom. 8.14.
Balsdon, J. P. V. D., pp. 239, 241.

▣ VERANIA

(1st century C.E.) Roman: Italy
Credulous victim

Verania was swindled. She was a wealthy woman,
the daughter of Quintus Veranius, consul in 49
C.E. She married Lucius Calpurnius Piso, whom
the emperor Servius Sulpicius Galba adopted as
his successor on January 10, 69. Both men were
killed five days later. Verania ransomed her husband's head from his killers.

At about 60 years old, she became seriously ill,
and Marcus Regulus, whom she disliked as he was
an old enemy of her husband, had the audacity to
visit. He inquired the date and hour of her birth
and then informed her that she would survive her
illness. To confirm his assertion he consulted with

an expert in the examination of entrails, who was skilled in divining their meaning.

He returned to again reassure her. She rewrote her will and left him a handsome legacy. Shortly thereafter, she took a turn for the worse and cursed him before she died. The sources accuse Regulus of habitually insinuating himself with the seriously ill to secure a legacy.

Plin., Ep. 2.20.
Tac., Hist. 1.47.
PW 19.

⊞ VERGINIA (1)

(5th century B.C.E.)   Roman: Rome
Heroine

Verginia was the daughter of Lucius Verginius, a plebeian who served as a centurion of the first rank. She was to marry a former tribune, Lucius Icilius. In 449 B.C.E. Appius Claudius tried to seduce her. He was a patrician and leader of the *decemveri*, the magistrates selected to decide on a code of laws to replace the suspended constitution. Despite his offers of money and gifts, she resisted.

While her father was away, Appius Claudius arranged for his client, Marcus Claudius, to seize Verginia in the Forum. Claudius claimed that she was a slave who had been born in his house and secreted away by her father as a small child. A crowd gathered who knew her father, and Claudius agreed to take her case to court. The judge was the same Appius Claudius who lusted after Verginia. He allowed that Claudius could take Verginia to his house and produce her in court when her father returned. At this point, Verginia's fiancé and uncle arrived and demanded that she be allowed to return to her home until the trial. The crowd supported them. Appius Claudius gave way.

When her father returned, Appius Claudius ruled that Verginia was the slave of Marcus Claudius. Her father, fearing that efforts to keep Verginia out the clutches of Appius Claudius were futile, killed her. For him, her death was preferable to her enslavement.

Diod. 12.24
Livy 3.44–58
Val. Max. 6.1.2
Balsdon, J. P. V. D., pp. 28–29.
OCD, p. 1,588.
Pomeroy, S. B., *Goddesses*, p. 153.

⊞ VERGINIA (2)

(4th–3rd century B.C.E.)   Roman: Rome
Reformer

Verginia challenged the historical division between patrician and plebeian in the practice of religious rites among women. Born a patrician, Verginia married a plebeian, Lucius Volumnius, who became a consul. In 296 B.C.E. omens portending possible troubles for Rome led the Senate to request special attention to religious rites that would assure Rome's safety.

Verginia had always been a member of the patrician women's community and had participated in the rites restricted to patrician women. Despite the high office held by her husband, however, his plebeian birth barred her from further participation and the women would not admit her to the rites. She argued that her marriage did not alter her birth and that she fulfilled the second criterion of having only married once, but to no avail. Not to be silenced or excluded, Verginia sought out a group of plebeian women who had been married only once. She enclosed a portion of her large house and erected an altar. She invited the women to practice the rites that celebrated chaste married women and the well-being of Rome.

Livy 10.23.1–10.
Bauman, R. A., pp. 15–16.
Fantham, E., et al., pp. 231–32.

⊞ VESPASIA POLLA

(1st century B.C.E.–1st century C.E.)   Roman: Italy
Mother of the emperor Vespasian

Vespasia Polla came from an honorable equestrian family in Nursia, some 80 miles northeast of Rome. Her father Vespasius Pollo, an officer, was three times tribune of the soldiers and a prefect of the camp. Her brother became praetor and senator. She married Flavius Sabinas, whose father, Titus Flavius Petro, was a native of Reate in the Sabine country and had fought on the side of Gnaeus Pompeius Magnus (Pompey the Great) in the civil war. He later became a tax collector. Her husband was not a military man and became a collector of import and export taxes in Asia. He later went into banking in what is now Switzerland, where he died. Vespasia was left with two children, Sabinus and the future emperor Titus Flavius Vespasian, who was born on November 17, 9 C.E.

Vespasian was brought up in Cosa on the coast northwest of Rome by his paternal grandmother, Tertulla, about whom we only know her name. Unlike his brother who became a prefect in Rome, Vespasian appeared in no hurry to enter political life. The sources claim that Vespasia pushed him. She was said to have used her sharp tongue and to have unfairly compared him with his brother in an effort to stir his ambition. She was successful; Vespasian became emperor in 69.

Suet., Ves. 1–2.2.
PW, pp. 1,710–11.

▣ VIBIDIA

(1st century C.E.) Roman: Rome
Priestess

Vibidia was senior Vestal Virgin when Valeria MESSALLINA, the wife of the emperor Claudius, was accused of marrying her lover Gaius Silius. Messallina appealed to Vibidia to ask for mercy from the emperor and to be allowed to plead her case. Narcissus, the powerful freedman secretary of the emperor, was determined to prevent an appeal, but he could not refuse to see Vibidia.

Vibidia argued that under Roman law a wife could not be killed without an opportunity to defend herself. Narcissus promised that Messallina would be allowed to state her case and dismissed Vibidia, but when he saw Claudius wavering, he gave the order for Messallina's execution.

Tac., Ann. 11.34, 37.
Balsdon, J. P. V. D., pp. 100–101.
Bauman, R. A., pp. 176–77.

▣ VICTORIA (VITRUVIA)

(3rd century C.E.) Roman: Gaul
Augusta; governor of Gaul

Victoria's family supported Marcus Cassianius Latinus Postumus, appointed by the future emperor Gallienus to protect the Rhine border of the empire during a period of general unrest, characterized by invasions, economic disruptions, and declining population. Postumus was killed by his own troops when he prohibited the sacking of what is now Mainz.

Victoria's son Victorinus served under Postumus and under Marcus Aurelius Claudius Augustus. He held de facto power for about two years, probably from 269 to 270 C.E. During the two-year period, Victoria took the title Mother of the Camp and Augusta. Coins were issued in her name. After her son died, Victoria supported a general known by the name of Tetricus to become the commander of Gaul. When he led troops in Spain, he was said to have left her in charge of Gaul.

SHA, TT, v. 3–4, 6.3; 24.1; 25.1; 31.2–3.

▣ VIPSANIA AGRIPPINA

(33 B.C.E.–20 C.E.) Roman: Italy
Very wealthy woman

Vipsania Agrippina stayed clear of direct engagement in the politics of succession, just as two generations earlier her grandfather had stayed clear of choosing sides in the politics of civil war. Vipsania's grandfather, Titus Pomponius Atticus, was an Epicurean and cultured collector of art as well as shrewd businessman who lived his life outside the deadly high stakes of late republican senatorial politics. Caecilia ATTICA, his only daughter and mother of Vipsania, was reputed to be one of the wealthiest women in Rome. She married Marcus Vipsanius Agrippa, Augustus's loyal friend and greatest general. Vipsania, their only child, was little more than a year old in 32 B.C.E. when her grandfather, already incurably ill, arranged with LIVIA her future marriage with Tiberius. Tiberius was Livia's 10-year-old son and the stepson of Octavian, proclaimed Augustus in 27 B.C.E.

The marriage arrangement was made nine years before the battle of Actium and the first settlement of 23 B.C.E. between a victorious Augustus and the Senate. With the Roman civil war far from over, Atticus's step to establish an alliance with the soon-to-be powerful Livia Drusilla was a bold move. The astute Livia recognized that the alliance strengthened her ties with her husband's confidant and general, Vipsania's father Agrippa, and probably eased very real financial pressures that were a leitmotiv of those years.

Vispania married Tiberius in 20 or 19 B.C.E., after her mother had probably died and her father had remarried, divorced, and married again, this time with JULIA (6), the only child of his friend Augustus in 27 B.C.E. With the civil war over and Augustus the victor, her widowed father's successive round robin of marriages reflected the new political circumstances. Tiberius and Vipsania were perilously close to these shifts of political fortune. At the time of their marriage there still appeared to be an ample number of heirs to Augustus from the Julian line. Vipsania gave birth to a son, Drusus Julius Caesar, in 13 B.C.E. who like his father, was a Claudian. They would come to the fore in the battles over succession only after others had died. However, in 12 B.C.E., even before Tiberius's own rise to emperor appeared imminent, Vipsania's father, Agrippa, died leaving his wife, Augustus's daughter Julia, a widow with five children. Ever practical, Augustus and Livia pressured Tiberius to divorce Vipsania and marry Julia in 11 B.C.E., thereby neatly conjoining their progeny in one couple and uniting the Julian and Claudian clans.

Vipsania did not stay unmarried long, nor did she choose another Julian or Claudian for a husband. In 11 B.C.E. she married Gaius Asinius Gallus, consul in 8 C.E. and son of the noted republican orator and writer Gaius Asinius Pollio, consul in 40 B.C.E. Vipsania and Gallus had five sons, some of whom were notable in public life of the post-Tiberius generation. Gallus, however, was no friend of Tiberius, even though he was linked to him through his stepson Drusus. Moreover, for reasons that are either illogical or obscure, Tiberius deeply resented the marriage of Vipsania and Gallus: Possibly, Gallus was too tied to the senatorial elite at a time when the Senate could still pose a problem to the emperor, or alternatively, the divorce with Vipsania did not free Tiberius from his feelings about her. Vipsania died in 20 C.E. the only one of Agrippa's children to die peacefully. Ten years later in 30, Tiberius had the Senate indict Gallus who was imprisoned in his own house and after three years, died of starvation.

Dio. 14.31.2; 57.2.7; 58.3.1–6.
Nep., Att. 19.4
Suet., Tib. 7.2–3.
Tac., Ann. 1.12–13; 3.19.
Balsdon, J. P. V. D., index.
Levick, B., *Tiberius,* index.
OCD, p. 1,601.
Syme, R., *Augustan Aristocracy,* index.
Syme, R., *Roman Revolution,* index.

⊞ VISTILIA

(1st century B.C.E.–? C.E.)   Roman: Italy
Much married woman

Vistilia came from Umbrian Iguvium in Italy. She was said to have had six husbands over a period of about 20 years and to have had children with each of them. One of her sons was the general Gnaeus Domitius Corbulo. Her daughter MILONIA CAESONIA married the emperor Gaius Caligula had one child, a daughter, and died with them.

Plin., NH 7.39.
Syme R., *Augustan Aristocracy*, pp. 74, 305.
Syme, R., "Domitius Corbulo," pp. 27 ff.

▣ VITIA

(? B.C.E.–32 C.E.)   Roman: Rome
Convicted of treason

Vitia was the mother of Fufius Geminus, consul in 29 C.E. Her son was a client of the powerful LIVIA DRUSILLA, the widow of Augustus and the emperor Tiberius's mother. Livia was instrumental in Geminus's advancement. His wife, MUTILIA PRISCA, was also protected by Livia. Tiberius, however, often held opinions that differed from those of his mother, and he disliked the sharp-tongued Geminus, especially since he was sometimes the object of Geminus's wit. Both Geminus and his wife supported Lucius Aelius Sejanus, the head of the Praetorian Guard who had Tiberius's ear and in the years after Tiberius retreated to Capri, was the conduit of information from Rome to the emperor.

After Livia's death, Tiberius accused Geminus of lacking respect and casting aspersions upon the emperor, which was treason under imperial law. Sejanus either could not or would not come to their aid. Geminus and Mutilia were forced to commit suicide. In 32, after the fall of Sejanus when the Senate was rife with treason trials, Vitia was tried for weeping over her son's death. Her tears were evidence enough of her treason, and she was convicted.

Tac., Ann. 6.10.

XANTHIPPE

(5th century B.C.E.) Greek: Athens
Wife of Socrates

Xanthippe married Socrates in the latter part of his life. She supposedly had a temper, and Socrates may well have been a difficult husband. He was said to have quipped to one of his more brilliant and erratic students that his wife's temper had prepared him to cope with other impudent and unreasonable people.

Xanthippe had one son, Lamprocles. There was, however, another woman in Socrates' life, MYRTO, with whom he had two additional children. The relationship among the three remains unclear.

Aul. Gell., NA 1.17.1.
Diog. Laert. 2.26.
Pomeroy, S. B., *Goddesses*, p. 67.

Z

ZENOBIA, SEPTIMIA

(3rd century C.E.) Syrian: Syria and
Asia Minor
Great general and ruler

Septimia Zenobia was a military leader with a talent for strategy, a student of philosophy, and a just ruler. She conquered much of Asia Minor and Egypt before Rome brought an end to her rule. Reported to have been incredibly beautiful, she was dark-complexioned with gleaming white teeth that were said to be like a strand of pearls. Stern in her demeanor, she was an accomplished horsewoman, walked miles with her troops, and enjoyed hunting. She drank with the Persians and the Armenians and often bettered them. She was greatly feared in the East; none dared oppose her.

There is some indication that Zenobia was attracted to Judaism, but she certainly was not a convert. She studied Greek language and literature with the philosopher and rhetorician Cassius Longinus, who became her principal adviser. Never accused of licentiousness, she was said to have had sex with her husband once a month for the purposes of procreation.

Her husband was Septimus Odenathus, who seized power and became ruler of Palmyra. He cleverly exploited Rome's weakness by becoming the main protector of their eastern territories against the Persians, whom he defeated. The emperor Gallienus put him in charge of the Roman army of the East with the title of *imperator*. In 267 C.E. he was assassinated in a dynastic quarrel. It is unclear whether or not Zenobia was implicated in his death; however, she immediately assumed power as guardian for their infant son, Septimus Vaballathus.

In an effort to limit her son's power, the Roman emperor restricted the boy's rule to Palmyra, but Zenobia was regent and continued to exercise control over Syria. As she successfully protected Rome's eastern frontiers, successive emperors bestowed his father's former titles of king of kings, consul, and *imperator* on the young boy. Unlike her husband, Zenobia was not content to act under the authority of Rome. She wanted an independent Palmyra. She exploited Roman disorder after the death of the emperor Claudius Gothicus in 270 by assuming control over Egypt and much of Asia Minor.

In September 271 the emperor Aurelian dispatched an army that retook Egypt. With the war raging, she took a final step toward independent rule. Zenobia declared her son Augustus and herself Augusta. Coins were struck with her image and new title. The war, however, did not go well. In the early part of 272, Aurelian reconquered Asia Minor and launched an attack on Antioch.

Zenobia took part in the battle. Her forces were defeated. She escaped with the remnants of her army to Emesa and then fled to Palmyra. She was captured as she was trying to cross the Euphrates after the city fell. Her life was spared, and she probably was paraded in Aurelian's triumph in Rome.

SHA, Aurel. 22.1; 25.1–6; 26.1–6; 27.1–6; 28.1–5; 30.1–4.
SHA, Gallien. 13.2–3.
SHA, TT 15.8; 30.1–27.
Downey, G., pp. 263 ff.
Millar, B. F., p. 13.

REGISTRY

Acte, Claudia, self-made woman; q.v. **Agrippina the Younger**	Roman: Italy	1st cent. C.E.
Acutia, convicted conspirator; q.v. **Livilla**	Roman: Rome	1st cent. C.E.
Aelia Iunilla, political victim; daughter of **Apicata;** q.v. **Antonia the Younger; Livilla**	Roman: Rome	?–31 C.E.
Aelia Paetina, political victim; mother of **Antonia (4)**; q.v. **Agrippina the Younger; Messallina**	Roman: Rome	1st cent. C.E.
Aemilia (1), condemned priestess; colleagues: **Licinia (4)** and **Marcia (1)**	Roman: Rome	2nd cent. B.C.E.
Aemilia (2), political wife; daughter of **Caecilia Metella (1)**; half sister of **Fausta;** q.v. **Antistia (2)**	Roman: Rome	1st cent. B.C.E.
Aemilia Lepida (1), political wife; mother of **Cornelia** (6)	Roman: Rome	1st cent. B.C.E.
Aemilia Lepida (2), unjustly convicted of adultery; daughter of **Cornelia (7)**; granddaughter of **Mucia Tertia** and **Junia (1)**	Roman: Rome	1st cent. B.C.E.– 1st cent. C.E.
Aemilia Lepida (3), political victim; daughter of **Julia (7)**; mother of **Junia Lepida** and **Junia Calvina;** granddaughter of **Julia (6)**; great-granddaughter of **Scribonia;** q.v. **Agrippina the Younger**	Roman: Rome	1st cent. B.C.E.–1st cent.– 1st cent. C.E.
Aemilia Lepida (4), duplicitous wife; sister-in-law of **Julia Drusilla (1)**	Roman: Rome	1st cent. C.E.

Aemilia Tertia, power broker; mother of **Cornelia (1)** and **Cornelia (2)**	Roman: Rome	2nd–1st cent. B.C.E.
Afriana (Carfania), lawyer	Roman: Rome	?–48 B.C.E.
Agariste (1), mother of the Athenian statesman Cleisthenes	Greek: Sicyon and Athens	6th cent. B.C.E.
Agariste (2), mother of the Athenian statesman Pericles; granddaughter of **Agariste (1)**	Greek: Athens	c. 520/510 B.C.E.–?
Agariste (3), witness	Greek: Athens	5th cent. B.C.E.
Agathocleia, adventurer and murderer; daughter of **Oenanthe;** q.v. **Arsinoë III Philopator**	Greek: Samos and Egypt	3rd cent. B.C.E.
Agesistrata, reformer; daughter of **Archidamia;** mother-in-law of **Agiatis**	Greek: Sparta	?–241 B.C.E.
Agiatis, reformer; daughter-in-law of **Agesistrata** mother-in-law of **Agiatis**	Greek: Sparta	3rd cent. B.C.E.
Agrippina the Elder, Vipsania, political player and power broker; daughter of **Julia (6);** daughter-in-law of **Antonia the Younger** mother of **Julia Agrippina the Younger, Julia Drusilla,** and **Julia Livilla;** granddaughter of **Scribonia;** q.v. **Livia Drusilla; Munatia Plancina; Octavia (2); Vipsania Agrippina**	Roman: Germany and Rome	c. 14 B.C.E.–33 C.E.
Agrippina the Younger, Julia, Augusta; political player; daughter of **Agrippina the Elder;** sister of **Julia Drusilla (1)** and **Julia Livilla;** great-granddaughter of **Julia (6);** q.v. **Acte; Domitia Lepida; Junia Calvina; Lollia Paulina; Messallina; Milonia Caesonia; Octavia, Claudia; Poppaea Sabina (2)**	Roman: Italy	c. 15–59 C.E.
Albucilla, alleged conspirator; convicted adulterer; q.v. **Agrippina the Younger**	Roman: Italy	1st cent. C.E.
Alce, self-made woman	Greek: Athens	4th cent. B.C.E.
Alexandra, conspirator; q.v. **Cleopatra VII**	Jewish: Judaea	1st cent. B.C.E.
Amastris, ruler; q.v. **Arsinoë II Philadelphus**	Persian: Asia Minor	4th–3rd cent. B.C.E.

Ancharia, mother of **Octavia (1)**; q.v. **Atia (1)**	Roman: Rome	1st cent. B.C.E.
Anteia, Stoic; q.v. **Arria the Younger; Fannia (2)**	Roman: Rome	1st cent. C.E.
Antigone, political wife; daughter of **Berenice I**	Greek: Macedonia, Egypt, and Epirus	3rd cent. B.C.E.
Antistia (1), reformer; mother of **Claudia (2)** and **Claudia (3)**; grandmother of **Clodia (2)**; q.v. **Cornelia (2)**	Roman: Rome	2nd cent. B.C.E.
Antistia (2), political victim; q.v. **Aemelia (2); Caecilia Metella (1)**	Roman: Rome	1st cent. B.C.E.
Antistia Pollitta, political victim; q.v. **Agrippina the Younger; Livia Drusilla; Octavia (2)**	Roman: Italy	?–65 C.E.
Antonia (1), captured by pirates	Roman: Rome	1st cent. B.C.E.
Antonia (2), adulterer; mother of **Antonia (3)**; q.v. **Tullia (2)**	Romam: Rome	1st cent. B.C.E.
Antonia (3), political wife; daughter of **Antonia (2)**; mother of **Pythodoris**; q.v. **Cleopatra VII**	Roman: Rome and Tralles	c. 54/49 B.C.E.–?
Antonia (4), possible conspirator; daughter of **Aelia Paetina**; q.v. **Messallina; Poppaea Sabina (2)**	Roman: Rome	28–66 C.E.
Antonia the Elder, political player; daughter of **Octavia (2)**; sister of **Antonia the Younger**; mother of **Domitia (1)** and **Domitia Lepida**; grandmother of Valeria **Messallina**; q.v. **Cleopatra VII; Fulvia (2)**	Roman: Rome	39 B.C.E.–?
Antonia the Younger, Augusta; political player; daughter of **Octavia (2)**; mother of Livia Julia Claudia **Livilla**; mother-in-law of **Agrippina the Elder**; grandmother of **Agrippina the Younger**; daughter-in-law of **Livia Drusilla**; q.v. **Berenice (1); Cleopatra VII; Julia Drusilla (1); Julia Livilla; Salome; Vipsania Agrippina**	Roman: Italy	January 31, 36 B.C.E.– May 1, 37 C.E.
Antonia Tryphaena, ruler; daughter of **Pythodoris**; great-granddaughter of **Antonia (2)**; q.v. **Livia (2)**	Roman: Asia Minor	1st cent. C.E.
Antye, lyric poet	Greek: Tegea	3rd cent. B.C.E.

Apama (1), progenitor of the Seleucid dynasty; q.v. **Stratonice (2)**	Persian: Persia and Antioch	4th–3rd cent. B.C.E.
Apama (2), ruler; daughter of **Stratonice (2)**; half sister of **Phila (2)**; sister of **Stratonice (3)**; mother of **Berenice II of Cyrene**	Greek: Cyrene	3rd cent. B.C.E.
Apega, political player	Greek: Sparta	3rd–2nd cent. B.C.E.
Apicata, avenger; mother of **Aelia Iunilla**; q.v. **Livilla**	Roman: Rome	1st cent. C.E.
Appuleia Varilla, convicted adulterer; grand-niece of Octavia (2); q.v. **Livia Drusilla**	Roman: Rome	1st cent. B.C.E.–1st cent. C.E.
Apronia, murder victim; q.v. **Fabia Numantina; Livia Drusilla; Urgulania**	Roman: Rome	1st cent. C.E.
Archidamia, reformer; mother of **Agesistrata;** q.v. **Agiatis**	Greek: Sparta	3rd cent. B.C.E.
Archippe (1), political wife	Greek: Athens	6th–5th cent. B.C.E.
Archippe (2), self-made woman	Greek: Athens	c. 410 B.C.E.–?
Archo, war victim; sister of **Theoxena**	Greek: Thessaly	2nd cent. B.C.E.
Aretaphila, avenger	Greek: Cyrene	1st cent. B.C.E.
Arete (1), philosopher	Greek: Cyrene and Greece	5th–4th cent. B.C.E.
Arete (2), political player; daughter of **Aristomache**	Greek: Syracuse	4th cent. B.C.E.
Aristomache, political player; mother of **Arete (2);** q.v. **Doris**	Greek: Syracuse	4th cent. B.C.E.
Arrecina Tertulla, young wife	Roman: Rome	1st cent. C.E.
Arria the Elder, Stoic; mother of **Arria the Younger;** grandmother of **Fannia (2)**; q.v. **Messallina**	Roman: Italy	1st cent. C.E.
Arria the Younger, Stoic; daughter of **Arria the Elder;** mother of **Fannia (2);** q.v. **Agrippina the Younger**	Roman: Italy	1st cent. C.E.
Arria Fadilla, mother of Antoninus Pius	Roman: Gaul	1st–2nd cent. C.E.

Arsinoë, progenitor of the Ptolemaic line	Greek: Macedonia	4th cent. B.C.E.
Arsinoë I, political player; daughter of **Nicaea (1)**; mother of **Berenice Syra;** sister-in-law of **Arsinoë II Philadelphus**	Greek: Greece and Egypt	300 B.C.E.–?
Arsinoë II Philadelphus, coruler; deified; daughter of **Berenice I;** half sister of **Lysandra** and **Antigone**	Greek: Egypt and Macedonia	c. 316–270 B.C.E.
Arsinoë III Philopator, ruler; daughter of **Berenice II of Cyrene;** killed by **Agathocleia;** q.v. **Oenanthe**		3rd cent. B.C.E.
Arsinoë Auletes, coruler; insurgent leader; sister of **Cleopatra VII;** q.v. **Cleopatra VI Tryphaena**	Greek: Egypt	65–43/40 B.C.E
Artacama, political wife	Persian: Persia	4th cent. B.C.E.
Artemisia I, ruler	Greek: Asia Minor	5th cent. B.C.E.
Artemisia II, ruler	Greek: Asia Minor	4th cent. B.C.E.
Artonis, political wife; sister of **Artacama**	Persian: Persia	4th cent. B.C.E.
Artoria Flaccilla, loyal wife	Roman: Rome	1st cent. C.E.
Aspasia, self-made woman; q.v. **Hipparete (1)**	Greek: Athens	5th cent. B.C.E.
Atia (1), daughter of **Julia (4)**; mother of **Octavia (2)** and the emperor Augustus; stepmother of **Octavia (1)**; sister of **Atia (2)**	Roman: Italy	1st cent. B.C.E.
Atia (2), daughter of **Julia 4**; younger sister of **Atia (1)**; mother of **Marcia (3)**	Roman: Italy	1st cent. B.C.E.
Atilia, accused adulterer	Roman: Italy	1st cent. B.C.E.
Attia Variola, litigant	Roman: Rome	1st cent. C.E.
Attica, Caecilia, heiress; daughter of **Pilia;** mother of **Vipsania Agrippina**	Roman: Rome	51 B.C.E.–?
Aurelia (1), mother of **Julia (3)**, **Julia (4)**, and Gaius Julius Caesar	Roman: Rome	2nd–1st cent. B.C.E.
Aurelia (2), woman of means	Roman: Rome	1st cent. C.E.
Aurelia Orestilla, possible conspirator	Roman: Rome	1st cent. B.C.E.

Aurelia Severa, condemned priestess; colleagues: **Cannutia Crescentina, Clodia Laeta,** and **Pomponia Rufina**	Roman: Rome	?–213 C.E.
Axiothea (1), philosopher	Greek: Greece	4th cent. B.C.E.
Axiothea (2), heroine	Greek: Cyprus	4th cent. B.C.E.
Balbilla, Julia, poet; q.v. **Sabina**	Greek: Asia Minor	2nd cent. C.E.
Barsine (1), adventurer	Persian: Asia Minor and Egypt	4th cent. B.C.E.
Barsine (2), political victim; wife of Alexander the Great; sister of **Drypetis;** q.v. **Roxane**	Persian: Persia	4th cent. B.C.E.
Bastia, hard-hearted woman	Roman: Rome	1st cent. B.C.E.
Berenice (1), political client; patron of **Antonia the Younger;** daughter of **Salome**	Jewish: Judaea	1st cent. B.C.E.– 1st cent. C.E.
Berenice (2), political player; sister and rival of **Drusilla (2)**	Jewish: Judaea and Rome	1st cent. C.E.
Berenice I, political player; deified; mother of **Antigone** and **Arsinoë II Philadelphus;** q.v. **Eurydice (3)**	Greek: Macedonia and Egypt	340–281/271 B.C.E.
Berenice II of Cyrene, ruler; daughter of **Apama (2);** mother of **Arsinoë III Philopator;** granddaughter of **Berenice I**	Greek: Cyrene and Egypt	c. 273–221 B.C.E.
Berenice III Cleopatra, ruler; daughter of **Cleopatra IV** or **Cleopatra V Selene**	Greek: Egypt	2nd–1st cent. B.C.E.
Berenice IV Cleopatra, coruler with **Cleopatra VI Tryphaena**	Greek: Egypt	1st cent. B.C.E.
Berenice Syra, ruler; daughter of **Arsinoë I;** q.v. Laodice I	Greek: Egypt and Antioch	c. 280–246 B.C.E.
Bilistiche, self-made woman	Greek or Phonecian: Egypt	3rd cent. B.C.E.
Boudicca, ruler of the Iceni	Celtic: Britain	1st cent. C.E.
Busa, patriot	Roman: Italy	3rd cent. B.C.E.
Caecilia, mother of Pliny the Younger	Roman: Italy	1st cent. C.E.

Caecilia Metella (1), power broker; mother of **Aemilia (2)** and **Fausta**	Roman: Rome	2nd–1st cent. B.C.E.
Caecilia Metella (2), political player; mother of two consular sons	Roman: Rome	2nd–1st cent. B.C.E.
Caedicia, possible conspirator	Roman: Rome	1st cent. C.E.
Caenis Antonia, self-made woman; freedwoman of **Antonia the Younger**	Roman: Rome	?–75 C.E.
Calpurnia (1), wife of Julius Caesar	Roman: Rome	1st cent. B.C.E.
Calpurnia (2), self-made woman; q.v. **Messallina**	Roman: Rome	1st cent. C.E.
Calpurnia (3), wife of Pliny the Younger; q.v. **Cornelia Hispulla**	Roman: Rome	1st–2nd cent. C.E.
Calpurnia Hispulla, woman of means; aunt of **Calpurnia (3)**	Roman: Italy	1st–2nd cent. C.E.
Calvia Crispinilla, political survivor; q.v. **Poppaea Sabina (2)**	Roman: Rome	1st cent. C.E.
Calvina, financial manager	Roman: Italy	1st–2nd cent. C.E.
Cannutia Crescentina, condemned priestess; colleagues: **Aurelia Severa, Clodia Laeta,** and **Pomponia Rufina**	Roman: Rome	?–213 C.E.
Cartimandua, ruler	Brigantian: Britain	1st cent. C.E.
Casta, Caecilia, acquitted of corruption charge	Roman: Rome	1st–2nd cent. C.E.
Celerina, Pompeia, wealthy woman; mother-in-law of Pliny the Younger	Roman: Rome	1st–2nd cent. C.E.
Chaerestrate, mother of philosopher Epicurus	Greek: Samos	4th cent. B.C.E.
Chelidon, office manager	Greek: Sicily	1st cent. B.C.E.
Chilonis (1), heroine	Greek: Sparta	7th cent. B.C.E.
Chilonis (2), heroine	Greek: Sparta	3rd cent. B.C.E.
Chilonis (3), heroine	Greek: Sparta	3rd cent. B.C.E.

Chiomara, avenger	Galatian: Asia Minor	4th cent. B.C.E.
Claudia (1), possibly tried for treason	Roman: Rome	3rd cent. B.C.E.
Claudia {2), reformer; daughter of **Antistia (1);** sister of **Claudia (3);** q.v. **Aemilia Tertia; Cornelia (2); Sempronia (1)**	Roman: Rome	2nd cent. B.C.E.
Claudia (3), priestess; sister of **Claudia (2)**	Roman: Rome	2nd cent. B.C.E.
Claudia (4), political player; niece of **Clodia (1), Clodia (2),** and **Clodia (3);** q.v. **Servilia (1)**	Roman: Rome	1st cent. B.C.E.
Claudia (5), political pawn; daughter of **Fulvia (2);** niece of **Clodia (1), Clodia (2),** and **Clodia (3)**	Roman: Rome	53 B.C.E.–?
Claudia (6), member of artistic circle	Roman: Italy	1st cent. C.E.
Claudia Pulchra, political player; daughter of **Claudia Marcella the Younger**	Roman: Rome	1st cent. C.E.
Cleito, mother of playwright Euripides	Greek: Greece	5th cent. B.C.E.
Cleoboule, fraud victim; mother of orator Demosthenes	Greek: Athens	c. 407/400 B.C.E.–?
Cleobuline, poet	Greek: Rhodes	6th cent. B.C.E.
Cleodice, mother of poet Pindar	Greek: Greece	6th cent. B.C.E.
Cleopatra (1), wife of two rulers	Greek: Macedonia	5th cent. B.C.E.
Cleopatra (2), political player; q.v. **Olympias (1)**	Greek: Macedonia	4th cent. B.C.E.
Cleopatra (3), coruler; daughter of **Olympias (1);** sister of Alexander the Great; q.v. **Nicaea (1)**	Greek: Macedonia, Epirus, and Asia Minor	c. 354–308 B.C.E
Cleopatra (4), self-made woman; q.v. **Calpurnia (2); Messallina**	Roman: Rome	1st cent. C.E.
Cleopatra (5), political client; friend of **Poppaea Sabina (2)**	Roman: Rome	1st cent. C.E.
Cleopatra I (the Syrian), ruler; daughter of **Laodice III;** mother of **Cleopatra II Philometor Soteira**	Greek: Asia Minor and Egypt	c. 215–176 B.C.E.

Cleopatra II Philometor Soteira, ruler; daughter of **Cleopatra I (the Syrian);** mother of **Cleopatra III** and **Cleopatra Thea**	Greek: Egypt	c. 185?–115 B.C.E.
Cleopatra III, ruler; daughter of **Cleopatra II Philometor Soteira;** sister of **Cleopatra Thea;** mother of **Cleopatra IV, Cleopatra Tryphaena,** and **Cleopatra V Selene**	Greek: Egypt	c. 165?–101 B.C.E.
Cleopatra IV, insurgent leader; daughter of **Cleopatra III;** sister of **Cleopatra Tryphaena** and **Cleopatra V Selene;** q.v. **Cleopatra Thea**	Greek: Egypt and Syria	2nd cent. B.C.E.
Cleopatra V Selene, political player; daughter of **Cleopatra III;** sister of **Cleopatra IV** and **Cleopatra Tryphaena**	Greek: Egypt and Syria	c. 131–130–69 B.C.E.
Cleopatra VI Tryphaena, coruler with **Berenice IV Cleopatra;** possibly mother of **Cleopatra VII** and **Arsinoë Auletes**	Greek: Egypt	?–57 B.C.E.
Cleopatra VII, ruler; sister of **Arsinoë Auletes;** mother of **Cleopatra Selene;** q.v. **Berenice IV Cleopatra; Cleopatra VI Tryphaena**	Greek: Egypt, Asia Minor, and Italy	c. 69–30 B.C.E.
Cleopatra Selene, coruler; daughter of **Cleopatra VII;** mother of **Drusilla (1);** q.v. **Octavia (2)**	Greek: Egypt, Italy and Mauritania	40 B.C.E.–? C.E.
Cleopatra Thea, coruler; daughter of **Cleopatra II Philometor Soteira;** q.v. **Cleopatra Tryphaena**	Greek: Egypt and Syria	2nd cent. B.C.E.
Cleopatra Tryphaena, military leader; daughter of **Cleopatra III;** sister of **Cleopatra IV** and **Cleopatra V Selene;** niece of **Cleopatra Thea**	Greek: Egypt and Syria	2nd cent. B.C.E.
Cleora, wife of ruler	Greek: Sparta	5th–4th cent. B.C.E.
Clodia (1), political wife; sister of **Clodia (2)** and Clodia (3)	Roman: Rome	1st cent. B.C.E.
Clodia (2), adventurer; sister of **Clodia (1)** and **Clodia (3)**	Roman: Italy	95–? B.C.E.
Clodia (3), convicted adulterer; sister of **Clodia (1)** and **Clodia (2)**	Roman: Rome	1st cent. B.C.E.
Clodia (4), long-lived woman	Roman: Rome	1st cent. B.C.E.– 1st cent. C.E.

Clodia Laeta, condemned priestess; colleagues: **Aurelia Severa, Cannutia Crescentina,** and **Pomponia Rufina**	Roman: Rome	?–213 C.E.
Cloelia (1), heroine	Roman: Rome and Etruria	6th cent. B.C.E.
Cloelia (2), faultless wife; divorced; q.v. **Caecilia Metella (1)**	Roman: Rome	1st cent. B.C.E.
Coesyra, political wife	Greek: Athens	6th cent. B.C.E.
Constantia, Flavia Julia, Augusta; early Christian; daughter of Flavia Maximiana **Theodora;** q.v. **Fausta, Flavia Maxima; Helena Flavia Julia**	Rome: Italy	?–329 C.E.
Corellia Hispulla, litigant	Roman: Italy	1st–2nd cent. C.E.
Corinna, poet	Greek: Tanagr	3rd cent. B.C.E.
Cornelia (1), political player; elder daughter of **Aemilia Tertia;** sister of **Cornelia (2)**	Roman: Rome	2nd cent. B.C.E.
Cornelia (2), political player; younger daughter of **Aemilia Tertia;** sister of **Cornelia (1);** mother of **Sempronia (1)**	Roman: Italy	c. 190s–121 B.C.E.of
Cornelia (3), great-grandmother of **Livia** Drusilla and great-great-grandmother of Tiberius	Roman: Rome	2nd–1st cent. B.C.E.
Cornelia (4), businesswoman; daughter of **Ilia;** mother of **Pompeia (1)**	Roman: Rome and	2nd–1st cent. B.C.E.
Cornelia (5), brave woman; mother of **Julia (5);** q.v. **Julia (1)**	Roman: Rome	?–68 B.C.E.
Cornelia (6), cultured woman; daughter of **Aemilia Lepida (1)**	Roman: Rome	1st cent. B.C.E.
Cornelia (7), political wife; daughter of **Pompeia (2);** daughter-in-law of **Junia (1);** mother of **Aemilia Lepida (2);** q.v. **Servilia (1)**	Roman: Rome	c. 46 B.C.E.–?
Cornelia (8), eulogized by poet Propertius; daughter of **Scribonia;** half sister of **Julia (6)**	Roman: Rome	?–16 B.C.E.

Cornelia (9), loyal wife	Roman: Rome	1st cent. B.C.E.– 1st cent. C.E.
Cornelia (10), priestess	Roman: Rome	1st cent. C.E.
Cornelia (11), adulterer	Roman: Rome and Germany	1st cent. C.E.
Cornelia (12), condemned priestess; q.v. **Oculata; Varronilla**	Roman: Rome	?–90 C.E.
Cornificia, political victim; daughter of **Faustina** **the Younger, Annia Galeria;** q.v. **Julia Domna**	Roman: Rome	?–211 C.E.
Cratesicleia, reformer	Greek: Sparta and Egypt	3rd cent. B.C.E.
Cratesipolis, ruler	Greek: Sicyon	4th cent. B.C.E.
Crispina, brave woman	Roman: Rome	1st cent. C.E.
Crispina Bruttia, political player; sister-in-law of Annia Aurelia Galeria **Lucilla**	Roman: Rome	2nd cent. C.E.
Cynane, political player; mother of **Eurydice (2)**	Greek: Macedonia and Asia Minor	?–322 B.C.E.
Cynisca, self-made woman	Greek: Sparta	4th cent. B.C.E.
Cytheris Volumnia, self-made woman	Roman: Rome	1st cent. B.C.E.
Danae, political player; daughter of **Leontion;** q.v. **Laodice I**	Greek: Athens and Syria	3rd cent. B.C.E.
Deinomache, mother of the Greek general Alcibiades	Greek: Athens	5th cent. B.C.E.
Demarete, political player	Greek: Syracuse	5th cent. B.C.E.
Domitia, political player; daughter of **Antonia** the Elder; granddaughter of **Octavia (2);** sister of **Domitia Lepida;** aunt of Valeria **Messallina;** q.v. **Agrippina the Younger;** **Junia Silana**	Roman: Rome	?–59 C.E.

Domitia Lepida, political player; younger daughter of **Antonia the Elder;** granddaughter of **Octavia (2);** sister of **Domitia;** mother of Valeria **Messallina;** sister-in-law of Julia **Agrippina the Younger**	Roman: Rome	?–54 C.E.
Domitia Longina, Augusta	Roman: Rome	?–c. 140 C.E.
Domitia Lucilla, political player	Roman: Rome	?–155/161 C.E.
Domitia Paulina (1), political player; mother of **Domitia Paulina (2)**	Roman: Spain	1st cent. C.E.
Domitia Paulina (2), political player; daughter of **Domitia Paulina (1)**	Roman: Rome	?–130 C.E.
Domitilla, Flavia (1), mother of emperors	Roman: Italy and North Africa	1st cent. C.E.
Domitilla, Flavia (2), political exile; niece of the emperor Domitian	Roman: Italy and Pandateria	1st cent. C.E.
Doris, political player; wife, along with **Aristomache,** of Dionysius I	Greek: Syracuse	5th–4th cent. B.C.E.
Drusilla (1), political wife; daughter of **Cleopatra Selene;** granddaughter of **Cleopatra VII**	Roman: Mauritania and Judaea	39 C.E.–?
Drusilla (2), political player; sister and rival of **Berenice (2)**	Jewish: Judaea and Rome	1st cent. C.E.
Drypetis, political player; sister of **Barsine (2);** q.v. **Roxane**	Persian: Persia	4th cent. B.C.E.
Duronia, criminal; q.v. **Hispala Faecenia**	Roman: Rome	2nd cent. B.C.E.
Egnatia Maximilla, loyal wife	Roman: Rome	1st cent. C.E.
Elpinice, well-known Athenian; daughter of **Hegesipyle**	Greek: Athens	c. 510 B.C.E.–?
Ennia Thrasylla, political player; reputed lover of Gaius Caligula	Roman: Rome	? B.C.E./C.E.–38 C.E.
Epicharis, conspirator	Roman: Rome	?–65 C.E.
Erinna, poet	Greek: Telos	4th cent. B.C.E.
Euboea, political player	Greek: Euboea	3rd–2nd cent. B.C.E.

Eurydice (1), political player; grandmother of **Cleopatra (3)** and Alexander the Great	Illyrian: Illyria and Macedonia	4th cent. B.C.E.
Eurydice (2) (Adea), political player; military leader; daughter of **Cynane;** q.v. **Olympias (1)**	Greek: Macedonia	c. 337–317 B.C.E.
Eurydice (3), political player; military leader; sister of **Nicaea (1)** and **Phila (1);** mother of **Lysandra;** q.v. **Berenice I**	Greek: Macedonia, Egypt, and Miletus	4th–3rd cent. B.C.E.
Eurydice (4), political player; daughter of **Nicaea (1);** sister of **Arsinoë I**	Greek: Thrace and Macedonia	4th–3rd cent. B.C.E.
Euryleonis, self-made woman	Greek: Sparta	4th cent. B.C.E.
Euthydice (Eurydice), political player	Greek: Athens, Cyrene, and Macedonia	4th–3rd cent. B.C.E.
Eutropia, Galeria Valeria, wife of co-emperor; early Christian; mother of Flavia Maxima **Fausta;** q.v. **Constantia; Helena Flavia Julia**	Roman: Syria, Italy, and Judaea	3rd–4th cent. C.E.
Fabia, priestess; half sister of **Terentia (1)**	Roman: Rome	1st cent. B.C.E.
Fadia, ignored wife	Roman: Italy and Greece	1st cent. B.C.E.
Fannia (1), litigant	Roman: Rome	1st cent. B.C.E.
Fannia (2), Stoic; exiled daughter of **Arria the Younger;** granddaughter of **Arria the Elder;** q.v. **Junia (3); Anteia**	Roman: Italy	?–107 C.E.
Fausta, political player; daughter of **Caecilia Metella (1);** half sister of **Aemilia (2)**	Roman: Rome	1st cent. B.C.E.
Fausta, Flavia Maxima, Augusta; younger daughter of **Eutropia;** daughter-in-law of **Helena Flavia Julia;** q.v. **Constantia**	Roman: Italy, Gaul, Asia, and North Africa	289/290–324/325 C.E.
Faustina the Elder, Annia Galeria, Augusta; mother of Annia Galeria **Faustina the Younger**	Roman: Baetica/ Narbonensis, Italy, and Asia	c. 94–140/141 C.E.
Faustina the Younger, Annia Galeria, Augusta; daughter of Annia Galeria, **Faustina the Elder;** mother of Annia Auvelia Galeria **Lucilla**	Roman: Italy, Asia, Gaul, and German	25/130–175 C.E.

Flora, self-made woman	Roman: Rome	1st cent. B.C.E.
Floronia, condemned priestess; colleague: **Opimia**	Roman: Rome	?–216 B.C.E.
Fulvia (1), political player; q.v. **Pompeia (1)**	Roman: Italy	1st cent. B.C.E.
Fulvia (2), political player; niece of **Sempronia (2);** mother of **Claudia (5);** q.v. **Julia (2); Octavia (2)**	Roman: Italy and Greece	?–40 B.C.E.
Galeria Fundana, political player; q.v. **Sextilia**	Roman: Rome	1st cent. C.E.
Gallitta, adulterer	Roman: Rome and Germany	1st cent. B.C.E.– 1st cent. C.E.
Glaphyra (1), political player; grandmother of **Glaphyra (2)**	Greek: Asia Minor	1st cent. B.C.E.
Glaphyra (2), adventurer; granddaughter of **Glaphyra (1)**	Greek (probably Roman citizen): Cappadocia and Judaea	1st cent. B.C.E.– 1st cent. C.E.
Glycera, self-made woman; q.v. **Pythonice**	Greek: Athens and Babylon	4th cent. B.C.E.
Gorgo, patriot	Greek: Sparta	5th cent. B.C.E.
Grattila, Stoic	Roman: Rome	1st cent. C.E.
Gygaea, political pawn	Greek: Macedonia	5th cent. B.C.E.
Hagesichora, choral leader	Greek: Sparta	7th cent. B.C.E.
Hedyto, mother of rhetorican Isocrates	Greek: Athens	5th cent. B.C.E.
Hegesipyle, mother of **Elpinice** and Athenian statesman Cimon	Thracian: Thrace and Athens	6th–5th cent. B.C.E.
Helena Flavia Julia, Augusta; early Christian; q.v. **Fausta Flavia Maxima; Theodora**	Roman: Italy, Germany, Judaea, Asia, and Syria	?–327 C.E.
Helvia, mother of Marcus Tullius Cicero	Roman: Italy	2nd–1st cent. B.C.E.
Herodias, loyal wife; daughter of **Berenice (1)**	Jewish: Judaea, and Gaul	Italy, 1st cent. C.E.

Herpyllis, companion of Aristotle	Greek: Greec	4th cent. B.C.E.
Hipparchia, philosopher	Greek: Greece	4th–3rd cent. B.C.E.
Hipparete (1), independent woman; mother of **Hipparete (2)**; daughter-in-law of **Elpinice**	Greek: Athens	6th–5th cent. B.C.E.
Hipparete (2), rich Athenian; daughter of **Hipparete (1)**	Greek: Athens	?–417/416 B.C.E.
Hispala Faecenia, patriot; q.v. **Duronia**	Roman: Rome	2nd cent. B.C.E.
Hispulla, family manager; mother of **Corellia Hispulla**	Roman: Italy	1st cent. C.E.
Horatia, war victim	Roman: Rome	7th cent. B.C.E.
Hortensia, orator; q.v. **Fulvia (2)**; **Livia Drusilla**; **Octavia (2)**	Roman: Rome	1st cent. B.C.E.
Hydna, patriot	Greek: Scione	5th cent. B.C.E.
Ilia, mother of **Cornelia (4)**	Roman: Rome	2nd–1st cent. B.C.E.
Ismenodora, self-made woman	Greek: Thespiae	1st cent. C.E.
Isodice, loyal wife	Greek: Athens	5th cent. B.C.E.
Julia (1), brave woman; aunt of Julius Caesar; q.v. **Cornelia (5)**	Roman: Rome	?–68 B.C.E.
Julia (2), power broker; mother of Mark Antony; mother-in-law of **Fulvia (2)** and **Octavia (2)**	Roman: Rome	1st cent. B.C.E.
Julia (3), politically well connected; elder sister of **Julia (4)**; daughter of **Aurelia (1)**	Roman: Rome	1st cent. B.C.E.
Julia (4), witness; daughter of **Aurelia (1)**; sister of **Julia (3)**; mother of **Atia (1)** and **Atia (2)**; grandmother of **Octavia (2)**; q.v. **Pompeia (1)**	Roman: Rome	?–51 B.C.E.
Julia (5), political wife; daughter of **Cornelia (5)**	Roman: Rome	83–54 B.C.E.
Julia (6), political player; daughter of **Scribonia**; mother of **Vipsania Agrippina the Elder** and **Julia (7)**; q.v. **Marcella the Elder**; **Octavia (2)**	Roman: Italy, Gaul, and Pandateria	39 B.C.E.–15 C.E.

Julia (7), political victim; daughter of Julia (6); elder sister of Vipsania Agrippina the Elder; mother of Aemilia Lepida (3); daughter-in-law of Cornelia (8)	Roman: Italy	19 B.C.E.–28 C.E.
Julia (8), political victim; daughter of Livia Julia Claudia Livilla; daughter-in-law of Vipsania Agrippina the Elder; granddaughter of Octavia (2 and Livia Drusilla; q.v. Messallina	Roman: Rome	?–43 C.E.
Julia Aquilia Severa, married priestess	Roman: Rome	3rd cent. C.E.
Julia Avita Mamaea, power broker; younger daughter of Julia Maesa; sister of Julia Soaemias Bassiana; niece of Julia Domna; q.v. Orbiana	Roman: Syria and Italy	?–235 C.E.
Julia Cornelia Paula, Augusta; daughter-in-law of Julia Soaemias Bassiana	Roman: Italy	3rd cent. C.E.
Julia Domna, Augusta; sister of Julia Maesa; aunt of Julia Soaemias Bassiana and Julia Avita Mamaea; q.v. Plautilla	Roman: Syria and Italy	2nd cent.–218 C.E.
Julia Drusilla (1), deified; daughter of Vipsania Agrippina the Elder; sister of Julia Agrippina the Younger and Julia Livilla	Roman: Rome	16–38 C.E.
Julia Drusilla (2), political victim; daughter of Milonia Caesonia	Roman: Rome	40–January 24, 41 C.E.
Julia Flavia, Augusta; deified; daughter of Marcia Furnilla	Roman: Rome	65–91 C.E
Julia Livilla, political player; daughter of Vipsania Agrippina the Elder; sister of Julia Agrippina the Younger and Julia Drusilla (1)	Roman: Italy, Germany, and Gaul	18–41 C.E.
Julia Maesa, power broker; sister of Julia Domna; mother of Julia Avita Mamaea and Julia Soaemias Bassiana	Roman: Syria, Asia, and Rome	2nd cent.–224 C.E.
Julia Phoebe, loyal attendant, freedwoman of Julia (6)	Roman: Rome	1st cent. B.C.E.–1st cent. C.E.
Julia Procilla, murder victim	Roman: Gallia Narbonensis and Rome	?–69 C.E.

Julia Soaemias Bassiana, Augusta; elder daughter of **Julia Maesa;** sister of **Julia Avita Mamaea;** niece of **Julia Domna**	Roman: Syria and Italy	2nd cent.–222 C.E.
Junia (1), conspirator; daughter of **Servilia (1);** sister of **Junia (2)** and **Junia Tertia**	Roman: Rome	1st cent. B.C.E.
Junia (2), political player; daughter of **Servilia** (1); sister of **Junia (1)** and **Junia Tertia;** mother of **Servilia (3)**	Roman: Rome	1st cent. B.C.E.
Junia (3), priestess; q.v. **Fannia (2)**	Roman: Rome	1st–2nd cent. C.E.
Junia Calvina, long-lived woman; daughter of **Aemilia Lepida (3);** sister of **Junia Lepida;** last descendant of Augustus; q.v. **Julia (6)**	Roman: Italy	?–79 C.E.
Junia Claudilla, political wife; sister of **Junia Silana**	Roman: Rome	1st cent. C.E.
Junia Lepida, political player; daughter of **Aemilia Lepida (3);** sister of **Junia Calvina**	Roman: Italy	1st cent. C.E.
Junia Silana, political player; sister of **Junia** Claudilla; q.v. **Agrippina the Younger; Messallina**	Roman: Italy	?–c. 59 C.E.
Junia Tertia, political player; youngest daughter of **Servilia (1);** sister of **Junia (1)** and **Junia (2)**	Roman: Italy	73 B.C.E.–22 C.E.
Junia Torquata, priestess	Roman: Rome	1st cent. B.C.E.–1st cent. C.E.
Labda, heroine	Greek: Corinth	7th cent. B.C.E.
Laelia, orator; mother of two daughters named **Mucia;** grandmother of **Licinia (1)** and **Licinia (2)**	Roman: Rome	2nd–1st cent. B.C.E.
Laïs self-made woman	Greek: Sicily, Corinth, and Thessaly	5th–4th cent. B.C.E.
Lamia, flutist	Cyprian: Cyprus and Egypt	4th–3rd cent. B.C.E.
Lanassa, political player	Greek: Syracuse, Corcyra, and Greece	4th–3rd cent. B.C.E.

Laodice I, ruler; q.v. **Berenice Syra; Danae**	Greek: Syria and Asia Minor	3rd cent. B.C.E.
Laodice III, philanthropist; mother of **Cleopatra I** (the Syrian)	Persian: Asia Minor and Asia	3rd–2nd cent. B.C.E.
Lastheneia, philosopher	Greek: Greece	4th cent. B.C.E.
Leaena, brave woman	Greek: Athens	6th cent. B.C.E.
Leontion, philosopher; mother of **Danae**	Greek: Athens	4th–3rd cent. B.C.E.
Licinia (1), convicted murderer along with **Publilia (1)**	Roman: Rome	?–154 B.C.E.
Licinia (2), reformer; elder sister of **Licinia (3)**	Roman: Rome	2nd cent. B.C.E.
Licinia (3), reformer; younger sister of **Licinia (2)**	Roman: Rome	2nd cent. B.C.E.
Licinia (4), condemned priestess; colleagues: **Aemilia (1)** and **Marcia (1)**	Roman: Rome	?–113 B.C.E.
Licinia (5), elegant conversationalist; daughter of **Mucia;** sister of **Licinia (6)**	Roman: Rome	1st cent. B.C.E.
Licinia (6), elegant conversationalist; daughter of **Mucia;** sister of **Licinia (5)**	Roman: Rome	1st cent. B.C.E.
Licinia (7), priestess	Roman: Rome	1st cent. B.C.E.
Livia, political wife; mother of **Servilia (1)** and **Servilia (2)**	Roman: Rome	?–92 B.C.E.
Livia Drusilla, power broker; rival of **Octavia (2)**; mother-in-law of **Antonia the Younger;** close friend of **Munatia Plancina** and **Urgulania;** friend and patron of **Salome;** q.v. **Julia Drusilla (1); Julia Livilla; Marcella the Elder; Marcella the Younger; Scribonia**	Roman: Italy	January 30, 58 B.C.E. –29 C.E.
Livia Ocellina, political player; q.v. **Mummia** Achaica	Roman: Rome	1st cent. C.E.
Livia Orestilla, political victim	Roman: Rome	1st cent. C.E.
Livilla, Livia Julia Claudia, conspirator; daughter of **Antonia the Younger;** granddaughter of Octavia (2) and **Livia Drusilla;** mother of **Julia (8)**	Roman: Rome	c. 13 B.C.E.–31 C.E.

Lollia Paulina, political player	Roman: Italy	1st cent. C.E.
Lucilia, mother of Gnaeus Pompeius (Pompey the Great)	Roman: Rome	2nd–1st cent. B.C.E.
Lucilla, Annia Aurelia Galeria, Augusta; daughter of Annia Galeria **Faustina the Younger;** q.v. **Crispina Bruttia**	Roman: Asia, Africa, Germany, and Rome	148–182 C.E.
Lucretia, heroine	Roman: Rome	6th cent. B.C.E.
Lysandra, power broker; daughter of Eurydice (3); daughter-in-law of **Thessalonice;** half sister of **Arsinoë II Philadelphus**	Greek: Egypt, Macedonia, and Syria	4th–3rd cent. B.C.E.
Maecia Faustina, ruler for son	Roman: Italy and North Africa	3rd cent. C.E.
Maesia, lawyer	Roman: Umbria and Rome	1st cent. B.C.E.
Magia, mother of Virgil	Roman: Italy	1st cent. B.C.E.
Mallonia, political victim	Roman: Rome	1st cent. C.E.
Marcella the Elder, Claudia, political player; daughter of **Octavia (2);** sister of Claudia **Marcella the Younger;** q.v. **Julia (4)**	Roman: Italy	43 B.C.E.–? B.C.E./C.E.
Marcella the Younger, Claudia, political wife; daughter of **Octavia (2);** sister of Claudia **Marcella the Elder;** mother of **Claudia Pulchra;** mother-in-law of **Domitia Lepida;** grandmother of Valeria **Messallina;** q.v. **Julia (4); Octavia (2)**	Roman: Rome	39 B.C.E.–? C.E.
Marcia (1), condemned priestess; colleagues: **Aemilia (1)** and **Licinia (4)**	Roman: Rome	?–113 B.C.E.
Marcia (2), political wife; stepdaughter of **Atia (1)**	Roman: Rome	1st cent. B.C.E.
Marcia (3), patron of the arts; daughter of **Atia (2);** stepniece of **Octavia (2);** mother of Fabia **Numantina;** friend of **Livia Drusilla**	Roman: Italy, Cyprus, Asia, and Spain	1st cent. B.C.E.– 1st cent. C.E.
Marcia (4), conspirator; q.v. Lucilla	Roman: Rome	?–193 C.E.
Marcia Furnilla, political wife; mother of Julia Flavia	Roman: Rome	1st cent. C.E.

Marciana, Ulpia, Augusta; deified; sister-in-law of Pompeia **Plotina;** mother of **Matidia (1);** q.v. **Sabina**	Roman: Spain, Germany, Italy, and Asia	?–112 C.E.
Martina, poisoner; friend of **Munatia Plancina;** q.v. **Agrippina the Elder**	Syrian: Syria and Italy	? B.C.E.–19/20 C.E.
Matidia (1), Augusta; deified; daughter of Ulpia **Marciana;** mother of Vibia **Sabina** and **Matidia (2);** q.v. **Plotina**	Roman: Italy, Asia, and Germany	68–119 C.E.
Matidia (2), never married; wealthy daughter of **Matidia (1);** half sister of Vibia **Sabina;** q.v. **Faustina the Younger; Plotina**	Roman: Italy, Asia, Germany, and Egypt	1st–2nd cent. C.E.
Melinno, poet	Greek: Italy	2nd cent. B.C.E.
Melissa, murder victim	Greek: Greece	7th cent. B.C.E.
Messallina, Valeria, power broker; daughter of **Domitia Lepida;** mother of Claudia **Octavia;** q.v. **Aelia Patina; Agrippina the Elder; Calpurnia (2); Cleopatra (4); Julia Livilla; Junia Silana; Livia Drusilla; Poppaea Sabina**	Roman: Rome	c. 20–48 C.E.
Milonia Caesonia, political player; mother of **Julia Drusilla (2);** daughter of **Vistilia**	Roman: Rome	c. 5–41 C.E.
Minervina, lover of Constantine; q.v. Flavia Maxima **Fausta**	Roman: Asia	3rd–4th cent. C.E.
Minucia, convicted priestess	Roman: Rome	?–337 B.C.E.
Mucia, elegant speaker; daughter of **Laelia;** mother of **Licinia (5)** and **Licinia (6)**	Roman: Italy	2nd–1st cent. B.C.E.
Mucia Tertia, power broker; mother of **Pompeia (2);** q.v. **Scribonia**	Roman: Italy	1st cent. B.C.E.
Mummia Achaica, mother of emperor Servius Sulpicius Galba	Roman: Rome	1st cent. B.C.E.–1st cent. C.E.
Munatia Plancina, political player; close friend of **Livia Drusilla;** q.v. **Agrippina the Elder; Antonia the Younger**	Roman: Italy, Asia, and Syria	?–33 C.E.
Musa, Thea Urania, ruler	Italian: Italy and Parthia	st cent. B.C.E.–1st cent. C.E.

Mutilia Prisca, political victim; friend of **Livia Drusilla**	Roman: Rome	? B.C.E.–30 C.E.
Myrrhine, loyal wife	Greek: Athens and Asia Minor	6th–5th cent. B.C.E.
Myrtis, poet; q.v. **Corinna**	Greek: Greece	5th cent. B.C.E.?
Myrto, wife of philosopher Socrates; q.v. **Xanthippe**	Greek: Athens	5th–4th cent. B.C.E.
Neaera, self-made woman; mother of Phano	Greek: Corinth and Athens	4th cent. B.C.E.
Nicaea (1), political pawn; sister of **Phila (1)** and **Eurydice (3);** mother of **Arsinoë I;** q.v. **Cleopatra (3); Olympias (1)**	Greek: Macedonia and Thrace	4th cent. B.C.E.
Nicaea (2), ruler	Greek: Corinth	3rd cent. B.C.E.
Nicopolis, self-made woman	Roman: Rome	2nd cent. B.C.E.
Nossis, poet	Greek: Locri	3rd cent. B.C.E.
Numantina, Fabia, litigant; daughter of **Marcia (3);** granddaughter of **Atia (2);** q.v. **Apronia; Atia (1)**	Roman: Rome	1st cent. C.E.
Occia, priestess	Roman: Rome	? B.C.E.–19 C.E.
Octavia (1), half sister of **Octavia (2)** and Augustus; daughter of **Ancharia;** grandmother of **Appuleia Varilla**	Roman: Rome	1st cent. B.C.E.
Octavia (2), power broker; daughter of **Atia (1);** mother of Claudia **Marcella the Elder,** Claudia **Marcella the Younger, Antonia the Elder, and Antonia the Younger;** q.v. **Cleopatra VII; Julia (6); Livia Drusilla**	Roman: Italy and Greece	69–11 B.C.E.
Octavia, Claudia, faultless wife; banished; daughter of Valeria **Messallina;** q.v. **Acte; Agrippina the Younger; Poppaea Sabina (2)**	Roman: Italy	39/40–62 C.E.
Oculata and her sister of the same name, convicted priestesses; colleague: **Varronilla**	Roman: Rome	1st cent. C.E.

Oenanthe, conspirator and murderer; mother of **Agathocleia;** q.v. **Arsinoë II**	Greek: Samos and Egypt	3rd cent. B.C.E.
Olympias (1), ruler; mother of **Cleopatra (3)** and Alexander the Great; q.v. **Cleopatra (2); Eurydice (2); Philinna; Roxane**	Greek: Epirus and Macedonia	4th cent. B.C.E.
Olympias (2), ruler; mother of **Phthia;** q.v. **Stratonice**	Greek: Epirus	3rd cent. B.C.E.
Opimia, condemned priestess; colleague: **Floronia**	Roman: Rome	?–216 B.C.E.
Orbiana, Augusta; exiled and murdered; q.v. **Julia Avita Mamaea**	Roman: Italy and Libya	3rd cent. C.E.
Papiria, divorced, financially strapped noble woman; q.v. **Aemilia Tertia**	Roman: Rome	3rd–2nd cent. B.C.E.
Paulina, victim of deception	Roman: Rome	1st cent. C.E.
Paxaea, charged with treason and extortion	Roman: Italy and the Balkans	1st cent. C.E.
Perictione, mother of **Potone** and Plato	Greek: Athens	5th cent. B.C.E.
Petronia, political player	Roman: Rome	1st cent. C.E.
Phaenarete, mother of Socrates	Greek: Athens	5th cent. B.C.E.
Phila (1), wise and loyal wife; sister of **Nicaea (1)** and **Eurydice (3);** mother of **Stratonice (2)**	Greek: Macedonia	c. 351–283 B.C.E.
Phila (2), power broker; daughter of **Stratonice (2);** half sister of **Stratonice (3) and Apama (2)**	Greek: Asia, Asia Minor, and Macedonia	3rd cent. B.C.E.
Philesia, wife of philosopher Xenophon	Greek: Athens, Sparta, and Corinth	5th–4th cent. B.C.E.
Philinna, cowife with **Olympias (1)** of Philip II	Greek: Thessaly and Macedonia	4th cent. B.C.E.
Phryne, self-made woman	Greek: Greece	5th cent. B.C.E.
Phthia, coruler; daughter of **Olympias (2)**	Greek: Epirus and Macedonia	3rd cent. B.C.E.

Pilia, loyal wife and friend; mother of Caecilia **Attica**	Roman: Rome and Italy	1st cent. B.C.E.
Pipa (Pipara), young lover; q.v. **Solonina**	German: Germany and Italy	3rd cent. C.E.
Plangon, independent woman	Greek: Athens	404 B.C.E.–?
Plathane, wife of rhetorician Isocrates	Greek: Athens	5th–4th cent. B.C.E.
Plautia Urgulanilla, political player; grand-daughter of **Urgulania;** q.v. **Apronia;** Livia Drusilla	Roman: Italy	1st cent. B.C.E.– 1st cent. C.E.
Plautilla, Augusta; banished and executed; q.v. **Julia Domna**	Roman: Italy and Lipara	2nd–3rd cent. C.E.
Plotina, Pompeia, Augusta; sister-in-law of Ulpia **Marciana;** aunt of **Matidia (1);** great-aunt of Vibia **Sabina** and **Matidia (2)**	Roman: Gaul, Italy, Asia, Egypt, Germany, Syria, and Greece	1st–2nd cent. C.E.
Pompeia (1), political wife; daughter of **Cornelia (4);** q.v. **Aurelia (1); Ilia**	Roman: Rome	1st cent. B.C.E.
Pompeia (2), political wife; daughter of **Mucia Tertia;** mother of **Cornelia (7)**	Roman: Italy	1st cent. B.C.E.
Pompeia Macrina, conspirator	Roman Greek: Lesbos and Sparta	1st cent. C.E.
Pompeia Paulina, political victim	Roman: Italy	1st cent. C.E.
Pomponia (1), mother of Publius Cornelius Scipio Africanus	Roman: Rome	3rd–2nd cent. B.C.E.
Pomponia (2), angry wife; q.v. **Attica; Pila; Terentia (1); Tullia (2)**	Roman: Italy	1st cent. B.C.E.
Pomponia Galla, disinherited her son	Roman: Italy	1st cent. C.E.
Pomponia Graecina, political player; friend of **Julia (8)**	Roman: Italy	?–c. 83 C.E.
Pomponia Rufina, convicted priestess; colleagues: **Aurelia Severa, Cannutia Crescentina,** and **Clodia Laeta**	Roman: Rome	?–213 C.E.

Popilia, loyal wife; honored in public	Roman: Rome	?–102 B.C.E.
Poppaea Sabina (1), political player; mother of **Poppaea Sabina (2);** q.v. **Messallina**	Roman: Italy	?–47 C.E.
Poppaea Sabina (2), Augusta; daughter of **Poppaea Sabina (1);** q.v. **Agrippina the Younger; Messallina; Octavia, Claudia**	Roman: Italy	31?–65 C.E.
Porcia, political player; daughter of **Atilia;** q.v. **Junia Tertia; Servilia (1)**	Roman: Italy	?–43 B.C.E.
Potone, sister of philosopher Plato, daughter of **Perictione**	Greek: Athens	5th–4th cent. B.C.E.
Praecia, self-made woman; political player	Roman: Rome	1st cent. B.C.E.
Praxilla, poet	Greek: Sicyon	5th cent. B.C.E.
Prisca, politically influential wife of emperor; early Christian sympathizer; mother of **Valeria (2)**	Roman: Balkans, Syria, Italy, Asia, and Greece	3rd cent.–c. 316 C.E.
Publilia (1), convicted murderer along with **Licinia (1)**	Roman: Italy	2nd cent. B.C.E.
Publilia (2), ill-used second wife of Marcus Tullius Cicero; q.v. **Terentia (1); Tullia (2)**	Roman: Italy	1st cent. B.C.E.
Pudentilla, Aemilia, independent woman	Roman: North Africa	2nd cent. C.E.
Pythias, wife of Aristotle	Greek: Asia Minor	?–c. 335 B.C.E.
Pythodoris, Roman client ruler; daughter of **Antonia (3);** granddaughter of **Antonia (2);** mother of **Antonia Tryphaena;** q.v. **Livia Drusilla**	Roman: Asia	1st cent. B.C.E.– 1st cent. C.E.
Pythonice, self-made woman	Greek: Greece, Asia Minor, and Babylon	4th cent. B.C.E.
Quarta Hostilia, convicted murderer	Roman: Rome	?–c. 179 B.C.E.
Rhea, devoted mother	Roman: Italy	2nd–1st cent. B.C.E.
Rhodopis, self-made woman; q.v. **Sappho**	Thracian: Samos and Egypt	6th cent. B.C.E.

Roxane, political player; wife of Alexander the great; daughter-in-law of **Olympias (1)**; sister-in-law of **Cleopatra (3)**; q.v. **Eurydice (2)**	Persian: Asia Minor and Greece	?–313 B.C.E.
Rubria, priestess	Roman: Rome	1st cent. C.E.
Sabina, Vibia, Augusta; daughter of **Matidia (1)**; half sister of **Matidia (2)**; q.v. **Julia Balbilla; Plotina**	Roman: Greece, Italy, Britain, Asia, Syria, Palestine, and Egypt	c. 87/88–136 C.E.
Salome, client and friend of **Livia Drusilla;** mother of **Berenice (1)**	Jewish: Judaea	1st cent. B.C.E.– 1st cent. C.E.
Salonina, Cornelia, Augusta	Greek: Asia Minor and Italy	3rd cent. C.E.
Sancia, convicted of treason	Roman: Rome	? B.C.E.–33 C.E.
Sappho, poet; q.v. **Rhodopis**	Greek: Lesbos and Sicily	c. 612 B.C.E.–?
Sassia, victim	Roman: Italy	1st cent. B.C.E.
Satria Galla, political player	Roman: Rome	1st cent. C.E.
Scribonia, political player; mother of **Cornelia (8)** and **Julia (6)**; grandmother of **Julia (7)** and Vipsania **Agrippina the Elder;** q.v. **Livia Drusilla**	Roman: Italy	70 B.C.E.–? C.E.
Sempronia (1), political player; daughter of **Cornelia (2)**; granddaughter of **Aemilia Tertia**	Roman: Italy	2nd cent. B.C.E.
Sempronia (2), possible conspirator	Roman: Rome	1st cent. B.C.E.
Servilia (1), power broker; daughter of **Livia;** mother of **Junia (1), Junia (2), Junia Tertia,** and Marcus Junius Brutus; q.v. **Pompeia (1); Porcia**	Roman: Italy	1st cent. B.C.E.
Servilia (2), political wife; sister of **Servilia (1)**; aunt of **Junia (1), Junia (2),** and **Junia Tertia;** q.v. **Clodia (3)**	Roman: Italy, Asia, and Rhodes	1st cent. B.C.E.
Servilia (3), political wife; daughter of **Junia** (2); granddaughter of **Servilia (1)**; niece of **Junia (1)** and **Junia Tertia**	Roman: Italy	1st cent. B.C.E.

Servilia (4), victim	Roman: Rome	c. 46–66 C.E.
Sextia (1), committed suicide; political victim; q.v. **Livilla**	Roman: Rome	? B.C.E.–34 C.E.
Sextia (2), political victim; grandmother of **Antistia Pollita**	Roman: Italy	?–65 C.E.
Sextilia, independent woman; Augusta; q.v. **Agrippina the Younger; Roman: Rome Galeria Fundana; Petronia**	Roman: Italy	?–c. 69 C.E.
Silia, exile	Roman: Italy	1st cent. C.E.
Sosia Gallia, exile	Roman: Italy, Asia, and Germany(?)	? B.C.E.–c. 24 C.E.
Statilia, political survivor; q.v. **Statilia Messallina**	Roman: Italy, Asia, Samos	26 B.C.E.–? C.E.
Statilia Messallina, political player; q.v. **Agrippina the Younger; Sulpicia (2)**	Roman: Italy	1st cent. C.E.
Stratonice (1), political wife	Greek: Macedonia and Thrace	5th cent. B.C.E.
Stratonice (2), political wife and player; daughter of **Phila (1)**; mother of **Phila (2)**, **Stratonice (3)**, and **Apama (2)**; q.v. **Apama (1)**	Greek: Macedonia and Asia	?–254 B.C.E.
Stratonice (3), political leader; daughter of **Stratonice (2)**; sister of **Apama (2)**; half sister of **Phila (2)**; q.v. **Olympias (2)**	Greek: Asia and Macedonia	3rd cent. B.C.E.
Sulpicia (1), poet	Roman: Rome	1st cent. B.C.E.
Sulpicia (2), poet	Roman: Italy	?–94/98 C.E.
Tanaquil, heroine	Etruscan: Rome	7th–6th cent. B.C.E.
Telesilla, poet and military leader	Greek: Greece	5th cent. B.C.E.
Terentia (1), financial manager; mother of **Tullia (2)**; half sister of **Fabia**; q.v. **Clodia (2)**	Roman: Italy	1st cent. B.C.E.
Terentia (2), literary patron; reputed lover of Augustus; q.v. **Cleopatra VII; Livia Drusilla**	Roman: Rome	1st cent. B.C.E.– ? C.E.

Tettia Etrusc, virtuous wife	Roman: Italy and Asia(?)	?–60 C.E.
Teuta, ruler	Greek: Illyricum	3rd cent. B.C.E.
Thaïs, self-made woman; wife of Ptolemy I Soter	Greek: Athens, Asia, and Egypt	4th cent. B.C.E.
Thebe, avenger	Greek: Pherae and Thessaly	4th cent. B.C.E.
Themista, philosopher	Greek: Athens	4th–3rd cent. B.C.E.
Theodora, Flavia Maximiana, Augusta; possible daughter of Galeria Valeria **Eutropia;** mother of Flavia Julia **Constantia**	Roman: Italy, Britain, Gaul, Spain, and Germany	3rd–4th cent. C.E.
Theoxena, heroine; sister of Archo	Greek: Thessaly and Macedonia	3rd–2nd cent. B.C.E.
Thessalonice, ruler; stepdaughter of **Olympias (1);** half sister of **Cleopatra (3)** and Alexander the Great; q.v. **Olympias (1)**	Greek: Thessaly and Macedonia	c. 346/340– 298/294 B.C.E.
Timaea, wife of Agis II; lover of Alcibiades	Greek: Sparta	5th cent. B.C.E.
Timandra, faithful lover of Alcibiades; mother of **Laïs**	Greek: Sicily and Greece	5th–4th cent. B.C.E.
Timo, heroine	Greek: Greek Islands	6th–5th cent. B.C.E.
Timocleia, avenger	Greek: Thebes	4th cent. B.C.E.
Triaria, political player	Roman: Italy	1st cent. C.E.
Tullia (1), political player	Roman: Rome	6th cent. B.C.E.
Tullia (2), victim; daughter of **Terentia (1)** and Marcus Tullius Cicero	Roman: Italy	c. 79–49 B.C.E.
Urgulania, political player; close friend of **Livia** Drusilla; grandmother of **Plautia Urgulanilla**	Roman: Italy	1st cent. B.C.E.– 1st cent. C.E.
Valeria (1), self-made woman	Roman: Rome	1st cent. B.C.E.
Valeria (2), Augusta; exiled and murdered along with her mother **Prisca**	Roman: Germany, Dalmatia, Syria, Asia(?), and Italy	3rd–4th cent. B.C.E.

Varronilla, condemned priestess; colleagues: **Oculata** sisters	Roman: Rome	?–83 C.E.
Verania, credulous victim	Roman: Italy	1st cent. C.E.
Verginia (1), heroine	Roman: Rome	5th cent. B.C.E.
Verginia (2), reformer	Roman: Rome	4th–3rd cent. B.C.E.
Vespasia Polla, mother of the emperor Vespasian	Roman: Italy	1st cent. B.C.E. –1st cent. C.E.
Vibidia, priestess	Roman: Rome	1st cent. C.E.
Victoria (Vitruvia), Augusta; governor of Gaul	Roman: Gaul	3rd cent. C.E.
Vipsania Agrippina, wealthy woman; daughter of Caecilia **Attica;** q.v. **Livia Drusilla**	Roman: Rome	33 B.C.E.–20 C.E.
Vistilia, much married woman; mother of **Milonia Caesonia**	Roman: Ital	1st cent. B.C.E.–? C.E.
Vitia, convicted of treason; mother-in-law of **Mutilia Prisca;** q.v. **Livia Drusilla**	Roman: Rome	? B.C.E.–32 C.E.
Xanthippe, wife of Socrates; q.v. **Myrto**	Greek: Athens	5th cent. B.C.E.
Zenobia, Septimia, great general and ruler	Syrian: Syria and Asia Minor	3rd cent. C.E.

GLOSSARY

aedile Roman magistrate responsible for overseeing public order, the food supply, the markets, and public games

Aeneas Mythological Trojan leader whom the Augustan poet Virgil credited with the founding of Rome in the *Aeneid*

archon A chief magistrate in a Greek city-state

Atellan farce Latin bawdy comedy performed in the country and on the streets

augur Roman priest who interpreted omens

Augusta Highest imperial title for a woman during the Roman Empire

Augustus Title conferred on the leader of the Roman Empire after 27 B.C.E.

Bona Dea Roman goddess of chastity and fertility, whose rites were restricted to well-born Roman women

censor Roman official who registered citizens

Centumviral Court Roman board of judges that decided civil suits, especially inheritance

centurion Professional officer in the Roman army

civic tribune Official or military commander who administered civil affairs in large cities in the later Roman Empire

client Free person allied with some more powerful man, woman, or family in a relationship with mutual responsibilities and obligations

client-king Independent ruler under the authority of a more powerful ruler

Concordia Goddess of peace and harmony

consuls Either of two highest civil and judicial magistrates of Rome, elected annually

consul designate Consul-elect during period between election in August and assumption of office on January 1

consul suffectus Consul chosen to complete another consul's term

Cynic Follower of a Greek philosophy that preached a life of virtue lived with few material possessions

decemviri Early Roman court of noblemen

deme Main local political unit in Attica; membership was hereditary

dictator Roman magistrate given unlimited but temporary emergency powers

diva/divus Goddess or god

docta puella Well-educated and well-spoken woman, in Latin

drachma Greek monetary unit or coin

Epicureanism Greek philosophy that emphasized the physical and sense-based aspects of the world

eques, equites Wealthy landowning and commercial families that constituted the highest Roman order after the senators

fasces Bundle of elm or beechwood rods bound together with an ax that symbolized Roman magisterial authority

Flavians   Roman emperors of the Flavian family, from Titus through Domitian, 69–96 C.E.

freedman, freedwoman   Emancipated slave

Ides of March   March 15

imperator   Originally a Roman title for military commander, bestowed by troops after victory; came to denote the emperor's supreme military power

imperium   Power vested in Roman magistrates

Julio-Claudians   Members of the Julian and Claudian families, who ruled Rome from the time of Livia and Augustus, 27 B.C.E., until the death of Nero in 68 C.E.

legate   Deputy or staff member of a military commander, provincial governor, or emperor

legion   Roman army unit consisting of 4,200–6,000 troops, in 10 cohorts of foot soldiers and 300 cavalrymen

lex Falcidia   Roman law of 40 B.C.E. limiting the amount of an estate that could be willed to nonheirs through legacies; stipulated that the heir must receive at least one-quarter of the estate

lictors   Attendant of Roman magistrates

magistrate   General designation for all elected Roman officials except tribunes

military tribune   Any one of six most senior officers of a Roman legion, each assumed command for a two-month period

mina   Greek monetary unit equal to 100 drachmas

Neo-Platonism   Reinterpretation of Platonic philosophy begun by Plotinus during third century C.E.

noble   Roman who had consul(s) in the family

obverse/reverse   Front/back of coins; the obverse usually bears a portrait

optimates   Roman faction that favored conservative, aristocratic interests

patrician   Member of one of the original aristocratic families of Rome

pax deorum   Literally, "Peace of the gods": Roman concept of harmonious relations between humans and divinities

phratry   Hereditary Greek social group with jurisdiction over various matters including citizenship and inheritance

plebeian/pleb   Free-born Roman who was not a patrician

pontifex maximus   Leading priestly official during the Roman republic; became the equivalent of high priest during the reign of Augustus; afterward was routinely included among imperial offices and titles

praetor   High Roman magistrate whose duties included presiding over criminal courts, administering provinces, and leading armies

Praetorian Guard   Military bodyguard of the emperor and his family

prefect of Egypt   Roman governor of Egypt beginning with the reign of Augustus

proconsul/propraetor   Former consul or praetor who was appointed as provincial governor or military commander; as imperial agent, duties included collecting taxes, civil administration, paying and provisioning troops, and administering justice

proscription   Process of publicly declaring certain Roman citizens outlaws and making their property liable to confiscation

quaestio   Roman court established to investigate and try criminal cases; a praetor presided over a panel of 30 or more jurors

quaestor   Magistrate who oversaw finances in Rome and the provinces

satrap   Persian title for governor of a territory called a satrapy

sestertium, sesterces   Small Roman silver coin

sophist   Traveling lecturer or teacher who expressed many of the most advanced and controversial ideas in the Greek world during the fifth and fourth centuries B.C.E.

Stoic   Practitioner of a philosophy that stressed the importance of virtue and reason

talent   Greek monetary unit equal to 60 minas

toga virilis   White garment worn by free-born Roman males

tribune of the plebs   Any one of 10 representatives of the Roman people elected annually to defend against illegal and abusive acts by patricians; office and person of the tribunes were sacrosanct

tribunicia potestas Public power exercised by a tribune

triumph Roman military commander's public celebration of victory, including a parade to the temple of Jupiter on the Capitol

triumvir Literally, "One of the three men": denoting member of a personal alliance aimed at gaining political supremacy in Rome during the Republic

tutor Roman citizen acting as guardian and financial administrator for a minor, a woman, or another person who lacked right to transact legal and business affairs

tyrant Usurper of rule in a Greek city-state, often with support of the people against the aristocracy

Vesta Roman goddess of the hearth

Vestal Virgin Priestess of Vesta charged with keeping Rome's sacred hearth flame burning; usually selected from senatorial families; had to remain virgin during her 30 or more years of service on pain of death

vigiles Police and fire brigade of city of Rome

BIBLIOGRAPHY

A. Ancient Authors

Andocides	*On the Mysteries*
Appian	*Roman History: Bella civilia (Civil Wars), Syrian Wars*
Apuleius	*Apologia*
	Metamorphoses (The Golden Ass)
Aristotle	*Politics*
Arrian	*Anabasis of Alexander*
	Successors
Asconius	Commentary on Cicero's *Pro Milone*
Athenaeus	*Deipnosophistae*
Aulus Gellius	*Noctes Atticae*
Catullus	Poems
Cicero	*Brutus, De amicitia, De domo sua, De lege agraria, De oratores, Epistulae ad Atticum, Epistulae ad Brutum, Epistulae ad familiares, Epistulae ad Quintum fratrem, In Catalinum, In Verrum, Orationes Philippicae, Pro Caelio, Pro Cluentio, Pro Milone*
Demosthenes	*In Neaeram*
	Private Orations
Dio Cassius	*Roman History*
Diodorus Siculus	*Library of History*
Diogenes Laertius	*Lives of the Eminent Philosophers*
	Epitome Caesaris
Eusebius	*Vita Constantini*
Eutropius	*Breviarium ab urbe condita*
Fronto	*Epistulae*
Herodian	*History of the Empire*
Herodotus	*The Persian Wars*
Horace	*Odes*
Isaeus	Speeches of Isaeus

Josephus	*Antiquitates Judaicae* (*Jewish Antiquities*)
	Bellum Judaicum (*Jewish Wars*)
	Vitae
Justin	*Epitome*
Juvenal	*Satires*
Lactantius	*De Mortibus Persecutorum*
Livy	*From the Founding of the City* (vols. 1–14), including the *Epitomae* and *Periochae*
Lucan	*Pharsalia*
Macrobius	*Saturnalia*
Martial	*Epigrammata*
Nepos	*Atticus*
	Cimon
	Letter of Cornelia
Orosius	*Seven Books of History Against the Pagans*
Ovid	*Amores*
Pausanias	*Description of Greece*
Plato	*Alcibiades*
	Charmides
	Epistulae
	Gorgias
	Menexemus
	Meno
Pliny the Elder	*Naturalis Historia*
Pliny the Younger	*Epistulae*
	Panegyricus
Plutarch	*Moralia: Amatorius, De fortunata Romanorum, De liberis educandis, De mulierum virtutibus, Quaestiones Graecae, Quaestione Romanae*
	Vitae Parallelae (*Parallel Lives*): *Aemilius Paulus, Agesilaus, Agis, Alcibiades, Alexander, Antonius, Aratus, Brutus, Caesar, Cato Minor, Cicero, Cimon, Cleomenes, Crassus, Demetrius, Demosthenes, Dion, Eumenes, Gaius Gracchus, Lucullus, Marius, Nicias, Pelopidas, Pericles, Phocion, Pompeius, Pyrrhus, Sertorius, Sulla, Themistocles, Tiberius Gracchus*
Polyaenus	*Strategemata*
Polybius	*Histories*
Propertius	*Elegies*
Quintilian	*Institutio Oratoria*
Sallust	*Bellum Catilinae*
Scriptores Historiae Augustae	Alexander Severus, Antoninus Pius, Aurelian, Commodus, Didius Julianus, Gallienus, Gordian, Hadrian, Marcus Aurelius Antoninus (Caracalla), Marcus Aurelius Antoninus (Marcus Aurelius), Maximinus, Pertinax, Tyranni Triginta (Thirty Tyrants)

Seneca	*Ad Marciam de consolatione*
	De beneficiis
	Epistulae
Statius	*Silvae*
Strabo	*Geography*
Suetonius	*The Lives of the Caesars: Augustus, Caesar, Claudius, Domitian, Gaius Caligula, Galba, Nero, Otho, Tiberius, Titus, Vespasian, Vitellius*
	The Lives of Illustrious Men: De grammaticis (Grammarians), Virgil
Tacitus	*Agricola*
	Annales
	Historiae
Thucydides	*History of the Peloponnesian War*
Ulpian	*The Civil Law*
Valerius Maximus	*Factorum ac dictorum memorabilium libri IX*
Valleius Paterculus	*Historiae Romanae libri II*
Xenophon	*The Hellenica*
	The Anabasis of Cyrus
Zonaras	*Annales*
Zosimus	*New History*

B. Modern Authors

Alfoldi, Andros. *Early Rome and the Latins.* Ann Arbor: University of Michigan Press, 1965.

Babcock, Charles L. "The Early Career of Fulvia." *American Journal of Philology* 86 (1965): 1–32.

Balsdon, J. P. V. D. *Roman Women.* New York: John Day Comp., 1963.

Barnes, Timothy. *Constantine and Eusebius.* Cambridge: Harvard University Press, 1981.

———. *The New Empire of Diocletian and Constantine.* Cambridge: Harvard University Press, 1982.

Barrett, Anthony A. *Agrippina: Sex, Power, and Politics in the Early Empire.* New Haven, Conn.: Yale University Press, 1996.

Bauman, Richard A. *Women and Politics in Ancient Rome.* London: Routledge, 1994.

Berger, Adolf. *Encyclopedic Dictionary of Roman Law.* Philadelphia: American Philosophical Society, 1953.

Best, E. E. "Cicero, Livy and Educated Roman Women." *Classical Journal* 65 (1970): 199–204.

Bevan, Edwyn B. *The House of Selecus.* 2 vols. London: Edward Arnold, 1902.

Bing, Peter. *Games of Venus: An Anthology of Greek and Roman Erotic Verse from Sappho to Ovid.* New York: Routledge, Chapman and Hall, 1993.

Birley, Anthony Richard. *Marcus Aurelius: Emperor of Rome.* Boston: Little Brown, 1966.

———. *Septimius Severus: The African Emperor.* New Haven, Conn.: Yale University Press, 1989.

Blundell, Sue. *Women in Ancient Greece.* London: British Museum Press, 1995.

Bowie, E. L. "Greek Poetry in the Antonine Age." In *Antonine Literature,* ed. by D. A. Russell. Oxford: Clarendon Press, 1990.

Bowra, C. M. *Greek Lyric Poetry from Alcman to Simonides.* 2d ed. Oxford: Clarendon Press, 1967.

———. "Melinno's Hymn to Rome." *Journal of Roman History* 47 (1957): 21–28.

Burn, Andrew Robert. *Alexander the Great and the Hellenistic World.* London: English Universities Press, 1964.

———. *Persia and the Greeks: The Defense of the West, c. 546–478 B.C.* New York: St. Martin's Press, 1962.

Burstein, Stanley Mayer. "Arsinoe II Philadelphos: A Revisionist View." In *Philip II, Alexander the Great, and the Macedonian Heritage,* ed. by W. Lindsay Adams and Eugene N. Borza. Washington, D.C.: University Press of America, 1982.

The Cambridge Ancient History. 3d. ed. New York: Cambridge University Press, 1970–.

Cameron, Averil, and Aemlie Kuhrt, eds. *Images of Women in Antiquity.* Detroit, Mich.: Wayne University Press, 1983.

Campbell, David A. *Greek Lyric.* 5 vols. Cambridge: Harvard University Press, 1982–93.

Carney, Elizabeth D. "The Career of Adea-Eurydice." *Historia* 36 (1987): 496–502.

———. "Olympias." *Ancient Society* 18 (1987): 496–502.

———. "The Sisters of Alexander the Great: Royal Relicts." *Historia* 37 (1988): 385–404.

———. "What's in a Name?" In *Women's History and Ancient History,* ed. by Sarah B. Pomeroy. Chapel Hill: University of North Carolina Press, 1991.

Cartledge, Paul. "Spartan Wives: Liberation or License." *Classical Quarterly* 31 (1981): 84–109.

Cary, M. *A History of the Greek World from 323 to 146 B.C.* London: Methuen, 1951.

Charles-Picard, Gilbert. *Augustus and Nero: The Secret of the Empire.* Trans. by Len Ortzen. New York: Thomas Y. Crowell Comp., 1965.

Cluett, Ronald. "Roman Women and Triumviral Politics, 43–37 B.C." *Classical Views* (1998).

Cohen, G. M. "The Marriage of Lysimachus and Nicaea." *Historia* 22 (1973): 354–56.

Creekmore, Hubert, trans. *The Erotic Elegies of Albius Tib3ullus.* New York: Washington Square Press, 1966.

Davies, J. K. *Athenian Propertied Families, 600–300 B.C.* Oxford: Clarendon Press, 1971.

D'Avino, Michele. *The Women of Pompei.* Naples, Italy: Loffredo, 1967.

Debevoise, Nielson Carel. *A Political History of Parthia.* Chicago: University of Chicago Press, 1938.

DeForest, Mary, ed. *Woman's Power, Man's Game: Essays on Classical Antiquity in Honor of Joy K. King.* Wauconda, Ill.: Bolchazy-Carducci, 1993.

Delia, Diana. "Fulvia Reconsidered." In *Women's History and Ancient History,* ed. by Sarah B. Pomeroy. Chapel Hill: University of North Carolina Press, 1991.

Der Kleine Pauly; Lexikon der Antike, ed. by Konrat Julius Furchtegott and Walther Sontheimer. Stuttgart, Germany: A. Druckenmuller, 1984–.

Dixon, Suzanne. "Family Finances: Terentia and Tullia." In *The Family in Ancient Rome: New Perspectives,* ed. by Beryl Rawson. Ithaca, N.Y.: Cornell University Press, 1986.

Downey, Glanville. *A History of Antioch in Syria from Seleucus to the Arab Conquest.* Princeton, N.J.: Princeton University Press, 1961.

Drake, H. A. *In Praise of Constantine: A Historical Study and New Translation of Eusebius' Tricennial Orations.* Berkeley: University of California Press, 1976.

Dudley, Donald R., and Graham Webster. *The Rebellion of Boudicca.* New York: Barnes and Noble, 1962.

Edmonds, J. M., ed. and trans. *Lyra Graeca: Being the Remains of All the Greek Lyric Poets from Eumelus to Timotheus, Excepting Pindar.* Rev. ed. 3 vols. Cambridge: Harvard University Press, 1959.

Fantham, Elaine, et al. *Women in the Classical World.* New York: Oxford University Press, 1994.

Ferrill, A. "Augustus and His Daughters: A Modern Myth." In *Studies in Latin Literature and Roman History,* ed. by C. Deroux. Brussells, Belgium: Latomus, 1986.

———. *Caligula: Emperor of Rome.* London: Thames and Hudson, 1991.

Fischler, Susan. "Social Stereotypes and Historical Analysis: The Case of the Imperial Women in Rome." In *Women in Ancient Societies: An Illusion of the Night,* ed. by Leonie J. Archer, Susan

Fischler, and Maria Wyke. New York: Routledge, 1994.

Fitton, J. W. "That Was No Lady, That Was. . . ." *Classical Quarterly* 64 (1970): 56–66.

Flaceliere, Robert. *Love in Ancient Greece*. Trans. by James Cleugh. New York: Crown Publishers, 1962.

Forrest, W. G. A. *A History of Sparta*. London: Hutchinson, 1968.

Gardner, Jane F. *Women in Roman Law and Society*. London: Routledge, 1995.

Geoghegan, D. *Antye: A Critical Edition with Commentary*. Rome: Edizioni dell'Ateneo & Bizzarri, 1979.

Gibbon, Edward. *The Decline and Fall of the Roman Empire*. New York: Heritage Press, 1946.

Godolphin, Francis B., ed. *The Greek Historians: The Complete and Unabridged Historical Works of Herodotus translated by George Rawlinson, Thucydides translated by Benjamin Jowett, Xenophon translated by Henry G. Dakyns, Arrian translated by Edward J. Chinnock*. 2 vols. New York: Random House, 1942.

Gordon, Hattie. "The Eternal Triangle, First Century B.C." *Classical Journal* 28 (1933): 574–78.

Gow, Andrew S. F., and Denys L. Page. *The Greek Anthology: Hellenistic Epigrams*. 2 vols. Cambridge, England: Cambridge University Press, 1965.

Grant, Michael. *The Jews in the Roman World*. New York: Charles Scribner's Sons, 1973.

Green, Peter. *Alexander to Actium*. Berkeley: University of California Press, 1990.

———. *Alexander of Macedon, 356–323 B.C.* Berkeley: University of California Press, 1991.

Greenwalt, W. S. "The Search for Philip Arrhidaeus." *Ancient World* 10 (1984): 69–77.

Griffin, Marian T. *Nero: The End of a Dynasty*. New Haven, Conn.: Yale University Press, 1985.

Grimal, Pierre. *Love in Ancient Rome*. Trans. by Arthur Train, Jr. New York: Crown Publishers, 1967.

Haley, Shelly P. "The Five Wives of Pompey the Great." In *Women in Antiquity*, ed. by Ian McAuslan and Peter Walcot. Oxford: Oxford University Press, 1996.

Hallett, Judith. *Fathers and Daughters in Roman Society: Women and the Elite Family*. Princeton, N.J.: Princeton University Press, 1984.

———. "Perusinae Glandes and the Changing Image of Augustus." *American Journal of Ancient History* 2 (1977): 151–71.

Hammond, N. G. L. *A History of Greece*. Oxford: Oxford University Press, 1967.

———. "Illyris, Rome and Macedon in 229–205 B.C." *Journal of Roman Studies* (1968): 1–21.

Hammond, N. G. L., and G. T. Griffith. *A History of Macedonia*. 2 vols. Oxford: Oxford University Press, 1972–79.

Hammond, N. G. L., and H. H. Scullard eds. *The Oxford Classical Dictionary*. 2d ed. Oxford: Clarendon Press, 1996.

Harris, H. A. *Sport in Greece and Rome*. Ithaca, N.Y.: Cornell University Press, 1972.

Hawley, Richard. "The Problem of Women Philosophers in Ancient Greece." In *Women in Ancient Societies: An Illusion of the Night*, ed. by Leonie J. Archer, Susan Fischler, and Maria Wyke. New York: Routledge, 1994.

Heckel, Waldemar. "Philip and Olympias." In *Classical Contributions: Studies in Honor of Malcolm Francis McGregor*, ed. by G. S. Shrimpton and D. J. McCargar. Locust Valley, N.Y.: J. J. Augustin, 1981.

Hemelrijk, Emily A. "Women's Demonstrations in Republican Rome." In *Sexual Asymmetry: Studies in Ancient Societies*, ed. by Josine Blok and Peter Mason. Amsterdam: J. C. Giebon, 1987.

Hillard, Tom. "On Stage, Behind the Curtain: Images of Politically Active Women in the Late Roman Republic." In *Stereotypes of Women in Power: Historical Perspectives and Revisionist Views*, ed. by Barbara Garlick, Suzanne Dixon, and Pauline Allen. New York: Greenwood Press, 1992.

Hoenigswald, Gabriele S. "The Murder Charges in Cicero's Pro Cluentio." *Transactions and Proceedings of the American Philological Association* 93 (1962): 109–23.

Horsfall, Nicholas. *Cornelius Nepos: A Selection Including the Lives of Cato and Atticus*. New York: Oxford University Press, 1989.

Huzar, Eleanor G. "Mark Antony: Marriages vs. Careers." *Classical Journal* 81 (1986): 86–111.

Johnson, W. H. "The Sister-in-Law of Cicero." *Classical Journal* 8 (1913): 160–65.

Jones, A. H. M. *The Herods of Judaea.* Rev. ed. Oxford: Clarendon Press, 1967.

———. *The Later Roman Empire.* 2 vols. Norman: Oklahoma University Press, 1964.

Lacey, W. K. *The Family in Classical Greece.* Ithaca, N.Y.: Cornell University Press, 1968.

Lane Fox, Robin. *Pagans and Christians.* New York: Alfred A. Knopf, 1987.

Leon, Harry J. *The Jews of Ancient Rome.* Philadelphia: Jewish Publication Society of America, 1960.

Levick, Barbara. *Claudius: The Corruption of Power.* New Haven, Conn.: Yale University Press, 1993.

———. *Tiberius the Politician.* London: Thames and Hudson, 1976.

Licht, Hans. *Sexual Life in Ancient Greece.* Trans. by J. H. Freese. London: Abbey Library, 1971.

Luck, Georg. *The Latin Love Elegy.* London: Methuen, 1959.

McCabe, Joseph. *The Empresses of Rome.* New York: Henry Holt, 1911.

McAuslan, Ian, and Peter Walcot, eds. *Women in Antiquity.* Oxford: Oxford University Press, 1996.

Macdowell, Doulas M., ed. *Audokides on the Mysteries.* Oxford: Clarendon Press, 1962.

MacMullen, Ramsey. "Women in Public in the Roman Empire." *Historia* 29 (1980): 208–18.

Macurdy, Grace. *Hellenistic Queens.* Reprint. Chicago: Ares Publishers, 1985.

Magie, David. *Roman Rule in Asia Minor, to the End of the Third Century after Christ.* 2 vols. Princeton, N.J.: Princeton University Press, 1950.

Marsh, Frank Burr. *The Reign of Tiberius.* New York: Barnes and Noble, 1931.

Marshall, A. J. "Ladies at Law: The Role of Women in the Roman Civil Courts." In *Studies in Latin Literature and Roman History,* ed. by C. Deroux. Brussels, Belgium: Latomus, 1989.

———. "Women on Trial before the Roman Senate." *Classical Views* 34 (1990): 333–66.

Miller, Fergus. "Paul of Samosata, Zenobia and Aurelian: The Church, Local Culture and Political Allegience in Third-Century Syria." *Journal of Roman Studies* 61 (1971): 1–17.

Mosse, Claude. "Women in the Spartan Revolutions of the Third Century B.C." In *Women's History and Ancient History,* ed. by Sarah B. Pomeroy. Chapel Hill: University of North Carolina Press, 1991.

Munzer, Friedrich. *Romische Adelsparteien und Adelsfamilien.* Stuttgart, Germany: J. B. Metzler, 1920.

Murray, Gilbert. *Euripides and His Age.* London: Oxford University Press, 1965.

Oxford Classical Dictionary, ed. by Simon Hornblower and Antony Spawforth. 3d. ed. New York: Oxford University Press, 1996.

Page, Dennys L. *Alcman: The Partheneion.* Oxford: Clarendon Press, 1951.

———. *Corinna.* London: Society for the Promotion of Hellenic Studies, 1953.

Pauly, A., G. Wissowa, and W. Kroll. *Real-Encyclopadie d. Klassischen Altertumswissenschaft 1893–.* (Germany: multiple publishers.)

Perowne, Stewart. *Hadrian.* Reprint. Westport, Conn.: Greenwood Publishing, 1976.

———. *The Later Herods: The Political Background of the New Testament.* New York: Abingdon Press, 1950.

Pomeroy, Sarah B. *Goddesses, Whores, Wives, and Slaves: Women in Classical Antiquity.* New York: Schocken Books, 1975.

———. *Women in Hellenistic Egypt.* New York: Schocken, 1984.

Pomeroy, Sarah B., ed. *Women's History and Ancient History.* Chapel Hill: University of North Carolina Press, 1991.

Quinn, Kenneth, ed. *Catullus: The Poems.* 2d. ed. New York: St. Martin's Press, 1977.

Rabinowitz, Nancy Sorkin, and Amy Richlin, eds. *Feminist Theory and the Classics.* New York: Routledge, 1993.

Rawson, Beryl. *Marriage, Divorce, and Children in Ancient Rome.* Canberra, Australia: Clarendon Press, 1991.

Rawson, Beryl, ed. *The Family in Ancient Rome.* Ithaca, N.Y.: Cornell University Press, 1986.

Richardson, Keith. *Daggers in the Forum: The Revolutionary Lives and Violent Deaths of the Gracchus Brothers.* London: Cassell, 1976.

Richlin, A. "Julia's Jokes. Galla Placidia and the Roman Use of Women as Political Icons." In *Stereotypes of Women in Power: Historical Perspectives and*

Revisionist Views, ed. by B. Garlick, S. Dixon, and P. Allen. New York: Greenwood Press, 1992.

Richmond, I. A. "Queen Cartimandua." *Journal of Roman Studies* (1954): 43 ff.

Schulz, Fritz. *Classical Roman Law.* Oxford: Clarendon Press, 1969.

Scullard, H. H. *From the Gracchi to Nero: A History of Rome from 133 B.C. to A.D. 68.* New York: Frederick Praeger, 1963.

———. *A History of the Roman World, 753 to 146 B.C.* London: Routledge, 1980.

———. *Scipio Africanus: Soldier and Politician.* Ithaca, N.Y.: Cornell University Press, 1970.

Sealey, R. "On Lawful Concubinage in Athens." *Classical Antiquity* 3 (1984): 111–33.

Seltman, Charles. *Women in Antiquity.* Westport, Conn.: Hyperion Press, 1979.

Shackleton Bailey. D. R. *Cicero.* New York: Charles Scribner's Sons, 1971.

Singer, Mary White. "The Problem of Octavia Minor and Octavia Maior." *Transactions of the American Philological Association* (1948): 268–74.

Skeat, Theodore Cressy. *The Reigns of the Ptolemies.* Munich: Beck, 1969.

Skinner, Marilyn B. "Clodia Metelli." *Transactions of the American Philological Associaton* 113 (1983): 273–87.

———. "Nossis Thelyglossos: The Private Text and the Public Book." In *Women's History and Ancient History,* ed. by Sarah B. Pomeroy. Chapel Hill: University of North Carolina Press, 1991.

Skinner, Marilyn B., ed. "Rescuing Creusa: New Methodological Approaches to Women in Antiquity." *Helios* 13, no. 2 (1986).

Smallwood, E. Mary. "The Alleged Jewish Tendencies of Poppaea Sabina." *Journal of Theological Studies* (1959): 29–35.

Snyder, Jane Mcintosh. "Public Occasion and Private Passion in the Lyrics of Sappho of Lesbos." In *Women's History and Ancient History,* ed. by Sarah B. Pomeroy. Chapel Hill: University of North Carolina Press, 1991.

Stockton, David. *The Gracchi.* Oxford: Clarendon Press, 1979.

Syme, Ronald. *The Augustan Aristocracy.* Oxford: Clarendon Press, 1986.

———. "Domitius Corbulo." *Journal of Roman Studies* 60 (1970): 27–39.

———. *History in Ovid.* New York: Oxford University Press, 1978.

———. *The Roman Revolution.* London: Oxford University Press, 1963.

———. *Sallust.* Berkeley: University of California Press, 1974.

———. *Tacitus.* 2 vols. Oxford: Clarendon Press, 1958.

Tarn, William Woodthorpe. *Alexander the Great.* 2 vols. Boston: Beacon Press, 1956.

———. *Hellenistic Civilization.* London: Methuen, 1966.

———. "Phthia-Chryseis." In *Athenian Studies Presented to William Scott Ferguson.* Cambridge: Harvard University Press, 1940.

Townsend, G. B. "Traces in Dio Cassius of Cluvius, Aufidius and Pliny." *Hermes* 89 (1961) 227–48.

Townsend, Prescott W. "The Administration of Gordian III." *Yale Classical Studies* 15 (1955): 59–132.

———. "The Revolution of A.D. 238: The Leaders and Their Aims." *Yale Classical Studies* 14 (1955): 49–97.

Walbank, Frank. *Philip V of Macedon.* Cambridge, England: Cambridge University Press, 1940.

Walcot, Peter. "Plato's Mother and Other Terrible Women." In *Women in Antiquity,* ed. by Ian McAuslan and Peter Walcot. Oxford: Oxford University Press, 1996.

Walter, Gerard. *Nero.* Trans. by Emma Craufurd. Westport, Conn.: Greenwood Press, 1976.

Walters, K. R. "Women and Power in Classical Athens." In *Woman's Power, Man's Game: Essays on Classical Antiquity in Honor of Joy K. King,* ed. by Mary DeForest. Wauconda, Ill.: Bolchazy-Carducci, 1993.

Warmington, B. H. *Nero: Reality and Legend.* New York: W. W. Norton and Comp., 1969.

Weaver, P. R. C. *Familia Caesaris: A Social History of the Emperor's Freedmen and Slaves.* Cambridge, England: Cambridge University Press, 1972.

Weimar, W. *Quintus Tullius Cicero.*

William, Stephen. *Diocletian and the Roman Recovery.* New York: Routledge, 1996.

INDEX